New World Literature Series: 28

THE IMAGE OF INDIA
IN ENGLISH FICTION

(Studies in Kipling, Myers and Raja Rao)

K.C. Belliappa

1991

B.R. Publishing Corporation
[A Division of D.K. Publishers Distributors Pvt. Ltd.]
DELHI - 110 007

Sales Office:
D.K. Publishers Distributors (P) Ltd.
1, Ansari Road, Darya Ganj
New Delhi-110002.
Phones: 3278368, 3261465

© 1991 K.C.Belliappa (b.1950 –)
ISBN 81-7018-609-9
Code No. I 00530

All rights reserved with the publishers including the right to translate or to reproduce this book or parts thereof except for brief quotations in critical articles or reviews.

Published by: B.R. Publishing Corporation [Division of D.K. Publishers Distributors (P) Ltd.], 29/9, Nangia Park, Shakti Nagar, Delhi-110007. Phone: 7120113
Laser typeset by: Lustre Prints, Delhi.
Printed at: D.K.Fine Art Press, Delhi.

PRINTED IN INDIA

TO THE MEMORY

OF MY FATHER

LATE SRI KAMBEYANDA CARIAPPA

Foreword

The Image of India in English Fiction is the product of K.C. Belliappa's research under the Ph.D. programme with which I was associated as his supervisor. Belliappa mapped out the difficult terrain, located a number of writers whom he has noticed in passing, and chose to focus on three important figures, in writing on whom he has pursued his own line of thinking and maintained his critical independence. Reading through the press copy I find it a very rewarding piece of work — rewarding to both of us, to scholars working in the area of Indian English fiction and generally to anyone interested in Indian history and the literary scene.

Not long ago, the history of India was chiefly written by Englishmen for whom, as Jawaharlal Nehru observes in *The Discovery of India,* it "virtually began with the advent of Englishmen into India and all that went before is in some mystic kind of way a preparation for the divine consummation". Much Anglo-Indian fiction did no better as it gave us India and no Indians in it." Yes, victors write history!

But it is naive to talk of British bias against India. After all, British interest in trade with India and the eventual political expansion culminating in the greatest empire in history has, predictably, led to various shades of self-justification. One hastens to add, that Indian actuality with its undoubted shortcomings must have invited what must appear to us today as adverse comment by the British. What should interest us however, after making allowances for it, is how even the intelligent and apparently cultivated Englishmen — historian, social scientist, literary figure and artist — presumably by virtue of their being the cultural elite of their society and therefore cast in the role of conscience keepers, may have felt an added responsibility to explain British rule over India. And the explanations, not being qualitatively different from those in political affairs, solidified over a length of time into stereotypes. Close examination reveals these are less the result of a capacity for thinking than the quality of experience and the attitudes to life the writers brought to their task.

It has been seen the Orientalists were, like the cultural anthropologists, though in a different way, generally impressed by the metaphysical aspects of Indian life while they were repelled by the social practices and the extraordinary 'ineffectiveness' of the Indians for which they were looked down upon. On the other hand, a writer like E.M.Forster, because of his Liberal sympathies, intended to reach out, but found rapproachment difficult between the rulers and the ruled. Even so, it is good to know as Belliappa reminds us, that for Forster, 'the Mediterranean was the norm'. In any case, Forster's sympathies were not matched by an understanding of India. It is my hope that someone would bring into focus Forster's 'Bridge Party' in *A Passage to India,* Kipling's short story, *Bridge-Builders,* and Raja Rao's 'rope bridges in the Himalayas' in *The Serpent and the Rope,* and shed light on the varying images of India in fiction. It is amazing how *A Passage to India* dealing with surface realities received the kind of critical attention it did. Did Indian scholars feel placated that where other Englishmen were contemptuous of India, Forster atleast was different! The bizarre trial and its spill-over in the rest of the novel which renders it close to a thriller must have done the rest.

Belliappa deserves to be congratulated for leaving Forster alone and choosing instead Kipling, who knew his India incomparably better. Actually no student of Indian English fiction, or for that matter no writer of fiction in English or any of the Indian languages can afford to be ignorant of Kipling. Indeed their interest must start with him. Apart from his Indian birth and living and working in India long enough which makes him an outside-insider, his acquaintance with India—its hills, jungles, vast plains and the pitiless seasons and the Grand Trunk Road gave him a chance to know Indian humanity in the mass as well as its individuals at festivals, processions, bazaars, railway stations which should remain the envy of many an Indian writer. He even Indianized his English so as to be faithful to the contours of Indian experience. This is not to say he neglected the British presence in India. Only his interest in the English officials was largely as men with a mission doing a tough job under a hostile sky away from home, which led him to admire their high sense of duty to the King and country, and which in turn earned him the unfair appellation, 'imperialist' from his own countrymen who apparently used him to salvage their conscience in respect of India.

Foreword

But which English writer has shown Kipling's kind of compassion, and condescension, yes, for the Indian poor and disadvantaged? So, is his impeccable understanding and assessment of the unique organization of traditional Indian society. It is a stroke of genius which brought together, in a chance encounter, the Buddhist Lama and the admiring Irish (a loaded word in the context) boy, Kim, and through them an exploration of Indian concerns, social, religious and spiritual. All these have been admirably presented by Belliappa in their particularities in his analysis of *Kim* and selected short stories. His close reading of the work in front of him is always a point in his favour.

Belliappa's chapter on L.H. Myers is something to be grateful for. The initial attention won for Myers by the *Scrutiny* group led by Dr. Leavis who called *The Root and the Flower* a 'very remarkable novel', and its reading 'a memorable experience' was not pursued by any Indian scholar in a serious way, and Belliappa has done well to give Myers a whole chapter of incisive analysis and evaluation without overlooking his shortcomings. Myers had the courage and the integrity to admit he, 'counted on the ignorance' of his readers in his choice of a remote age of Indian history because of the freedom it conferred on his inventive mind to people it with the men and women of his choice to work out the end in view, namely, a quest for an answer to the corroding materialism of our age. Indian thought and the values enshrined in it fascinated Myers as they did T.S. Eliot who looked upto to India with a view to ordering the anarchy of contemporary existence. Belliappa should be complimented for perceiving in Myers' choice of Akbar's time, an affinity between the novelist's own search and that of Akbar for a serene life.

A good man, says Myers, 'exhales an atmosphere of serenity', and so chooses a Guru as Kipling chooses the Lama, in *Kim,* and T.S.Eliot the psychiatrist in *A Cocktail Party,* all three drawing sustenance from timeless India. Belliappa sees in Myers' 'deft handling of a difficult theme' a reverent understanding of the Hindu pantheon of gods to the last detail. And yet, like T.S. Eliot, Myers had no chance of visiting India. He says 'he struck a compromise between philosophy and fiction' (no compromise, but a welcome reconciliation in the light of D.H.Lawrence's observation that philosophy and fiction had parted like a nagging couple which provoked him to pronounce 'surgery or bomb' for the English novel) and says disarmingly that for this reason, his novel was foredoomed from the beginning to great defects. If so, much may be forgiven an English novelist who sought to seriously counteract the growing trivialization (T.S. Eliot called it 'secularization') of fiction and the life it portrayed.

I shall not, for fear of saying too much in a foreword, dwell on Raja Rao whose reputation as a major novelist is now beyond question despite the weakness of *The Chessmaster*. I should like to say, however, that Belliappa's inclusion of Raja Rao in this volume helps to impart to it a variety and depth, in addition to providing opportunities for comparison with the other two. He boldly disagrees with several critics who have written extensively on Raja Rao. And one respects him for it.

C.D. Narasimhaiah

Preface

It is perhaps not an exaggeration to claim that a country projects its most authentic image through its art and literature. And literature has a most intimate nexus with the larger cultural ethos. Indeed it is this nexus that imparts to literature vitality. It is an interesting endeavour to explore how an old civilization such as India comes through in the perceptions of writers 'alien' to it. It is rewarding to compare these perceptions with one not alien by birth but seemingly distanced from it.

The present study critically examines the image of India in the fictional works of Rudyard Kipling, L.H. Myers and Raja Rao. It considers how their attitude to Indian actuality and the spirit of India affects their fiction in terms of their major preoccupations in particular their delineation of human relationships. An attempt is made to see how far their fictional techniques are determined by their attitudes and concerns. The adequacy of the English language for their creative purposes is also discussed by highlighting the departures made by them from 'Standard English' to mediate experiences 'alien' to it. This book is an edited version of the thesis submitted to the University of Mysore for the award of a doctoral degree.

I wish to acknowledge with gratitude now, as I did then, the help and encouragement I received from Professor C.D. Narasimhaiah in writing this thesis. He has been generous with his time and many of his suggestions have helped me to give the thesis its present form. The writing of this thesis, is in fact, the culmination of my studentship under him.

I must also thank my friend and colleague Dr. D.A. Shankar with whom I spent many rewarding hours discussing the problems of my study. I am also grateful to my teacher Dr. U.R. Ananthamurthy for the keen interest he evinced in my work and the insights he shared with me and to late Professor K.B. Ramakrishna Rao for clarifying many issues relating to Indian Philosophy.

I owe special thanks to my friends Professor V.K. Natraj and Dr. R. Ramachandra who have been a constant source of inspiration to me.

I dedicate this book to the memory of my dear father Late Sri Kambeyanda Cariappa.

K.C. BELLIAPPA

Contents

	Foreword	iv
	Preface	ix
1.	Introduction	1
2.	Rudyard Kipling	23
3.	L.H. Myers	131
4.	Raja Rao	191
5.	Towards Conclusion	303
	Appendices	341
	Bibliography	357
	Index	373

Chapter - 1

Introduction

I

When the East India Company was permitted by Emperor Jehangir in 1608 to hire a house for the purposes of setting up a factory on the banks of the river Tapti at Surat, the British had unconsciously taken the first step towards building an empire in India. This empire was the result of a few ambitious Britishers, not foreseen by many of them when they first landed in India. What was initially merely a commercial enterprise went beyond their early plans. Interestingly enough, at that time India was not considered a good commercial proposition by the British, and this made them delve deeper into the local conditions with greater effort and insight than either the French or the Dutch who preceded them. This "provided (them) an unconscious preparation for their later debut on the Indian political state."[1] And it could be rightly said that, "the Indian empire was born when the British trading concern was caught in the chain-drive of Indian power politics."[2]

The real British interest in India had come with Clive's exploits and Hastings's organization of Bengal. However, very soon the initial euphoria of having begun to rule a potentially big empire turned into grave misgivings because of the chaotic conditions and total disorder prevalent within the country. These misgivings were of two kinds. On the one hand, Hastings saw the conditions of the times being disorderly and the oppression of people maximum, while his opponents perceived rank corruption in the company officials themselves. The logical culmination was the trial of Warren Hastings. It is appropriate that one should begin a study of British attitudes towards India with Hastings. Not only was he "the real founder of the British dominion in India,"[3] but as the first governor general he made a sincere attempt — something never attempted so far — to be familiar with the local conditions and also with Indian culture. This interest in Indian culture led Hastings "to an affectionate respect for many Indians such as was uncommon in his times."⁴ He had a number of Sanskrit Dharma Sastras translated into English. He got Charles Wilkins to translate the *Bhagavadgita* to which he contributed a foreword. He had the courage to assert that "these will survive when the British Dominion in India shall have long ceased to exist."⁵ He also established a College of Arabic and Persian studies in Calcutta in 1781.

These interests of Hastings have come in for sharp criticism. No doubt, all these as well as his desire to govern India according to her own traditional laws were, to some degree, determined by political necessity. Some historians have been more than unfair to Hastings in dubbing him an imperialist in the making. But when viewed against his successors, he does emerge as a towering figure, for his attitude towards India was never a supercilious one. And he did not suffer from either a feeling of moral righteousness or racial superiority seen so very often in the later British rulers. His rule in Bengal was very popular and he "laid the foundation of a better, more secure regime than India had known since Akbar."⁶

The willingness of Hastings to learn about the natives cannot be in the ultimate analysis, regarded only as a matter of political expediency since it is known that he admired Indian manners and customs; mastered the Persian language; gathered Indian paintings and manuscripts and in his letters to his wife he used to quote from the *Bhagavadgita* which he found a great source of inspiration. In his efforts at understanding the people, he unknowingly offered an ideal for the rulers that was worthy of emulation. However, it was callously disregarded by the latter-day rulers with tragic results, both for themselves and the ruled. In terms of categorising attitudes, Hastings's was basically conservative, something he shared rather ironically with his political adversary, Edmund Burke.

About the same time, Burke emerged as a leading figure in British politics who was genuinely concerned about India. His role in the impeachment of Warren Hastings has to be seen in relation to his distress at the effect corruption and mismanagement in India was likely to have upon the preservation of the British Constitution. Burke studied extensively many works about various aspects of India—its culture, economy and history and showed good understanding of Indian conditions. He was always inclined to take a philosophical view of political problems. He was essentially concerned with having political action correspond with the nature of the political order under God. He formulated a conservative theory of Indian society, culture and government and wanted it preserved.

Burke's genuine respect for India made him declare:

> "Faults this nation may have, but God forbid we should pass judgement upon a people who formed their laws and institutions prior to our insect origins of yesterday."[7]

As pointed out by George D. Bearce, it was after Burke that "the British were obliged to establish a trained civil service for India, well enough paid to avoid graft and corruption, and in its political policy in India, Britain had to recognize the needs and peculiar characteristics of that country."[8] But subsequently, Burke's conservatism was diluted to satisfy the needs of reactionary elements to suit their imperial interests. To the imperialist, British power in India had to be strengthened at any cost and this meant not allowing Indian ways to prosper. But then, they also realised that a partial encouragement would be strategically ideal to completely stall India's rise to modernity and independence — a thing that would be potentially dangerous.

The rule by the next governor-generals such as Cornwallis, Wellesley, Minto, Lord Hastings and Amherst saw a consolidation of the British imperial power in India, which was justified on the basis of the material and social reform it brought about in the country. All of them invariably spoke of the 'blessings of the British rule' and strongly believed that the British presence made for 'the inestimable benefits of civilization' in India.

Along with the conservative and imperial reactions to India, we notice the emergence of Liberal and Humanitarian attitudes which contributed new ideas to the British task of ruling India. These attitudes have their basis in the rapid changes taking place in England at the time. England which saw the birth pangs of industrial revolution was now acquiring a new economic theory, *laissez-faire*, to serve its new, vigorous economic development.[9] Liberal and democratic thinkers like Jeremy Bentham and Tom Paine were advocating sweeping political and legal changes in Britain. James Mill was perhaps the most important spokesman of the Liberal movement with his *The History of British India* (1817). Written from a Liberal and Utilitarian viewpoint he gained the important position of an examiner of correspondence in the Company's offices in London. Like Burke, he never visited India and believed that this made for greater objectivity and detachment in his views. But this was not true, for his view of India was determined by his being "a Utilitarian reformer, a prophet of progress, and a critic of the backward, medieval and aristocratic institutions of both Britain and India."[10]

Mill's views of India are historically significant, for they established what came to be the standard reactions of the English to the country in the coming years. He was excited at the prospect of what the English could do in India: "There was an opportunity in India to which the history of the world presents not a parallel."[11] To Mill, India was in urgent need of reforms and for men like him, "India seemed very much like a blank page."[12] This opinion was shared by the Evangelical Wilberforce. But the difference lay in their methods, for "the Utilitarians hoped to improve morals by reforming society, Evangelicals hoped to improve society by reforming morals."[13] They replaced the earlier view of India as a rich and highly developed civilization offered by Conservatives like Hastings and Burke with the one which pictured India as existing in the grossest sort of degradation. In Mill's judgement of Indian people, institutions and culture, his own conception of civilization provided the touchstone. For him, civilization was to be found only in ancient Greece and modern Europe. India and medieval Europe were, on the contrary, rude societies, India being the ruder. His formulations on India were based on this premise and hence, India was regarded by him as a backward place, a society that was still barbaric, a picture that was on the whole, negative. His view of India is that of an eighteenth century rationalist for whom reason was the sole guiding principle. In fact, the Utilitarian thinkers of the nineteenth century saw themselves as the philosophers of rationalism.

Mill argued that the prevalent conditions in India were similar to those found in rude societies anywhere else, may it be that of the Red Indian or the primitive Anglo-Saxon. To him, Hindu conceptions of God appeared to resemble those possessed by "the rude tribes of America, wandering naked in the woods."[14] Hindu notions of caste reminded him of the "Druids among the ancient Britons, as there was a striking similarity in many of the doctrines which they taught, also possessed many similar privileges and distinctions to those of the Brahmens."[15]

Mill found, as did most of his successors, that there was nothing to be admired in the Hindu ideal of asceticism. He characterized it as, "an absolute renunciation of all moral duties, and moral affections. 'Exemption from attachments, and affection for children, wife, and home'..."[16] He believed that the Hindu social system produced indolence, avarice, lack of cleanliness, venality, and ignorance. Of Indian education he said: "the attention of the Hindu is more engaged by frivolous observances, than by objects of utility."[17] He dismissed Indian history as only absurd legends and was equally severe on Hindu metaphysics: "The propensity to abstract speculations is then the natural result of the state of the human mind in a rude and ignorant age."[18] He was oblivious of the aesthetic merits of Indian art and literature. Hindu sculpture, architecture and painting did not appeal to him. He found the great Indian epics "excessively prolix and insipid."[19]

It is against this background that we should understand his enthusiasm for what the British could do in India with a proper government to establish an ideal society. No doubt, his emphasis on oriental despotism in India suited the requirements of an imperial government. Though H.H. Wilson, the well known Orientalist edited the later editions of Mill's History and made elaborate footnotes to correct many of the wrong theories propounded by Mill, the damage had been done. As Wilson himself pointed out, Mill's description of the Hindus was

> calculated to destroy all sympathy between the rulers and the ruled... There is a reason to fear that these consequences are not imaginary, and that a harsh and illiberal spirit has of late years prevailed in the conduct and councils of the rising service in India, which owes its origin to impressions imbibed in early life from the History of Mr. Mill.[20]

As a matter of fact, incalculable harm had been done to race relations. Mill's image of India and Indians projected in his history has found almost a universal acceptance in the minds of the British down the years. This near-total acceptance has contributed stereotyped images of the land and its people. Thanks to the definition of Mill, civilization has come to mean exclusively the European kind, and India despite its rich and ancient past, has been characterised as a primitive and barbaric society. Added to this image, there was the logical corollary of the image of the people who were regarded as childlike, innocent and primitive who needed to be looked after and ruled by the Englishmen, the representatives of an immeasurably superior culture. Mill's book became a basic text in Haileybury College, where the civil servants going out to India were trained. And so they already had an image of India in their minds which only needed a little more evidence on coming into contact with the real India. A predisposed mind like that will selectively choose only such facts in the native life as will corroborate the image already present. This also brings home another important truth that the image of India was more often created in England, a fact that speaks volumes for the accuracy, or to be more precise, the lack of it in such an image.

The Evangelicalism represented by Charles Grant, William Wilberforce and Bishop Heber, as suggested earlier, had similar notions about India so much so that the image of the land and the people found in Mill is reinforced further. Note for instance, Charles Grant's conception of the Indian character:

> We cannot avoid recognizing in the people of Hindustan a race of men lamentably degenerate and base; retaining but a feeble sense of moral obligation; yet obstinate in their disregard of what they know to be right, governed by malevolent and licentious passions, strongly exemplifying the effects produced on society by a great and general corruption of manners.[21]

Even the humanitarian missionary Bishop Heber was not free from superciliousness in his compassion towards a people, "so goodly, so gentle, and how so misled and blinded."[22] The missionaries' view of India was also based on the conviction of British superiority in religious, social and intellectual life. Wilberforce passionately argued that,

> Our religion is sublime, pure and beneficent. Theirs is mean, licentious, and cruel. Of our civil principles and conditions, the common right of all ranks and classes to be governed, and punished by equal laws, is the fundamental principle. Equality, in short, is the vital essence and the very glory of our English laws. Of theirs, the essential and universal pervading general character is inequality, despotism in the higher classes, degradation and oppression in the lower.[23]

The missionaries believed that "Christianity would bring not only a moral and spiritual improvement but also a political, legal and social improvement."[24] Christianity, in other words, would be the beacon of light that would drive darkness out of India. The supreme irony of both the Utilitarian and Evangelical movements was that they were more successful in a negative way by discrediting Indian society rather than encouraging any enthusiasm for reform, which was their original intention. This is borne out by the fact that the later generations of Englishmen were more inclined to view Indian society with contempt and with little or hardly any concern for reform.

In a consideration of the British attitudes towards India, one notices, however, an occasional departure from the main trends. Such departures appear to grow rarer with the consolidation of the British rule in India. One such instance is seen in the case of Thomas Munro, who was the Governor of Madras from 1820 to 1827. He was Conservative in outlook and his opinions about India come as a refreshing contrast to that of the Utilitarians and Evangelicals. He was generous in his praise of the literature, and the religious and social laws of India. That he could never accept the belief in the cultural inferiority of India is evident in his remark:

> "If civilization is to become an article of trade between the two countries, I am convinced that this country (Britain) will gain by the import cargo."[25]

Munro had this to say of the British treatment of Indians:

> "Foreign conquerors have treated the natives with violence and often with great cruelty, but none has treated them with so much scorn as we."[26]

He believed that an Anglo-Indian official "must not be led away by fanciful theories founded on European models."[27] And he asserted that "we cannot be qualified to govern men against whom we are prejudiced."[28]

The reasons for this unusual sympathy in Munro for India is not difficult to seek. He had spent nearly fifty years in the country in various positions both military and civilian, and had developed an acute understanding of the country. He recognized, what his contemporaries and the latter-day imperialists failed to perceive, that India had a civilization of its own; that the British were far from being fair to the natives and that they committed the monumental folly of trying to view India from their own predilections and prejudices. In this, lies the clue to the failure of the relationship between the Indians and the English. This also provides us with an insight into the basic tenets of imperialism.

Though such voices of sanity as that of Munro were heard now and then, the imperialist assumptions of the British grew in strength. The

Mutiny of 1857 saw a further justification of the imperial attitude of the British. The East India Company was abolished and India came under the direct rule of the Crown. As Hutchins points out, "the main significance of the abolition of the Company was this symbolic endorsement of British permanence in India, whose credibility and justifiability had been slowly growing in the preceding decades."[29]

Here are two classical justifications of the Empire. Curzon's high flown rhetoric attempts to suggest that an empire meant not merely a rule by alien races but for him, constituted a storehouse of ideals:

> "But let it be our ideal all the same. To fight for the right, to abhor the imperfect, the unjust, or the mean, to swerve neither to the right hand nor to the left, to care nothing for flattery or applause or odium or abuse — it is so easy to have any of them in India — never to let your enthusiasm be soured or your courage grow dim, but to remember that the Almighty has placed your hand on the greatest of His ploughs, in whose furrow the nations of the future are germinating and taking shape, to drive the blade a little forward in your time, and to feel that somewhere among these millions you have left a little justice or happiness or prosperity, a sense of manliness or moral dignity, a spring of patriotism, a dawn of intellectual enlightenment, or a stirring of duty where it did not exist before — that is enough. That is the Englishman's justification in India."[30]

About the same time, a more vehement and less ambiguous justification for the British in India was made by Chamberlain where we notice a racist bias:

> "I believe in the British Empire and ... I believe in the British race. I believe that the British race is the greatest of governing races that the world has ever seen."[31]

For a different but unusual view, we should turn to John Seeley. He entirely endorsed the British imperial mission in India but not because of Indian inferiority. In him, we have an imperialist free from the racial prejudice of Chamberlain, who is able to recognise the merits of the ruled, something of a rarity. Note his assessment of the Hindu in relation to the British:

> We are not cleverer than the Hindu; our minds are not

> richer or larger than his. We cannot astonish him, as we astonish the barbarian, by putting before him ideas that he never dreamed of. He can match from his poetry our sublimest thoughts; even our science perhaps has few conceptions that are altogether novel to him.[32]

The imperialist posture built on feelings of racial superiority naturally led to a life of exclusiveness in the British in India. It is this sense of separateness that primarily prevented them from assimilating anything from the rich culture of India. And so it is not surprising that,

> the influence of things Indian on Europeans, and in particular, British life seems very small for so long a connection.[33]

But then such an assimilation has to be viewed from the postulates of the colonial relationship as well:

> To say that the colonizer could or should accept assimilation and, hence, the colonized's emancipation, means to topple the colonial relationship.[34]

It can now be said, there were certain minor variations in the British attitudes towards India, but the general trend did not undergo any perceptible change since the British continued to have the illusory feeling of permanence in India till the beginning of the twentieth century.

Historically speaking, the imperial idea suffered a severe setback for the first time with the Boer War at the turn of the century. This war "disillusioned even the most utopian, intellectual imperialists, and destroyed for good the dream of an Empire dedicated to internationalism, liberalism and humanitarianism."[35] Darwin's theory of evolution which had earlier been used to justify imperialism, gave way to new trends in the field of anthropology led by Malinowski and others. Studies of native cultures and institutions were undertaken as a means of achieving a total view of society. The Post-Darwinian method is characterized by the approach to an alien experience which is 'what does it mean to them?' and not 'how strange it seems to me.' That is to say they were examined in their own right and not from the point of view of an European model. This made it impossible for the white man to still believe in his superiority and that of his civilization. Simultaneously, the rise of nationalism and the political and economic changes of the times along with the Second World War destroyed the idea of imperialism. India won her freedom in 1947 and the rest of the empire disintegrated soon after.

II

India has exercised a powerful influence on the English literary imagination over the last four hundred years. Initially India was regarded as a land of riches, pearls, magic, rope trick and mysticism. The conception was mainly romantic as is evident from the following references. Perhaps the first ever reference to India occurs in Christopher Marlowe's play, *Tamburlaine* (1587):

> "Whereas the Terrene and the Red Sea meet
> Being distant less than a hundred leagues,
> I mean to cut a channel to them both
> That men might quickly sail to India."[36]

Marlowe's Faustus cries, "I'll have them fly to India for gold."[37] In Shakespeare, we have "the base Indian"[38] in *Othello* while *As You Like It* speaks of "From the east to western Ind / No jewel is like Rosalind."[39] In *Henry the Fourth* we notice, "as bountiful / As the mines of India",[40] and read in *Twelfth Night,* "How now, my metal of India."[41] While Andrew Marvell promises his coy mistress "by the *Indian Ganges* side / Shoulds't Rubies Find,"[42] Milton, obviously inspired by *The Journal of Sir Thomas Roe* described Satan's exalted position in 'Paradise Lost' as

> High on a Throne of Royal State, which far
> Outshone the wealth of *Ormus* and of *Ind*.[43]

A slightly different response is noticed in Cowper, who aware of the political relationship between the two countries, seems to rather surprisingly sympathize with the plight of the native:

> Is India free? and does she wear her plumed
> And jewelled turban with a smile of peace
> Or do we grind her still?[44]

However, it is in fiction that the British response to India finds predominant expression. In A.G. Bhupal Singh's book *A Survey of Anglo-Indian Fiction* (1934),[45] one can count over a thousand fictional works by Englishmen on India and the number has continued to increase in the last fifty years. One of the first Anglo-Indian novels is Sir Walter Scott's *The Surgeon's Daughter* (1827). This novel of eighteenth century India opens in Scotland and ends in the domains of Haider Ali and Tipu Sultan. It is a romantic view of India as seen by one who had never been to India. The novel tells the story of Richard Middlemas, a soldier who induces his sweetheart to come to India. He offers her to Tipu Sultan in return for the command of Tipu's main fort and then tries to betray his master to the British. Middlemas's duplicity is discovered and he is trampled to death by an elephant. Though it reads more like a tale of adventure, *The Surgeon's Daughter* can also be regarded as "a historical parable of British rule in India."[46]

Middlemas was attracted to India as he considered it to be land of diamonds where "Indian streams flowed over sands of gold."[47] In his desire to visit a far off land in pursuit of wealth, Middlemas represents the British urge to explore. Scott also painted India rather bleakly, for we have a Brahmin Paupaiah who is portrayed as an Indian Machiavelli and a Muslim holy man who is seen to be praying endlessly and at the same time spying. Haider Ali and Tipu Sultan are presented as despots. However, Scott's insight into Indians is particularly impressive when he describes them as the "patient Hindu," the "warlike Rajpoot" and the "haughty Moslemah." He is also aware of the Indian conventions. In chapter X, when Dr. Hartley meets Barak el Hodgi at the tomb of Cara Razi, we read that, "complying with the Mohammedan custom, our friend Hartley laid aside his shoes."[48]

Given Scott's limitations, *The Surgeon's Daughter* is a considerable achievement since he had successfully "romanticized British imperialism in India, and he had many literary successors in this genre."[49] Though the romantic view prevailed in early writers like Scott, Britain's official attitudes towards India were based on the ideas of progress and imperialism. The attitude of the average educated Englishman in the nineteenth century was determined by this official policy. In 1844, according to George D. Bearce

> *The Quarterly Review* made a perceptive analysis of these opinions of India held by the general public. (1) To some

Britons, India was still a land of fable and marvels, a region of inexhaustible wealth—gold, gems, sultans on peacock thrones, palaces paved with jasper and onyx—and Arabian nights. (2) To some, India was a large uniform land, occupied by a feeble and unwarlike people, tyrannized by the Brahmins, living in a rigid caste system, darkened with superstitions and offending religious practices, characterized by the worst vices of slaves—baseness, cruelty, falseness, cowardice. (3) Some viewed India as a place to make fortunes, where younger sons of established families could find lucrative employment, where a trifle of capital would grow into the wealth of a Rothschild. (4) Some men knew that there was literature, philosophy, and science in India, though they disdained to study this culture and condemned it all as 'oriental extravagance and hyperbole.[50]

All these attitudes in some form or the other, no doubt in varying degrees, have continued to characterize western response to India even to this day. This points to either a basic conservatism in the western attitude or lends credence to the often levelled charge against India that it was always a stagnant culture. But what is of interest in view of the nature of this study, is that these formulations have also formed the basis for basic conceptions towards India in the tradition of Anglo-Indian fiction. But for an extraordinary range of attitudes to India and the role of the British in India, we should look to William Delafield Arnold's novel, *Oakfield: or, Fellowship in the East* [51] published in 1853, four years before the mutiny. It is this range that makes him a true forerunner of novelists like Rudyard Kipling, Flora Annie Steel, E.M.Forster, Edward Thompson and George Orwell who have all reacted differently to the British empire in India.

Oakfield, disillusioned by both Oxford and the Church of England comes to India in search of a new environment where he hopes to make a fresh start and

> try once more to realise his theory of bringing religion into daily life, without the necessity of denying it at every turn in obedience to some fashion or dogma of society. (Vol. I, p. 16.)

Though he is ignorant of India, he wishes to work out his experiment there of bringing about a synthesis between "the utmost freedom of thought and a firm belief in the New Testament." (p. 25.) As he arrives in India, he looks upon himself as part of Europe's civilizing mission, for "was not every European in India engaged in the grand work of civilising Asia?" (p. 16.) But when his friend Stanton tells him of his inability to understand why Oakfield should have given up a promising career in England "to come to this wretched country," he replies, "In the first place, in spite of your experience, I am disposed to hope that it is not a wretched country." (p. 2.)

Though India and Indians are discussed in the novel by Oakfield and his friends, curiously there is very little mention of the landscape of the country and even the eternally present native servant of Anglo-Indian fiction is absent in *Oakfield*. In fact, E.M. Forster points out how "the English lakes gleam in the pages of the book with a radiance denied to the Ganges."[52] The novel operates more on the level of a narrative which is "expository, reflective and dialectical."[53] And so we see the characters in the novel always mouthing new ideas, but these ideas are never realized in terms of situations and incidents in the novel. This certainly points to a major defect in *Oakfield* as a fictional work. However, our interest in the novel is because of the richly complex attitudes present in it and not due to its literary merit.

First, let us consider William Arnold's view of India and Indians. When Wykham, in a conversation with Oakfield refers to the natives as "brutes," Oakfield refutes him:

> "It is grievous to live among men, and feed the idea of fraternity thwarted by facts; and yet the idea must not be abandoned as false or hopeless. We must not resign ourselves, without a struggle, to calling them brutes."
>
> "I think we may call them what they are"
>
> "Yes, but be sure of what they are first; you know yourself that there are many good points in the natives." (Vol. II, p. 139.)

This certainly reveals a sympathetic attempt by Oakfield to understand the natives and recognise the "many good points" in them. And he continues his defence by arguing further that

> "We esteem them the better, the more we know them. Why? because we learn to look a things from their view, instead of arrogantly assuming our own as the true one,

and condemning them for not coming up to it. So if we
know them well (which, neither you nor I do), we should
find them men even as we are, looking at truth from a different point of view, and a much worse one, which is their
misfortune; but still their view is as honest as ours, and in
some things as sufficient." (Vol. II, p. 141.)

In saying this, Oakfield is in the true Victorian liberal tradition. He seems to be aware of a very important truth in colonial relationships as he realises that the inability of the coloniser to judge the colonised in his cultural context has led to lack of understanding and meaningful relationships between the two. But Oakfield, as a representative of the rulers in India, is also convinced of the inferiority of the Indian race. His own tragic plight is an outcome of his difficulty in practising his liberal ideas in India as he himself rather helplessly admits:

"But after all, I grant freely that they are a deplorably in-
ferior race, but I do not see why they should be considered
hopelessly so. I know they have souls; and I believe their
souls to be as glorious and majestic as yours or mine,
though perhaps more terribly hampered. But I grant freely, Wykham, that it is much easier to say all this than to
believe and act upon it; indeed this latter is so hard as to
constitute, as I said, one of the 'drawbacks to happiness in
India'." (pp. 141-43.)

This painful awareness makes Oakfield feel like an exile throughout his stay in India. The climate of India, "the ugliness of the country," (p. 138.) and the natives themselves are regarded by him as constituting the major problems for the Englishmen in India. That is why, he tries to dissuade his brother Herby from his intention of entering the Indian service. Oakfield's friend Wykham goes to Herby's public school to persuade him from coming over to India and warns him ominously:

"... I tell you Herby, you would hate India; everybody does.
The best men, such as your brother, who work hard, and it
is said, *get on,* hate it, idle, good for nothing dogs, like
myself, hate it. Perhaps the worse like it best..." (p. 192.)

Herby heeds to the warning, and Oakfield is so delighted that he writes a letter to Wykham thanking him, which incidentally reveals his own conception of India:

Introduction

> "In the first place let me thank you, my dear Fred, most heartily, for your very kind and wise treatment of poor Herby. Indeed it would be a sad disappointment to me if he were to come out here; one of a family is enough for this place of torment; speaking seriously, you know how often we have agreed that for one man whose character is refined and strengthened by the fiery furnace of the Indian temptation, there are ten who are carried away, withered up and destroyed by it. It is a risk to which I never wish to see kith and kin of mine exposed." (p. 218.)

Significantly, Oakfield, for all his liberal beliefs, is here emphasizing "what India does *to* people, rather than what people can do *for* India."54 Elsewhere Oakfield confesses:

> "You know I never liked India, but one always takes a sort of stoical pleasure in doing a very unpleasant duty. You may imagine what zest stable duty may acquire by being regarded as a chronic martyrdom." (p. 268.)

This debilitating effect of India on the Englishmen carrying on the imperial task of governing the natives is seen to be a recurring theme in Anglo-Indian fiction.

But what distinguishes William Arnold's novel from the run-of-the-mill Anglo-Indian novel is that he not merely emphasises the deadening impact of India on the English, but also pointedly blames the moral bankruptcy of the English for the wretchedness of India, a surprising insight in such an early writer. After spending a few weeks with his regiment, Oakfield writes to his friend Stanton:

> "Where is the energy by which British India has been conquered? Not in the army—at least in the officers. These are really, in nine cases out of ten, so far as I have seen, mere animals, with no single idea on any subject in the world beyond their carcasses." (Vol. I, p. 39.)

This makes Oakfield call for a change of heart in the British, both in the army and in the bureaucracy. Such a desire for the moral reform of the British, apart from finding a powerful expression in the novel is explicitly stated in Arnold's dedication to the novel:

> "But whatever the people of England may talk, or think, or do about India, whether they get their cotton from it or

not, I know that all will still depend upon the Englishmen who are in India; and the most sanguine and the most conservative will hardly deny that reform is wanted there. They speak ignorantly who speak in sweeping disparagement of the two services; there is much of gallantry and patient endurance in the one, much intelligence and laborious energy in the other of them. But it cannot be denied that there is a want of earnestness, a want of moral tone, and together with much superficial scepticism that would pass for freedom of thought, a want of liberality, greater than exists in corresponding classes of society at home." (pp. vii-viii.)

In his plea for reform of the English in India, we find an interesting reversal of the position of the Utilitarians and Evangelicals who had both called for a reform of the Indian society. On account of this passionate belief in reform, his ideal of an Englishman in India was the character of a duty-bound, morally upright officer whose allegiance was to his work and a complete moral code. It is this ideal that came to be glorified in later Anglo-Indian fiction especially in Kipling.

William Arnold's views on imperialism coming as it does in 1853 when the British Empire was coasting along merrily, comes as another of the many surprising revelations in the novel. In a letter to his friend Wykham in England, Oakfield writes:

"There is an utter want of nobleness in the Government of India; it still retains the mark of its commercial origin... its evil is a money-getting earthly mind, that dares to view a larger portion of God's world, and many millions of God's creatures, as a more or less profitable investment, as a good return for money laid out upon them, as a providential asylum for younger ones." (Vol. II, p. 223.)

Such a severe indictment of the empire as only a commercial enterprise is very rare in Anglo-Indian fiction, the other notable example being George Orwell's *Burmese Days*. But even in Orwell, Arnold's religious overtones are absent. For Arnold, the British failed in India not only because of the cultural incompatibility between the two races, but because they had become worshippers of Mammon in India. Oakfield writes to his friend Wykham:

"... when this spirit of philosophy, and poetry, and godli-

Introduction 17

ness shall move across the world, and begin to dawn even upon the Englishmen in the East — when the philosopher-reformer shall come out here as Governor-General, — then the spirit of Mammon may tremble for its empire, but not till then." (p. 225).

William Arnold's novel *Oakfield* is probably the most significant work to emerge in the entire Anglo-Indian fiction of the nineteenth century outside Kipling. Despite the absence of Indians in the novel and its artistic limitations, it exhibits a profound involvement with the Indian situation that has contributed to the presence of a whole range of attitudes so central to our understanding of the fiction of the colonial empire. In many of these, Arnold was well ahead of his times, a true sign of his genius. Notice the range in a brief restatement of Arnold's major preoccupations in the novel: his healthy respect for India despite his recognition of its inferiority; his ideas of cultural incompatibility between India and England; his scathing criticism of British officialdom; his enthusiastic plea for the white man's stoic commitment to duty in India; his fears about the danger to the empire owing to the insensitivity and moral and spiritual bankruptcy of the British army and bureaucracy in India; his view of the British in India as living in exile; his disarmingly frank exposure of the empire as a commercial enterprise; his own awareness of the white man's burden in India and his concern for better understanding between the two races. Arnold's preoccupations thus constitute the major features of the tradition of Anglo-Indian fiction. And it is these features that determine the nature of the image of India* in British writing on India.

III

In a consideration of the image of India in the works of fiction, attention will be drawn to the major constituents that contribute towards this fictional image. The first constituent of the image of India is the presence of the Englishmen in India. The focus is naturally on

---

* For a detailed discussion of the image of India as it appears in (a) the Orientalists and (b) the British historians, indologists and art critics, see Appendix A and B.

the Englishman whether he is a civilian or a soldier. In the picture of India, the problems of the Englishman receive greater attention at the hands of the writer. Hence, we find that it is not the Indian situation that is described, but the situation of the Englishman in India. The emphasis is invariably on his sacrifices, hardships and struggles, all carried out to save the soul of the benighted heathen! Even here, a stereotype is likely to emerge when the other side of the life of the Englishman in India like his comforts and his having an unduly large retinue of servants is purposefully played down. This portrayal is also important to discover the impact of India on the English.

Secondly, we have the portrayal of the Indians themselves. One discerns a neat formula in the characterisation of the Indians by the British writers. Most of these Indians are two dimensional characters who can all be rather easily lumped together under one stereotyped figure of *the* Indian. The colonial relationship necessitated the British writer to regard the native as one who is innocent, childlike and easily led. The category of people who fitted this description admirably well were the loyal servants and sepoys. Kipling's Imam Din and Gunga Din are the prototypes of this category. When the British writer went beyond this class, he depicted either the middle class or the westernized Indian. Most of the time, his portrayals of these classes produce only types which make one suspect whether he shuns complexity in his treatment of the native or refuses to grant it to the Indian solely for political reasons. The exceptions to this general trend are few and far between. Among them, mention could be made of Kipling's Lama, E.M.Forster's Aziz, Edward Thompson's Sadhu Jayananda and Paul Scott's Hari Kumar. In view of this, one is tempted to generalise that in Anglo-Indian fiction, we have an India without Indians.

The third aspect is the outcome of the first two in relation to each other, that is, the relationship between Indians and Englishmen. We see in many novels the absence of meaningful contact between the two races, for theirs is a parent-child, master-servant, teacher-pupil relationship that has been predetermined by the imperial ideology. But almost all the major Anglo-Indian novelists reveal a serious interest in the coming together of the races. Within the limitations imposed on them by the colonial situation, they have explored into this aspect with varying degrees of complexity and success.

Then we have India, the land with its emphasis on religion and philosophy. How well has the English writer been able to comprehend this either through intuition, observation or scholarship is the question. The responses have varied from extreme enthusiasm to supercilious dismissal. In addition, his depiction of the Indian Gods, myths, rituals, festivals, social conventions and behavioural patterns bring out not only his knowledge of India but more significantly his attitude towards these facets of Indian life. Here, one should refer to a conception which has been assiduously built up by these writers, that of the inscrutability of the orient.

Finally, the physical image of India plays a particularly notable role in creating a solid world that is recognizably Indian. The descriptions of the Indian landscape, its flora and fauna can be generally regarded as the forte of the English writer on India. This should have led to a very authentic image of at least the land in Anglo-Indian fiction but surprisingly even here stereotyped images seem to emerge as a consequence of the emphasis on the fantastic heat, dust and extreme climatic conditions. This emphasis on climate is seen to have another function, in that it is regarded as one of the main causes for the indolence, passivity and deceitfulness of the natives. The different areas of the country which are used as locales in Anglo-Indian novels will give us an idea of the fictional representation of India as a geographical entity.

All these constituents that go to form the image of India will be examined in the fictional works of Kipling, L.H. Myers and Raja Rao. A certain flexibility in approach is a precondition in a study of this kind, since the interest in India in these three writers is not the same. While Kipling's interest in the country is most representative of the more sensitive English writers on India, Myers's fascination is more for the philosophy and religion of the land than for its history which however is not ignored. In contrast to them, we get the insider's image of India in Raja Rao's works.

Notes

1. Percival Spear, *A History of India: Volume Two* (1965, rpt. Harmondsworth: Penguin Books Ltd. 1975), p. 68.
2. Nirad C.Chaudhuri, *Clive of India: A Political and Psychological Essay* (London: Barrie & Jenkins, 1975), p. 14.
3. Percival Spear, *A History of India,* p. 92.
4. Dennis Kincaid, *British Social Life in India: 1608-1937* (London: Routeledge, 1938), p. 109.
5. Quoted in S.N.Mukherjee, *Sir William Jones: A Study in Eighteenth-Century British Attitudes to India* (Cambridge: Cambridge University Press, 1968), p. 115.
6. Edward Thompson and G.T.Garratt, *The Rise and Fulfilment of British Rule* (London: Macmillan & Co., 1934), p. 166.
7. Quoted in Francis G.Hutchins, *The Illusion of Permanence: British Imperialism in India* (Princeton: Princeton University Press, 1967), p. 8.
8. George D.Bearce, *British Attitudes Towards India 1784- 1858* (London: Oxford University Press, 1961), p. 19.
9. Ibid., p. 65.
10. Ibid., p. 70.
11. James Mill, *The History of British India* (London: Macmillan, 1817), V, p. 416.
12. Francis G.Hutchins, *The Illusion of Permanence,* p.ix.
13. Ibid., p. 10.
14. James Mill, *The History of British India,* I, p. 342.
15. Ibid., p. 188.
16. Ibid., pp. 364-65.
17. Ibid., p. 378.
18. James Mill, *The History of British India,* II, pp. 70-71.
19. *Ibid.*, p. 46.
20. Mill, *The History of British India* (London: Macmillan, 1840), I, p. vii.
21. Quoted in James Morris, *Heaven's Command: An Imperial Progress* (1973; rpt. Harmondsworth: Penguin Books, 1979), p. 84.
22. Quoted in Bearce, p. 85.
23. Quoted in Bearce, p. 82.
24. Bearce, p. 82.
25. Quoted in Bearce, p. 125.
26. Quoted in James Morris, *Pax Britannica: The Climax of an Empire* (1968; rpt. Harmondsworth: Penguin Books, 1982), p. 139.

27. Quoted in Bearce, p. 133.
28. Quoted in Bearce, p. 134.
29. Hutchins, *The Illusion of Permanence,* p. 99.
30. Quoted in George Bennett (ed.), *The Concept of Empire: Burke to Atlee, 1774-1947* (London: Black, 1953), p. 105.
31. Quoted in George Bennett, p. 315.
32. J.R.Seeley, *The Expansion of England* (1883; rpt. London: Macmillan & Co., Ltd., 1920), p. 283.
33. Michael Edwardes, *British India, 1772-1947: A Survey of the Nature and Effects of Alien Rule* (London: Sidgwick & Jackson, 1967), p. 312.
34. Albert Memmi, trans., *The Colonizer and the Colonized* (New York: The Orion Press, 1965), p. 126.
35. Shamsul Islam, *Chronicles of the Raj: A Study of Literary Reaction to the Imperial Idea towards the End of the Raj* (London: Macmillan, 1979), p. 4.
36. Christopher Marlowe, *Tamburlaine The Great* (London: Methuen & Co., Ltd., 1951), Part II.V. iii. 132-35.
37. Christopher Marlowe, *The Tragical History of Doctor Faustus* (Madras: Macmillan, 1976), I.i. 80.
38. William Shakespeare, *Othello (*London: Macmillan & Co., Ltd., 1965), V .ii . 346.
39. William Shakespeare, *As You Like It* (London: Macmillan, 1928), III. ii. 69-70.
40. William Shakespeare, *Henry The Fourth (Part I)* (New York, Washington Square Press, Inc., 1961), III. i.1 80-81.
41. William Shakespeare, *Twelfth Night* (Cambridge: Cambridge University Press, 1971), II. v. 14-15.
42. 'To His Coy Mistress', *The Metaphysical Poets,* ed. Helen Gardner (1957; rpt. Calcutta: Rupa & Co., 1978), 4-5.
43. 'Paradise Lost', *Complete Poetry and Selected Prose of John Milton* (New York: Modern Library, 1950), Book II. 1-2.
44. 'The Task', *The Complete Poetical Works of William Cowper,* ed. H.S.Milford (London: Oxford University Press, 1913), IV. 28-30.
45. A.G.Bhupal Singh, *A Survey of Anglo-Indian Fiction* (London: Oxford University Press, 1934).
46. Bearce, p. 11.
47. Walter Scott, *The Surgeon's Daughter* (London: Ward, Lock & Co., 1827), p. 14
48. Walter Scott, *The Surgeon's Daughter,* p. 130.
49. Bearce, p. 112.
50. Bearce, p. 242.
51. W.D.Arnold, *Oakfield: or, Fellowship in the East* (1853; rpt. Leicester: Leicester University Press, 1973). Subsequent quotations referred to in the text are from this edition.
52. E.M.Forster, 'William Arnold', in *Two Cheers for Democracy* (London: Edward Arnold, 1951), p. 204.
53. Shirley Chew, "Vain Empires: The Response of some recent British Writers to the East," Diss. Singapore 1976, p. 6.
54. Hutchins, The Illusion of Permanence, p. 36.

Chapter - 2
Rudyard Kipling

Among the English writers who have written extensively on India, Rudyard Kipling occupies a singularly unique position. He spent the first five and a half years of his life in Bombay before he was sent to England along with his sister to be educated. And naturally, his earliest recorded impressions are of the streets of Bombay, his native servants and the Hindu Gods:

> My first impression is of daybreak, light and colour and golden and purple fruits at the level of my shoulder. This would be the memory of early morning walks to the Bombay fruit market with my *ayah* and later with my sister in her perambulator, and of our returns with our purchases piled high on the bows of it. Our *ayah* was a Portuguese Roman Catholic who would pray—I beside her—at a wayside Cross. Meeta, my Hindu bearer, would sometimes go into little Hindu temples where, being below the age of caste, I held his hand and looked at the dimly-seen, friendly Gods.[1]

The children those days were so constantly in the company of servants that they "thought and dreamed" in Hindustani. Kipling remembers how he was sent into the dining room after being dressed, with the caution, 'Speak English now to Papa and Mamma.'

Kipling's stay in England at Southsea in the house of a retired naval officer was far from happy as he went through "calculated torture— religious as well as scientific."[2] His experiences are recorded most movingly in one of his early stories, 'Baa, Baa, Black Sheep'. At Lorne Lodge (named 'House of Desolation'[3] by Kipling) he was treated badly, dissuaded from asking questions, separated from his sister, in short, treated as "a sort of moral leper."[4] But it had its redeeming side as well. It "drained [him] of any capacity for real, personal hate for the rest of [his] days."⁵ He had to invent lies to escape punishment and he felt that possibly in this, lay "the foundation of literary effort." This entire period seemed to him not "an unsuitable preparation for [his] future."⁶

After a little over five years at Southsea, Kipling was educated at the United Services College at Westward Ho! The principal, Mr. Cormell Price, a family friend of the Kiplings and one who had connections with the artists and intellectuals in London, successfully nurtured the latent literary talents in Kipling. His acute shortsight kept him out of the army or the tough Indian Civil Service examination. He began writing poems and also editing the *United Services College Chronicle*. The choice was soon made and Kipling was to be a writer. While in College, he made good use of Uncle Crom's library which stood him in good stead later on.

The Kiplings couldn't afford to send their son to Oxford for further studies, and so his father secured for him the job of an assistant editor of the *Civil and Military Gazette* published from Lahore. He wrote to a friend in December 1881 that "Ruddy thirsts for a man's life and a man's work."⁷ As a practising journalist, Kipling found just that kind of life and work at Lahore, and later on at Allahabad where he worked for the *Pioneer*.

After nearly seven years stay, he left India for good to return only once to Lahore to see his parents. This time he went from Colombo through southern India which he had not seen before. And he said, "this was my last look round the only real home I had yet known."⁸ Even while in London, already a famous literary figure, he was so homesick for India that he "clung to anyone who could remind him of it."⁹ Later on in Vermont he said, "there are only two places in the world where I want to live — Bombay and Brattleboro. And I can't live at either."¹⁰ Such was his predicament. Perhaps he did not belong anywhere, though he was, in an important sense, an Englishman. Still he could write to his friend, C.E.Norton that "England is a wonderful land. It is the most marvellous of all foreign countries that I have ever been in."¹¹ This rootlessness and the absence of a sense of belonging in Kipling was responsible for "one of the earliest of the recurrent recognitions about life ... that of the loneliness of man"¹² in his works. His entire life was marked by his attempts to overcome this feeling of loneliness and isolation through the security of his family (the Foursquare as his mother called it), Freemasonry, Mithraism, and the mystique of Empire.

India occupies a central position in Kipling's writings since the land, as suggested earlier, had a special place in his heart. He had spent his impressionable years as a child and the formative years of his life as a young man, in India. Wherever he went, whether it was London, Sussex or Vermont, he carried his India within his mind. And so it is no wonder that India serves as the single largest background to his creative writings. That is why, Alan Sandison thinks that "the main character in the stories is not the tired, tough, dedicated administrator nor the resourceful subaltern: the main character *is India itself*"[13] (emphasis mine). Kipling experienced India with an intensity and completeness that made it possible for him to show "the many faces of [the] country in all their *beauty, power* and *truth*"[14] cemphasis mine). It is no exaggeration to suggest that as a writer on the Indian scene, Kipling is unmatched by any English writer who came either before or after him, both in terms of the quality of perceptions and the bulk of his literary output.

In addition to his own genius and the influence of his father, his rich and eventful life as a journalist contributed in no small measure to his success in projecting the image or rather images of India. To begin with, Kipling had "a truly insatiable curiosity, prodigious powers of observation and a staggering memory."[15] Actually, one of his father's friends, a Parsee gentlemen "lived to record, sixty years afterwards, that Rudyard, at five years old, never forgot a face or a name."[16] All creative writers, it is commonly acknowledged, rely on memory to a very great extent. In his middle period, Kipling relied on this powerful memory of his, to drew from the subterranean depths of his being, remarkable portraits of India and its people. Kay Robinson, editor of the *Civil and Military Gazette* speaks of Kipling's extraordinary abilities in comprehending the Indian reality:

> While possessing a marvellous faculty for assimilating local colour without apparent effort, Kipling neglected no chance and spared no labor in acquiring experience that might serve a literary purpose. Of the various races of India, whom the ordinary Englishman lumps together as "natives", Kipling knew the quaintest details respecting habits, language, and distinctive ways of thought...No half-note in the wide gamut of native ideas and customs was unfamiliar to him: just as he had left no phase of white life in India unexplored.[17]

As a young man, "he acquired in the bazaar", said Sir Louis Dane to Lord Birkenhead, the author of a recent biography of Kipling, "an immense knowledge of Indian ways, language, and trade customs. He was extraordinarily accurate in his Indian details. What he could not get from personal exploration, he was able to get from his father."[18] He was indeed perceptive and sensitive to the Indian reality, but his father's influence on him in this regard needs to be examined in some detail. Of course, Lockwood Kipling had lived long enough in India and his Principalship of the School of Art in Bombay and the Curatorship of the Lahore Museum later, and the fact that he was the author of the book, *Beast and Man in India* made him an authoritative voice on India. Kipling also tells of his indebtedness to his father in writing that remarkable work, *Kim*. What is quite revealing in the few extracts reproduced below from his book is that, Lockwood Kipling was far from being completely free from some of the common prejudices that marked the white man's attitude towards India and its people.

> First-hand observation and accurate statement of fact seem almost impossible to the Oriental, and education has not hitherto availed to help him. In the West, public instruction becomes more real and vital year by year, but in the East, it is still bound hard and fast to the corpse of dead literature.[19]

> There are many lies in History, but Hindu writers are remarkable for having deliberately and of set principle ignored all the facts of life. All is done, however, with such an air of conviction and pious purpose that we must use Dr. Johnson's kindly discrimination and say they are not inexcusable, but consecrated liars.[20]

The attitude revealed here is very much the same that one notices in Macaulay's brazen dismissal of the sacred books of Hindus as being "false history, false astronomy, false medicine ...[and] false religion."[21] Like Macaulay, Lockwood Kipling goes wrong because he applies his own standards of judgement in his attempt to understand a radically different civilization. He not only fails to comprehend the basic aspects of Hindu mythology, but is unable to distinguish between legend and reality. He also believed "that only a fool will pretend to say with absolute confidence what a native thinks."[22] This inscrutability of the Oriental mind is another oft repeated charge made by the Europeans. And so we see that Lockwood Kipling, despite his inwardness with Indian life, responded in a surprisingly conventional fashion. He treads the beaten track especially when he attempts generalizations about Indian attitudes to life and the Indian mind. This is inevitable, since *"Beast and Man in India* came from books and travellers' reports, not from any first-hand knowledge of Indian cities, villages or jungle."[23] Therefore, Lockwood Kipling was not altogether a healthy influence on his son, a fact generally overlooked by Kipling critics. With his admiration and an almost uncritical reverence for his father, Rudyard Kipling was always susceptible to be swayed by the latter's views on India. Although many Kipling stories suffer from similar biases, he is like all great writers, able to transcend them in his best work.

And finally to his life as a journalist which launched him on his literary career and also made for a complete exposure to the Indian reality. He termed his life in India as "Seven Years' hard."[24] When his parents and sister went over to the Hills during summer, he was all alone in Lahore with only the heat, sickness and nightmares for company. Because of his belief that "much of real Indian life goes on in the hot-weather nights,"[25] he usually went on long jaunts during nights. One such wandering in Lahore is evoked brilliantly in his story. The City of Dreadful Night. During the day,

> I never worked less than ten hours and seldom more than fifteen per diem; and as our paper came out in the evening, did not see the midday sun except on Sundays. I had fever too, regular and persistent, to which I added for a while chronic dysentry. Yet I discovered that a man can work with a temperature of 104, even though next day he has to ask the office who wrote the article.[26]

Even while he talks of the various privileges he enjoyed as a sahib like having his own carriage and servants, he points out how,

> One must set these things against the taste of fever in one's mouth, and the buzz for quinine in one's ears; the temper frayed by heat to breaking-point but for sanity's sake held back from the break; the descending darkness of intolerable dusks; and the less supportable dawns of fierce, stale heat through half of the year.[27]

In addition to these tremendous hardships, there was also the fragility of human effort and the continuous proximity of death:

> ... my world was filled with boys, but a few years older than I, who lived utterly alone, and died from typhoid mostly at the regulation age of twenty-two ... Death was always our near companion. When there was an outbreak of eleven cases of typhoid in our white community of seventy, and professional nurses had not been invented, the men sat up with the men and the women with the women. We lost four of our invalids and thought we had done well. Otherwise, men and women dropped where they stood ... The dead of all times were about us — in the vast forgotten Muslim cemeteries round the Station, where one's horse's hoof of a morning might break through to the corpse below ...[28]

These hardships had revealed to Kipling an important aspect of the imperial experience. The trying conditions under which the white men, both civilians and soldiers living in India performed their duties heroically, trying to administer this vast, unmanageable land with its teeming masses and their diverse religions, elicited a profound admiration from Kipling.

At the same time, he became keenly aware of the rigid caste-like structure of the British society in India. There were two major castes, 'Officers' and 'Other ranks.' Marriage was permitted only within the group. They did not even dine together and they were further subdivided, something very similar to the Indian caste system. And there was at the end of the *Civil List,* a list of different groups arranged in their order of precedence and it showed everyone's pay and his exact place in the hierarchy.[29] Much to Kipling's own discomfiture, it did not include reporters for the *Civil and Military Gazette.*[30] And so Kipling found himself a sort of an outcaste in the Anglo-Indian society.

This feeling of being an oddity in his own society is, in a sense, a continuation of his nightmarish experiences earlier at the Lorne Lodge, and the frustrations of Westward Ho! In other words, he was "someone who had spent six years in a concentration camp as a child; he never got over it. As a very young man, he spent seven years in India that confirmed his belief in concentration camps, he never got over this either."[31] In spite of the slight overstatement in this assessment, Jarrel's is a fair description of Kipling's situation. Though he felt victimised for no fault of his, paradoxically, his concerns in his stories, are never for the victim, except in a story like 'Baa, Baa, Black Sheep' which is perhaps explained by its being largely autobiographical. Where his stories accept the basic assumptions of imperialism without any questioning, the feelings of the victim are completely subordinated to that of the victimiser, in this case, the ruler. One must also add that in the stories, where Kipling regards the white man himself as the victim of his work in India, his sympathies are interestingly very much with the white man.

Seen from a totally different perspective, one notices the less unpleasant aspects of Kipling's life in British India which are more relevant to a study of the image of India in his writings. Being a newspaperman, he was able to see the working of the British administrative machinery from close quarters. He also came into contact with the entire cross-section of the British working in India. In the Punjab Club, and elsewhere he admits:

> ... I met none except picked men at their definite work — Civilians, Army, Education, Canals, Forestry, Engineering, Irrigation, Railways, Doctors, and Lawyers — samples of each branch and each talking his own shop. It follows then that 'show of technical knowledge' for which I was blamed later came to me from the horse's mouth, even to boredom.[32]

And he

> Would wander till dawn in all manner of odd places — liquor-shops, gambling-and-opium-dens, which are not a bit mysterious, wayside entertainments such as puppet-shows, native dances; or in and about the narrow gullies under the Mosque of Wazir Khan for the sheer sake of looking.[33]

And so we see how his Indian writings are the result of close observation, fidelity to detail and total involvement. With these actual facts staring in one's face, one cannot suggest that "Kipling ... took one look at India — perhaps one sniff as well — and began to write."[34] This would only have resulted in a very superficial account of the country, something the run-of-the-mill Anglo-Indian novelists endlessly achieved.

So well did Kipling know the soldiers, that Lord Roberts the Commander-in-chief of the British army once asked him in Simla as to what the men thought of their living conditions. He justifiably regarded it as "the proudest moment of [his] young life."36 Put briefly, Kipling was eminently qualified to be the chronicler of colonial India of the nineteenth century. He served the cause of the Empire with great devotion and was able to bring home to his countrymen in England, through his writings, the conditions under which Englishmen toiled in their 'civilising mission' in India.

It is this anxiety of Kipling to justify the empire that has resulted in his being dubbed, "a jingo imperialist ... morally insensitive and aesthetically disgusting"36; as a writer whose "imperialism is reprehensible not because it *is* imperialism but because it is puny and mindless imperialism"37; as a writer who "discarded his own moral intelligence in favour of the point of view of a dominant political party."38 These attacks by the three well-known twentieth century critics are not hard to understand in view of the present day contempt and derision for imperialism as a political ideology and all that it stands for, but the violence of their attack is surely indefensible. They are impatient and are in a hurry to reach definite conclusions. Not only do they take a wholly simplistic view of Kipling's complex attitudes towards his major material and political faith, that is India and Imperialism respectively, they also fail to draw a line between his political beliefs and creative writings. None of them rely entirely on the creative works in their assessment of Kipling the writer, thus ignoring one of the basic premises of literary criticism.39 And it is even more sad when one looks in vain for greater sympathy in Indian critics like Bhaskara Rao40 and Syed Sajjad Husain.41 In their evaluation of Kipling in relation to his works set in India, surprisingly, textual evidence is conspicuous by its relative absence—a feature fairly common in most Kipling critics. Only Benita Parry42 shows an admirable and enviable mixture of sympathy and understanding along with an incisive mind that lays bare all the subtleties and factual distinctions in Kipling's response to India, a response that matches the complexity underlying India.

Kipling's image of India is, largely the result of two, not contrary, but developing attitudes. The early attitude is the typical response of the coloniser, one who is given to having fixed notions about the colonised. The emergent image from such an attitude is not only static but, in many ways, easily predictable. Whereas the later attitude, in sharp contrast, is more personal and genuine and it accounts for greater probing into the Indian reality. Because of this probing, the earlier stock responses gradually disappear and we have a series of images that can be described as authentic. It is rather difficult to pinpoint accurately the period when the earlier attitude ends and the later begins. Perhaps it is the year 1889 that is crucial, for it was in March that year that Kipling left India for good. This distancing from his subject both in space and time perhaps gave him a better perspective and the necessary detachment as well. Though a few stories remain exceptions to this kind of rigid classification, this division by and large holds good.

A study of the image of India as revealed in Kipling's fictional writings has to be both exhaustive and inclusive. Firstly, in the depiction of the English in India, a certain historical perspective is necessary in view of the British imperial rule in India. The attitudes of the English men and women living in India were largely conditioned by their role as rulers of the country. They were, more often than not, rulers first and human beings only next. Secondly, his portrayal of the landscape of India and its people needs to be examined. In other words, how far are Kipling's descriptions of the Indian landscape accurate? Is there a deliberate or unintentional, whichever it be, overemphasis on a particular feature of the landscape that makes for some kind of distortion? Of course, this problem applies as well as to the question of the image of India in its entirety. The study of the portrayal of the Indian peoples must take into account their attitudes to life, their religions, myths and superstitions together with their strengths and weaknesses as a race. And finally, perhaps the most significant of all, is the delineation of the relationship between the Indians and the Englishmen.

More important is Kipling's own allegiance to the imperialistic credo that assumes a central significance in all these three aspects that contribute to his image of India. Syed Sajjad Hussain says that Kipling "subordinate(d) his artistic sensibilities to a political creed."[43] It is true that Kipling was not able to overcome this allegiance in many of his early stories. But in quite a few of his later ones, and particularly in *Kim*, coincidentally his better artistic efforts, he achieves a vision of India where art triumphs over ideology.

The first story that Kipling wrote, as we have on Cornell's[44] authority, is 'The Gate of the Hundred Sorrows'. It is about an Eurasian opium addict and is written as a sort of dramatic monologue in prose. It should be recalled here, that Kipling was a great admirer of Browning while at school. It does not tell us a story, nor does it dramatise a moral but is only "an exercise in texture and mood."[45] It conveys dramatically through the use of simple but evocative words, the feelings of an opium addict and his eventual disintegration. Kipling occasionally employs devices of poetry like refrain, to heighten the effect. All the related problems of this addict such as Black Smoke, money and death are linked with each other in an intensely personal way to produce a powerful story.

And as Louis Cornell points out "we note the author's neutrality towards his material."[46] Here the narrator, though involved in what he narrates, is able to dramatise the entire situation with an admirable mixture of objectivity and involvement. But it has to be said at once, that Kipling did not always attain this kind of neutrality towards his material. This usually happened only in his best work while in his less satisfying works, he is seen as a writer who is easily swayed by his prejudices, be they political or racial. In this story, he succeeded since he was only trying to create a particular mood and describe the predicament of an individual—whose race did not matter to Kipling —with a weakness for opium.

His first collection of stories, *Plain Tales from the Hills,* opens with 'Lispeth', a fine portrait of an Indian hill girl. Though an early story, there are already signs of the mature Kipling who refused to take fixed positions in his attitudes towards the Indian and the Englishman. Originally a Pahari, but converted into Christianity when she was only five weeks old, Lispeth lives a "half-servant, half-companion" to the wife of the Chaplain of Kotgarh Mission. She accidentally finds a badly injured Englishman, nurses him back to health and while doing so falls in love with him. When he fails to turn up, contrary to his word, she curses the English as liars and goes back to her people.

Lispeth is an extremely beautiful woman, "the original Diana of the Romans." Among the native women, Kipling idealised the Hill-woman because he believed that she, "can in six months master most of the ways of her English sisters"[47] and so she was for him the nearest approximation to the English woman. Kipling exhibits some of his biases when he makes neat demarcations initially in the story. She is savage and hides no feelings of hers from the Englishman. She is instinctive and falls in love at first sight, one of the "uncivilized Eastern instincts." In contrast, the Englishman made of "a superior clay" goes about feigning love for Lispeth calling her pet names that "meant nothing at all to him."

A consideration of Kipling's attitude here would be necessary. When the Chaplain's wife remarks at the end of the story that, "there is no law whereby you can account for the vagaries of the heathen ... that Lispeth was always at heart an infidel,"[48] Kipling sardonically comments that the girl was with them from "the mature age of five weeks." Despite this failure of the missionaries, Kipling seems to suggest that Lispeth has found her true self in going back to her own people. What does Kipling think of the Englishman? We are told that he "wrote a book on the East afterwards. Lispeth's name did not appear there. — "[49] a man who is callous enough to not even mention the name of the person who saved him, perhaps from death itself, in contrast to a woman who shows selfless concern for another. It is apparent which of the two is better.

'The Judgement of Dungara' has a similar theme in that it also depicts the failure of the missionaries in India when they try to meddle with the native ways of life. Rev. Justus, the missionary ignores the warning of Gallio, the Assistant Collector and succeeds in drawing the people of Buria Kol away from their local goddess, Dungara. Angered at this, Athon Daze, the High Priest retaliates in a telling manner. As the converts, forty strong, all dressed up stand to welcome Gallio and his wife, they feel a burning sensation and run away helter skelter. Their clothes begin to burn as it is made from Nilgiri Nettle, given by Athon Daze, a fibre which literally means 'woven fire.' As is to be expected in such circumstances, the natives attributing it to Dungara's anger return to her fold.

Kipling's view of the missionaries is more complex in this story. He seems to believe that the task of the missionaries is an almost hopeless one, for they are dealing with natives who have "the simplicity of childhood, the experience of man and the subtlety of the savage."[50] They have to fight against all possible odds and the only spur for their actions is that they are fighting against the Devil itself. They suffer immensely:

....The reports are silent here, because heroism, failure, doubt, despair and self-abnegation on the part of a mere cultured white men are things of no weight as compared to the saving of one half-human soul from a fantastic faith in wood-spirits, goblins of the rock, and river-fiends.[51]

Though Kipling is a little cynical of the devious means adopted by the missionaries, his attitude is far from being a straight forward condemnation of their activities. As a matter of fact, he looks at the natives from the empirical European standpoint. That is the reason why he seems to suggest that the natives are beyond redemption and expresses almost a reverential admiration for the difficulties the missionaries endure:

> Do you know what life at a mission outpost means? Try to imagine a loneliness exceeding that of the smallest station to which government has ever sent you—isolation that weighs upon the waking eyelids and drives you by force headlong into the labours of the day. There is no post, there is no one of your own colour to speak to, there are no roads: there is, indeed, food to keep you alive, but it is not pleasant to eat; and whatever of good or beauty or interest there is in your life, must come from yourself and the grace that may be planted in you.[52]

While Kipling made derisive remarks against the Chaplain's wife in 'Lispeth', he seems to view them in, 'The Judgement of Dungara,' as noble individuals toiling heroically undaunted by the fear of failure. And so we have quite contrary attitudes in Kipling towards the missionaries and their work. This brings us to one of the general features in Kipling's response to India. To read Kipling's writings on India is to get into a maze of contradictions. To begin with, one can explain it by referring to the conflicting pulls he underwent throughout his literary career. While Kipling responded to India as one who deeply loved the country and its people, he was also constantly aware of his being an Englishman, a representative of the governing class that religiously followed 'Law, Order, Duty an' Restraint, Obedience, Discipline'[53] in performing the imperial mission in India. This duality of response, in other words, is the outcome of his near total identification with the cause of the Empire interfering with his integrity as a writer. The consequence of it is that in the entire body of his fictional work set in India, these two impulses are often at variance with each other. The particular impulse that predominates in a given work determines the nature of Kipling's response and the eventual image of India that emerges from it.

A related problem of Kipling's opinion of religions other than his own can be discussed here. Bonamy Dobree believed that Kipling "intuitively sympathised with races quite different from his own."[54] Religion was, for Kipling, something so deeply ingrained into one's nature that it is very hard, even impossible, for one to change. One of his characters, Grish Chunder, remarks "once a Hindu, always a

Hindu."⁵⁵ Kipling did not think it right to trifle with the beliefs of other people. That is why, Fleete, is made to go through a traumatic experience after he insultingly grinds his cigar into the statue of Hanuman in 'The Mark of the Beast.'⁵⁶ And finally to his views on missionaries expressed in a letter:

> It is my fortune to have been born and to a large extent brought up among those whom white men call "heathen"; and while I recognize the paramount duty of every white man to follow the teachings of his creed and conscience as "a debtor to the whole law" it seems to me cruel that white man, whose governments are armed with the most murderous weapons known to science, should amaze and confound their fellow creatures with a doctrine of salvation imperfectly understood by themselves and a code of ethics foreign to the climate and instincts of those races whose most cherished customs they outrage and whose gods they insult.⁵⁷

These are indeed words of a civilized man who has a basic respect for other religions, and *not* a 'jingo imperialist' who invariably thinks in terms of the superiority of his religion and for whom conversion to Christianity amounts to a civilizing mission.

Of the two impulses referred to before, the impulse to justify the Empire dominates Kipling's earlier work such as *Plain Tales from the Hills, Soldiers Three* and *Wee Willie Winkie.* These creative exercises in the defence of the Empire describe how the English gave India "internal security, communications, precautions against famine, irrigation, afforestation, even the rudiment of an educational system, on a scale that no other country in continental Asia or Africa could approach."⁵⁸ He glorifies their work with emphasis invariably on their physical hardships, feelings of loneliness and isolation and their distressing working conditions. And for the English, Kipling has, as is to be expected, nothing but sympathy and praise. In his anxiety to commend the 'White man's burden,' he almost always, overlooks the predicament of the native. The result is that we have a *fixed* perspective in these stories, thus making it easier sometimes even to anticipate the turn of the narrative. Another outcome of this, is the inevitable focus on the English in his Indian stories, and in terms of the image of India we have an India that is preponderantly English.

And hence it is but logical that most of these early stories should be grounded in certain basic assumptions. The natives, like little children, cannot look after themselves and hence need the English made of 'superior clay' to govern them. The English, trained in public schools surely make better rulers of India. And as a race, they are superior to Indians both physically and morally and, curiously, this is endorsed by the Indians themselves without question.

When some of these assumptions are carried beyond tolerable limits, Kipling becomes guilty of racial prejudice, which could take on distasteful proportions as in his story, 'His Chance in Life.' For Kipling, to be a white man is to be in possession of supreme authority to which the helpless native meekly submits. Even the Eurasian can rise to great heights occasionally, thanks to the presence of the white blood in him. Michele D'Cruze, the telegraph signaller, a Eurasian, is "very black" and he "looked down on natives as only a man with seven-eighths native blood in his veins can."[59] He is in love with Miss Vezzis, and Mrs Vezzis agrees to their marriage on condition that he should at least earn fifty rupees a month, while he presently drew a salary of only thirty five rupees. And his chance comes when he is in Tibasu. There is a 'little Mohurrum riot,' started by the native muslims because of their contempt for the Hindu Sub-Judge. And Kipling warns:

> Never forget that unless the outward and visible signs of
> Our Authority are always before a native he is an incapable as a child of understanding what authority means,
> or where is the danger of disobeying it. (p. 81.)

This is, of course, a basic premise of the colonial situation. The rioters march towards the Telegraph Office. Michele's co-worker, a Bengali Babu "put on his cap and quietly dropped out of the window." Kipling's proverbial contempt for the Bengali is evident even in this early story. When the native police inspector addresses Michele as Sahib, he realises that he "was the only representative of English authority in the place." He fires at the crowd and is able to successfully quell the riot. He is, in fact, in control of the town till next morning when the assistant collector arrives.

Kipling's racial prejudice is evident in his description of the pathetic manner in which Michele disintegrates when confronted by a pure white man :

> ... Michele went down the road, musket in hand, to meet
> the Assistant Collector who had ridden in to quell Tibasu.

> But, in the presence of this young Englishman, Michele felt himself slipping back and more into the native; and the tale of the Tibasu Riots ended, with the strain on the teller, in an hysterical outburst of tears, bred by sorrow that he had killed a man, shame that he could not feel as uplifted as he had felt through the night, and childish anger that his tongue could not do justice to his great deeds. It was the White drop in Michele's veins dying out, though he did not know it. (p. 83.)

Though Kipling tries to suggest that Michele rose to great heights of heroism because of his love for Miss Vezzis, the story makes it clear that it is the one-eighth white blood in him that was responsible for his action. To possess white blood is to be in possession of power and authority! And to possess even a little bit of it is sure to make one into a hero. This also confirms Kipling's belief in the innate superiority of the white man over the native.

This belief is even better illustrated in his story, 'The Head of the District'. On the death of the English Deputy Commissioner, Yardly-Orde, the Viceroy decides to appoint a Bengali to administer Kot-Kumharsen district. Kipling's tongue-in-cheek response makes his attitude clear:

> The very simplicity of the notion was its charm. What more easy to win a reputation for far-seeing statesmanship, originality, and, above all, deference to the desires of the people, than by appointing a child of the country to the rule of that country?[60]

Elsewhere in the story, he regards it as "a piece of cruel folly!" a remark that the story plainly justifies. Interestingly, Kipling had little respect for the liberal policies of Prime Minister Gladstone and Viceroy Lord Ripon; obviously the above remark is directed against the latter.

We have a foretaste of what is to come in the manner in which the new appointee is introduced:

> There was a gentleman and a member of the Bengal Civil Service who had won his place and a University degree *to boot* in fair and open competition with the sons of the English. He was cultured, of the world, and, *if report spoke truly*, had wisely and, above all, sympathetically ruled a

crowded district of South-Eastern Bengal. He had been to England and charmed many drawing rooms there. His name, if the Viceroy recollected aright, was *Mr.* Grish Chunder De, *M.A.* (p.123.)   (Emphasis mine)

It is made up of innuendoes, 'to boot'; doubts about his efficiency, 'if report spoke truly; mocking tone evident in both the prefix and suffix to his name and there is a dig at the Viceroy too.

Grish Chunder De's earlier success in governing a district in South-Eastern Bengal, Kipling makes it plain, is not to be interpreted as a sign of his administrative capabilities. For "he did no more than turn the place into a pleasant little family preserve, allowed his subordinates to do what they liked, and let everybody have a chance at the shekels." (p. 126.) But this does not work in the turbulent border district of Kot-Kumharsen where trouble starts brewing immediately after his arrival. And Grish Chunder De flees for his life,

> thanking gods entirely unknown to the most catholic of universities that he had not taken charge of the district, and could still — happy resource of a fertile race — fail sick. (p. 138.)

Kipling's irony directed against the natives as a race is savage here. As is to be expected, the trouble is put down by Tallantire, the English assistant without much ado.

A significant aspect of the colonial situation is revealed in the story through Kipling's delineation of the relationship between the rulers and the ruled. The rulers' concern for the ruled, the personal sacrifices made by them and their status as gods are all made explicit in the advice given by the dying Yardly-Orde to his subjects:

> ... You must be good men when I am not here. Such of you as live in our borders must pay your taxes quietly as before. I have spoken of the villages to be gently treated this year. Such of you as live in the hills must refrain from cattle-lifting, and burn no more thatch, and turn a deaf ear to the voice of the priests, who, not knowing the strength of the Government, would lead you into foolish wars, wherein you will surely die and your crops be eaten by strangers. And you must not sack any caravans, and must leave your arms at the police-post when you come in; as has been your custom and my order. And Tallantire Sahib will be

with you, but I do not know who takes my place. I speak now true talk, for I am as it were already dead, my children, — for though ye be strong men, ye are children. (pp. 120-21.)

Their leader Khoda Dad Khan's reply reveals both the helplessness and the sense of dependence of the ruled:

"And thou art our father and our mother. What shall we do, now there is no one to speak for us, or to teach us to go wisely." (p. 121.)

Thus we see Kipling define the colonial relationship through Parent-child and God-worshipper associations. The native, who have made gods and parents of their rulers are convinced that only the white man is capable of ruling them. This points to a basic premise of the colonial situation. Albert Memmi perceptively remarks that the coloniser

enjoys the preference and respect of the colonised themselves, who grant him more than those who are the best of their own people; who, for example, have more faith in his word than in that of their own population.[61]

The colonial rule was intended to prove, among other things, the indispensability of the British as rulers. The story is, no doubt, a defence of the English point of view but it is a defence which is based on racial bias. What is difficult to comprehend is that Kipling does not allow Grish Chunder De to prove himself even as a failure. The only redeeming feature is that Kipling never repeated such a blatantly prejudiced point of view in any of the future stories. It is possibly stories like 'His Chance in Life' and 'The Head of the District', that made George Orwell remark that, "it is no use pretending that Kipling's view of life, as a whole, can be accepted or even forgiven by any civilized person."[62]

In Kipling's portrayal of the people of India and England, a fairly neat classification is possible. His Anglo-Indians were mostly workers whether they be soldiers, civilians, engineers or the highly fashionable set at Simla. His Indians were drawn from both the educated and the uneducated classes. It is interesting to note that the illiterate native servant is one of the most commonly depicted characters in Kipling. A major reason could be that he knew them well and possibly liked them, having grown up amidst them. The upper and the middle classes receive much less attention at his hands. In fact, his reluctance to portray the educated Indian, makes his image of India incomplete to that extent. After all, it is the middle class Indian who reacted strongly against the English rule, and did succeed in initiating the movement for political freedom. However, it is not difficult to locate the reason for this reluctance in Kipling. Kipling the 'imperialist' perhaps knew that if there was any threat to the infallible British Empire, it came from this particular class. Perhaps this explains his consistently hostile attitude towards the educated Indian, whether he was a rajah or he belonged to the middle classes. But in the story, 'On the City Wall' he was able to, through his sheer artistic integrity, anticipate the actual dangers that would destroy the Empire in future.

'On the City Wall' portrays, among other things, the supreme power of the British the unreliability of the educated Indian in a moment of crisis and his problems as he is caught between two worlds — his own and that of the British. The narrator, a young Englishman is very friendly and intimate with Wali Dad and Lalun, a beautiful courtesan. He unwillingly becomes an accomplice in their plan to smuggle out Khem Singh, a professed rebel, who, they hope will once again successfully lead the fight against the British.

To deviate for a while, a short passage from the story reveals a rich cross-section of Indian society that meet in Lalun's place:

> Shiahs of the grimmest and most uncompromising persuasion; Sufis who had lost all belief in the Prophet and retained but little in God; wandering Hindu priests passing southward on their way to the Central India fairs and other affairs; Pundits in black gowns, with spectacles on their noses and undigested wisdom in their 'insides,' bearded headman of the wards; sikhs with all the details of the latest ecclesiastical scandal in the Golden Temple; red-eyed priests from beyond the Border, looking like trapped wolves and talking like ravens; M.A's of the University, very superior and very voluble...[63]

Here is a description that would do credit to an Indian novelist! How well has Kipling been able to capture such a disparate crowd of Indians. Each group is individualised with that minimal detail, the hallmark of a mature writer. These little details, in addition, offer us clues to the character of each group. There is nothing superficial or journalistic in this description that comes from Kipling, the man who had known India so well that he had absorbed it into his system. This description, in miniature, anticipates his brilliant evocation of Indian life on the Grand Trunk Road in *Kim*.

In Wali Dad, Kipling has portrayed a convincing picture of an individual who is 'suffering acutely' from English education, and has "spent two years experimenting with the creeds of the Earth." His predicament is indeed pathetic, for he "was always mourning over something or other — the country of which he despaired, or the creed in which he had lost faith, or the life of the English which he could by no means understand." (p. 330.) And hence, he is bitterly scornful of his Faith and its manifestations. Mohurrum to him is "a most disgraceful exhibition." Many a contemporary English educated Indian may well be inclined to identify himself with the predicament of Wali Dad!

What is, of course, revealing is that when the riots break out between the Muslims and Hindus, he forgets his role in the planned rescue of Khem Singh — this, despite his English education, remarks Kipling — and plunges "into the thick of the fight." And at the end of it all, the narrator finds Wali Dad, the confirmed "Agnostic and Unbeliever" sobbing hysterically. Kipling has sensitively portrayed in him, "the westernized Indian weary of west and east, poised between eras."[64]

He seems to be suggesting that India needs the moral authority of the British, in view of the unreliability of even educated Indians like Wali Dad. So he felt that their attempts at nationalism were all doomed to failure. What Kipling did not fully foresee, was that educated Indians in future would be able to resist this kind of negative retreat into the past, and succeed where Wali Dad had failed. As a matter of fact, the seeds of liquidation of the British Empire were sown in the very act of deciding to educate the natives, a truth borne out by Indian history. Wali Dad had said earlier to the narrator:

> "Thanks to your Government, all our heads are protected and with the educational facilities at my command I might be a distinguished member of the local administration. Perhaps, in time, I might even be a member of a Legislative Council." (p. 331.)

There are places where the reader can detect the tone of doubt and uncertainty in Kipling, when he points out that some of the natives, though uneducated,

> hope to administer the country in their own way — that is to say, with a garnish of Red Sauce. Such men must exist among two hundred million people, and, if they are not attended to, may cause trouble and even break the great idol called *Pax Britannica,* which, as the newspapers say, lives between Peshawar and Cape Comorin...(pp. 325-26.)

It is these remarks that have given the story the ring of a political prophecy.

At this juncture, it would be appropriate to briefly consider his story, 'The Enlightenments of Pagett, M.P.,'[65] wherein we find "an unrestrained attack on the totality of Indian norms and customs."[66] Perhaps, there is no other story in the entire corpus of Kipling's writings where India and Indians are treated so harshly, his customary sympathy being conspicuous by its absence. Apart from his own dislike of the Liberal talk in London about India at the time, Kipling's father is said to have assisted him in the writing of this story.[67]

Pagett, a Member of Parliament for three terms, interested in Indian affairs, visits the country with an open mind to see for himself the problems confronting it. While in India, he "intends to study the political aspect of things and the possibility of bestowing electoral institutions on the people." (p. 352.) He is rather anxious to learn of the impact of the Congress movement on the masses and during his stay with Orde, the deputy commissioner, he gets his opportunity when he comes into contact with a cross section of Indian society. Pagett's anxiety is matched by the callous contempt Orde has for Congress.

Pagett meets Bishen Singh, a Sikh carpenter; Rasul Ali Khan, the Mohammedan landholder and Jelloo, the Jat farmer, all of whom confide to Orde that they had never even heard of Congress and knew nothing about it. Unlike these Indians, Dina Nath, a middle class Bengali student regards Congress as "the greatest movement of modern times, and one in which all educated men ...*must* join." (p. 346.) But this Bengali Babu is, as in other Kipling stories, the target of satire of a rather vicious kind. He speaks formal, idiomatic English that sounds stilted and funny, airs "vague generalities" and "the crudity of his views" make Pagett confess to Orde that he regards young India as "Curious, very curious — and callow." (p. 247)

At the end, we see Pagett still unable to share Orde's view that the Congress is "merely a class movement of a local and temporary character." (p. 354) To this doubt, comes Orde's oracular pronouncement:

"Believe me, Pagett, to deal with India you want first-hand knowledge and experience", pagett can only tamely answer: "India's a very curious place." (P. 355)

Though the story offers a few revealing truths about the influence of the family in India, the need to protect India from exploitation by selfish interests (including British) through a strong government, it emphasises only the deaths and disasters in India, divisions based on caste and class, horrifying social evils to reiterate the need for British rule in India and not for reforms as suggested by Pagett. That Kipling should dismiss the Congress movement as "the work of a limited class, a microscopic minority" ignoring the larger historical truth that all such movements are the handiwork of an influential, educated minority, and that he should regard Indian customs and habits as being inimical to happiness and health of the people, points to a certain illiberal frame of mind in him. And Alan Sandison, otherwise a sensitive critic of Kipling, finds in this story,"a *reasoned* and *responsible* defence of the Anglo-Indian point of view"[68] (emphasis mine). This is nothing short of a total misreading of the story. What is, however, redeeming is that not only did Kipling refuse to take such a viewpoint in any of his later stories, but also that he wisely excluded this from the collected edition of his works, a sure sign of penitence!

When we speak of India in Kipling's works, it is really British India that we are talking about. This is true of all major Anglo-Indian writers. And in a depiction of this India, it is inevitable given their kind of predilections, that major attention should be focussed on the presentation of the British in India. A study of Kipling's portrayal of the British in India cannot be divorced from his views on the Empire. The basic assumptions that govern his earlier stories, are largely those of an imperialist. Kipling's faith in the Empire can be explained by its utility value, in that it helped maintain order and promote the cause of civilization. Perhaps more important is the psychological reason that the mystique of Empire offered him a feeling of security and a sense of belonging in a hostile universe that had made him feel like a "Stranger upon Earth."[69] Having been a journalist, Kipling had watched the Empire in action from a vantage point of view. He saw the disinterested devotion of the Englishmen who carried out the work of the Empire. He also believed that but for their authoritative presence in the country, India would not have been able to escape "banditry, massacre, flood, drought, famine, plague."[70] The Empire that did such heroic deeds and inspired complete loyalty in its servants must indeed be, Kipling felt, a noble institution.

This was but inevitable, as Kipling lived and began writing during the heyday of the British Empire. He was to be disillusioned later by the Boer War. But it must be added, that Kipling was indeed aware of the dangers of Imperialism though he tended to play it down especially in his earlier writings. He was not unaware, as alleged by George Orwell, of the economic implications of Imperialism. It is also rather curious to note that the always used the word 'Imperialism' in inverted commas in his autobiography, *Something of Myself*. He understood, if only occasionally, the plight of the colonised as is evident, for instance, in his poem, 'A Pict Song':

> Rome never looks where she treads
> Always her heavy hooves fall,
> On our stomachs, our hearts, or our heads;
> And Rome never heeds when we bawl. [71]

However, one should not forget that this particular point of view, that of the colonised seldom appears in his work.

For Kipling, "authority, discipline, fidelity, devotion, fortitude and self-sacrifice constitute the ideal imperial servant."[72] His Englishmen, to whichever category they belong, have these virtues and Kipling, in story after story, brings them out with a sympathy that is born of a total admiration for their work. The Soldiers and Civilians, form the two major groups in Kipling's writings. The soldier stories in Kipling are the products of his close observation and fidelity to detail which make for a remarkable verisimilitude. And it is, no doubt, true that in the entire English literature "you will find no treatment of the English soldier on any adequate scale between Shakespeare and Kipling."[73] His most memorable creations are, of course, the famous trio of Mulvaney, Leraoyd and Ortheris. They are real tommies and this is achieved in no small measure by Kipling's evocation of their speech in all its slangy, picturesque detail.

Kipling's depiction of the other Englishmen in India keeping the machinery of the Empire in motion is equally fascinating, and has a greater degree of complexity because of the variety of their professional roles. For Kipling's Empire-builders, the public school provided both the inspiration and a code of conduct:

> The game is more than the player of the game,
> And the ship is more than the crew![74]

The public schools inculcated, in the words of Dr. Arnold, Headmaster at Rugby, "religious and moral principles, gentlemanly conduct and intellectual ability,"[75] into its pupils. These were the men who were needed to administer the Empire. They had to be "men of courage, endurance and fortitude: men who saw their duty clearly and simply: men who could fulfil their responsibilities with fairness, firmness and justice: men who could willingly sacrifice all they had in the interest of their country's cause."[76] The best of Kipling's men like Findlayson, Scott, Dicky Hatt possess these qualities. His admiration is reserved for these men who lived in most terrible conditions, at far off places, where work was their only reward; they were the men on the spot, those that did the real work of the Empire. He had a deep dislike for the bureaucrats because he believed they did not know the people whom they were supposed to administer and were full of wrong notions about them. Also they did not really know how to go about their work. In 'The Bridge-Builders,' he tells of how Findlayson's planning for months is destroyed at one stroke, "when the Government of India, at the last moment, added two feet to the width of the bridge, under the impression that bridges were cut out of paper, and so brought to ruin at least half an acre of calculations."[77]

It is not the bureaucrats nor the members of Parliament who govern the country but ordinary civilians. In Kipling's presentation of the English civilians in India, the emphasis is, without fail, on the hard work they perform, the sacrifices they make and their horrid living conditions. And in India the English civilians

> do their work, and grow to think that there is nothing but their work, and nothing like their work, and that they are the real pivots on which the Administration turns.[78]

And in India

> Sickness does not matter, because it's all in the day's work, and if you die, another man takes over your place and your office in the eight hours between death and burial.[79]

But in his writings on India, Kipling is not merely presenting the image of the English civilian as a heroic figure in possession of infinitely superior qualities and moral authority. He offers us, in addition, a very important perspective to his existence in India, a perspective that is an outcome of the probing we witness in all great writers. It is this which reveals to us a deeper truth about his life as a ruler. He who is said to govern the land is, far from being an infallible individual, a victim himself, an irony that Kipling was profoundly aware of. He saw Otis Yeere as a civilian who lived in

> the seething, whining, weakly hive, impotent to help itself, but strong in its power to cripple, thwart, and annoy the sunken-eyed man, who, by official irony, was said to be 'in charge' of it.[80]

No doubt, Kipling's sympathies are with the tragic plight of the rulers. The work they do has had a crushing and debilitating effect on them. Mrs. Mallowe speaks of her husband:

> "... Government has eaten him up. All his ideas and powers of conversation – he really used to be a good talker, even to his wife, in the old days – are taken from him by this – this kitchen-sink of a Government. That's the case with every man up here who is at work. I don't suppose a Russian convict under the knout is able to amuse the rest of his gang; and all our men-folk here are gilded convicts." (pp. 7-8)

'Convicts' may seem a strong word but that is most appropriate in the colonial context. This is indeed one of the terrible ironies of colonialism. Mrs. Mallowe has no illusions about the superiority of the white man and her position is hardly that of an arrogant coloniser. She grieves over the change that has come over her husband:

> "... we are only little bits of dirt on the hillsides – here one day and blown down the *Khud* the next. We have lost the art of talking – at least our men have. We have no cohesion – " (p. 9)

Apart from the consciousness of their plight as victims of the Game (Imperialism) they themselves have invented, they also have to encounter problems of loneliness and face unknown dangers as depicted powerfully in the story 'At the End of the Passage.' Hummil, the Assistant Engineer, is the tragic victim of a terrible nightmare that is positively the outcome of his work in India. Moriarty of 'In Error' and 'The Boy' of "Thrown Away" are the other victims of the terrible monotony of official work in India. Both of them commit suicide.

Kipling's preoccupation with work not only highlights its negative and deadening effects on human beings — in this case, on English

Civilians in India — but also its creative influences that lead to fulfilment in them. It was work, as Kipling seems to say emphatically in some of his stories, that gave the English in India a sense of purpose and a belief that they were doing something highly beneficial whether it be to expand and protect the Empire, or help 'civilizing' the natives. It is this all-embracing concern with work that made C.S.Lewis consider Kipling "first and foremost the poet of work ... it is really remarkable how poetry and fiction before his time had avoided the subject."[81] It was no doubt, work that gave them a sense of identity and also a meaning to their life. It helped them successfully establish closer ties with fellow human beings. That is, perhaps, what Lewis meant when he remarked that Kipling "love(d) work for the sake of professional brotherhood."[82] It is this concern of Kipling that finds expression in one of his later stories, 'William the Conqueror'. In this story, he takes a more inclusive view of work relating it to the public and the private, the professional and the personal in the lives of the Englishman, and hence justifies a detailed analysis. In a world which is normally inhabited by men, Kipling chose to focus his attention on a woman William, a strange nickname indeed for a lady. We are not told her first name but the nickname perhaps reveals "her having been admitted on a man's terms to a man's world."[83]

Scott, an Officer in the Irrigation department and Martyn, William's brother, an acting District Superintendent of Police are posted to South India from Lahore to assist in the Famine relief work being supervised by Jimmy Hawkins. The reason for their choice is a comment upon the amount of work expected of the Anglo-Indian official: "every man who isn't doing two men's work seems to have been called upon."[84]

The story opens with reference to the terrible heat of Lahore, evoked almost poetically:

> It was a hot, dark, breathless evening, heavy with the smell of the newly-watered Mall. The flowers in the Club Gardens were dead and black on their stalks, the little lotus-pond was a circle of caked mud, and the tamarisk-trees were white with the dust of days. (pp. 181-82)

This is matched only by the terrible and unrelieved monotony of their dreary lives:

> From time to time a man would ride at a foot-pace into the

Club compound and listlessly loaf over to the white-washed barracks beside the main building. These were supposed to be chambers. Men lived in them, meeting the same faces night after night at dinner, and drawing out their office-work till the latest possible hour, that they might escape that doleful company. (p. 182)

And we also have a very rare description, worth quoting in full, of the inside of an Englishman's bungalow in which Scott lives. This throws much light on the actual comforts they 'enjoyed' in a "little four-roomed bungalow" such as this one:

There were the usual blue-and-white striped jail-made rugs on the uneven floor; the usual glass-studded Amritsar *Phulkaris* draped to nails driven into the flaking white wash of the walls; the usual half-doozen chairs that did not match, picked up at sales of dead man's effects; and the usual streak of black grease where the leather punka-thong rang through the wall. It was as though everything had been unpacked the night before to be repacked next morning. Not a door in the house was true on its hinges. The little windows, fifteen feet up, were darkened with waspnets, and lizards hunted flies between the beams of the wood-ceiled roof. (p. 185)

Royal comforts indeed! The repetition of the word 'usual' is obviously intended to drive home the point that this bungalow is no exception but the most common of its kind.

William accompanies them to Madras preferring it to a journey to the Hills, a more natural choice for a young woman like her. But then William is an unusual woman, like her unusual nickname. She likes to be where the action is and prefers "men who do things." Shades of Kipling!

So we see that William is made of sterner stuff than most English ladies and is indeed a worthy companion to the two men. She is one of the very few 'round' female characters in Kipling's entire fiction. What strikes the reader is her adaptability:

Life with men who had a great deal of work to do, and very little time to do it in, had taught her the wisdom of effacing as well as of fending for herself. She did not by word or deed suggest that she would be useful, comforting, or beautiful, in their travels, but continued about her business serenely: put the cups back without clatter when tea was ended, and made cigarettes for her guests. (p. 194)

At the Famine headquarters, she assists Mrs. Hawkins in looking after the women and children and performs her duties religiously. Scott and Martyn immediately set off on relief work. The focus from now onwards is on Scott. With a convoy of bullock-carts he travels down the "baked Gehenna of the South," transporting the starved masses to the relief camp, supplying food grains, picking up emaciated children dying of hunger and learning to feed them with goat milk. As he literally crawls along, he learns of the astonishing size of India and its people, rice-eaters of the south who refuse to eat the "strange hard grains" consumed in the North. Then the rains fall and he is entrusted with the distribution work of seed, grain and money to buy oxen, and he carries on despite bad roads and mutinous drivers. Primarily his work is all manual labour, mechanical and grinding and "he did it again and again, and yet again, while Jim Hawkins, fifty miles away, marked off on a big map the tracks of his wheels gridironing the stricken lands." (p. 214) He works like a devil and as he performs his duties, Kipling would have us believe as the descriptions and the tone suggest, that is surely gives him a sense of direction and meaning to his life. This sharply contrasts with his early dreary life at Lahore.

A new dimension to the story is added by Kipling in the flowering of love between Scott and William. It was only subtly suggested in Part I and is made more explicit in Part II. This actually gives him a stake in his work. Scott demonstrates to William through his work involving various sacrifices, how deserving he is of her love and affection. And thus Kipling relates the personal and the professional in a convincing manner. It is not to be mistaken for a device to add a romantic touch to the story as alleged by some critics. As he returns to the camp surrounded by goats and starving children, we have a splendid description:

> He had no desire to make any dramatic entry, but an accident of the sunset ordered it that, when he had taken off his helmet to get the evening breeze, the low light should fall across his forehead, and he could not see what was before him; while one waiting at the tent door beheld, with new eyes, a young man, beautiful as Paris, a god ia a halo of golden dust, walking slowly at the head of his flocks, while at his knee ran small naked Cupids. (p. 205)

The simile of god is appropriate "not only because of the pastoral grouping, but because Scott has indeed the preserver of life and restorer of hope."[85] William in return "laughed consumedly" and she learns from Scott to milk the goats. And later we are told that,

> She dreamed for the twentieth time of the god in the golden dust, and woke refreshed to feed loathsome black children, scores of them, wastrels picked up by the wayside, their bones almost breaking their skin, terrible, and covered with sores. (p. 216.)

In places like this, we see how Kipling's purpose is basically to emphasise the sacrifices of the English, with the result that he tends to ignore the sufferings of the natives during the famine. And even his occasional references to the natives make his attitude clear. The native children are both 'loathsome' and 'black' and elsewhere are referred to as 'the little beggars.' It is his imperial preoccupation that accounts for his condescending attitude towards the natives.

After a series of discriptions of the endless difficulties encountered by both Scott and William in their famine relief operations, it is a welcome relief to come across references to love and moments of true happiness. And the story concludes on a sentimental note with the singing of Christmas carols and wiping of tears of joy.

'William the Conqueror' is a refreshingly different story in that it not only celebrates work, but Kipling observes how love and duty, work and pleasure did co-exist, however occasionally, in the life of the Englishman in India. He demonstrates credibly, in the course of the story, how in his life of work, discipline and duty, moments of emotional fulfilment were present for the Englishman. Though the overall emphasis in Kipling is more on the harsher realities, 'William the Conqueror' proves that he was not oblivious of the softer and the more pleasant aspects of their life. Such an awareness helps Kipling overcome the danger of either romanticizing or sentimentalizing them and thus project an authentic image of the British in India.

The life of the British in India, as a consequence of the overwhelming emphasis by Kipling, forms an integral part of his image of India. A brief discussion of the image of Simla in his writings, will throw light on a hitherto unexplored aspect of the British way of life in India. Simla was the little England of the British Empire. It was to this hill station that the Viceroy, officers and civilians and their families went during the hot summer season. Kipling speaks of the various diversions available to the British in Simla:

> There are garden-parties, and tennis-parties, and picnics, and luncheons at Annandale, and rifle-matches, and dinners and balls; besides rides and walks...[86]

But beneath this exterior, there also lay the sordid Simla society with its social scandals, midnight revelries, illicit affairs and broken marriages that are pictured most convincingly in nearly twenty short stories that appear in the three collections, *Plain Tales from the Hills, Soldiers Three* and *Wee Willie Winkie*. Mrs. Hauksbee, "the most wonderful woman in India" is the centre of attraction in a large number of these stories. She is a charming, kind and compassionate woman who mends broken marriages, helps secure better posts for gifted young men without 'connections' and rescues eligible but innocent young men from the clutches of devouring females. In fact, Mrs. Hauksbee "uses her wit and intelligence and flair to humanize the hard and lonely white world of Kipling's India."[87]

Even the wonderful landscape of Simla, a city perched on the slopes of the Himalayan foothills in a series of descending terraces, steeply overhung, so that the houses looked ready to pitch off the edges and start sliding down the mountainside, is described in story after story with that rare power, we have by now come to associate with Kipling's writings. No doubt, Kipling knew his Simla:

> After two months of riding, first round Jakko, then Elysium, then Summer Hill, then observatory Hill, then under Jutogh, and lastly up and down the Cart Road, as far as the Tara Devi gap in the dust...[88]

These are the famous landmarks of Simla. In addition, we also come across Peliti's Grand Hotel, the Mall and the ubiquitous rikshaw.

Simla, like all centres of political power, seethed with ambition and intrigue. Kipling's powerful satire is directed against both these and the superficialities in English life. To achieve this, he had to heighten his effects but notwithstanding this, Kipling's image of Simla is a convincingly realistic portrayal.

One of the last stories (December, 1887) that Kipling wrote before he left India, 'The Man who would be King'[89] probes into a hitherto unexplored facet of imperialism. Whereas Kipling had all along emphasised the nobility and sacrifices involved in playing the role of the coloniser, he now takes a closer look at the darker sides of imperialism in this story. The 'civilizing' myth of the imperialist is unmasked and his motives are revealed in all their sordid details despite, perhaps, Kipling's actual intentions.

Kipling dramatises in this story—described variously as the 'myth of imperialism,' 'parable of empire building'—how with the determination and resourcefulness of the white man an Empire could be successfully established. Daniel Dravot and Peachy Carnehan, two loafers, posing as gods, manage to build an Empire in Kafiristan with the help of superior technology, both military and agriculture, gunpowder and religion (here, freemasonry).

The narrative technique employed by Kipling in the story is very significant since it is the narrator, a newspaper editor with a strong resemblance to Kipling himself, who guides and mediates our response to these two larger-than-life-figures. We see that he would rather have white loafers as his railway-carriage companions than the natives:

> There are no cushions in the Intermediate class, and the population are either Intermediate, which is Eurasian, or native, which for a long night is nasty, or Loafer, which is amusing though intoxicated. Intermediates do not buy from refreshment-rooms. They carry their food in bundles and pots, and buy sweets from the native sweetmeat-sellers, and drink the road-side water. That is why in the hot weather Intermediates are taken out of the carriages dead, and in all weathers are most properly looked down upon. (pp. 202-3)

While the narrator finds both the Eurasian and the native 'nasty', he exhibits a kind of amused tolerance towards the loafer by referring even to his drunken state as 'intoxicated.' Even though he is aware of the horrible practices of the loafers' looting the native rulers through nefarious means, his target for attack is not Carnehan and loafers like him, as it should be here, but revealingly the native states themselves:

> I had heard, more than once, of men personating correspondents of newspapers and bleeding small Native States with threats of exposure, but I had never met any of the caste before. They lead a hard life, and generally die with great suddenness. The Native States have a wholesome horror of English newspapers which may throw light on their peculiar methods of government, and

> do their best to choke correspondents with champagne, or drive them out of their mind with four-in-hand barouches. They do not understand that nobody cares a straw for the internal administration of Native States so long as oppression and crime are kept within decent limits, and the ruler is not drugged, drunk, or diseased from one end of the year to the other. They are the dark places of the earth, full of unimaginable cruelty, touching the Railway and the Telegraph on the one side, and on the other, the days of Harun-al-Raschid. (pp. 206-7.)

Phrases such as 'peculiar methods of government', 'oppression and crime,' 'dark places of the earth,' 'unimaginable cruelty' reveal the narrator's sweeping assessment of the native states. Even the mode of killing the loafers is intended more to elicit our sympathy for them. He seems only to accuse them, that too lightly and rather reluctantly, of possibly being guilty of ordinary blackmail. And the intended irony in the remark, 'they lead a hard life' fails to come through in view of what he tells of his own experience in the native states :

> When I left the train I did business with divers kings, and in eight days passed through many changes of life. Sometimes I wore dress-clothes and consorted with Princes and Politicals, drinking from crystal and eating from silver. Sometimes I lay out upon the ground and devoured what I could get, from a plate made of leaves, and drank the running water, and slept under the same rug as my servant. (p. 207.)

Dravot and Carnehan are profoundly dissatisfied with their life despite its rich variety:

> "...we have been boiler-fitters, engine-drivers, petty contractors, and all that, and we have decided that India isn't big enough for such as us." (p. 213.)

This is because :

> The country isn't half worked out because they that governs it won't let you touch it. They spend all their blessed time in governing it, and you can't lift a spade, nor chip a rock, nor look for oil, nor anything like that without the Government saying, "Leave it alone, and let us

govern." Therefore, such as it is, we will let it alone, and go away to some other place where a man isn't crowded and can come to his own..." (p. 214.)

And so for these two enterprising individuals, India offers no scope and hence they go into Kafiristan in search of greener pastures where they can do things with greater freedom. What is to be noted is that these two individuals who find the administrative machinery of the Anglo-Indian Government too critical of their adventures, later on bestow virtually no thought on what they have been doing to the natives of Kafiristan. Of course, the native are altogether uncivilized and, in the words of the narrator, "are utter brutes."

As Dravot and Carnehan share their plan of action with the narrator, their physical size is emphasised. In the small newspaper office, "Dravot's beard seemed to fill half the room and Carnehan's shoulders the other half, as they sat on the big table." (pp. 213-14.) They are now "big men with big dreams and capable of big achievements."[90] In order to succeed in their mission, they have all the necessary "attributes which characterize colonizers, pioneers and freebooters — the readiness to take risks, to act promptly and without scruple, to utilize every propitious occasion in pursuit of their ends."[91] They manage to reach Kafiristan through disguise and other devious means. And once they are there, Carnehan and Dravot join the battle between two warring tribes, support the weaker side and establish themselves as rulers. And in co-operation with the Priests and the village Chiefs, Dravot administers justice. They "pick out twenty good men and show them how to click off a rifle, and form fours, and advance in line, and they were very pleased to do so, and clever to see the hang of it." (p. 229.) In this way, they are able to gather a small force which gradually grows into a powerful army.

Carnehan, in this process of empire building, plays a vital role in both civil and military affairs:

> My work was to help the people plough, and now and again go out with some of the Army and see what the other villagers were doing, and make 'em throw rope-bridges across the ravines which cut up the country horridly. (p. 237.)

But it is Dravot who is the moving spirit behind this imperialist programme. He is the visionary who is inspired to build an empire:

> "I won't make a Nation ... I'll make an Empire! These men

aren't niggers; they're English! ... There must be a fair two million of 'em in these hills. The villages are full o'little children. Two million people—two hundred and fifty thousand men, ready to cut in on Russia's right flank when she tries for India! Peachey, man ... we shall be Emperors —Emperors of the Earth! ... I'll treat with the Viceroy on equal terms ... when everything was ship-shape, I'd hand over the crown—this crown I'm wearing now—to Queen Victoria on my knees, and she'd say: 'Rise up, Sir Daniel Dravot' oh, it's big' it's big, I tell you." (pp. 238-39).

It is significant that repeated references are made to the fair complexion of the people of Kafiristan. The way Dravot and Carnehan regard them as sub-human beings lends a curious twist of irony to the whole issue of colour. As a matter of fact, they are seen as individuals who have no identity of their own, and have to be given "names according as they was like men we had known in India — Billy Fish, Holly Dilworth, Pikky Kergan."

All through their stay in Kafiristan, Kipling's tone insistently demands that we admire Dravot and Carnehan for their efficiency, courage, energy, and even their fantastic bluff. They have now became kings and gods in Kafiristan, thanks to their attributes and also to the willing compliance of the natives. However the seemingly endless situation of peace and stability is shattered not on account of the natives, but because of Dravot's intentions of marrying a native girl. Dravot arrogantly pays no heed to the pleas of Carnehan and Billy Fish to give up this foolhardy thought and more importantly, he breaks the vital clause in their 'contrack'[92] which they had agreed to follow before they had set out on their adventure.

The native girls are reluctant since "there are all sorts of gods and devils in these mountains, and now and again a girl marries one of them and isn't seem anymore." (p. 243.) And finally a bride is found, who prompted by the rebellious priests bites Dravot during the marriage ritual. He bleeds and the priests howl triumphantly that he was "neither God nor Devil but a man!" The entire structure of their empire collapses with this discovery that they are merely men and not gods. In the classic imperial situation, the natives always make Gods out of the rulers and place them, on a high pedestal. Any attempt of the ruler to come down from this pedestal is bound to result in disastrous consequences as it would be construed as a sign of their weakness. This situation has been brilliantly analysed by Mannoni:

> *a colonial situation* is created so to speak the very instant a white man, even if he is alone, appears in the midst of a tribe, even if it is independent, so long as he is thought to be rich or powerful or merely immune to the local forces of magic, and so long as he derives from his position, even though only in his most secret self, a feeling of his own superiority. The man-in-the street will say instinctively and without experience, that if the white man who goes amongst the Negroes avoids being eaten, he will become King.[93]

Carnehan tells Dravot that "this business is our 'Fifty- Seven', "a reference to the Indian mutiny. This experience has made him wiser as we see when he asserts, "there's no accounting for natives." The natives noiselessly capture them, "they just closed tight, and I tell you their furs stunk," remarks Carnehan. Once again, we see how in the colonial situation, the responses are conditioned towards eliciting sympathy for the white coloniser, always at the expense of the natives. Here, we are expected to pity the plight of Dravot and Carnehan, although earlier the feelings of the natives at the time of their defeat had been wholly ignored. While Dravot is flung to death ironically from one of the rope-bridges that they had built, Carnehan is crucified and is allowed to crawl back to India. He dies after he has recounted his experience to the first person narrator.

Jeffrey Meyers believes that the theme is, "the need for moral authority represented by the law of the British Empire"[94] though by their terrible deaths Kipling attempts to 'vindicate' the character of the adventurers which Meyers regards as a serious flaw in the story. Benita Parry takes an almost similar view: "the portrayal of Dravot and Carnehan suggests Kipling's failure to discriminate between a sympathetic understanding of his characters and a sanctioning of their conduct. As avaricious, unscrupulous and brave adventurers, the talented outcastes of respectable societies who have no use for their gifts, they are marvellously realized; but as heroic figures they exist only through the author's legerdemain."[95]

What troubles both Meyers and Parry, is the way Kipling simultaneously makes Dravot and Carnehan avaricious and greedy loafers, as well as tragic figures who compel our admiration and sympathy. By choosing to adopt the first person narrative scheme, Kipling has been able successfully to guide our response to Dravot and Carnehan who emerge, through their adventures, as impressive and admirable individuals. As pointed out earlier, from the very beginning of the story, we see the narrator's preference for the loafers, and that is made clear in his tacit approval of all their actions. The narration is carried on in such a way as to highlight only their initiative, enthusiasm and superior skills–all that constitutes the essential expertise of the colonizer, and gloss over the avarice, greed and ambition which are their true motives. It is not through "legerdemain" but through a deliberate and careful use of the first person narrative technique that Kipling elevates them into heroic figures.

Dravot and Carnehan fail as empire-builders not because the natives offer any resistance, nor through an awareness in the natives of their exploitation, but because Dravot failed to retain his self-image in the eyes of the natives. By deciding to marry a native girl, he was ignoring one of the basic tenets of colonialism, that is, to always maintain a necessary distance from the ruled. By failing to do this, he only proved to the natives that he was merely someone like themselves and hence, seriously undermined his own moral authority.

Apart from being a successful parable of imperialism, 'The Man who would be King' is the only story wherein Kipling probed deeply into the manner of building an empire, while the rest of Kipling's work is more concerned with how to hold an empire together after it is built. That is the reason why the industrious, morally upright English civil servant or soldier is not found in this story. And so certain truths–rather unpleasant ones–of the imperial experience that are wholly ignored in his entire fiction are revealed here. Thus the story demonstrates how the empire builder is not always motivated by nobler reasons, as suggested in the entire corpus of Kipling's work, but by "avarice, the thirst for personal glory, the satisfactions of feeding on the homage of dependent people,"[96] a fact that comes through, in spite of Kipling's anxiety to present Dravot and Carnehan as heroic figures.

While 'The Man who would be King' is an authentic image of British rule and its ulterior motives, 'The Tomb of His Ancestors', a story written nearly after ten years, is an accurate depiction of the nineteenth century imperial situation in India. It is about the Chinns, one of the English families that spent its time administering the Central Indian states and their relationship with the Bhils, "the strangest of the many strange races in India." The Bhils were "wild men, furtive, shy, full of untold superstitions." Centuries of oppression and massacre, Kipling tells us, had made the Bhil a cruel and half-crazy thief and cattle stealer. And it was John Chinn's—the hero of the story—grandfather who had brought about a noticeable change in the Bhils. He

> went in his [Bhil] country, lived with him, learned his language, shot the deer that stole his poor crops, and won his confidence, so that some Bhils learned to plough and sow, while others were coaxed into the Company's service to police their friends.[97]

These were the classic methods employed by the nineteenth century imperialist in his civilizing mission. The English with bluff and limited use of physical force demonstrated their superior powers to the natives over whom they held total sway. Their strength and powers naturally made them gods in the eyes of the natives, to the point of sometimes causing them acute embarrassment. The white man seemed infallible to the native.

John Chinn closely resembles his grandfather and also has the dull-red birth-mark on his shoulder (seen by the Bhils) which confirms their belief that he is indeed the reincarnation of his late grandfather. Kipling's attitude is clear:

> Because the savage and the child who plays lonely games have one horror of being laughed at or questioned, the little folk kept their convictions to themselves; and the colonel, who thought he knew his regiment, never guessed that each one of the six hundred quick-footed, beady-eyed rank-and-file, at attention beside their rifles, believed serenely and unshakenly that the subaltern in the left flank of the line was a demi-god twice born—tutelary deity of their land and people. The Earth-gods themselves had stamped the incarnation, and who would dare to doubt the handiwork of the Earth-gods? (p. 121.)

The entire passage is marked by Kipling's amused and indulgent tone towards the naive belief of the native Bhils.

When the Bhils begin to see the vision of John Chinn's grandfather riding a clouded tiger during nights, Bukta, their leader asks John the reason for this. John is, of course, helpless for a moment, but, overcoming his awkwardness at having to answer this question "invent(s) a specious lie" that his grandfather has been appearing only to see how his people were doing. So the white man whatever his feelings be, has to retain his self-image, the image that the natives have of him.

When the government sends a Mahratta State-educated vaccinator to the Satpura Bhils to inoculate them against smallpox, they resist this attempt by detaining him. Then the Colonel sends John Chinn, as he knows of the "hereditary influence" he has over the Bhils. Where the black native had failed, John Chinn manages to succeed through tact and diplomacy. He does some straight talking but it is to be remembered that the Bhils have absolute faith in him. And so, in a remarkable turnabout of events, we see the earlier crisis ending up as

> a child's sport, for the vaccinated chased the unvaccinated to treatment, vowing that all the tribe must suffer equally. The women shrieked, and the children ran howling; but Chinn laughed, and waved the pink-tipped lancet. (p. 137.)

Then finally, he further confirms their beliefs by shooting down the much dreaded clouded tiger. And truly John Chinn is "not simply a British official, but the hereditary ruler of an aboriginal tribe."[98]

In stories like these, Kipling's political beliefs, instead of acting as a hindrance, actually sustain his artistic efforts. Here his efforts are directed towards projecting an image of Indians and their country. The image projected in 'The Tomb of His Ancestors' may seem 'imperialist' but one should not overlook the historical accuracy of the picture presented. However distasteful and degrading one might find the relationship that is depicted between John Chinn and the Bhils, it is to be conceded that the nature of this relationship offers a clue to our understanding of imperialism not only as a political ideology but as it was *actually* practised by the British imperialists in nineteenth century India. Such stories entirely give the lie to George Orwell's accusation that Kipling's picture of the nineteenth century Anglo-India is "tawdry and shallow."[99]

However, there are also a few early stories of Kipling which, interestingly, depict the Englishman as a helpless figure and not a figure of authority who inspires awe in natives like John Chinn. That imperialism, the success ideology of the white man will not always succeed, is made manifestly clear in 'The House of Suddhoo.' Suddhoo, a native, has become a victim of the black art of the seel-cutter and is fast losing all his money to him. Here is a white man, the narrator who is a party to this, in the sense he has been an onlooker all the while but is unable to do anything, for he has no hope of getting any witness to his defence. And it is "the sense of futility which emerges from the depiction of imperialism"[100] in the story. There is also another weird story of Jukes, a civil engineer who accidentally stumbles into the hideous village of the Dead and goes through a traumatic experience, before he is rescued by his servant. Aptly termed "a genuine Anglo-Indian nightmare,"[101] 'The Strange Ride of Morrobie Jukes' reveals to us in Jukes, "a Sahib, a representative of the dominant race, helpless as a child and completely at the mercy of his native neighbours."[102] Here, for once, the roles seem reversed. And hence, it is surprising to read Angus Wilson regard this story as a 'brilliant horror allegory of British rule."[103]

In his portrayal of the Indians, it is the lower classes, the native servant and their children, in addition to women and the 'Bengali Babu' who receive predominant attention. Whether it is his portrayal of Little Tobrah or Muhammad Din, they are characterised by Kipling's genuine sympathy that enables him to see them as human beings. These two stories are "rare miniatures about the precarious beauties and all too prevalent horrors of Indian Childhood."[104] The latter is a moving story of the loving, tender relationship between an Englishmen, who is also the narrator and Muhammad Din, a young boy, "a tiny, plump figure in a ridiculously inadequate shirt which came, per haps, half-way down the tubby stomach."[105] After the young boy's ignorant entry into the sahib's dining room and punishment for it, there grows a beautiful relationship between the two though their conversation is limited to only 'Talaam Tahib' from the boy's side and 'Salaam, Muhammad Din' from the sahib's. The story ends with the unexpected death of the little boy. The English doctor's brutal comment that "they have no stamina, these brats," has made Cornell regard this story as "symbolic of England's helplessness in the face of India's frailty, her triple curse of poverty, starvation and disease."[106]

Bhaskara Rao in his anxiety to prove that "Kipling's Anglo-Indian world was a world bereft of human relationships" finds "condescension"[107] in the Englishman's attitude towards Muhammad Din. The story, in fact, proves just the contrary, for this relationship, despite the differences in age and colour, has blossomed into something wonderful and human. The story ends thus:

    A week later, though I would have given much to have

avoided it, I met on the road to the Mussulman burying-ground Imam Din, accompanied by one other friend, carrying in his arms, wrapped in a white cloth, all that was left of little Muhammad Din.[108]

The response of the narrator is one of a profound sense of loss at this unexpected death of the child. The last brief paragraph also reveals how Kipling could occasionally shed his journalistic devices and produce an unexpectedly moving effect by relying on "quintessential simplicity."[109]

We should consider the poem, 'Gunga Din'[110] for an exceptional treatment of the lower class Indian. It is about Gunga Din, the Indian water-carrier, who is singled out by Kipling for his deep devotion to duty and compassion for the poor, thirsty, English soldiers:

> Of all them blackfaced crew
> The finest man I knew
> Was our regimental bhisti, Gunga Din.

He is to be found everywhere on the battlefield with his water skin bag on his back ever ready and ever willing to quench the thirst of the fighting tommies. It is this admirable spirit of sacrifice that makes Kipling exclaim:

> An' for all 'is dirty 'ide
> 'E was white, clear white, inside.

It is easy to dismiss these lines, as many critics have done, by accusing Kipling of racial prejudice and condescension. But one should remember that, "in the eighteen-nineties, the phrase, 'a white man,' did not only mean man with an unpigmented skin; it had a secondary symbolic meaning: a man with the moral standards of the civilized world."[111] With this knowledge, one is sure to have the right perspective in determining Kipling's deeply felt regard for Gunga Din. This is, most emphatically stated in the last two lines revealing his unqualified praise for the man:

> By the livin' Gawd that made you
> You're a better man than I am, Gunga Din!

These lines, are also, in the nature of self-admonition. In a similar vein, his approbation is reserved for Sudanese soldier, Fuzzy-Wuzzy:[112]

> So 'ere's *to* you, Fuzzy-wuzzy, at your'ome in the Soudan;

> You're a pore benighted heathen but a first-class fightin'
> man;
> We gives you your certificate, an' if you want it signed
> We'll come an' 'ave a romp with you whenever you're in-
> clined.

And also because:

> You big black boundin' beggar — for you broke a British
> square!

In these poems, the colour of either Gunga Din or Fuzzy-Wuzzy is no hindrance to Kipling's recognition of the essential qualities of selfless sacrifice and bravery in them. He is thus able to transcend, even though occasionally, the imperialist assumptions that govern his artistic vision in these poems, and in stories like 'Without Benefit of Clergy', and 'The Miracle of Purun Bhagat.'

In his stories set in the North-West Frontier, the likes of Khoda Dad Khan ('The Head of the District') and the other tribal folk are depicted with some admiration by Kipling because of their martial qualities. We also have in this category of illiterate Indians, peasants[113] like Jelloo, land-holders such as Rasul Ali ('The Enlightenments of Pagett, M.P.') and small merchants like the sweet-meat-seller, Naboth ('Naboth').

In the second category of Indians, the portrait of the Bengali Babu is most representative though there are exceptions like Wali Dad ('On the City Wall'). While the portrait of Grish Chunder De ('The Head of the District') is a study in some depth, there are some 'flat' figures in 'His chance in Life', 'The Enlightenments of Pagett, M.P.' and other stories. No doubt, Kipling is ridiculing the entire educated Indian community by making the Bengali a typical representative of this class. Reasons for this have to be sought outside literature. The province of Bengal was one of the earliest to come under British rule. Before the Charter Act of 1853, the Bengal province consisted of Bengal, Assam, Orissa, Bihar, the whole of the United Provinces, Delhi and a part of Punjab. And so it could perhaps be said that at the beginning of the nineteenth century, Bengal practically meant India.[114] In addition, the Bengali had come to mean in Anglo-Indian fiction one who is bookish, cowardly, impractical, mean and contemptible. Kipling conveniently falls into this line except in his portrayal of Hurree Babu in *Kim*.

To look at the physical image of India in Kipling is a fascinating experience. To look for one single image of India is to seek something that does not exist in actuality. The problem with India is that there is not *one* India but, in an important sense, many Indias. So, what we discover is the composite image of India that emerges from the body of Kipling's work.

There are numerous splendid evocations of the Indian landscape in Kipling. Here are a few significant ones. As pointed out earlier, the toughest demand on the Englishmen is made by the land itself. The most striking feature of the land is its heat, especially during summer. And it is intensely felt within the four walls:

> Every door and window was shut, for the outside air was that of an oven. The atmosphere within was only 104°, as the thermometer bore witness, and heavy with the foul smell of badly-trimmed kerosene lamps; and this stench, combined with that of native tobacco, baked brick, and dried earth, sends the heart of many a strong man down to his boots, for it is the smell of the Great Indian Empire when she turns herself for six months into a house of torment.[115]

The heat transforms the very face of this land, the "house of torment" and to live in it is a hellish experience. And one such moment is captured vividly in the story "The City of Dreadful Night', the title being borrowed from James Thomson. Kipling's mind registers the various impressions most effectively as he, unable to sleep, walks through the city of Lahore after midnight seeing streets littered with "sleeping men who lay like sheeted corpses." Here is a small passage, picked at random:

> More corpses: more stretches of moonlit, white road; a string of sleeping camels at rest by the wayside; a vision of scudding jackals; ekka-ponies asleep — the harness still on their backs, and the brass-studded country carts, winking in the moonlight — and again more corpses.[116]

It is Kipling's eye for these little details that makes the picture accurate and memorable and also helps him succeed in evoking the heat in an almost tactile and palpable manner.

India is not only a "baked Gehenna" but also a "Swampy, sour green" land where

> the soil spawned humanity, as it bred frogs in the rains,

and the gap of the sickness of one season was filled to overflowing by the fecundity of the next. [117]

In the rainy season, it is the turn of the floods to torment the work of the English bridge-builders:

> ...the face of the river whitened from bank to bank between the stone facings, and the far-away spurs went out in spouts of foam. Mother Gunga had come bank-high in haste, and a wall of chocolate-coloured water was her messenger........After the first down stream plunge there came no more walls of water, but the river lifted herself bodily, as a snake when she drinks in midsummer...[118]

When there is no rain, it is the turn of the famine to drive the Englishman to a state of feverish work. The plight of the victims is indeed unimaginably miserable. Note the deep compassion that has gone into the portrayal.

> Here the people crawled to the side of the train, holding their little ones in their arms; and a loaded truck would be left behind, men and women clustering round and above it like ants by spilled honey. Once in the twilight they saw on a dusty plain a segment of little brown men, each bearing a body over his shoulder; and when the train stopped to leave yet another truck, they perceived that the burdens were not corpses, but only foodless folk picked up beside their dead oxen by a corps of Irregular troops... [White] men staved off the rush of wailing, walking skeletons, putting them down three at a time in heaps, with their own hands uncoupling the marked trucks...[119]

If these are the malevolent weather conditions that characterise India, it is the rough terrain of the land that further adds to the misery. Kot-Kumharsen is a typical hill district and

> it lay cut lengthways by the Indus under the line of the Khusru hills—ramparts of useless earth and tumbled stone. It was seventy miles long by fifty broad, maintained a population of something less than two hundred thousand, and paid taxes to the extent of forty thousand pounds a year on an area that was by rather more than half sheer, hopeless waste. The cultivators were not gentle

> people, the miners for salt were less gentle still, and the
> cattle-breeders least gentle of all. A police-post in the top
> right-hand corner prevented as much salt-smuggling and
> cattle-lifting as the influence of the civilians could not put
> down; and in the bottom right-hand corner lay Jumala, the
> district headquarters — a pitiful knot of lime-washed barns
> facetiously rented as houses, reeking with frontier fever,
> leaking in the rain and ovens in the summer.[120]

In Kipling, as is evident in this description, the landscape and the people living on it is significantly related. The peoples are what they are, largely because of the conditions in which they live. Their strength and weaknesses are thus determined. While the hilly people are tough and robust, the people on the plains, are weak and feeble. But for a rich image of the Indian landscape, one has to wait till *Kim*.

Next, the image of India as a geographical entity in Kipling's works needs to be considered. As one who had lived in Lahore, Simla and Allahabad at different times during his stay in India, and also as one who had travelled fairly widely within the country, we see, naturally, a close parallel between the various places of his acquaintance and the places that figure in his work, be they under their actual names or pseudonyms as in the two *Jungle Book (s)* and *The Naulahka*. Thus we notice that Lahore and Simla provide the setting to the majority of his stories. Then there is, of course, the Himalayas, Rajasthan, the Seonee Hills of Central India, vast areas of the North-Western parts of India and the teeming Grand Trunk Road. It is in *Kim* that we have the most satisfying and complete image of India that encompasses all the places depicted earlier on in his works. Incidentally, his travel accounts can be seen in the two volumes of *From Sea to Sea*. As one from South India, it is interesting to note that the only reference to the South occurs in 'William the Conqueror'. As a matter of fact, Kipling had only once travelled in this part of the country, which was during his last visit to India when he went to Lahore from Colombo by train. These are the two brief references:

> Then they came to an India more strange to them than to
> the untravelled Englishman — the flat, red India of palm-
> tree, palmyra-palm, and rice, the India of the picture-
> books, of *Little Henry and His Bearer* — all dead and dry in
> the baking heat. (pp. 195-96.)

> The South of pagodas and palm-trees, the over-populated Hindu South was done with. (p. 225.)

And then we have a fairly good number of generalisations about India that reveal Kipling's attitude to the country. Though they are, at times, contradictory, they are of great help in determining the true nature of the various images of India that occur in his writings. Kipling occasionally lapses, though there is much genuine understanding of India to redeem him, into the standardised responses that India evokes in the Westerner: "India, as everyone knows, is divided equally between jungle, tigers, cobras, cholera, and sepoys."[121] In one of his earlier stories, 'Thrown Away,' he generalises:

> India is a place beyond all others where one must not take things too seriously—the midday sun always excepted ... It is a slack country.[122]

He suggests that one should not take anything seriously in India whether it is good work or bad work, amusement or sickness. Otherwise one is sure to meet the fate of 'The Boy', who pays a heavy price for taking things seriously: he shoots himself. In the other stories, there is a slight variation of this attitude since Kipling repeatedly describes men who have become lonely, isolated beings because of taking their work seriously in India. There is, of course, the other side of this view, where work assumes a positive role in that it gives meaning to an otherwise dreary existence.

These variations offer us an insight into the creative method at work in Kipling. We see how he is able to perceptively view life in its entirety and hence the presence of various shades in his work. He probes into life and does not merely skim the surface. If he were only an imperialist, as alleged by Orwell and Trilling, Kipling would have taken only formulated positions and there would have been only stereotyped images of India and its people. And hence, it could be said justifiably of Kipling, that his works defy such oversimplified assessments made by numerous critics. A reference to India in 'Georgie Porgie' makes this very evident. When Georgiana, the Burmese Woman goes all over the north western parts of India in search of her missing English husband:

> She could not understand the language of the people: but *India is infinitely charitable*, and the women-folk along the Grand Trunk gave her food.[123]
> (emphasis mine)

Then there is the notion that India is a land that defies all theories, and this finds expression in 'The Conversion of Aurelian McGoggin.' Kipling warns us at the very outset that "this is not a tale exactly. It is a tract." It is about Aurelian McGoggin, a civil servant, who is "brilliantly clever," has read Comte and Spencer and believes that men had no souls and that there was no God and no hereafter. He is shown working hard, finally breaks down under the strain and has an attack of aphasia. The story concludes with his conversion to a man of faith. On one level, it is a satire on the dry sort of intellectual who has no respect for either religion or god, but more importantly it is offered as an evidence of what happens to one's intellectual convictions when confronted by the Indian reality:

> But in India, where you really see humanity—raw, brown, naked humanity—with nothing between it and the blazing sky, and only the used-up, over-handled earth underfoot, the notion somehow dies away, and most folk come back to simpler theories. Life, in India, is not long enough to waste in proving that there is no one in particular at the head of affairs.[124]

Yet another perspective is added to India when Kipling chose to portray it as a 'land of mystery', a country wherein the supernatural and the irrational were so predominant that Western rationalism almost always failed to unravel its 'mystery.' In 'The Bisara of Pooree', there is a passing mention of this aspect of India:

> All kinds of magic are out of date and done away with, except in India, where nothing changes in spite of the shiny, top-scum stuff that people call 'civilisation'[125]

The Bisara of Pooree is "a tiny square box of silver," "the only regularly working, trust-worthy love-charm in the country." In the story, Kipling hhas an Englishman who believes in its potent powers:

> He was an Englishman, but knew how to believe. Which shows that he was different from most Englishmen. He knew that it was dangerous to have any share in the little box when working or dormant; for Love unsought is terrible gift. (p. 263.)

Significantly, the entire story is narrated without any scepticism by Kipling. Interestingly India doesn't come in for censure just because magic and supernatural powers still seem to work there. Hence, he names the Englishman who accepts the powers of the Bisara of Pooree as 'The Man Who Knew', which suggests that Kipling has a sneaking sympathy for this aspect of India.

A similar story, 'By Word of Mouth' opens:

> This tale may be explained by those who know how souls are made, and where the bounds of the Possible are put down. I have lived long enough in this India to know that it is best to know nothing, and can only write the story as it happened. [126]

Dumoise, the Civil Surgeon's wife dies of typhoid. His bearer Ram Dass sees the dead Mem Sahib who is said to have told him that she will meet his master at Nuddea in the coming month. And truly, as foretold, Dumoise is transferred to Nuddea and is dead eleven days hence. Though there is a touch of amusement in the narrator's tone, he is nowhere sceptical and is merely reporting the event "as it happened". It is such experiences that make Kipling remark that:

> India ... is not a golden country though poets have sung otherwise. There men die with great swiftness, and those who live suffer many and curious things.[127]

One such "curious" occurrence is the basis of the story, 'The Mark of the Beast,' which also has a significant opening:

> East of Suez, some hold, the direct control of providence ceases; Man being there handed over to the power of the Gods and Devils of Asia, and the Church of England Providence only exercising an occasional and modified supervision in the case of Englishmen.[128]

This accounts for "the more unnecessary horrors of life in India", but in the above remark we see that Kipling is quite ironic of the Church of England as well. It is the story of Fleete who, on New Year's Eve, in a drunken state, grinds the ashes of his cigarbutt into the forehead of the red stone image of Hanuman. He is bitten by the leper at the temple and this begins to tell on him. He behaves like a beast and though diagnosed by the doctor as hydrophobia, Strickland of the Police, with his will-informed knowledge of Indian life, knows that "the affair was beyond any human and rational experience." And also that "this isn't any doctor's work." So he begins to work on the leper with hot irons and Fleete returns to normalcy. Though Kipling's intentions are clear, his recourse to asterisks at the vital moment in the story prefaced by the statement, "This part is not to be printed" is a rather poor artistic strategy. Though he says he has put the story in print on Strickland's suggestion, his concluding paragraph is quite consistent with his attitude discussed in the two earlier stories:

> I cannot myself see that this step is likely to clear up the mystery; because, in the first place, no one will believe a rather unpleasant story, and, in the second, it is well known to every right-minded man that the gods of the heathen are stone and brass, and any attempt to deal with them otherwise is justly condemned.(p. 259.)

The phrase "right-minded man" is ironical in the context of the story, for the nightmarish experiences of Fleete are far too real to regard the "gods of the heathen" as merely "stone and brass." And so we see in Kipling, rather curiously, almost a total acceptance of the mystery that seems to pervade India.

To finally turn to Kipling's descriptions of the relationships between Englishmen and Indians which is central to the study of the image of India, is to enter into an area that is at once complex and fascinating, perceptive and revealing. It is the way these relationships are worked out that produces a knot of attitudes which contribute to the overall richness of the Indian image in Kipling's fictional work. It is one thing to examine the English and the Indians in isolation, and another to attempt to bring them together into close contact with each other. That is to say, we have here the colonial encounters as seen in the actual coming together of the English and Indians as human beings. And in this encounter, truths about them as human beings both in their individual capacities and in their sense of togetherness come to the surface.

The basic premise in the colonial situation is that the coloniser and the colonised are two entirely different peoples belonging to altogether distinct races. And also as Philip Woodruff remarks

> Between people so different there could be courtesy, kindliness and liking, there could be affection, but no dealing on equal terms. The relationship was paternal, accepted on both sides. It was fixed and settled, like caste; the district officer and his family were one kind of human

beings, the people of his district another. There was no thought of equality.[129]

In, 'On the City Wall', the English narrator tells Wali Dad,

> "... you never speak to us about your women-folk and we never speak about ours to you. That is the bar between us." (p. 339.)

But Wali Dad is more perceptive and knows that he will never be accepted by the English though

> "I might wear an English coat and trousers. I might be a leading Mohammedan pleader. I might be even received at the Commissioner's tennis–parties where the English stand on one side and the natives on the other, in order to promote social intercourse throughout the Empire...(p. 339.)

These words anticipate Forster's "Bridge Party" in *A Passage to India*.

The sense of separateness and the barriers between the two races, naturally, lead to a loss of communication. This, in turn, makes for a total absence of understanding between them. This also results in a feeling of superiority in the coloniser, and the innately ingrained inferiority complex of the colonised. The coloniser, invariably ignorant of the ways of the colonised, takes the easy way our and lays the blame squarely on the native:

> "You cannot explain things to the Oriental. You must *show*."[130]   (emphasis mine)

This is the "inscrutability" of the oriental.[131] And while the native is too happy obeying the rulers and making gods of them, the coloniser in his complacency makes no attempt at understanding him.

The coloniser is a figure of supreme authority for the native, an accepted fact of life for both of them. And so, one need not be surprised by Kipling's interesting presentation of a young boy, Wee Willie Winkie, who asserts his authority in no uncertain manner. Wee Willie Winkie, is a precocious "six and three-quarters" year old who is able to guard a helpless Miss Allardyce from the bad men of the hills and emerges a *"pukka* hero" in the event. He is not made into a totally incredible figure, as suggested by Kipling critics, since the author is aware of the responses in both the child and the tribesmen. When the tribesmen are threateningly close to them, Kipling tells us how

it needed all Wee Willie Winkie's training to prevent him
from bursting into tears. But he felt that to cry before a
native, excepting only his mother's *ayah*, would be an in-
famy greater than any mutiny. Moreover, he, as future
Colonel of the 195th, had that grim regiment at his back.[132]

And on the other hand, while they contemplate kidnapping the two, one of their men speaks of the dangers involved:

"... He is the heart's heart of those white troops... I say that
this child is their God, and that they will spare none of us,
nor our women, if we harm him."[133]

These are explanations that convince us of the action of Wee Willie Winkie. What is more important in the story, is that it reveals how even in such a young boy the feelings and values that form the backbone of the British Raj are drilled in.

In the colonial context, the two races never meet as equals. In this also, lies the key to the breakdown of attempts of bring the races nearer and establish meaningful relationships. And hence whether is it at all possible for the two races to come together, is the question that keeps recurring in Kipling's writings. It is raised in a very fundamental way in his well known poem, 'The Ballad of East and West.'[134] The opening lines have achieved a near proverbial status:

Oh, East is East, and West is West, and never the twain
   shall meet,
Till Earth and Sky stand presently at God's great
   Judgement Seat;

While the next two lines, though less known for obvious reasons, are more significant in view of Kipling's acknowledgement of the possibility of such a coming together:

But there is neither East nor West, Border, nor Bread,
   or Birth,
When two strong men stand face to face, though they
   come from the ends of the earth!

The poem is about an encounter between the Colonel's son and Kamal, the frontier Pathan who has stolen the colonel's mare, 'That is the Colonel's pride'. They meet, and recognise, in the words of Kamal that 'we be two strong men.' And so Kamal asks his son to go with the

Colonel's son, for he has gifted him to the white man in recognition of their new-born friendship:

> "Now here is thy master," Kamal said, "who leads a troop of the Guides,"
>
> "And thou must ride at his left side as shield on shoulder rides."
>
> "Till Death or I cut loose the tie, at camp and board and bed,"
>
> "Thy life is his — thy fate it is to guard him with thy head."
>
> "So, thou must eat the White Queen's meat, and all her foes are thine,"
>
> "And thou must harry thy father's hold for the peace of the Border-line."
>
> "And thou must take a trooper tough and hack thy way to power—
>
> "Belike they will raise thee to Ressaldar when I am hanged in Peshawar!"

Though the nobility of Kamal's gesture is laudable, it is a little difficult to reconcile to the tone of these lines. One suspects a streak of servility in Kamals asking his son to completely identify himself with the white man at the cost of even losing his own identity completely. Despite this slightly jarring note, the poem makes clear, through the first four lines occurring again at the end of the poem, Kipling's answer to this question of the meeting of the two races. He believes that such a coming together is indeed a possibility, a contention supported by a few of his stories as well, when two exceptional individuals come face to face.

Kipling was concerned in his works, in different ways, with this relationship, and in probing into its true nature, he was successful in bringing out both the reasons for their failure and the limitations that lie on both sides. And he was convinced that unless the British came down to the level of the native, that is, meet him on an equal footing, there was no possibility of any understanding between the two. This theme is taken up in his memorable story, 'Tods' Amendment.' Very rightly considered a "political allegory"[135] by Edmund Gosse, it is about Tods, "an utterly fearless young pagan, about six years old, and the only baby who ever broke the holy calm of the Supreme Legislative Council."[136] Tods knew the lower class natives very well; he spoke Urdu and was precocious for his age, and his mixing with natives had taught him some of the more bitter truths of life; the meanness and the sordidness of it. (p. 198.)

And so, Tods is able to give the legal member, the opinion of the natives about the proposed Bill for the Sub-Montane Tracts. It is accepted with gratitude by the legal member, since Tods has allowed him a glimpse of the working of a native's mind.

Tods emerges as a credible picture of a precocious child, for he is portrayed by Kipling as a child first, and only then as someone who is on very intimate terms with the natives. Added to this, the awareness that the use of Tods is also a strategy to describe the imperial situation, makes Kipling's purposes manifestly clear.

The story provides some significant insights into the colonial situation. Kipling satirises the complete ignorance of the Englishman in the ways of the native. As they finalise the draft of the bill, he mocks at their pretensions:

> As if any Englishman legislating for natives knows enough to know which one are the minor and which are the major points, from the native point of view, of any measure! (p. 198.)

They are not aware that, "no man can tell what natives think unless he mixes with them with the varnish off." (p. 199.) This is an important insight of Kipling's. Unless the Englishman is able to overcome his feelings of superiority and condescension and meet the native on his own grounds, he has little chance of understanding the native mind. And it is precisely because of their inability to do this that the learned members of the legislative council are so completely ignorant of the ways of the native, whereas Tods, even though a young boy, succeeds since he has not only access to the natives but feels one among them. Moreover he speaks and thinks in their vernacular.

There is, in the story, an interesting comment made on the educated Indian. He is treated with contempt by Kipling even in such an early story: "The native members of Council knew as much about Punjabis as he knew about Charring Cross." (p. 199.) That is perhaps, the reason why the Legal Member after his conversation with Tods "was filled with an uneasy suspicion that Native Members represent very little, except the orders they carry on their bosoms." But then "he put the thought from him as illiberal. He was a most Liberal man." (p.

203.) Kipling's sarcasm is indeed, bitting, when the Indian under question is educated.

An older version of Tods is seen in Strickland, the Police Officer who appears in stories such as 'Miss Youghals Sais, The Bronckhorst Divorce-Case, The Return of Imray and The Mark of the Beast.' He "held the extra-ordinary theory that a Policemen in India should try to know as much about the natives as the natives themselves."[137] And so he educated himself for seven years among the "native riff- raff." In the story, however, this ability of Strickland helps him win over the consent of Miss Youghal's parents to his marriage with her. Though the narrator does not seem to approve of this "outlandish custom of prying into native life," the story reveals the view that it is not possible to understand the native from any other point of view but his own. That is why, Strickland believes "that no man can appreciate Simla properly till he has seen it from the *Sais's* point of view."(p. 31.) And he wants to write a book on his experiences. The narrator adds, "that book will be worth buying: and even more worth suppressing."(p. 32.) This is possibly because the book is going to reveal unpleasant truths about the rulers, feels Kipling perceptively. Though Strickland agrees to give up his old ways, after his marriage to Miss Youghal, we are told that

> it was a sore trial to him, for the streets and the bazaars, and the sounds in them, were full of meaning to Strickland, and these called to him to come back and take up his wanderings and his discoveries. (p. 34.)

In fact, he breaks his promise to help Biel out of a false charge hoisted on him which is supported solely by the false evidence of the native servants. Before the trial, Strickland threatens the servants of grave consequences and they tell the truth in the Court and Biel's reputation is saved. Once again, it is Strickland's familiarity with the native mode of life that makes him a much dreaded figure for the natives. Similarly, he is able to solve the mystery of Imray's disappearance and rescue Fleete from certain death. Kipling's meaning is clear in all these stories: What Strickland does should be emulated by the other Englishmen. Only this can bring about a change of heart in the rulers and make for a more human relationship with the ruled. Such an understanding would surely be outside the perceptions of an imperialist, if Kipling was merely that, as alleged by his detractors.

In his explorations into discovering meaningful relationships between the rulers and the ruled within the imperial system, Kipling finds that Love is one of the significant emotions that makes such a relationship possible, however brief, remote and tragic it might be.

'Beyond the Pale'[138] is the first tale in this series. The story has a Hindu proverb for its epigraph, "Love heeds not caste nor sleep a broken bed. I went in search of Love and lost myself." But the very opening sentence of the story seems to contradict the epigraph, "A man should, whatever happens, keep to his own caste, race, and breed. Let the White go to the White and Black to the Black. Then, whatever trouble falls, is in the ordinary course of things — neither sudden, alien nor unexpected." And so when one defies the dictum, as Trejago does in loving Bisesa, a native Hindu woman, the crisis is shown to be "sudden, alien and unexpected." Bisesa tells Trejago, "You are an Englishman. I am only a Black girl." Kipling's comment on this that "she was fairer than bar-gold in the Mint" almost amounts to a denial of the sentiment expressed in the opening sentence.

The affair between the two is carried on secretly. "Bisesa was an endless delight to Trejago." She was ignorant as a bird and is regarded as a "child" by him. But when she discovers that Trejago is in love with a white memsahib, she displays the characteristic "Oriental Passion and impulsiveness" and wants him to break off that relationship. In this desire of hers, Bisesa anticipates the possessiveness that is delineated more finely in the character of Ameera in 'Without Benefit of Clergy.'

This secret affair is discovered and her hands are cut off, while he is wounded in the groin and is left with a slight limp for the rest of his life. And so both Bisesa and Trejago have to pay a heavy price for their "folly" and "madness" (Kipling's words). It should be noted, however, that paradoxically "It was because they met in defiance of casts, race and breed that their love was so affirmative."[139] Despite the tragic end, the emphasis in the story is undoubtedly on the possibility of the existence of such a relationship between the two races based on love, a relationship that is virtually non-existent in the official and public roles of the two races.

In portraying the white man-native woman union, Kipling is able to transcend, at one stroke as it were, all the imperialist assumptions that govern many of his stories. In two such instances, 'Yoked with an Unbeliever' and 'Georgie Porgie', he highlights the spirit of sacrifice and generosity of the native woman and the cruelty and inhumanity of the white man. In the former, he depicts Dunmaya, a hill woman — an improved version of Lispeth — who, in addition to being a handsome girl, is able to convert Phil Garron into a better man. Agnes Laiter with whom Phil was earlier in love, had married another man and, on his death, comes to India to live with Phil who is now married to Dunmaya. Phil decides to take Agnes, and Dunmaya is very nice to her and Kipling comments:

> Worst of all, Dunmaya is making a decent man of him; and he will ultimately be saved from perdition through her training.[140]

And he adds, this is the "sin and shame of the whole business" and reaffirms that it is "manifestly unfair." Here it is evident that all his sympathies are on the side of Dunmaya.

"Georgie Porgie' is set in Burma. Georgie Porgie marries a native Burmese girl, calls her Georgina and leads a very happily married life for

> No race, men say who know, produces such good wives and heads of households as the Burmese.[141]

And for this, Georgie Porgie is envied by a visiting Subaltern "from the bottom of his heart." But the happiness does not last long. Soon Georgie Porgie realises how much more comfortable he would have been if married to a "sweet English maiden who would not smoke cheroots, and would play upon a Piano instead of banjo?" And he wishes to marry "a girl with Georgina's eyes and most of her ways. But not all. She could be improved upon." (p. 385.)

So giving a false reason to Georgina he goes to England and finds an English wife and returns with her to a different place. Meanwhile, for Georgina "there was no peace or comfort." She goes in search of Georgie Porgie and finally locates him. She takes just one look at the bride and runs away shrieking : "I am going away. I swear that I am going away." (p. 392.) Such is her faithfulness and generosity, that she emerges in a much better light as a loving woman than the ungrateful Georgie Porgie. The depiction by Kipling of the miseries suffered by Dunmaya and Georgina contradicts Bhaskara Rao's view that "he [Kipling] completely and conveniently forgot the hardships and humiliations that the Indians suffered at the hands of the British."[142]

But for fuller treatment of the white man — native woman union, we should turn to 'Without Benefit of Clergy',[143] easily one of Kipling's most memorable short stories. This is the story of Ameera, a young woman of sixteen and Holden, an English civil servant. Ameera gives Holden such joy that his "unlovely" existence is transformed into perfect happiness. She gives him, more than anything, a home. The arrival of their baby is resented by Holden and he regards it as an interference to their blissful existence while for Ameera it meant strengthening of their love for, "the love of a man, and particularly a white man, was at best an inconstant affair." (p. 151.)

A son is born to them and their living from now onwards is one of delight. Ameera's love and concern for Holden turns into an obsessive fear for the white woman, a good perception of Kipling, something natural in a native woman, who has won the affection of a white man, in short, someone who has achieved the impossible. In terms of a cultural encounter, India and England have come together in Ameera and Holden, and such an encounter is made possible, Kipling suggests, through the universal feeling of love. And we see how they participate in each other's rituals with respect and without any scepticism. For instance, Holden willingly kills two goats with his own hands to ward off the evil spirits to ensure the safety and welfare of his child. Occasionally, there is a suggestion of the possibility of a discordant note in this coming together of the two races, but it is soon overcome. Ameera asks Holden:

"... But, my life, what little name shall we give him?"

....

....

"There is the answer", said Holden. "Mian Mittu has spoken. He shall be the Parrot. When he is ready he will talk mightily and run about. Mian Mittu is the parrot in thy — in the Mussulman tongue, is it not?"

"Why put me so far off?" said Ameera fretfully.

"Let it be like unto some English name — but not wholly. For he is mine."

"Then call him Tota, for that is likest English!"

"Ay, Tota and that is still the Parrot. Forgive me, my Lord, for a minute ago, but in truth he is too little to wear all the weight of Mian Mittu for name. He shall be Tota — our Tota to us. Hearest thou, oh, small one? Littlest, thou art Tota." (p. 161.)

Note also Ameera's prayer:

"I have prayed for two things. First, that I may die in thy stead if thy death is demanded, and in the second that I may die in the place of the child. I have prayed to the Prophet and to Beebee Miriam [the Virgin Mary] Thinkest thou either will hear?" (p. 162.)

Here Ameera is not a "bazaar prostitute"[144] as alleged by Nirad C. Chaudhuri but an utterly selfless woman who prays to both their Gods, the outcome of her total identification with Holden. Chaudhuri's rather puerile criticism overlooks the possibility of sincerity of emotions in someone like Ameera, but Kipling recognises the influence of true love on an individual irrespective of one's class or caste.

They live a life of secrecy necessitated by the circumstances, "shut in behind he wooden gate that Pir Khan guarded." And eventually

The delight of that life was too perfect to endure. Therefore it was taken away as many things are taken away in India—suddenly and without warning. (p. 167.)

Though Kipling momentarily associates the unexpected and the tragic with India, he is able to raise the story from the racial to the universal level. The child Tota dies of autumnal fever. While the pain of this loss dawns on Holden slowly, Ameera is shattered completely. As cholera strikes, "Nature's going to audit her accounts with a big red pencil." In spite of Holden's piteous pleas, Ameera refuses to go to the hills. She tells him:

"... My lord and my love, let there be no more foolish talk of going away. Where thou art, I am. It is enough." (p. 175.)

In her decision to live by his side, at grave danger to her own life, we see how for Ameera, life without her love, Holden, has no meaning. She emerges from the story, as a woman very much superior to the 'mem-log' who rush to the hills leaving their husbands behind, in times of heat and disease. It is this knowledge about the white women that has turned her earlier envy into disdain now.

Finally, as she herself succumbs to black cholera, she whispers to Holden:

"... Remember only that I was thine and bore thee a son. Though thou wed a white woman tomorrow, the pleasure of receiving in thy arms thy first son is taken from thee for

> ever. Remember me when thy son is born—the one that shall carry thy name before all men. His misfortunes be on my head. I bear witness—I bear witness—'the lips were forming the words on his ear—*'that there is no God but—thee, beloved."* (pp. 177-78.)   (emphasis mine)

Ameera's dying words reveal her profound realisation that love is the only reality in her life, and it is love that gave meaning to her existence. And it is again, this very love that has brought the two races—the coloniser and the colonised—together and performed the miracle, a perceptive insight of Kipling.

Even while Kipling's emphasis is on love, it does not make his "attitude toward(s) colonialism irrelevant in [the] context"[145] of the story as suggested by Elliot L.Gilbert. One has come to accept by now that work is one of the leading metaphors in Kipling's fiction. Work assumes a richly significant position in the imperial situation. This aspect of colonialism is adequately examined by Kipling in the life of Holden. He suggests, almost insistently, that it is work that offers solace and comfort to Holden in moments of deep personal anguish. After the child's death

> One mercy only was granted to Holden. He rode to his office in broad daylight and found waiting him an unusually heavy mail that demanded concentrated attention and hard work. He was not, however, alive to this kindness of the gods. (p. 167.)

And Kipling attributes this to the "kindness of the Gods." Also, after Ameera's death, he is to proceed immediately to relieve a dying colleague. And so, for Holden, the representative of the ruling class, work not merely offers refuge but is a necessary occupation for survival as well. In the face of such evidence from the story, it is hard to understand how Elliot L.Gilbert, in an otherwise admirable analysis, could remark that "Holden's office duties do not relieve him of anxiety and pain."[146]

Thus we see Kipling capable of rising above his political beliefs in this sensitive dramatisation of the personal relationships between the two races. "Here, Kipling the artist, is at his purest, and the politician almost entirely absent."[147] Where officialdom failed to bring the East and West together, love is shown to succeed, although briefly. The tragic end to the love affair between Holden and Ameera does not "symbolise the impossibility of fusing British and Indian culture through love,"[148] as Noel Annan suggests taking a rather simplistic position, rather their love reminds us of Romeo and Juliet and Laila and Majnu. Such instances of complete happiness come to their inevitable end, brought about by the inexplicable logic of life. And so in conclusion, it should be said in fairness to Kipling that in 'Without Benefit of Clergy' he was able to, "if only briefly, relate the diverse worlds of India—the personal and the official, the native and the imperialistic—through the common concerns of love, work and death."[149]

If love was a significant factor that enabled Kipling to project an authentic image of India in all its entirety, religion was another. It is hard, perhaps even impossible, to understand India as a country without possessing an abiding interest in its religion and metaphysics. Kipling had lived long enough in the country to have acquired a more than superficial knowledge of its religions. And hence, he was able to get into the heart of the Indian reality, when religion was central to his vision of India. This is very much evident in his stories, 'The Bridge-Builders and The Miracle of Purun Bhagat' and of course, in his great novel, *Kim*.

'The Bridge-Builders' is a short story that not only examines the value of work in the larger context of human experience but it also brings together two different attitudes to life—western rationalism set against eastern mysticism and spirituality.

The Kashi Bridge built over the Ganga to facilitate quick travel and better trade is a marvel of Findlayson's engineering skill. Findlayson and his assistant, Hitchcock had endured all sorts of difficulties and their last three years

> covered storm, sudden freshets, death in every manner and shape, violent and awful rage against red tape half frenzying a mind that knows it should be busy on other things, drought, sanitation, finance; birth, wedding, burial, and riot in the village of twenty warring castes; argument, expostulation, persuasion, and the blank despair that a man goes to bed upon, thankful that his rifle is all in pieces in the gun-case.[150]

And after all these difficulties were overcome, Findlayson sees

> his bridge, raw and ugly as original sin, but pukka—per-

manent—to endure when all memory of the builder, yea, even of the splendid Findlayson truss, had perished. (p.3.)

The bridge is a symbol of modern progress, also of British power over India ("at either end rose towers of red brick, loopholed for musketry and pierced for big guns"). Findlayson is typically British in his attitude to life. Rooted in his own social milieu, he is wholly involved in his work and has a very pragmatic and rational attitude towards life. He is not only oblivious of other attitudes to life but even refuses to accept, for instance, the Indian attitude as revealed to him in the vision of the *Punchayat* of Gods.

Another significant character is Peroo, the Indian sailor. He "is the personification of East meeting West and is in this sense a true bridge builder."[151] He is efficient, hard working, skilled and very loyal. Quite a remarkable man indeed, for "there was no one like Peroo." He has had enough of western influences to be free from religious superstitions but still desists from being dogmatic. But he is essentially Indian, though he prays to the dome of St. Paul's while in London, and to the low-press cylinder while in the engine room of a steamer. That is why he tells Findlayson

"... London is London, Sahib. Sydney is Sydney, and Port Darwin is Port Darwin. Also Mother Gunga is Mother Gunga, and when I come back to her banks I know this and worship..." (p. 10.)

He has premonitions of the coming danger:

"We have bitted and bridled her. She is not like the sea, that can beat against a soft beach. She is Mother Gunga—in irons." (p. 10.)

Findlayson is only amused. But when the flood-warning comes, Peroo submits to fate, but only after vigorously participating in the various works to protect the bridge. And Findlayson

went over it (bridge) in his head, plate by plate, span by span, brick by brick, pier by pier, remembering, comparing, estimating, and recalculating, lest there should be any mistake... (p. 20.)

Peroo is annoyed at Findlayson's refusal to eat and also by his remark that "The bridge is mine; I cannot leave it." And so he can only laugh at Findlayson's hopeless anxiety:

"Wilt thou hold it up on with thy hands, then? ... I was troubled for my boats and sheers *before* the flood came. Now we are in the hands of the Gods..." (p. 22.)

While the first half of the story reveals Kipling's astounding knowledge of technical information regarding bridges, the second half is still more remarkable for his perceptive understanding of Hinduism as a religion. His awareness is different from the typically western attitudes since he knows the nuances and subtleties of the Hindu religion.

Findlayson and Peroo swallow some opium to guard themselves against fever. And the story from now onwards works on the allegorical level "to reveal the many faces of India, for the drug is a bridge to a lucid vision of India as it exists in its phenomenal form and as it is conceived in metaphysical speculation and given form in legend and myth."[152] Findlayson, under the influence of opium, thinks he can save the loosened boats and in attempting to do so, drifts along and is wrecked on an island downstream. There he and Peroo witness a *Punchayat* of the Gods. The Indian Gods appear in the form in which they are popularly known. Thus Shiva appears as the Bull, Mother Gunga as Crocodile, Hanuman as the Grey Ape, Indra as Buck, Ganesha as Elephant, Kali as Tigress and Sitala as the Ass.

Mother Gunga is angry because of the construction of the bridge and seeks justice from the gods through vengeance on the bridge builders. The responses of the various gods make illuminating reading. Ganesh the Elephant, points out how the fire-carriages have by connecting far-off towns, brought about economic changes resulting in prosperity to his worshippers, the fat money-lenders. This offers a clue to the essential irony of imperialism in that it has in it seeds of self-destruction. The imperialist lays roads and railway lines, builds bridges and does many more things of utilitarian value to achieve his own ends, that is, to strengthen his own hold over the natives. But ironically, it is these very things that give the native, in the long run, the necessary strength and self-confidence which enables him to launch an attack on the rulers. The illusion that the imperialist tries to create in the mind of the native that he is out to help him turns into a reality eventually, in spite of his intentions and also, perhaps, because of his work. Kipling is very much aware of this irony here, and as well in 'The Man who would be King'. He did know that the empire "is primarily a money-making concern,"[153] and not otherwise as alleged by George

Orwell. In his anxiety to damn Kipling for ever, Orwell goes to the extent of accusing Kipling of not possessing a basic insight into the imperial situation, when he says that Kipling "could not foresee... that the same motives which brought the Empire into existence would end by destroying it."[154]

Mother Ganga is sad that

> "they [English] have changed the face of the land—which is my land. They have killed and made new towns on my banks."

And Ganesh answers:

> "It is but the shifting of a little dirt. Let the dirt dig in the dirt if it pleases the dirt." (p. 32.)

How revealing is this statement and how perceptive is Kipling to the actual truth about the Indian reality. India, unlike many other countries of the world, has gone through numerous foreign invasions and absorbed all those influences to retain its identity, thanks to the inner strength of her people and the sustaining spirit of her religions. The process of these changes is referred to as "the shifting of a little dirt," truly a poetic masterstroke of Kipling in his choice of the phrase.

Hanuman's response throws light on another aspect of India:

> "For my own part it pleases me well to watch these men, remembering that I also built no small bridge in the world's youth." (p. 31.)

A clear reference to his exploits at Lanka. He further adds

> "... I am the builder of bridges indeed—bridges between this and that, and each bridge leads surely to us in the end. Be content, Gunga. Neither these men nor those that can follow them mock thee at all... but the fire carriages bring me new worshippers from beyond the Black Water—the men who believe that their God is toil. I run before them beckoning, and they follow Hanuman. (pp. 34-35.)

Hanuman's cool confidence is characteristic. Like Ganesha, he believes no harm will come to India because of the English. Here he is not implying the conversion of men of other religions into Hinduism, but his boast "is simply a statement of Hinduism's ability to absorb new influences, of India's enormous assimilative powers and of the people's devotion to tradition."[155]

The less secular gods but those of the higher pantheon like Indra reproach Mother Ganga:

> "Does Mother Ganga die, then, in a year, that she is so anxious to see vengeance now? The deep sea was where she runs but yesterday, and tomorrow the sea shall cover her again as the Gods count that which men call time. Can any say that this their bridge endures till tomorrow."
> (pp. 30- 31.)

At this crucial juncture, Krishna, the God who identifies himself with mankind, arrives on the scene, implores Mother Gunga to have pity on his people and refrain from destroying the bridge. In the words of Benita Parry, "though he is divine, his incarnation as a man embraces the transient and the infinite, the relative and the absolute."[156] Initially, he tries to convince the Gods of the benefits to be reaped because of the bridge:

> "... And the fire-carriage feeds your shrines, ye say? And the fire-carriages bring a thousand pilgrimages where but (ten) came in the old years?..." (p. 39.)

But then he prophecies about the future:

> ".... They [men] do not think of the Heavenly ones altogether. They think of the fire-carriage and the other things that the brige-builders have done, and when your priests thrust forward hands asking alms, they give unwillingly a little..." (p. 40.)

To this threat, Hanuman replies:

> "Their Gods came, and we changed them. I took the Woman and made her twelve-armed. So shall we twist all their Gods." (pp. 40-41.)

And Krishna disagrees:

> "Their Gods! This is no question of their Gods — one or three — man or woman. The matter is with the people. *They* move, and not the Gods of the bridge-builders."
> (p. 41.)

Krishna is, in other words, foretelling that western modes of living and their rational view of life will transform the traditional modes of living of the native.

It is Indra who finally pronounces his judgment with the riddle of the Gods:

> "... When Brahm ceases to dream, the Heavens and the Hells and Earth disappear. Be content. Brahm dreams still. The dreams come and go, and the nature of the dreams changes, but still Brahm dreams. Krishna has walked too long upon earth, and yet I love him the more for the tale he has told. The Gods change, beloved – all save one! ... Brahm dreams – and till He wakes the Gods die not." (pp. 42-43.)

This is the satisfactory resolution, for Brahm is the All-pervading Godhead who is immanent and transcendent. If Brahm dreams still, "the Gods die not." The riddle also makes clear the existence of the Gods in relation to man's spiritual needs and desires, since Brahman is the in-dwelling spirit in man, the Self or *Atman*. Man shapes his God according to his dreams. Dynamic changes introduced by the white man affect the Gods as well. If the old Gods represent dreams which still persist among the people, they will not die. And so we see how "Krishna's humane plea [is] reabsorbed into the eternal cycles of the cosmic processes in which the phenomenal universe is subject to permanent alteration while the world-spirit, who is immanent and transcendent, persists as the unvarying reality, indissoluble and immutable."[157]

At dawn, Findlayson still preoccupied with the bridge, has no recollection of the *punchayat* for, "in that clear light there was no room for a man to think of dreams of the dark." Hence, for him, the Gods do not exist, in other words, they die. In contrast, for Peroo the whole experience has been profoundly enlightening:

> "Oho! Then it *is* true. "When Brahm ceases to dream, the Gods die." Now I know, indeed, what he meant. Once, too, the *guru* said as much to me; but then I did not understand. Now I am wise." (p. 44.)

Recalling how his life was in danger during a typhoon, he concludes:

> "... I have seen the Gods. They are good for live men, but for the dead – They have spoken themselves... When Brahm ceases to dream, the Gods go." (pp. 45-46.)

Thus we see Kipling, in his artistic involvement with Hinduism, able to project an Indian vision of life with not only sympathy but with understanding. 'The Bridge-Builders' dramatises this vision "that the phenomenal world is but a momentary expression of the ultimate and enduring reality, but that this does not deprive the empirical world of meaning or life of value."[158] Kipling knew of this duality in Indian philosophy that the empirical world was not merely illusory in nature but, in fact, was part of the Ultimate Reality. S.Radhakrishnan's commentary on the point, supports Kipling's contention:

> The manifold world is not an illusion; it is being, though of a lower order, subject to change, waxing and waning, growing and shrinking... For the Hindu thinkers the objective world exists. It is not an illusion. It is real not in being ultimate, but in being a form, an expression of the ultimate. To regard the world as ultimately real is delusion (*moha*).[159]

The two different attitudes to life — the western and the eastern — are dramatized in Findlayson and the *punchayat* of Gods. For Findlayson, his own work in the face of severe natural disasters is the only reality. But it is Peroo, who is the true bridge-builder, for he has gained insight into the riddle of the gods, and is also able to fill his pace in the material world most admirably. Kipling's contempt is reserved for the Rao Sahib of Baraon, the local ruler who appears at the end of the story. He is a truly monstrous hybrid of the east and the west. He is dressed incongruously in "tweed shooting-suit and a seven-hued turban." He owns a steam-launch but does not, in his own words, "understand steam-engines" and for him, his own religious ceremonies are "dam-bore." Kipling did not fancy such men like the Rao Sahib making for a better understanding between the east and west. And hence, he makes him, justifiably, into a wholly ridiculous figure, a parody of the true bridge-builder like Peroo.

From the point of view of this study, 'The Bridge-Builders' is one of the finest stories of Kipling that presents an *authentic* image of India. Kipling was finally able to discover this elusive truth that had so far prevented him from comprehending the Indian reality fully. That is, the knowledge that India in essence could be captured only through its religion. And this made him see "beyond the bewildering variety and apparent inflexibility to an India, which, like Brahm, is Many but one and which, like Peroo, endures even while it changes."[160] India is not only made up of many Indias but ultimately there is only one India.

'The Miracle of Purun Bhagat' is a beautifully structured story that shows Kipling entirely free from any racial bias whatsoever in his sympathetic understanding of the Hindu way of life and in the memorable portrayal of an Indian, Purun Bhagat. Purun Dass, thanks to his English education rose to be the Prime Minister of Mohiniwala, a native state in the north-western part of India. All his values and ideals are English based; naturally he and his young ruler

> established schools for little girls, made roads, and started State dispensaries and shows of agricultural implements, and published a yearly blue-book on the 'Moral and Material Progress of the State,' and the Foreign Office and the Government of India were delighted.[161]

In short, because of this wisdom and foresight, Purun Dass became the honoured friend of the British from the Viceroy downwards. Finally he goes to England where he

> was given honorary degrees by learned universities, and he made speeches and talked of Hindu social reform to English ladies in evening dress, till all London cried, 'This is the most fascinating man we have ever met at dinner since cloths were first laid.' (p. 37.)

It is significant that he is a *man* and not just another Indian.

That Kipling knew the prevalent Hindu custom is clear from his reference to Purun Dass paying enormous sums to the priests on his return from England "for even so high-caste a Brahmin as Purun Dass lost caste by crossing the black sea." On his return to India, he is knighted, a fitting climax to an illustrious career. On this occasion, "replying to the toast of his master's health, [he] made a speech few Englishmen could have bettered." The genuine praise that Kipling has for the man cannot go unnoticed. And the very next month, "he did a thing no Englishman would have dreamed of doing; for, so far as the world's affairs went, he died." He wore ochre robes, took a begging bowl and walked out a sanyasi into the wide world. Kipling points out:

> He had been, as the old Law recommends, twenty years a youth, twenty years a fighter, — though he had never carried a weapon in his life, — and twenty years head of a household. (p. 38.)

Kipling is aware of the four stages of life as enshrined in Hindu religion and this is stated without any trace of irony or ridicule, thus avoiding the stock response to Hinduism of the Anglo-Indian novelists.

Purun Dass now calls himself Purun Bhagat. He wanders all over India, "depending on his neighbours for his daily bread, and so long as there is a morsel to divide in India, neither priest nor beggar starves." (p. 39.) He finally goes to the Himalayas where he hopes to find, in his own words, "knowledge" and "peace." His meditations that lead him towards this goal are sensitively described:

> He would repeat a Name softly to himself a hundred times, till, at each repetition, he seemed to move more and more out of his body, sweeping upto the doors of some tremendous discovery; but, just as the door was opening, his body would drag him back, and, with grief, he felt he was locked up again in the flesh and bones of Purun Bhagat. (p. 45.)

The power of the flesh is enormous and the time is not yet ripe for his release from this world.

Purun Bhagat subsists on the food brought to him by the hillfolk from the village down below. In the meanwhile, there grows a very intimate relationship between him and the animals that live there like the *langurs,* the big gray-whiskered monkeys; *barasingh,* the big deers; *muschiknabha,* the musk deer, *minauls,* the Himalayan pheasants and *Sona,* the Himalayan black bear. He "called them all 'my brothers,' and his low call of! *'Bhai! Bhai!'* would draw them from the forest at noon if they were within earshot." (p. 48.) Many years go by, and one summer it rains incessantly and "in the black heart of the night," he is woken up by the langur to warn him of the impending landslide. One look at the empty begging bowl, Purun Bhagat is reminded of the villagers below and he swings into action immediately. He rushes down the hilly slopes with the animals to warn the villagers of the imminent danger to their lives. Kipling adds:

> He was no longer a holy man, but Sir Purun Dass, K.C.I.E., Prime Minister of no small State, a man accustomed to command, going out to save life. (p. 53.)

The villagers are saved and next morning they find him "dead, sitting cross-legged, his back against a tree, his crutch under his armpit, and his face turned to the north-east." (p. 56.) They build a temple to the holy man and "they worship there with lights and flowers and offerings to this day." Kipling's conclusion gives us his point of view:

> But they do not know that the saint of their worship is the late Sir Purun Dass, K.C.I.E., D.C.L., Ph.D., etc., once Prime Minister of the progressive and enlightened State of Mohiniwala, and honorary or corresponding member of more learned and scientific societies than will ever do any good in this world or the next. (pp. 56-57.)

From this ending, it is apparent that Kipling makes a neat distinction between Purun Dass, the man of action and Purun Bhagat, the man of contemplation. While Shamsul Islam suggests that in Purun Bhagat "the roles of a man of action and a man of contemplation are fused together in a single personality,"[162] Angus Wilson interprets the story in view of its end as "a tribute to the western code of action rather than to the Hindu way of passivity ... He [Kipling] is attempting to pay tribute to both systems and yet to suggest that the Western creed of human concern will assert itself in a crisis."[163] Surely, both of them are right, but only partially.

This division of a man's life into two exclusive aspects, that of action and contemplation, is a typical western view of life. Kipling's knowledge of Hinduism was admirable but it was not deep enough for him to know that a life of renunciation did not preclude action in a crisis. In the Hindu view of life, action and contemplation are mutually inclusive. However, what is significant in a study of the image of India, is that Kipling, may be unknowingly, has given us in Purun Bhagat, a moving and *true* picture of an extraordinary Indian.

But for Kipling's classic on India, we should still look to his great novel *Kim*.[164] While Nirad Chaudhuri hails it as "the finest novel in the English language with an Indian theme, but also one of the greatest English novels in spite of the theme,"[165] J.M.S.Tompkins believes that "the vision is romantic in that, though complex in detail, it is simplified in impact."[166] As suggested at the beginning of this chapter, Kipling's works written after 1889, the year of his departure from India, reveal a maturity of attitude, a greater poise and a refusal to take sides easily. India by then had become a part of his system and writing about it while away from the land certainly gave him a better perspective. This is confirmed by his artistic achievement most notably in 'Without Benefit of Clergy', 'The Bridge-Builders' and 'The

Miracle of Purun Bhagat'. And *Kim* is distanced more so both in time and space since it was conceived in Vermont sometime during 1893, and was written between the autumn of 1899 and the summer of 1900. It is because Kipling was operating from this vantage ground, that he was able to achieve such an extraordinary success.

Kim is mainly concerned with the quest of two individuals, Kim, a fourteen year old Irish orphan brought up by a Eurasian woman and Teshoo Lama, the holy man from Tibet. Whereas Kim is in pursuit of "a great Red Bull on a green field," Lama, a "follower of the Middle Way" is in search of a River "whose nature ... is that whoso bathes in it washes away all taint and speckle of sin" (p. 14.) and thus can free himself from the Wheel of Life. Kim, though a white boy, is "burned black as any native... spoke the vernacular by preference, and his mother-tongue in a clipped uncertain sing-song ... consorted on terms of perfect equality with the small boys of the bazar." (p. 1.) He is appropriately nicknamed, 'Little Friend of all the World.' On seeing the Lama near Lahore Museum, a strange looking man in a strange garb, Kim's curiosity is roused. He finds him "entirely new to all his experience, and he meant to investigate further." (p. 17.) He is moved by the holy man's sincerity and innocence, begs food for him and thus begins an exceptional relationship between the master and the pupil, the *guru* and the *chela*.

Irish by birth, he has in him inner reserves of strength and power, but at the same time he is aware that he belongs to India, "this great and beautiful land." He seems to understand both the cultures, though at the beginning of the novel, he feels very much like an Indian. As a matter of fact, *Kim* at one level dramatises the growth of his awareness of being a Sahib. It is this chameleon like quality that makes him a fascinating character who can perform different roles be it a Hindu low-caste street boy, a Mohammedan horse-boy or for that matter, a holy man's *chela,* all with supreme ease and panache. But then what sets Kim apart is that he is able to, unlike most of Kipling's English civilians, unite love and work, thanks to the loving care and supervision shown by people around him especially the Lama and the Pathan.

As the Lama and Kim begin their journey first by train, then on foot, we are given remarkable descriptions of the Indian landscape and her peoples. It is here that a majority of Anglo-Indian novelists had failed, and a clue to Kipling's success is offered by the epigraph to the second chapter:

> And whoso will, from Pride released,
> Contemplating neither creed nor priest,
> May feel the Soul of all the East About him at Kamakura.

Pride, mainly a result of the feeling of racial superiority, has been for the Anglo-Indian writer, the major hurdle in getting to know the "Soul of all the East." Kipling, free from this pride is able to capture Indian reality in all its verisimilitude. First, the Lama and Kim travel by train from Lahore to Umballa. As the train roars into the railway station:

> The sleepers sprang to life, and the station filled with clamour and shoutings, cries of water and sweetmeat vendor, shouts of native policemen, and shrill yells of women gathering up their baskets, their families, and their husbands. (p. 38.)

There couldn't have been a more accurate picture of the din and bustle that accompanies the arrival of a train at an Indian railway station. And even inside the railway compartment the variety is striking. Note Kipling's eye for little details. We have a burly bearded Sikh artisan; a "blue-turbaned" Jat farmer and his loud-mouthed wife; a young Dogra soldier, a fat Hindu money-lender, "his folded account-book in a cloth under his arm" and an Amritsar courtesan "making eyes at the young sepoy... [from] behind her head drapery." (p. 40.)

From Umballa, the Lama and Kim set out walking on the Grand Trunk Road, "the backbone of all Hind":

> And truly the Grand Trunk Road is a wonderful spectacle. It runs straight, bearing without crowding India's traffic for fifteen hundred miles — such a river of life as nowhere else exists in the world. (p. 81.)

This road which is alive with teeming humanity brings distinctly different responses from the Lama and Kim. While the Lama who is trying to get away from life, the Wheel of Things, is "deep in meditation," Kim is greatly excited at viewing this "broad smiling river of life." He finds "new people and new sights at every stride":

> a troop of long-haired, strong-scented Sansis with baskets of lizards and other unclean food on their backs, their lean dogs sniffing at their heels. These people kept their own side of the road, moving at a quick, furtive jog-trot, and all other castes gave them ample room; for the Sansi is deep

pollution ... an Akali, a wild-eyed, wild-haired Sikh devotee in the blue-checked clothes of his faith, with polished steel quoits glistening on the cone of his tall blue turban ... gaily dressed crowds of whole villages turning out to some local fair; the women, with their babes on their hips, walking behind the men, the older boys prancing on sticks of sugar-cane, dragging rude brass models of locomotives such as they sell for a halfpenny, or flashing the sun into the eyes of their betters from cheap toy mirrors ... These merry-makers stepped slowly, calling one to the other and stopping to haggle with sweetmeat-sellers, or to make prayer before one of the wayside shrines — sometimes Hindu, sometimes Mussulman — which the low-caste of both creeds share with beautiful impartiality ... a gang of *changars* — the women ... [who were] flat-footed, big-bosomed, strong-limbed, blue-petticoated clan of earth-carriers, hurrying north on news of a job and wasting no time by the road. They belong to the caste whose men do not count, and they walked with squared elbows, swinging hips, and heads on high, as suits women who carry heavy weights. A little later a marriage procession would strike into the Grand Trunk with music and shoutings, and a smell of marigold and jasmine stronger even than the reek of the dust ... the money-lender on his goose-rumped pony, hastening along to collect the cruel interest ... the long-shouting, deep-voiced little mob ... of native soldiers on leave, rejoicing to be rid of their breeches and puttees, and saying the most outrageous things to the most respectable women in sight .... (pp. 86-88.)

While Kim "was in the seventh heaven of joy," Lama "never raised his eyes" because all these people are "bound upon the Wheel. Bound from life after life. To none of these has the way been shown." So much for their different views of life. But what is remarkable about this long passage is not merely the marvellous ability of Kipling to evoke various groups of Indians — something given to a lesser novelist as well — but his capacity to individualise each of them and give us an insight into their true nature, and also into the complex social realities of India. It could have only come from one who loved not only the land but also the people without any bias or prejudice, either racial or political. The Kipling of 'The Head of the District' and 'The Enlightenments of Pagett, M.P.', seems to have gone into oblivion, and in his place has emerged a new Kipling who has deep compassion and understanding for the Indian peoples. Having been away for ten years from the land that he regarded as his only home, must surely account for this positive development.

A little incident should clarify the essential disparity in the attitude to life in the Lama and Kim. This is when they come across a snake. Kim's instantaneous reaction is to look for a stick to kill it, for he hates snakes because "no native training can quench the white man's horror of the Serpent." On the other hand, the Lama calmly points out to Kim:

> '... He is upon the Wheel as we are—a life ascending or descending—very far from deliverance. Great evil must the soul have done that is cast into this shape ... Let him live out his life.'

And then goes on to address the snake directly:

> 'May thy release come soon, brother: ... Hast *thou* knowledge, by chance, of my River?'

Kim, overwhelmed at this, can only express his wonder to the Lama:

> 'Never have I seen such a man as thou art
> ... Do the very snakes understand thy talk?' (pp. 61-62.)

Kim's response is typically Western and that of the Lama Buddhist, typically Eastern, but paradoxically, the earlier devotion he had felt for the Lama turns into love from this moment onwards. The personal tie between the two grow stronger. Though, by instinct, he belongs to the world of action and rejects the Lama's world of renunciation, Kim feels strongly attached to him more than anyone else. And this is one of the curiously charming aspects of the novel.

Kim's search comes to an end with his sighting the regimental device of the Mavericks, the great Red Bull on a background of Irish Green. He is caught by Father Bennett and his parentage is established. Father Bennett and Father Victor discuss what should be done with Kim. Kipling's attitude towards these missionaries needs to be examined. While Father Bennett is attacked quite scornfully many a time by referring to him as 'Church of England' and not by his name,

Father Victor is treated with a little more sympathy. Bennett's view of the Lama reveals to us without doubt, that Kipling's sympathies lie entirely with the latter:

> Bennett looked at him [the Lama] with the triple-ringed uninterest of the creed that lumps nine-tenths of the world under the title of 'heathen.' (p. 124.)

Father Victor calls the Lama 'a street-beggar,' 'old beggar-man' and keeps repeatedly invoking the 'Powers of Darkness below!' as being the cause of Kim's wildness. When the Lama offers to pay for Kim's education, Father Victor can only exclaim, 'takin' a heathen's money to give a child a Christian education.' The missionaries do not know what to make of this strange figure, Kim, but Father Victor is hopeful since he believes, 'once a Sahib is always a Sahib' and he tells Kim, 'They'll make a man o' you, O'Hara, at St. Xavier's — a white man, an' I hope, a good man...' (p. 166.)

While one search — that of his parentage comes to an end, another begins, his search for identity. Kim has "a double personality and is torn by the antithetical demands of the East and West."[167] It is the case of a conflict between genes and environment. To begin with, let us consider the influence of the environment on Kim. Most important is his use of language. He constantly shifts from the vernacular to English, and back again but undoubtedly he is his natural self while speaking in the former. Note, for instance, his ability to squat:

> Mechanically Kim squatted beside him,–squatted as only the natives can, –in spite of the abominable clinging trousers. (p. 143.)

Kim finds eating "at one table in public ... particularly revolting [as he] preferred to turn his back on the world at meals." (p. 149.) He can sleep soundly even beside the railway lines, for "he had all the Oriental's indifference to mere noise." (pp. 198-99.) While he extracts from Mehbub Ali more and more money for giving valuable information, he is referred to as "mechanically following the huckster instinct of the East." (p. 191.)

It is this Kim who is sent to St. Xavier's to be trained as a chain-man in the Survey of India, another name for a spy in the Great Game. On the eve of his departure to St. Xavier's, when Mahbub Ali tells him, "Once a Sahib, always a Sahib," he confesses to him, "I do not want to be a Sahib." (pp. 151-52.) It is in this state of mind, that he travels to St.

Xavier's at Lucknow alone in a second class bogie which he finds "very different from that joyful down-journey in the third-class with the lama." And he sadly reflects:

> '*Hai mai:* I go from one place to another as it might be a Kick-ball. It is my *Kismet*. No man can escape his *Kismet*. But I am to pray to Bibi Miriam, and I am a Sahib ... No, I am Kim. This is the great world, and I am only Kim. Who is Kim?' He considered his own identity, a thing he had never done before, till his head swam. He was one insignificant person in all this roaring whirl of India, going southward to he knew not what fate. (p. 167.)

Kim repeats this question twice more in the course of the novel, without perhaps being able to find an entirely satisfactory answer. His own search for identity contrasts quite sharply with Lama's attempts at denying his identity.

While at St. Xavier's he begins to enjoy himself, for "the atmosphere suited him and he throve by inches." But he learns another aspect of his new life, as he realises that he cannot share his early experiences in the bazaar with the other boys at school when they reminisce about their experiences, because

> St. Xavier's looks down on boys who 'go native altogether.' One must never forget that one is a Sahib, and that some day, when examinations are passed, one will command natives. Kim made a note of this, for he began to understand where examinations led. (p.177.)

Despite this knowledge, when holidays come, the pull of his early life is too strong and insistent:

> Kim yearned for the caress of soft mud squishing up between the toes, as his mouth watered for mutton stewed with butter and cabbages, for rice speckled with strong-scented cardamoms, for the saffron-tinted rice, garlic and onions, and the forbidden greasy sweatmeats of the bazaars. (p. 178.)

And so, with the help of a dancing girl he is transformed into a low-caste Hindu boy. He travels third, and "in all India that night was no human being so joyful as Kim." (p. 181.) It is almost as if Kim has found his real identity. But it is not as simple as that, for we have him telling Mahbub Ali.

> '... In the *madrissah* I will be a Sahib. But when the *madrissah* is shut, then must I be free and go among my people ... [of] this great and beautiful land ...' (p. 193.)

He is now happy with the natives for "change of scene, service, and surroundings were the breath of his little nostrils." (p. 195.)

After finishing two more years at St. Xavier's, Kim is ready to enter the wide world of India to take his place in the Great Game. It is at this moment, that he is once again haunted by the spectre of loneliness.

> 'Now I am alone — all alone. In all India is no one so alone as I: If I die to-day, who shall bring the news — and to whom? ... Who is Kim — Kim — Kim?' (pp. 264-65.)

Kim is once again drawn towards the Lama, and joins him in his search for the healing River. He combines his desire to be with the Lama and his work as spy without arousing any suspicion in the innocent Lama. When Kim cures the young child of a Jat in Benares, Lama tells him:

> 'To heals the sick is to acquire merit ... That was wisely done, O Friend of all the World.' (p. 271.)

To this Kim replies, 'I was made wise by thee, Holy one' and

> forgetting the little play just ended; forgetting St. Xavier's; forgetting his white blood; forgetting even the Great Game as he stooped, Mohammedan-fashion, to touch his master's feet in the dust of the Jain temple. (p. 271.)

Such a spontaneous gesture is surely an indication of the loving relationship between the two, that continues till the end of the novel despite Kim's growing awareness that he is a sahib.

As the Lama and Kim proceed on their journey, we are made sharply aware of the differences between them. As a *chela*, Kim looks after the bodily needs of the Lama and also receives instructions regarding the Wheel of Life:

> When the shadows shortened and the Lama leaned more heavily upon Kim, there was always the Wheel of Life to draw forth, to hold flat under wiped stones, and with a long straw to expound cycle by cycle. ... Obediently, then with bowed head and brown finger alert to follow the

> pointer, did the *chela* study; but when they came to the Human world, busy and profitless, that is just above the Hells, his mind was distracted; for by the roadside trundled the very Wheel itself, eating, drinking, trading, marrying, and quarreling — all warmly alive. (p. 302.)

Though he is not critical of the Lama's search, he cannot share his philosophy of life and is instinctively drawn towards life on the Grand Trunk Road. The difference is reiterated once again in this dialogue between the two:

> 'To abstain from action is well — except to acquire merit.'
>
> 'At the Gates of Learning we were taught that to abstain from action was unbefitting a Sahib. And I am a Sahib.' (p. 303.)

Kim never regards the material life, as illusion as the Lama does, but as they travel together, an important change comes over him. He moves gradually away from his race and his mother-tongue and slips "back to thinking and dreaming in the vernacular, and mechanically followed the Lama's ceremonial observances at eating, drinking and the like." (p. 304.) This is an indication that he has moved into the Lama's world.

And at this time, Hurree Chunder Mookerjee, a fellow spy informs Kim of the presence of the French and Russian spies in the Hills, and seeks his assistance in pursuing them. Kim conveniently leads the Lama to the hills, for is it not said, 'Who goes to the Hills goes to his mother.' (p. 328.) In their encounter with the spies, the Russian strikes the holy man full on the face and Kim immediately retaliates by hitting him, for "the blow had waked every unknown Irish devil in the boy's blood." (p. 346.) In the melée, all the important papers are taken away from the spies and Kim's mission is complete.

The Lama's search constitutes the final movement of the novel. The Lama, after the incident with the Russian is remorse stricken. He tells Kim:

> '... The blow was but a shadow upon a shadow. Evil in itself — my legs weary apace these latter days! — it met evil in me — anger, rage, and a lust to return to evil ... Had I been less passionless, the evil blow would have done only bodily evil — a scar, a bruise — which is illusion. But my mind was *not* abstracted, for rushed in straightaway a lust to let the

> Spiti men kill. In fighting that lust, my soul was torn and wrenched beyond a thousand blows. Not till I had repeated the Blessings' (he meant the Buddhist beatitudes) 'did I achieve calm ....' (p. 360.)

This blow awakens the Lama to the presence of evil in himself and his pursuit suffers a temporary setback. But paradoxically, it is this awareness that also brings him nearer to his search. Because he now realises that his visit to the Hills made him physically stronger letting him forget his search. And the blow comes as a sign to him that his place is not in the hills, but down below on the plains.

As they go down the hills, Kim performs all the duties of a *chela* with supreme devotion:

> He begged in the dawn, set blankets for the lama's meditation, held the weary head on his lap through the noonday heats, fanning away the flies till his wrists ached, begged again in the evenings, and rubbed the lama's feet ...
> (pp. 385-86.)

The Lama is moved with infinite compassion at Kim's devotion and wonders whether he has not served him more faithfully than Ananda did Buddha. His tribute is genuine:

> '... never was such a *chela*. Temperate, kindly, wise, of ungrudging disposition, a merry heart upon the road, never forgetting, learned, truthful, courteous...' (pp. 404- 5.)

It is this devotion in Kim that raises a very important issue in the novel. As we have seen, Kim is caught between two worlds. There is the world of India as opposed to the British world of St. Xavier's school and that of the Great Game. In addition, there is the world of action, excitement and adventure in the world of Mahbub Ali, in contrast to the Lama's world of contemplation, renunciation and tranquility. Kim no doubt moves, as only he can, with enviable ease from one world to another. When referred to as a sahib by the Lama, Kim retorts:

> 'Thou hast said there is neither black nor white. Why plague me with this talk, Holy One? Let me rub the other foot. It vexes me. I am *not* a Sahib. I am thy *chela,* and my head is heavy on my shoulders.' (p. 386.)

This is perhaps the most significant remark in the entire novel viewed from the angle of Kim's identity. Kim says this at the end of the novel when he is stepping into manhood. That he can have these feelings in spite of his schooling at St. Xavier's, points to the hold of the Lama on the personality of Kim. If only someone could take from him the material that he has taken away from the foreign agents, "the Great Game might play itself for aught he ... cared." (p. 387.) That he can entertain thoughts of giving up the most cherished ambition of his life for the love of the lama, is an important revelation offered by Kipling into the character of Kim. Even Mahbub Ali is aware of this as he later tells the Lama, "Thou hast turned one man that I know from the path of strife." (p. 408.)

As he reaches the plains and while he regains his health under the kindly care of the woman from Kulu, he finds "that his soul was out of gear with its surroundings — a cog-wheel unconnected with any machinery." And again comes the insistent questioning for the third time:

> 'I am Kim, I am Kim. And what is Kim?' His soul repeated it again and again.
>
> He did not want to cry, — had never felt less like crying in his life, — but of a sudden easy, stupid tears trickled down his nose, and with an almost audible click he felt the wheels of his being lock up anew on the world without. Things that rode meaningless on the eyeball an instant before, slid into proper proportion. Roads were meant to be walked upon, houses to be lived in, cattle to be driven, fields to be tilled, and men and women to be talked to. They were all real and true — solidly planted upon the feet perfectly comprehensible — clay of his clay, neither more nor less ... (p. 403.)

Kim's question has not been really answered but he knows that his life should be lived here and now, in this world. The Lama's path of renunciation is not for him, though it is the same Lama who has brought home to him the profound truth of life that "there is neither black nor white." After this, Kim can no longer be a mere sahib though he might still choose to take part in the Great Game.

As Kim's search ends, simultaneously, that of the Lama also comes to its conclusive end. He gives up food and water, sits in meditation for two days and two nights. And on the second night, the Lama tells Kim:

> '... my Soul went free, and, wheeling like an eagle, saw in-

deed that there was no Teshoo Lama nor any other soul. As a drop draws to water, so my Soul drew near to the Great Soul which is beyond all things ... I knew the Soul had passed this I knew that I was free.' (p. 416.)

Even in this state of blissful freedom, he thinks of Kim, and says: "I will return to my *chela*, lest he miss the way." (p. 412.) His conviction that he will be able to free Kim from the Wheel is apparent from the final sentence of the novel:

"He crossed his hands on his lap and smiled, as a man may, who has won salvation for himself and his beloved."(p. 413.)

What is Kipling trying to say in *Kim*? Critics have offered various explanations and among them Edmund Wilson's views are worth serious consideration as they help clarify certain important issues in the novel, even if it is through disagreement. Writing about the ending of the novel, Wilson believes that

... what the reader tends to expect is that Kim will come eventually to realise that he is delivering into bondage to the British invaders those whom he has always considered his own people, and that a struggle between allegiances will result. Kipling has established for the reader — and established with considerable dramatic effect — the contrast between the East, with its mysticism and sensuality, its extremes of saintliness and roguery, and the English, with their superior organization, their confidence in modern method, their instinct to brush away like cobwebs the native myths and beliefs. We have been shown two entirely different worlds existing side by side, with neither really understanding the other, and we have watched the oscillations of Kim, as he passes to and fro between them. But the parallel lines never meet; the alternating attractions felt by Kim never give rise to genuine struggle. And the climax itself is double: the adventures of the Lama and of Kim simply arrive at different consummations without any final victory or synthesis ever being allowed to take place. Instead, there are a pair of victories, which occur on separate planes and do not influence one another: the Lama attains to a condition of trance which releases him from what the Buddhists call the Wheel of Things at the same moment that the young Anglo-Indian achieves promotion in the British Secret Service.[168]

The basic problem with Edmund Wilson's approach is that he has politicised the entire novel and then finds that certain conflicts, inevitable in a political context, are absent from it. But when one reads the novel, the political overtones are provided only by the Great Game, the main function of which, at least as suggested in the novel, is to protect the British empire in India from dangers, both internal and external, from the princes of small native states and notably Russia among the neighbouring countries. Kim's wonderful relationship is with the ordinary people of India and he wouldn't give this up for anything in life, the Great Game included. From the novel, it is plain that he sees no threat to this relationship because of his role in the secret service. After all, he believes and he is right, that he is helping the British Government to maintain law and order and save India from anarchy and misrule. Given this kind of conviction in Kim, it is a futile endeavour to look for a conflict of allegiances in him.

Kim, in the course of the novel does move between the two worlds, —the Indian and the English—but to say that these worlds do not understand each other is to misread the novel. In fact, it is Kim with "the Irish and the Oriental in his soul," who is able to comprehend both the Indian and the English with an ease that is at once credible and astounding. Kim succeeds, where many of Kipling's earlier heroes had failed, because he is endowed with an enormous amount of sympathy for the native way of life; is free from any feeling of racial superiority, and also possibly because he has gone native himself in many of his daily habits.

And it is far from true to say that the alternating attractions in Kim "never give rise to a genuine struggle," when we have had clear evidence of the struggle in him that almost made him give up the Great Game, because of the genuine love and affection that he has for the Lama. And it is through this relationship based on love, that the East and the West can be said to have truly met in the novel. To suggest, as Edmund Wilson does that the Lama and Kim "arrive at different consummations" is to take a too simplistic view. Though this may be true of the Lama, but as regards Kim's final decision, there is a teasing ambiguity about it. It is clear that he prefers a life of action to a life of contemplation as represented by the Lama, but he has also realised at the end, that he is not just a sahib and that "there is neither black nor white." Mahbub Ali wants to take him "beyond Balkh in six months," but what lies "beyond Balkh" is not stated by Kipling though one could perhaps suggest that Kim will continue to play an active part in the Great Game because of his instinctive love of adventure.

One can legitimately expect "synthesis" in a novel but certainly not "victory." Why should one way of life be shown to be necessarily superior to another? As a matter of actual fact, Kipling was occasionally guilty of this in his earlier works, but is seen to be totally free from it in *Kim*. Actually the ambiguity referred to earlier in the character of Kim is cleared for us if we interpret him as a figure of synthesis. This is because he is able to absorb the best of both worlds. There is also a strong suggestion of the mutual need between the two. Kim tells the Lama :

> 'Thou leanest on me in the body, Holy One, but I lean on thee for some other things...' (p. 389.)

And Angus Wilson rightly takes this for the theme of the novel:

> The story of Kim and the Lama is, in the last resort, beneath all its superbly realized human and topical detail, an allegory of that seldom portrayed ideal, the world in the service of spiritual goodness, and, even less usual, spiritual goodness recognizing its debt to the world's protection.[169]

Shamsul Islam also takes a similar view when he remarks that, "the part in Kim which the Lama cannot satisfy gets its satisfaction in the activity of the Game."[170] Kim thirsts for the world of action but at the same time, he learns from the Lama, "that there is neither black nor white", and such an awareness makes for a more human and meaningful existence in this world. That is to say, moving between two worlds has given Kim this insight into life which presumably enables him to take an unified rather than a fragmented view of the world in which he lives.

A brief discussion of the other aspects of the novel that have not been emphasised so far, can now be taken up. First, the characterisation of Indians. Hurree Chunder Mookerjee, the Bengali Babu, who "represents in little India in transition — the monstrous hybridism of East and West" is one of the ten best agents in the Great Game. He is "tough, intrepid, resourceful; everything that the Bengali Babu is traditionally not."[171] Hurree as a spy can perform miracles because of his ability to change roles almost in the twinkling of an eye. Kipling gives him a peculiarly idiosyncratic language that has now come to be known as Babu English. Though there is an element of satire in this portrayal, it is satire tinged with humour and sympathy and it is very different from the vicious satire directed against the Bengalis in Kipling's earlier stories.

Mahbub Ali, the Pathan horse-dealer is Kim's secular teacher just as the Lama was the spiritual teacher. He is the one who initiated Kim into the spying game even as he was a young boy. He is cautious, amorous, full of intrigues and acts in a dare-devil fashion when occasion demands. With Kipling's known admiration for the Pathans, it is no wonder that his character emerges as that of a man who is good, wise and tolerant. Note the way he speaks of the value of information, the faiths of different people and emotional attachments:

> "News is not meant to be thrown about like dung-cakes, but used sparingly—like *bhang*." (p. 191.)

> "...Faiths are like the horses. Each has merit in its own country." (p. 204.)

> "Hearts are like horses. They come and they go against bit or spur." (p. 204.)

One cannot miss their appropriateness as Mahbub Ali deals with horses.

There is yet another memorable creation in the woman of Kulu, easily Kipling's best portrait of an Indian woman. She is dictatorial, cantankerous but loving and affectionate at the same time. She is the matriarchal head of a large family, who is busy seeking charms from holy men for her numerous grandchildren. Her torrents of abuse at her servants shocks even Kim who is himself a pastmaster in this art. At the same time she is full of high spirits and relishes repartees. She is delighted to be called 'a Moon of Paradise', 'a Disturber of Integrity' and 'Dispenser of Delights' by an English District Superintendent of Police, more so because she learns from him that he was suckled by "a Pahareen—a hillwoman." In view of this, she believes that men like him are "the [right] sort to oversee justice. They know the land and the customs of the land." But she regards "the others, all new from Europe, suckled by white women and learning our tongue from books, are worse than the pestilence." (p. 107.) Here is native wisdom of the woman commenting on the reasons for the failure of the British in India. She plays the host to the Lama quite often, and towards the end of the novel, nurses Kim back to health as only a mother can. For this act of kindness, Kim can only exclaim, "Mother, I owe my life to thee. How shall I make thanks?" (p. 395.)

There is also the woman of Shamlegh who tries to seduce Kim, but without success. She had earlier appeared as Lispeth in the story of the same name. In addition, there are a host of minor characters like Chota Lal and Abdullah, Kim's playmates; a Kayeth letter-writer; Prostitutes like the Flower of Delight who drugs Mahbub Ali and the Dancing girl at Lucknow who helps Kim change into a native's dress; the Hillman such as the Ao-Chung man; the Hindu boy with the astonishing memory who works for Lurgan Sahib; the North-east secret agent E 23 who is rescued by Kim and many more. Added to this, there are references to "Brahmins and chumars, bankers and tinkers, barbers and baunias, pilgrims and potter's" on the Grand Trunk Road. It is almost as though Kipling is attempting to exhaust the inexhaustible variety and diversity of India in his novel. And in fairness to him, it must be conceded that he nearly succeeds in doing so.

While Kipling describes the Indian landscape in *Kim*, the emphasis is no longer on the terrifying heat that we have come to associate with many of his earlier stories. This absence can be explained, on one level, by the absence of British civilians in the novel. When they were present, Kipling's main purpose was to win our attention to their life of sacrifice and hardships, and hence dwelling in detail on the adverse climatic conditions of India was inevitable. But more significantly, the Kipling of *Kim* is an altogether different writer who dwells on India with tenderness and nostalgia accompanied by profound understanding. It is as though he had waited all these years to absorb India into his system, to utter his final word on the country in the novel *Kim*, "that prose Odyssey of Hindustan."[172]

Observe his description of the twilight accompanying the sunset:

> By this time the sun was driving broad golden spokes through the lower branches of the mango-trees; the parakeets and doves were coming home in their hundreds; the chattering, grey-backed seven Sisters, talking over the day's adventures, walked back and forth in twos and threes almost under the feet of the travellers; and shufflings and scufflings in the branches showed that the bats were ready

to go out on the night-picket. Swiftly the light gathered itself together, painted for an instant the faces and the cart-wheels and the bullocks' horns as red as blood. Then the night fell, changing the touch of the air, drawing a low, even haze, like a gossamer veil of blue, across the face of the country and bringing out, keen and distinct, the smell of wood-smoke and cattle and the good scent of wheaten cakes cooked on ashes. The evening patrol hurried out of the police-station with important coughings and reiterated orders; and a live charcoal ball in the cup of a wayside carter's hookah glowed red while Kim's eye mechanically watched the last flicker of the sun on the brass tweezers. (pp. 90-91.)

In his close attention to little details lies Kipling's real strength. And at his best, as in this case, he was able to use language in a way that "every word should tell, carry, weigh, taste and, if need were smell."[173] He can evoke India in a simple sentence with effortless ease :

All India was at work in the fields, to the creaking of well-wheels, the shouting of ploughmen behind their cattle, and the clamour of the crows. (p.73.):

Kipling's picture of Brahminee bull:

The huge, mouse-coloured Brahmini bull of the ward was shouldering his way through the many-coloured crowd, a stolen plantain hanging out of his mouth. He headed straight for the shop, well knowing his privileges as a sacred beast, lowered his head, and puffed heavily along the line of baskets ere making his choice. (p. 19.)

Kipling knows Indian food habits, different modes of dress, social conventions, superstitions, behavioural patterns and in short, the Indian way of life in its entirety. A completeness of this magnitude is unparalleled in the entire Anglo-Indian fiction. A few more illustrations should prove this point conclusively. Mahbub Ali gives Kim "a dress of honour" and tells him :

'Upon a Wednesday, and in the morning, to put on new clothes is auspicious.' (p. 243.)

If this is a typical Indian superstition, notice the characteristic Indian abuse as uttered by Kim :

> Thy father was a Pastry-cook, thy mother stole the *ghi*.
> (p. 5.)
>
> Go to Jehannum and abide there with thy reputationless aunt. (p. 173.)

And then there are numerous Indian proverbs :

> 'Trust a Brahmin before a snake, and a snake before an harlot, and an harlot before a Pathan...' (p. 156.)
>
> 'God made the Hare and the Bengali...' (p. 320.)
>
> 'For the sick cow a crow; for the sick man a Brahmin.' (p. 103.)

Only one who knew India intimately could have come out with the following generalisations :

> Keeping only one anna in each rupee... as his [Kim's] commission — the immemorial commission of Asia. (p. 38.)
>
> Ticket-collecting is a slow business in the East, where people secrete their tickets in all sorts of curious places. (p. 42.)
>
> One does not own to the possession of money in India. (p. 282.)
>
> ... for native police mean extortion to the native all India over. (p. 296.)
>
> He [Hurree] stowed the entire trove about his body, as only Orientals can. (p. 398.)

In conclusion, one can only invoke what Dryden said of Chaucer's *Canterbury Tales:*

> There is such a variety of Game springing up before me, that I am distracted in my Choice, and know not which to follow. 'Tis sufficient to say ... here is God's plenty'.[174]

Indeed as in Chaucer, for anyone wishing to discover India, there is 'God's plenty' in *Kim.* Not only is there so much of India in the novel but it is all *real* and *authentic.* If there is a false note in the whole of the novel, it is perhaps in Kim's response to Benares. We are told that

"Benares struck him as a peculiarly filthy city." (p. 266.) Angus Wilson explains:

> This rather English tourist's reaction may be considered to be the single example in that book of the palpable effect upon Kim of his years at St.Xavier's exemplary public school. He would hardly have survived his nomadic city life if he had usually cared so much about dirt.[175]

This sounds quite plausible, but the textual evidence points to the contrary. Life at St. Xavier's makes Kim realise that he is now a sahib and brings about a few definite changes in him. But his desire to be close to the bazaar life and be where the action is, has not in the least lessened in spite of his schooling. This is confirmed by his lifestyle during the vacation which approximates to that of the natives. To give one instance, notice the ability of Kim to sleep in open air during his first vacation:

> ... Kim lay out behind the little knot of Mahbub's followers, almost under the wheels of a horse-truck, a borrowed blanket for covering. Now a bed among brickbats and ballast-refuse on a damp night, between overcrowded horses and unwashen Baltis, would not appeal to many white boys; *but Kim was utterly happy*. Change of scene, service, and surroundings were the breath of his little nostrils, and thinking of the neat white cots of St. Xavier's all arow under the punkah *gave him joy* as keen as the repetition of the multiplication-table in English. (pp. 194- 95.)
>
> (emphasis mine)

In the light of this evidence, and despite Angus Wilson's explanation, one is right to contend that his reaction to Benares constitutes a false note.

It is interesting that Kipling opted for Buddhism rather than Hinduism and created a character like Teshoo Lama in a novel set in India. Kipling was certainly looking for a religion that was practical and spiritual at the same time. And with its simplicity, purity and castelessness, Buddhism certainly had a greater appeal to Kipling. Buddha's theory "strikes a mean between two extreme courses, e.g. believing neither in Being nor in non-Being, but in Becoming; believing neither in chance nor in necessity exclusively, but in conditioned happening ... Success lies in a middle course."[176] Buddha himself advocated avoidance of both the extremes, the life of pleasure and the life of mortification and advised his disciples to follow "the middle way which enlightens the eyes, enlightens the mind, which leads to rest, to knowledge, to enlightenment, to Nirvana."[177] And we know that the Lama is a "follower of the Middle Way." In Buddhism Kipling found the golden mean that he was always looking for.

And in terms of understanding, there is evidence to suggest that Kipling knew more about Buddhism than is often thought. While at school, he had read Edwin Arnold's *The Light of Asia*. His fascination for the Gandhara sculptures at the Lahore Museum continued this early interest. His father, Lockwood Kipling also helped him in this endeavour. Since India is the homeland of Buddhism, it is incorrect to suggest as some critics have done that it is a non-Indian religion. After all, Buddhism, an early form of Hinduism died a rather premature death in India for historical reasons but flourished in Japan, China and other South East Asian nations.

Nirad Chaudhuri offers another important reason when he argues that, "Hindu spirituality, even at its most unworldly and serene, has a suggestion of power and action, a kind of supermagical motivation which is not consistent with perfect beatitude and mystic quietism."[178] It is this "perfect beatitude and mystic quietism" that is dramatised in the life of the Lama. His life of contemplation and renunciation acts as a perfect foil to Kim's life of action and adventure. Kipling looking for an ideal synthesis between these two ways of life, couldn't have made a better choice than Buddhism.

But even the Lama's characterisation has been widely misinterpreted by critics. Whereas Martin Fido considers the Lama as "one of Kipling's major artistic triumphs [and that] he is the most successful representative of holiness in English literature,"[179] Jeffrey Meyers believes that "Kipling's portrayal of the Lama is shallow and superficial ... Kipling's attitude [towards the Lama] is one of tolerant pity that comes from a sense of inborn superiority."[180] Kipling triumphs because he brings his knowledge of Buddhism to full use in creating the character of the Lama. Lama's utter nobility and selflessness rarely leave the reader untouched. It happens precisely because Kipling, the artist, is free from "a sense of inborn superiority" that had characterised some of his earlier work. Alan Munro finds that "the main deficiency in the Lama's attitude to life is that in spite of its saintliness, it is totally removed from actuality and, is ultimately, self-centred."[181] And Alan Sandison takes a similar view in considering him as "wholly selfish."[182] This needs to be clarified. One who is self-centred would not have said to Kim, "To those who follow the Way there is neither black nor white, Hind nor Bhotiyal." (p. 303.) And it is this advice that affects most profoundly, as nothing else does, Kim's view of life. Moreover, even when he is singularly pursing his all-healing river, his attachment to his *chela* Kim, is most heart-warming because it is selfless. At the end, when the soul of the Lama leaves his body and sees whole of Hind and Ceylon in a vision, he withdraws from the Great Soul only for the sake of Kim lest he might miss the Way. And he is convinced at the end, as his smile indicates, that he has won salvation for both himself and Kim. What is significant is that the Lama can think of Kim even in that supreme moment, though Kipling's own preference for the world of action is entirely another matter.

In conclusion, it can be said that *"Kim* is the answer to nine-tenths of the charges levelled against Kipling and the refutation of most of the generalisations about him."[183] As a novel that projects the image of India, *Kim* marks an achievement that is yet to be equalled even after eighty years since it was written, despite the increasing number of novels on India by westerners. The major factor responsible for Kipling's success is his wise decision to let politics recede into the background. Whereas his political philosophy predominated his earlier writings on India, *Kim* turns out to be refreshingly different. Despite the presence of the Great Game, Kipling's view of India is not determined by his political philosophy. It is not the Kipling looking at India and its people from the viewpoint of the ruler, but the Kipling who nostalgically yearns for this land, which he referred to as his "Home" in many of his non-fictional writings, who is present in the novel. The other important reason for *Kim's* excellence lies in the choice of Kim, the eponymous hero of his novel. Here is a young boy who despite his Europeanness feels so much like an Indian that he can be legitimately called "a perfect specimen of the Indian boy."[184] And not for nothing has Kipling, an Englishman, chosen to make Kim an Irish boy. His being Irish makes for that sensibility to respond to the occult, the religious and the rituals in Indian life. As a matter of fact, there are several temperamental similarities between the Irish and the Indians. In other words, Kim looks at India, and so does his creator, like an *insider*. And it is only when one views India in its own terms, understanding becomes a distinct possibility. *Kim* is a classic instance of a work that triumphs as it is the outcome of love and sympathy and *not* cold reasoning, the bane of many a distinguished English writer on India.

Finally, to his novel *The Naulahka* which he wrote in collaboration with Wolcott Balestier. It is the love story of Nick Tarvin and Kate Sheriff. Kate comes to Rhatore in the province of Gokral Seetarun in Rajputna, after listening to "a heart-breaking-story" about the plight of Indian women. By working devotedly as a medical missionary, she hopes to ameliorate their living conditions. Tarvin tries to dissuade her by telling her that India is "no place for white men, let alone white women; there's no climate, no government, no drainage; and there's cholera, heat, and fighting."[185] But he fails, and soon he himself comes to India in pursuit of an invaluable necklace, the Naulahka. India is seen through the eyes of Kate and Tarvin. Her initial success in Rhatore come to nought because of the interference of a holy man in the working of her hospital. She was defeated by "thousands of years of traditions, and training, and habits of life." (p. 257.) She returns a disillusioned woman to her native town, Topaz.

Tarvin has, like the typical westerner, an entirely negative view of India. He always looks at

> Gokral Seetarun from his own point of view, dealing with the *dead East* from the standpoint of the *living West.* (p. 106.)   (emphasis mine)

Because of this bias, he can only describe the natives thus: "They're dead. They're mummies. They're wooden images." (p. 107.) Tarvin's reflections on seeing the inside of a Hindu temple where he finds the deity smeared with the dried blood of the sacrificed animal make interesting reading :

> Standing there, he recognised with fresh force how entirely the life, habits, and traditions of this strange people alienated them all that seemed good and right to him; and he was vaguely angered to know that it was the servants of these horrors who possessed a necklace which had the power to change the destiny of a Christian and civilized town like Topaz. (p. 212.)

Such stereotyped responses occur endlessly throughout the novel. Commenting on this passage, Benita Parry perceptively remarks that "it would have been impossible for Kipling to attach 'Christian' and 'Civilized' in any of his independent writings."[186] Even though Kipling, in some of his stories, reacts to Hindu religion from the western empirical standpoint, he never makes any overt suggestions about Hinduism being an uncivilized religion.

Tarvin goes to the Cow's Mouth looking for the Naulahka, and undergoes a terrifying experience. He hears in the Cow's Mouth "a malignant chuckle, half suppressed, which ended in a choking cough, ceased, and broke out anew." (p. 165.) He "shuddered from head to foot" as his heel crashed through a skull on the ground." (p. 169.) Then he realises that he is being observed by an alligator with pale emerald eyes and "horny eyelids, heavy with slime." In these moments, Tarvin had "tasted all the agonies of pure physical terror." (p. 170.) and he flees from the place. And this experience convinces him of "the purposelessness and emptiness of India, typified by a shrine in a dead city, and confirms his contempt for India as a denial of all he conceives of as important."[187] Finally, he leaves India without the Naulahka but with his fiancée Kate.

The novel ironically portrays India as the stronger power, in spite of Tarvin's contempt for her. After all, we see both Tarvin and Kate fail in their missions—he was the "white man from the West [who] came expressly to investigate the natural wealth of Hindustan" (p. 62) and she visited India to lighten the miseries of the natives. Kipling's attitude towards the missionaries is made abundantly clear in the following verse which he must have composed himself:

> Now, it is not good for the Christian's health to hustle the
> Aryan brown,
>
> For the Christian riles, and the Aryan smiles, and he
> weareth the Christian down;
>
> At the end of the fight is a tombstone white, with the name
> of the late deceased,
>
> And the epitaph drear; 'A fool lies here who tried to hustle
> the East.' (p. 56.)

Though it is mainly centred on Tarvin and Kate, *The Naulahka* gives us a glimpse of the goings on in a small princely state. We have brief but convincing portrayals of the Maharajah, the Queen and Sitabhai, the scheming but vivacious younger queen. There is also a memorable portrait of the young Prince, Maharajah Kunwar. His marriage is the occasion for brilliantly evocative descriptions of the festivities and the Indian streets. The Indian desert landscape is also realised in concrete terms in the novel. *The Naulahka* presents an image of princely India, a tradition that has been carried on in various works like *The Hill of Devi*, *The Hindoo Holiday* and *Heat and Dust*.

Before assessing the overall image of India in Kipling's fictional works, his fictional technique and the departures from standard English, also call for a critical examination. Kipling's genius was perhaps more suited to the short story form than that of the novel, since *The Light that Failed* is a seriously flawed work and *The Naulahka* is more of a popular thriller with all the sensational elements of love, sex, violence, intrigue and action thrown in. Only *Kim* proves to be an exception. The division that was made at the beginning of this chapter of Kipling's works into the Pre-1889 and Post-1889 periods to suggest the change in the quality of Kipling's response to India, holds good also with regard to his fictional technique. Most of the early stories with the notable exception of 'The Man who would be King' and to some extent, 'On the City Wall' are works that were written for publication in periodicals like, the *Civil and Military Gazette* and *Week's News*. And hence, they had to be "topical, arresting, and short, restricted to 2000 words."[188] This naturally imposed on Kipling certain limitations and did not allow for any probing in his portrayal of India and Indians. He is seen to be unable to transcend the imperialist assumptions that form the basis of these stories. And as a consequence, what we find in these early stories are stereotyped images of India and Indians.

Whereas, when we come to his later stories as in the collections, *Life's Handicap* (1891), and *The Day's Work* (1898), they are invariably longer and their length ranges from 10,000 to 12,000 words. There are, no doubt, a few stories of the first kind – the really short ones – in the first volume. But the significant difference lies in that the longer stories allow Kipling greater scope for exploration into his Indian themes. That all his best Indian stories such as 'Without Benefit of Clergy' 'The Bridge-Builders', and 'The Miracle of Purun Bhagat' are from this period is no mere coincidence. He is able to go beyond the stereo types and create memorable portraits of Indians like Ameera and Purun Bhagat and also respond perceptively to Hinduism and its tenets in 'The Bridge-Builders', while in the earlier phase his view tended to be superficial since his criterion of judgement was solely based on the empirical.

Kipling described *Kim* a little too modestly as "nakedly picaresque and plotless."[189] We are aware that in all great writers, interest in life is inseparable from an interest in art, that is the form of the work. And it is the content that determines the form as well. Here is Kipling dealing with the quest of two individuals, the Lama and Kim. This quest is seen in terms of their rich experience on the road. And so Kipling's choice of the picaresque form for a novel of the road like *Kim* was, in every sense, most appropriate. It is just the right mode to capture the bewildering variety and diversity of Indian life as well. Like the picaresque novel, *Kim* derives its unity from the continuous presence of Kim and the Lama. It is also episodic; but these episodes are all well related and integrated to the major themes of the novel giving it a clear pattern and recognizable plot. Structurally, one can divide the novel into three sections. The first five chapters tell us of the Lama's and Kim's search; the next five deal with the preparation of Kim for the Great Game, and the last five show Kim's success in the Great Game and the end of the Lama's quest and attempts a synthesis between the two way of life.

In his stories set in India, Kipling was mediating experiences 'alien' to the English language. Did this necessitate any departure from standard English? Unfortunately, this aspect of his art has received hardly any attention except for Vasant A. Shahane who devotes an entire chapter entitled 'Kipling's Idiolect' in his book.[190] Here, a general discussion of the stylistic features of Kipling's work is not attempted but only those devices which are used by him to convey the Indian experience are examined. The most striking and the single largest feature that characterises this attempt of Kipling is the extensive use of Hindustani dialect. In many of his Indian stories and especially in *Kim* there is a liberal sprinkling of Hindustani words. To choose perhaps the best example, we should examine a passage in *The Three Musketeers* Kipling's famous trio of soldiers, Mulvaney, Learoyd and Ortheris abduct Lord Benira Trig:

> Learoyd shows him wan down the sthreet, an' he sez, "How thruly Orientil! I will ride on a *hekka*." I saw thin that our Rigimintal Saint was for givin' Thrigg over to us neck an' brisket. I purshued a *hekka*, an' I sez to the dhriver-divil, I sez, "Ye black limb, there's a *Sahib* comin' for this *hekka*. He wants to go jildi to the Padsahi Jhil" 'twas about tu moiles away — "to shoot snipe — *chirria*. You dhrive *Jehannum ke marfik mallum* — like Hell? 'Tis no manner av use *bukkin;* to the *Sahib*, bekaze he doesn't

> *samjao* your talk. Av he bolos anything, just you *choop* and *chel.* Dekker? Go *arsty* for the first *arder* mile from Cantonmints. This *chel, Shaitan ke marfik,* an' the *chooper* you *choops* an' the *jildier* you chels the better *kooshy* will that *Sahib* be; an' here's a rupee for ye?"[191]

This is a brilliant rendition of the manner of speech the tommies use to a native servant. Urdu knowing Anglo-Indians of Kipling's time were delighted by this. If one is not familiar with Hindustani, the passage is sure to pose problems of comprehension. Shahane has analysed this passage effectively showing how Kipling not only used an admixture of Hindustani words but also anglicised Hindustani, expressions as when "bolo' is turned into 'bolos', 'choop' is turned into 'choops' and 'chel' is transformed into 'chels' in accordance with the English usage."[192] Though Shahane considers this passage as typical of Kipling, one can find no passage similar to this one except for a single sentence in his story, 'The God From The Machine':

> Take him away, an' av you iver say wan wurrud about what you've *dekkoed,* I'll *marrow* you till your own wife won't *sumjao* who you are![193]

It was indeed unfortunate that this most creative manner of combining Hindustani with English was given up Kipling after experimenting with it only in 'The Three Musketeers.' In the rest of his stories, what we find is a liberal use of Hindustani words with meanings given in parenthesis as in *darwaza band* [not at home] *burra-Khana* [dinner], *haramzadas* [scoundrels], Sais, *ghora lao* [bring my horse], Burra Sahib [a big man], Burra Sahib Bahadur [a very big man indeed], *Conjee* [rice-water] and innumerable others. Swear words such as *Hutt, Ya Illah,* are also occasionally used. But this cannot be in any sense regarded as creative departure from standard English. When Kipling used Hindustani words in this manner, one is reminded of Nehru's incisive observation on this habit in the Anglo-Indians. According to him, they

> evolved, with the help of their *Khansamahs* and *ayahs,* an extraordinary jargon, a kind of pidgin — Hindustani, which they imagine is the real article. Just as they take their facts about Indian life from their subordinates and sycophants, they take their ideas about Hindustani from their domestic servants, who make a point of speaking their pidgin lan-

guage to the sahib-log for fear that they would not understand anything else.[194]

Though one cannot accuse Kipling of this common ignorance in the British of the native life and their language, it is true that he also does not go beyond the use of "pidgin-Hindustani" in his creative exercises.

But once again, it is in *Kim* that he achieves his best stylistic effects. We see the familiar exclamations like 'oho:', 'Arre!', 'ohe!', 'Hai!', 'Hai mai!' and a very liberal usage of Hindustani words with meanings given as usual. But the real triumph of Kipling lay in his ability to convey the nuances of the speech patterns of both Kim and the Lama. Kim speaks most of the time in the vernacular and rarely does he switch over to English. Observe how Kipling is able to capture Kim's vernacular speech in English. Here are a few representative examples:

> "Ten thousand blessings", shrilled Kim, "O Holy one, a woman has given us in charity so that I can come with thee — a woman with a golden heart. I run for the *tikkut*." (p. 43.)

> "... Consider for a while, man with a mud head. Think you we came from the nearest pond like the frog, thy father-in-law. Hast thou ever heard the name of thy brother?" (p. 85.)

> "Five hundred — a thousand rupees could not buy them, he [Kim] thought sorrowfully. It was verree wasteful, but I have all their other stuff — everything they did — I hope. Now how the deuce am I to tell Hurree Babu, and *whatt* the deuce am I to do ..." (p. 363.)

Kim's speech is very different from that of a normal English boy. It is his native way of life that determines his mode of speaking. Kipling is able to capture this most effectively by using speech rhythms, proverbs, phraseology, syntax that are typically Indian. At the same time, it is not far removed from standard English to sound very quaint and stilted.

In contrast to this, notice Lama's language as in the following illustrations:

> "... It is manifest that from time to time I shall acquire merit — if before that I have not found my River — by assuring myself that thy feet are set on wisdom..." (p. 173.)

> "Yea, my Soul went free, and, wheeling like an eagle, saw indeed that there was no Teshoo Lama nor any other soul. As a drop draws to water, so my soul drew near to the Great Soul which is beyond all things..." (p. 411.)

While Kim's speech is earthy in keeping with his pragmatic view of life, that of the Lama's "is peculiarly airy, ethereal and abstract."[195] As a result of this, his use of language is seen to be essentially poetic.

Another variation of Kipling's use of English is found in the quaint Babu English spoken by Hurree Chunder Mookerjee. His spoken English with long-drawn vowels is accurately brought out in words like as 'opeenion,' 'offeecially,' 'verree good,' 'onlee' and 'releegion,'. His typical speeches go like this:

> "I am of opeenion it is not your old gentleman's precise releegion, but rather sub-variant of same. I have contributed rejected notes to *Asiatic Quarterly Review* on these subjects. Now it is curious that the old gentleman himself is totally devoid of releegiosity. He is not a dam' particular." (p. 258.)

> "This is fine! This is finest! Mister O'Hara! You have — ha! ha! swiped the whole bag of tricks — locks, stocks, and barrels. They told me it was eight month's work gone up the spouts! By Jove, how they beat me:...." (p. 398.)

Kipling's satire directed at this kind of English is one of tolerant amusement and definitely not vicious. He seems to be rather enjoying it himself as well. Apart from the emphasis on long vowels, there is the humorous mixture of formal and colloquial English and the ubiquitous English idiom. It is indeed a very picturesque language that is quite realistic since the educated Indians in those days did try to speak English like Chaucer and Shakespeare.[196]

Kipling through his use of Hindustani dialect, intended to "create an effect of actuality and verisimilitude."[197] And he succeeded in this by generously using Anglicized Hindustani since this was precisely the mode of speech of the Anglo-Indians during Kipling's time. In addition to this, Kipling was able to creatively explore into the English language in order to accommodate a truly Indian sensibility in the speeches of Kim, the Lama and Hurree Chunder Mookerjee.

By now, the nature of the image of India in Rudyard Kipling's works must be clear. The first component in the image of India in Kipling as in the other major Anglo-Indian novelists is the portrayal of the British in India. In the response of the British writer to India, the primary concern seems to be with the plight of the ruling race in the colonial context. And in the early phase of Kipling, this was also the case. He has highlighted only the hardships, sacrifices and the precarious existence of the British in India. Thus, India is seen as a country that has a debilitating effect on them because of its adverse climatic conditions. The emphasis has led Alan Sandison to speak in terms of "the vast threatening entity that is India."[198] Surely this is right seen from the point of view of the British, as Kipling does, in the majority of his stories. But Shamsul Islam goes a step further and equates India with "Kipling's vision of chaos",[199] which is to overstress this aspect ignoring Kipling's love for India that comes through in no uncertain terms in his later work.

The second component of the image of India in Kipling is the Indian landscape which is evoked with tremendous power. While the early stories concentrate solely on the heat and the seamier side of the land, the later works especially the two *Jungle Book(s)* and *Kim* present a very satisfying picture—both in terms of verisimilitude and artistic effects—of the country, its flora and fauna. Even in his early stories, Kipling—he is an unique exception in this—does not try to explain Indian character as having been predetermined by the climatic conditions as was the general practice of the Anglo-Indian novelists.

Then we have the portrayal of Indians. While the early Kipling depicted an India almost without Indians, except for native servants and the other low classes—Wali Dad of *On the City Wall* is an exception to this—the later Kipling created unforgettable Indians, most notable among them being Ameera, Puran Bhagat, the Lama, Mahbub Ali, the woman of Kulu and Hurree Chunder Mookerjee. T.S. Eliot believes that "in his Indian tales it is on the whole the Indian characters who have the greater reality, because they are treated with the understanding of love."[200] Though this statement is not entirely valid in respect of most Indian tales of Kipling, it does offer us an important insight into the basis of his success, when he did achieve it, in creating real Indian characters. Indeed, it was only when he wrote with this "understanding of love" that he could get beneath the skin of his Indian figures to produce rounded fictional characters. Added to this, he shows a greater understanding of Indian religions as in the *punchayat* of gods in 'The Bridge-Builders' and *Kim*. Here Kipling stands apart from the other Anglo-Indian novelists because of his "attitude of comprehensive tolerance"[201] towards religions other than his own, whereas the stock response in Anglo-Indian fiction to Indian religions was to treat them as dark, irrational, primitive and meaningless rituals.

And finally Kipling brings together the two races to explore the various reasons for the absence of a meaningful relationship between them. He discovers that while politics hardens the head, love can play quite a significant role in that it promises understanding and sympathetic communication between the races, at least as long as the relationship lasts. And in such an equation between the races, both the British and the Indians react to each other mainly as human beings first and then as people belonging to different nationalities. Consequently, this makes for a totally integrated image of India.

The early Kipling who gave us a fragmented image of India was more of a political being. And as Louis Cornell tells us, "his experience of India was sharply limited by his being a member of the conquering race."[202] While he viewed India from this perspective, he was able to produce, as we have seen, only stereotyped images of the land and its people. The journalist tended to overshadow the artist except in that remarkable story, 'The Man Who would be King'. But how does one explain the later phase in Kipling, the phase in which he wrote about India while living away from it? When in 1889 Kipling headed for London, he had spent a little more than half his twenty four years in India. All that he had seen, heard, smelt, and experienced in India was absorbed into his system. And when he was in London, Vermont and Sussex, like Wordsworth, he "was obsessed by a conscious or unconscious yearning to go back to the early enchanted hours. Upon the recollection of those hours he drew for his greatest literary achievement."[203] Recollection of the Indian experience also meant a great advantage in so far as he was distanced from India both in time and space. This brought home to him the profound realisation that India was in a very important sense his 'Home.' In one of his travel articles, he writes:

> "I want to go Home! I want to go back to India! I am miserable!"[204]

And even as late as 1913 when he visited Cairo he wrote:

> It is true that the call to prayer, the cadence of some of the

> street cries, and the cut of some of the garments differed a little from what I had been brought up to; but for the rest, the shadow on the dial had turned back twenty degrees for me, and I found myself saying, as perhaps the dead say when they have recovered their wits, 'This is my real world again!'"205

Cairo in the East brings to his mind compelling memories of India. But for a very personal and intimate account of his feelings for India, one should examine his article entitled 'Home' which was published in the Christmas Supplement of the *Civil and Military Gazette* in 1891 during his last visit to the country. 'Home' is a largely autobiographical account of his journey from Tuticorin in South India to Lahore and of his reminiscences about Lahore. He was returning to India after nearly thirty months. Even while he was in London, he was quite homesick. Carrington writes of Kipling's unhappy life in London: "So homesick was Kipling for India that he clung to anyone who could remind him of it."206 Kipling wrote to a friend on the Christmas Eve of 1889:

> there are five million people in London this night and, saving those who starve, I don't think there is one more heartsick or thoroughly wretched than that rising young author known to you as — Ruddy.207

That he experienced these emotions in spite of his fame and reputation in London being so high, can only point to his deep attachment for India which has been grossly underrated by many of his critics in their anxiety to dub him an 'imperialist.'

And as his boat the *Valetta* approached the Indian shores, the familiar smells of India invoke in him powerful feelings of nostalgia:

> A smell came out over the sea — a smell of damp earth, coconut oil, ginger, onions and mankind. It spoke with a strong voice, recalling many things; but the most curious revelation to one man was the sudden knowledge that under these skies lay home and the dearest places in all the world. Even the first sniff of London had not caused so big a choke in the throat, or so strict a tightening over the heart.208

And he continues:

> ... a big B.I. boat took charge of me to Tuticorin, and at the

first turn of her screw the first glimpse of the *Khitmatgars* on deck, Australia, the Cape, New Zealand and the British Isles dropped under the sea. (p. 3.)

The mere sight of the attendants brings back such a rush of memories to Kipling that all his other experiences are swept away at once. Such is the hold of India on him. And then he observes the strange, unfamiliar surroundings of South India:

> Then we stepped on to Indian soil under the green fig trees that face the beach, where the cotton trains go to and fro, and the Tamil women weave onion baskets of green reeds while their babies hang like cocoons in the bright of a loincloth flung over a branch. Allah be praised we stepped straight into India again ... But the beautiful smell was there, the brown, slow-moving crowds were there (white is rather a leprous tint when you come to think of it, and it doesn't match background), the crumbling *Kutcha* walls and the deep bowed bungalows were all waiting there. (p. 3.)

These are the reactions of an insider to the Indian landscape. No ordinary Englishman would have had either the courage or honesty to speak of the "leprous tint" of whites. This is the only description of South India in Kipling outside the brief references in his story 'William the Conqueror'. Interestingly, Kipling confesses his ignorance when he admits "that the Southern India papers point out that one writer at least does not describe India – their India."(p. 4.)

In contrast to "the memory of the murmurs of a little city called London – a city where there is neither colour nor light nor air," for Kipling Lahore was "the oldest and surely the most picturesque city in the world" and he was drunk with its charm and beauty for it was like "wine to a wearied man." (p. 5.) The country seems to "envelop him and fill his being with a new awareness of mythical reunion between the lost son and the waiting mother."[209] And it is no exaggeration to suggest that "Kipling's minute observation of external scenes filtered through his nostalgic vision, his extraordinary preception of colours and their myriad shades, and his effusion of love for India radiating through every line and image, are unparalleled in his writing."[210]

Kipling did know in 1891 that his parents were to soon return to England and so he knew that this would be his last look at India, his spiritual home:

> They [his parents] were coming "Home" for good soon: so this was my last look round the only real home I had yet known.[211]

Bonamy Dobree very rightly remarked, "indeed India is the place where he really belongs."[212] There is no other English writer who felt rooted to India the way Kipling did and this is the supremely important reason for the real India that emerges from his later works. Here it is the triumph of the artist over the 'imperialist.'

And one should sympathetically understand the contradictions in Kipling without which a complete response to his works becomes impossible. As he himself said in one of his poems:

> Much I owe to the Lands that grew—
> More to the Lives that fed—
> But most to Allah who gave me two
> Separate sides to my head.
> ....
> I would go without shirt or shoe,
> Friend, tobacco or bread,
> Sooner than lose for a minute the two
> Separate sides of my head![213]

It is this creative tension between the Kipling who was conscious of the 'White Man's Burden' and the Kipling who loved India that gave us his best work. He is unquestionably "the only English writer who will have a permanent place in English literature with books on Indian themes, and who will also be read by everyone who wants to know not only *British* India but also *timeless* India."[214] Kipling's image of India at its best is the image of an insider, who knew and loved her.

Notes

1. Rudyard Kipling, *Something of Myself: For My Friends Known and Unknown* (1937; rpt. London: Macmillan, 1951), pp. 1-2.
2. Ibid., p. 6.
3. Ibid., p. 9.
4. Ibid., p. 17.
5. Ibid., p. 16.
6. Ibid., p. 15.
7. Quoted in Charles Carrington, *Rudyard Kipling: His Life and Work* (London: Macmillan, 1955), p. 37.
8. Kipling, *Something of Myself*, p. 104.
9. Carrington, *Rudyard Kipling*, p. 141.
10. Quoted in Carrington, *Rudyard Kipling*, p. 239.
11. Letter to C.E. Norton, 30 November 1902. Quoted in Carrington, *Rudyard Kipling*, p. 369.
12. Bonamy Dobree, *Rudyard Kipling: Realist and Fabulist* (London: Oxford University Press, 1967), p. 28.
13. Alan Sandison, *The Wheel of Empire* (London: Macmillan, 1967), p. 78.
14. Nirad C. Chaudhuri, 'The Finest Story About India—In English', *Encounter*, VII, No. 4 (April 1957), p. 50.
15. Kingsley Amis, *Rudyard Kipling and his World* (London: Thames and Hudson, 1975), p. 20.
16. Carrington, *Rudyard Kipling*, p. 12.
17. Kay Robinson, "Kipling In India: Reminiscences by The Editor of The Newspaper On Which Kipling Served At Lahore," *McClure's Magazine*, VII, No. 2 (July, 1896), p. 104.
18. Quoted in Lord Birkenhead, *Rudyard Kipling* (London: Weidenfeld and Nicolson, 1978), p. 63.
19. John Lockwood Kipling, *Beast and Man in India* (London: Macmillan, 1891) p. 13.
20. Ibid., p. 239.
21. Macaulay, T.B., 'Minute on Education,' in *Sources of Indian Tradition*, ed. Theodre de Bary, 1958; rpt. New York: Columbia Univ. Press, 1959, p. 600.
22. J.L. Kipling, p. 15.
23. Angus Wilson, *The Strange Ride of Rudyard Kipling: His Life and Works* (1977; rpt. London: Granada Publishing Ltd., 1979), p. 143.
24. Kipling, *Something of Myself*, p. 39.

25. Ibid., p. 54.
26. Ibid., P. 41.
27. Ibid., p. 62.
28. Ibid., pp. 41-42.
29. Philip Mason, *Kipling: The Glass, The Shadow and The Fire* (London: Jonathan Cape, 1975), p. 49.
30. Ibid., p. 49.
31. Randall Jarrell, 'On Preparing to Read Kipling' in *Kipling and the Critics*, ed. Elliot L. Gilbert (London: Peter Owen, 1966), p. 141.
32. Kipling, *Something of Myself*, p. 43.
33. Ibid., pp. 53-54.
34. J.I.M. Stewart, *Rudyard Kipling* (London: Victor Gollancz, 1966), p. 45.
35. Kipling, *Something of Myself*, p. 57.
36. George Orwell, 'Rudyard Kipling' in *Kipling and the Critics*, ed. Elliot L. Gilbert (London: Peter Owen, 1966), pp. 74-75.
37. Lionel Trilling, 'Kipling' in *Kipling and the Critics*, p. 95.
38. Edmund Wilson, 'The Kipling that Nobody Read' , in *Kipling's Mind and Art*, ed. Andrew Rutherford (1964; rpt. Edinburgh and London: Oliver and Boyd, 1965), p. 48.
39. It is revealing that when Trilling's article was reproduced after 21 years, he told Andrew Rutherford, the editor of the collection, that 'if he were writing on Kipling now he would do so "less censoriously and with more affectionate admiration,", *Kipling Mind and Art*, p. 85.
40. Bhaskara Rao, K. *Rudyard Kipling's India* (Norman: University of Oklahoma Press, 1967).
41. Syed Sajjad Husain, *Kipling and India: An Inquiry into the Nature and Extent of Kipling's Knowledge of the Indian Sub-continent* (East Pakistan: The University of Dacca, 1964).
42. Benita Parry, *Delusions and Discoveries, Studies on India In the British Imagination 1880-1930,* (1972; rpt., New Delhi: Orient Longman, 1964)
43. Syed Sajjad Husain, p. 166.
44. Louis L. Cornell, *Kipling in India* (New York: Macmillan, 1966).
45. Ibid., p. 92.
46. Ibid., p. 93.
47. Kipling, 'Yoked With An Unbeliever,' *Plain Tales from The Hills* (1888; rpt. London: Macmillan, 1954), p. 39.
48. Kipling, 'Lispeth', *Plain Tales From The Hills*, p. 7.
49. Ibid., p. 6.
50. Kipling, 'The Judgement of Dungara', *Soldiers Three and Other Stories* (1888; rpt. London: Macmillan, 1960), pp. 246-47.
51. Ibid., p. 248.
52. Ibid., p. 246.
53. Kipling, 'McAndrews Hymn,' *Rudyard Kipling's Verse* (1940; rpt. London: Hodder and Stoughton, 1960), p. 126.
54. Bonamy Dobree, *Rudyard Kipling: Realist and Fabulist*, p. 16.
55. Kipling, *Many Inventions* (1893; rpt. London: Macmillan, 1949), p. 121.
56. Kipling, 'The Mark of the Beast,' *Life's Handicap* (1891; rpt. London: Macmillan, 1952).

57. Letter to Rev.J.Gillespie, 16 October 1895. Quoted in Carrington, *Rudyard Kipling*, p. 361.
58. Carrington, *Rudyard Kipling*, p. 83.
59. Kipling, 'His Chance in Life,' *Plain Tales from the Hills*, (1888; rpt. London: Macmillan, 1954), p. 79. Subsequent quotations referred to in the text are from this edition.
60. Kipling, 'The Head of the District', *Life's Handicap* (1891; rpt. London: Macmillan, 1952), p. 122. Subsequent quotations referred to in the text are from this edition.
61. Albert Memmi, *The Colonizer And The Colonized*, p. 12.
62. George Orwell 'Rudyard Kipling', *Kipling and the Critics*, p. 74.
63. Kipling, 'On the City Wall,' *Soldiers Three and other Stories*, p. 328. Subsequent Quotations referred to in the text are from this edition.
64. Benita Parry, *Delusions and Discoveries*, p. 242.
65. Kipling, *'The Enlightenments of Pagett, M.P.' in The Contemporary Review*, LVIII (September 1890), pp. 333-55. Subsequent references are incorporated in the text.
66. Benita Parry, *Delusions and Discoveries*, p. 214.
67. Angus Wilson, *The Strange Ride of Rudyard Kipling*, p. 160.
68. Alan Sandison, 'Kipling: The Artist and the Empire' in *Kipling's Mind And Art*, p. 148.
69. Philip Mason, *Kipling The Glass, The Shadow and the Fire* p. 302.
70. Kingsley Amis, *Rudyard Kipling and his World*, p. 53.
71. Kipling, 'A Pict Song', *Rudyard Kipling's Verse*, p. 548.
72. Alan Sandison, *The Wheel of Empire*, p. 200.
73. Carrington, *Rudyard Kipling*, p.106.
74. Kipling, 'A Song in Storm,' *Rudyard Kipling's Verse*, p. 149.
75. Quoted in Alan Sandison, *The Wheel of Empire*, p. 14.
76. Alan Sandison, *The Wheel of Empire*, p. 15.
77. Kipling, 'The Bridge-Builders,' *The Day's Work* (1898; rpt. London: Macmillan, 1955), pp. 4-5.
78. Kipling, 'Wressley of the Foreign Office,' *Plain Tales From the Hills*, p. 310.
79. Kipling, 'Thrown Away', *Plain Tales from the Hills*, p. 17.
80. Kipling, 'The Education of Otis Yeere,' *Wee Willie Winkie* (1888; rpt. London: Macmillan, 1951), pp. 20-21. Subsequent Quotations referred to in the text are from this edition.
81. Lewis, C.S., 'Kipling's World,' *Kipling and the Critics*, p. 102.
82. Ibid., p. 112.
83. Stewart, J.I.M. *Rudyard Kipling*, p. 66.
84. Kipling, 'William the Conqueror,' *The Day's Work*, (1898; rpt. London: Macmillan, 1955), p. 190. Subsequent quotations referred to in the text are from this edition.
85. Tompkins, J.M.S., *The Art of Rudyard Kipling* (1959; rpt. London: Methuen University Paperbacks, 1965), p. 158.
86. Kipling, 'On the Strength of a Likeness', *Plain Tales From the Hills*, p. 304.
87. Angus Wilson, *The Strange Ride of Rudyard Kipling*, p. 126.
88. Kipling, 'At the Pit's Mouth,' *Wee Willie Winkie*, p. 36.

89. Kipling, 'The Man who would be King', *Wee Willie Winkie* (1888; rpt. London: Macmillan, 1951). Subsequent Quotations referred to in the text are from this edition.
90. Benita Parry, *Delusions and Discoveries*, p. 217.
91. Ibid.
92. "That you and me will not, while this matter is being settled, look at any Liquor, nor any Woman black, white, or brown, so as to get mixed up with one or the other harmful," Kipling, 'The Man who would be King,' *Wee Willie Winkie*, p. 217.
93. Mannoni, O. trans., *Prospero and Caliban: The Psychology of Colonization* (London: Methuen & Co. Ltd., 1956), p. 18.
94. Jeffrey Meyers, *Fiction and the Colonial Empire* (Ipswitch: The Boydell Press, 1973), p. 14.
95. Benita Parry, *Delusions and Discoveries*, p. 222.
96. Ibid., p. 220.
97. Kipling, 'The Tomb of His Ancestors', *The Day's Work* (1898; rpt. London: Macmillan, 1955), p. 105. Subsequent Quotations referred to in the text are from this edition.
98. Hutchins, *The Illusion of Permanence*, p. 185.
99. George Orwell, 'Rudyard Kipling' in *Kipling and the Critics*, p. 78.
100. Elliot L.Gilbert, *The Good Kipling: Studies in the Short Story* (London: Manchester University Press, 1972), p. 152.
101. Louis L.Cornell, *Kipling in India*, p. 105.
102. Kipling, 'The Strange Ride of Morrowbie Jukes,' *Wee Willie Winkie*, p. 184.
103. Angus Wilson, *The Strange Ride of Rudyard Kipling*, p. 16.
104. James Harrison, *Rudyard Kipling* (Boston: Twayne Publishers, 1982), p. 147.
105. Kipling 'The Story of Muhammad Din,' *Plain Tales from the Hills*, p. 298.
106. Louis L. Cornell, *Kipling in India*, p. 114.
107. Bhaskara Rao, K., *Rudyard Kipling's India*, p. 50.
108. Kipling, 'The Story of Muhammad Din,' *Plain Tales from the Hills*, p. 301.
109. Tompkins, J.M.S., *The Art of Rudyard Kipling*, p. 86.
110. Kipling, 'Gunga Din,' *Rudyard Kipling's Verse*, pp. 406-08.
111. Carrington, *Rudyard Kipling*, p. 275.
112. Kipling, 'Fuzzy-Wuzzy', *Rudyard Kipling's Verse*, pp. 400-01.
113. For a memorable description of the Indian peasant, we should look at one of his poems:
    His speech is of mortgaged bedding,
    On his kine he borrows yet,
    At his heart is his daughter's wedding,
    In his eye foreknowledge of debt.
    He eats and hath indigestion,
    He toils and he may not stop;
    His life is a long-drawn question
    Between a crop and a crop.
    -'The Masque of Plenty',
    Rudyard Kipling's Verse, p. 39.
114. Bhaskara Rao.K., *Rudyard Kipling's India*, p. 93.
115. Kipling, 'At the End of the Passage', *Life's Handicap*, p. 198.

116. Kipling, 'The City of Dreadful Night', *Life's Handicap*, p. 373.
117. Kipling, 'The Education of Otis Yeere,' *Wee Willie Winkie*, p. 20.
118. Kipling, 'The Bridge-Builders,' *The Day's Work*, p. 18.
119. Kipling, 'William the Conqueror,' *The Day's Work*, p. 196.
120. Kipling, 'The Head of the District,' *Life's Handicap*, pp. 132-33.
121. Kipling, 'Yoked with an Unbeliever,' *Plain Tales from the Hills*, p. 35.
122. Kipling, 'Thrown Away,' *Plain Tales from the Hills*, pp. 16-17.
123. Kipling, 'Georgie Porgie', *Life's Handicap*, p. 390.
124. Kipling, 'The Conversion of Aurelian McGoggin,' *Plain Tales from the Hills*, p. 108.
125. Kipling, 'Bisara of Pooree', *Plain Tales from the Hills* (1888; rpt. London: Macmillan, 1954), p. 262. Subsequent Quotations referred to in the text are from this edition.
126. Kipling, 'By Word of Mouth,' *Plain Tales from the Hills*, p. 318.
127. Kipling, 'The Incarnation of Krishna Mulvaney,' *Life's Handicap*, p. 2.
128. Kipling, 'The Mark of the Beast,' *Life's Handicap* (1891; rpt. London: Macmillan, 1952), p. 240. Subsequent Quotations referred to in the text are from this edition.
129. Philip Woodruff, *The Men Who Ruled India* (London: Cape, 1953), II, pp. 172-73.
130. Kipling, 'Georgie Porgie', *Life's Handicap*, p. 391.
131. For a classic statement on the inscrutability of the Oriental, we should turn to one of his poems:
    You'll never plumb the Oriental mind,
    And if you did, it isn't worth the toil.
    Think of a sleek French Priest in Canada;
    Divide by twenty half-breeds. Multiply
    By twice the Sphinx's silence. There's your East,
    And you're as wise as ever. So am I.
    — 'One Viceroy Resigns', *Rudyard Kipling's Verse*, pp. 69-70.
132. Kipling, 'Wee Willie Winkie,' *Wee Willie Winkie*, pp. 268-69.
133. Ibid., p. 269.
134. Kipling, 'The Ballad of East and West,' *Rudyard Kipling's Verse*, pp. 234-37.
135. Edmund Gosse in *Kipling: The Critical Heritage*, ed., R.L. Green (London: Routledge and Kegan Paul, 1971), p. 120.
136. Kipling, 'Tods' Amendment,' *Plain Tales from the Hills* (1888; rpt. London: Macmillan, 1954), p. 196. Subsequent Quotations referred to in the text are from this edition.
137. Kipling, 'Miss Youghal's Sais,' *Plain Tales from the Hills* (1888; rpt. London: Macmillan, 1954), p. 27. Subsequent Quotations referred to in the text are from this edition.
138. Kipling, 'Beyond the Pale', *Plain Tales from the Hills*. (1888, rpt. London: Macmillan, 1954). Quotations referred in the text are from this edition.
139. Benita Parry, *Delusions and Discoveries*, p. 224.
140. Kipling, 'Yoked with an Unbeliever,' *Plain Tales from the Hills*, p. 41.
141. Kipling, 'Georgie Porgie', *Life's Handicap* (1891; rpt. London: Macmillan, 1952), p. 384. Subsequent Quotations referred to in the text are from this edition
142. Bhaskara Rao, *Rudyard Kipling's India*, p. 10.

143. Kipling, 'Without Benefit of Clergy', *Life's Handicap* (1891; rpt. London: Macmillan, 1952). All quotations referred to in the text are from this edition.
144. Nirad C.Chaudhuri, "The Finest Story About India-in English", *Encounter*, p. 49.
145. Elliot L. Gilbert, *The Good Kipling: Studies in the Short Story*, p. 118.
146. Elliot C. Gilbert, *The Good Kipling: Studies in Short Story*, p. 134.
147. Alan Sandison, "Kipling: The Artist and the Empire," in *Kipling's Mind and Art*, p. 159.
148. Noel Annan, "Kipling's place in the History of Ideas," in *Kipling's Mind and Art*, p. 110.
149. Shirley Chew, "Vain Empires" p. 60.
150. Kipling, 'The Bridge-Builders,' *The Days Work* (1898; rpt. London: Macmillan, 1955), pp. 5-6. Subsequent quotations referred to in the text are from this edition.
151. Benita Parry, *Delusions and Discoveries*, p. 229.
152. Ibid., p. 230.
153. George Orwell, "Rudyard Kipling" in *Kipling and the Critics*, pp. 76-77.
154. Ibid., p. 77.
155. Benita Parry, *Delusions and Discoveries*, p. 232.
156. Ibid., p. 234.
157. Ibid., p. 235.
158. Ibid., pp. 236-37.
159. Radhakrishnan, S., *Eastern Religions and Western Thought* (1939; rpt. London: Oxford University Press, 1958), pp. 30-31.
160. Benita Parry, *Delusions and Discoveries*, p. 238.
161. Kipling, 'The Miracle of Puran Bhagat,' **The Second Jungle Book** (1895; rpt. London: Macmillan, 1956), p. 36. Subsequent quotations referred to in the text are from this edition.
162. Shamsul Islam, *Kipling's 'Law': A Study of his Philosophy of Life* (London: Macmillans, 1975), p. 116.
163. Angus Wilson, *The Strange Ride of Rudyard Kipling*, p. 171.
164. Kipling, **Kim** (1901; rpt. London: Macmillan, 1958). All quotations referred to in the text are from this edition.
165. Nirad C. Chaudhuri, "The Finest Story About India-in English," *Encounter*, p. 47.
166. Tompkins, *The Art of Rudyard Kipling*, p. 22.
167. Jeffrey Meyers, *Fiction and the Colonial Empire*, p. 22.
168. Edmund Wilson, "The Kipling That Nobody Read," in *Kipling's Mind and Art*, p. 30.
169. Angus Wilson, *The Strange Ride of Rudyard Kipling*, pp. 183-84.
170. Shamsul Islam, *Kipling's Law'*, p. 118.
171. Henn, T.R., *Kipling* (Edinburgh and London: Oliver and Boyd, 1967), pp. 96-97.
172. Brander Matthews in *Kipling: The Critical Heritage*, p. 347.
173. Kipling, *Something of Myself*, p. 206.
174. John Dryden, "Preface to the Fables," *Dryden: Poetry, Prose and Plays*, ed. Douglas Grant, (London: Rupert Hart-Davis, 1952), pp. 484-85.
175. Angus Wilson, *The Strange Ride of Rudyard Kipling*, p. 132.

176. Hiriyanna, M., *Outlines of Indian Philosophy* (1932; rpt. London: George Allen & Unwin Ltd., 1958), p. 151.
177. Ibid.
178. Nirad C. Chaudhuri, "The Finest Story About India-in English," pp. 52-53.
179. Martin Fido, *Rudyard Kipling* (London: Hamlyn, 1974), p. 120.
180. Jeffrey Meyers, *Fiction and the Colonial Empire*, pp. 23-24.
181. Alan Munro, "Kipling's *Kim* and Co-Existence," *English Literature in Transition*, Vol. VII, No. 4 (1964), p. 226.
182. Alan Sandison, *The Wheel of Empire*, p. 97.
183. Mark Kinkead-Weeks, "Vision in Kipling's Novels" in *Kipling's Mind And Art*, p. 233.
184. Bhaskara Rao, *Rudyard Kipling's India*, p.130.
185. Kipling, *The Naulahka* (1892, rpt. London: Macmillan, 1917), p. 7. Subsequent quotations referred to in the text are from this edition.
186. Benita Parry, *Delusions and Discoveries*, p. 226. f.n.
187. Ibid., p. 227.
188. Carrington, 'Rudyard Kipling, p. 77.
189. Kipling, *Something of Myself*, p. 228.
190. Vasant A. Shahane, *Rudyard Kipling: Activist and Artist* (Carbondale: Southern Illinois University Press, 1973), pp. 125-31.
191. 'The Three Musketeers', *Plain Tales from the Hills*, pp. 71-72.
192. Shahane, *Rudyard Kipling*, p. 129.
193. 'The God From The Machine,' *Soldiers Three and Other Stories*, pp. 12-13.
194. Jawaharlal Nehru, *An Autobiography: With Musings on Recent Events in India* (1936; rpt. Bombay: Allied Publishers Private Ltd., 1962), p. 452.
195. Shahane, *Rudyard Kipling*, p. 131.
196. Bhaskara Rao, *Rudyard Kipling's India*, p. 151.
197. Shahane, *Rudyard Kipling*, p. 130.
198. Alan Sandison, *The Wheel of Empire*, p. 78.
199. Shamsul Islam, *Kipling's 'Law'*, p. 60.
200. T.S. Eliot, "Introduction", *A Choice of Kipling's Verse*, ed. T.S. Eliot (1941; rpt. London: Faber And Faber Ltd., 1954), p. 23.
201. Ibid., p. 24.
202. Louis L. Cornell, *Kipling in India*, p. 144.
203. Nelson S. Bushnell, "Kipling's Ken of India", *University of Toronto Quarterly*, 27, (October 1957), p. 72.
204. Quoted in Kingsley Amis, *Rudyard Kipling and his World*, p. 55.
205. Kipling. Quoted in Bonamy Dobree, 'Rudyard Kipling', *The Criterion*, VI, No. 6 (December 1927), p. 505.
206. Carrington, *Rudyard Kipling*, p. 141.
207. Quoted in Carrington, *Rudyard Kipling*, p. 144.
208. 'Home', *Civil and Military Gazette*, 25 December 1891, Christmas Supplement, p. 3. Subsequent references to the article are indicated in the text.
209. M. Enamul Karim "Kipling's Personal Vision of India in an Uncollected Article 'Home', *The Journal of Commonwealth Literature*, Vol. XIII, No. 1 (August 1978), p. 21.
210. Ibid., p. 24.
211. Kipling, *Something of Myself*, p. 104.

212. Bonamy Dobree, "Rudyard Kipling," *The Criterion*, p. 507.
213. Kipling, 'The Two Sided Man', *Rudyard Kipling's Verse*, pp. 587-88.
214. Nirad C. Chaudhuri; *The Continent of Circe: An Essay on the Peoples of India* (1965; rpt. Bombay: Jaico Publishing House, 1974), p. 8.

Chapter - 3
L.H. Myers

I

Leopold Hamilton Myers was the son of Frederic W. H. Myers, one of the founders of the Society for Psychical Research in 1882. This society attempted to prove the existence of the soul by scientific experiment. And so young Leopold grew up in Leckhampton House, Cambridge which became a centre of intellectual life where distinguished minds of the late Victorian era congregated. This undoubtedly had a profound impact on Myers. Rich and educated at Eton and Cambridge, he never needed to work for a living and except for a brief while at the Board of Trade during the First World War, he had no regular employment.

As a young man, he had a mystical experience in America. And throughout his life, "he retained a sense of powers extra-human and transcendental."[1] His concern with the spiritual life took the form of seeking answers to the question, 'Why do men choose to live?' His chief opponents in his pursuit of the answer were not scientific rationalists in the tradition of T.H.Huxley, the associate of Darwin, but aesthetes of the Bloomsbury group, who left moral experience to look after itself while they cultivated enjoyment of 'states of mind.' Myers also regarded the great influence of the French novelist Marcel Proust on English writing as pernicious, because Proust like the Bloomsbury group esteemed experience aesthetically and not morally. In his preface to *The Root and the Flower,* he remarks:

> When a novelist displays an attitude of detachment from the ordinary ethical and philosophical preoccupations of humanity, something in us protests ... Proust, for instance, by treating all sorts of sensibility as equal in importance, and all manifestations of character as standing on the same plane of significance, adds nothing to his achievement, but only draws attention to himself as aiming at the exaltation of a rather petty form of aestheticism.[2]

Myers believed that this "petty form of aestheticism" led to the trivializing of life. In his novels, he presents the opposition between those who interpret experience through moral discrimination and those who vulgarize it by regarding it as a means to aesthetic experience only. The latter gives rise to evil. He regarded civilized society as he knew it as corrupted by its moral indifference, and was convinced of the "deep-seated spiritual vulgarity that lies at the heart of our civilization."[3]

What characterises Myers's fiction is "the exercise of the moral judgement which actuates the discriminations among his characters."[4] And in his novels, he "investigated through his 'serious' characters ... the possibility of a way of life which should at once stand the test of a morally fastidious taste and end his feeling of social and personal isolation."[5] His basic concern is with "the theme of individual development in a civilized society, a society in which leisure and a tradition of culture make possible the practiced intelligence and sensibility which he takes to be necessary conditions of development."[6] And his major purpose "is to give form to his intuition of the undying conflict that exists between sensitive and cultured individuals and the world of commercial values and social competitiveness."[7] It is Myers's moral and ethical preoccupations that have certainly enthused both Harding and Leavis and made them assign a significant place to him among the novelists of the twentieth century. Curiously, they both overlook the serious limitations of Myers as a practitioner of the novel as an art form. However, it must be added that they are not unaware of these limitations – it could be said that here is a classic case of the critic ignoring the 'form' deliberately in view of his concern for the 'content' in the writer.

Myers occupies a unique place among the English writers who have written about India since his 'use' of India is very different from the others. No doubt, he shares certain similarities with writers from America like Thoreau, Melville, Emerson and Whitman who were profoundly influenced by Indian philosophical thought. But the major difference lies in the American writers' acknowledgement of their debt to India, while Myers's avowed intention is to exploit India only as a distancing device as he states in his preface to *The Near and the Far*:

> This is not a historical novel, although the action is placed in time of Akbar the Great Mogul (who was a contem-

porary of Queen Elizabeth), nor is it an attempt to portray Oriental modes of living and thinking. I have done what I liked with history and geography as well as with manners and customs. Facts have been used when they were useful, and ignored or distorted when they were inconvenient. Few of my characters bear the names of real people, and of these the only person drawn with any regard for historical truth is the Emperor.

In choosing sixteenth-century India as a setting, my object was to carry the reader out of our familiar world into one where I could — without doing violence to his sense of reality — give prominence to certain chosen aspects of human life, and illustrate their significance. It has certainly not been my intention to set aside the social and ethical problems that force themselves upon us at the present time. On the contrary, my hope has been that we might view them better from the distant vantage-ground of an imaginary world.[8]

He had earlier in his preface to *The Root and the Flower* said something in a similar vein:

My object has been to carry the reader away from the machinery of a life that is familiar to him, to avoid the mention of names or of places that hold associations that are foreign to my purpose, to obtain an attention undistracted by the social and economic problems of our day. I am aware, however, that it is dangerous to fly too far. The story-teller who soars out of our earthly geography and history altogether starts with too great an emptiness before him. He has to tell you everything from the beginning ... Such excessive freedom is tiresome to him and his readers alike. But take India in the reign of Akbar: enough and not too much, is at once outlined on the canvas. You see, I imagine, a vague picture of emperors and elephants, white marble palaces, palm trees and so on — nothing very precise, but plenty of fine, confused colouring for a background. And that is what I want. Your comfortable, normal ignorance is what I count upon. It supplies all that is necessary; the rest is my affair.[9]

This desire to escape from setting his novels locally, is typical of Myers's artistic intentions. If India provides the setting for *The Near and the Far,* the distant and almost fabulous district in Wales is the scene in *The Orissers,* the luxury yacht moving down the Amazon is the locale of *The Clio* and the moss-hung bayou of New Orleans is the place of action in *Strange Glory.* But it must said that by choosing to set his novels in exotic locales, Myers is not really trying to escape from the problems and preoccupations of his time. On the contrary, it is for him more a means of perceiving them with greater clarity. He seemed to believe that an unfamiliar background would help him to portray "certain chosen aspects of human life" more effectively, and their significance would come through with greater emphasis. In other words, the setting should not, by inviting attention to itself, divert the mind of the reader from discovering the real meaning behind his works. As a matter of fact, it is said that the idea of one of his characters walking down Piccadilly in London oppressed and frustrated Myers.

But then, there is also a very important difference between his use of locales in *The Orissers, The Clio* and *Strange Glory* on the one hand and the tetralogy, *The Near and the Far* on the other. Whereas the setting plays no significant role in the former novels, India is more than a mere backdrop in the latter. India operates not merely as a geographical landscape in *The Near and the Far* but its religious and philosophical thoughts have a central role in the scheme of the novel. While in the other novels, the relationship between the setting and the theme is at best tenuous, in *The Near and the Far* there is a meaningful interaction between the two. That is to say, India functions *not* as a distancing device in the novel as Myers claims, but through its ancient wisdom assists him to successfully convey his view of life. And it is this function of India in the novels of Myers that will receive detailed treatment.

It is certain that Myers did not primarily attempt to recreate the India of Akbar's time, in *The Near and the Far.* India provides the setting for his philosophical questions on the nature and problems of living. But what is interesting in view of the nature of this undertaking, namely to study the image of India, is that Myers's depiction of India emerges, but for minor deviations, as a faithful picture of the country in the sixteenth century. This makes it difficult to agree with Greenberger's contention that Myers's India "was solely the creation of his imagination."[10] There are numerous references to Indian religion, philosophy, history, manner of dress, social conventions, modes of behaviour etc, in the novels that successfully evoke the atmosphere of India. Myers never visited India (however, he did come to Ceylon, which was then virtually a part of India), but from a close reading of the novels, it is possible to demonstrate that he was widely read in Indian history and philosophy. And so it can be said with conviction that Myers chose the remote locale of India under Akbar not only because he wanted to escape from the secondary preoccupations of daily life in modern England, but mainly because he could treat the moral and spiritual issues with the large scope which the India of the sixteenth century with its multiple religions and philosophies offered him.

II

As in his other novels, Myers is concerned in *The Near and the Far* with the problem of living in a civilized society. His novels are the literary manifestations of his search for answers to the questions, 'Why do men choose to live?' and 'How to live?' And this search is primarily built around the conflict of "the hostility of the world to sensibility and intelligent living."[11] Though there are many strands running through this novel of 950 pages, Rajah Amar and Prince Jali are undoubtedly the major figures through whose lives Myers's major preoccupations are presented. Both of them are engaged in their own personal quest. While Rajah Amar's quest is that of a man who has lived his life to the full and is now contemplating renunciation, Prince Jali's is that of an adolescent coming to grips with the world around him in the search for a meaningful relationship with his environment.

Rajah Amar, the Rajput ruler of Vidyapur, a small state in Central India, is married to Sita, a Christian who was earlier known as Helen and has a son of twelve, Prince Jali. After thirteen years of married life, he embraces Buddhism because of his desire to lead a life of contemplation. And it is only now that he is aware of the spiritual disparities between him and Sita. While he desired to achieve holiness through renunciation, she found pleasure in this world, in "all the trivialities of daily living." He thinks he can dissociate the personal from the political, and go away to Ceylon as a monk in yellow robes with a begging bowl, but he discovers that such a dissociation is far from easy and has to go through a long, painful period before he can relinquish his responsibilities as a ruler.

In the novel, Rajah Amar emerges as the true representative of human goodness. He belongs to that category of characters in Myers, who are fastidious as opposed to the trivial. The fastidious are those "who stand over against society as it manifests itself in the life of social classes and institutions"[12] whereas the trivial only live by appearances. In this profound spiritual struggle between Good and Evil, one of the major themes of the novel, Myers's recourse to Buddhism to portray the Good provides an interesting comment on his creative use of an Indian religion. There is no denying that Buddhism had a tremendous impact on the Western mind. Anatole France, a confirmed sceptic, on seeing the statue of Buddha is said to have remarked, "if ever a God walked on this earth, I felt here was He."[13] Bertrand Russell said, "Of all religions which prevail in the world, I am attracted to early Buddhism."[14] This fascination can only be accounted for by the "deeply rational and profoundly spiritual"[15] message of the Buddha as suggested by S. Radhakrishnan. It is in the character of Rajah Amar that Myers's understanding of Buddhist doctrines is revealed. We have here the presence of India, with religion as an organic component in the novel.

After his conversion, Rajah Amar consciously fights his preoccupations with trivial thoughts and issues. Taking the traditional Buddhist line, he regards that "Evil springs from ignorance and delusion. The fires of lust and anger find no fuel when the delusions attached to individuality have been destroyed." (p. 41.) Amar's search from now on is for "the tranquility that is at the end of all desires." (p. 46.) Like a true Buddhist he knows that "the human affections are the most tenacious of all the chains." (p. 48.) So, naturally Amar's decision to renounce the world has its moments of self-doubt and uneasiness. When he is with his parents, he is "smitten with an agonizing uncertainty" and "he could not put away that particular knot of trivial concern; his pride was roused; he could not achieve inattention to self." (p. 130.) Thus there is this tortuous struggle in Rajah Amar. He finds that "worldly affairs drag on; one entanglement transforms itself into another." (p. 389.)

Rajah Amar has been waiting to hand over the care of his principality to Sita and Prince Jali and let them rule under the guidance of Gokal. The opportune moment never seems to come because of the bitter struggle that is going on between Daniyal and Salim to succeed Akbar. He is honest enough to tell Hari Khan, his brother-in-law, that his supporting either Salim or Daniyal is only "a question of political expedience." (p. 42.) But when he assesses both of them, he thinks he should extend his support to Daniyal, for he at least "appreciate(s) the worth of serious men such as Abu-l-Fazl, Man Singh, and Mobarek." (p. 85.) It is Srilata, his half-sister, who tells him that Daniyal is not the kind of person he should approve of. She is aware of Rajah Amar's dislike of the trivial. Amar tells her, "I understand that he is trivial-minded, an amateur of the Arts, and without much sense of the responsibilities of his position." (p. 85.)

When Amar meets Daniyal for the first time, he senses in Daniyal's presence

> an immediate impression of vulgarity — or of something, at any rate, which for want of a better word had to be called vulgarity. It was a pity no other term would fit, because the defect was reflected so shadowily on to the external man; it was a defect of spirit, of the innermost spirit — something that betrayed itself primarily to the moral sense. (p. 134.)

Rajah Amar's fastidiousness contrasts sharply with Daniyal's vulgarity. It is the moral core in Amar that is disturbed by the personality of Daniyal. This brief passage also offers a clue to Myers's method as a novelist. The meeting of Amar and Daniyal is described as seen through the eyes of Amar. What is revealing is that the meeting is *not* described as an incident, that is, as a physical happening, but only as a picture conceived in the mind of Amar. Here dialogue is conspicuous by its total absence. However, there are other situations in the novel where Myers relies on dialogues especially when intellectual issues are debated by individuals. But otherwise, the individual's thought process is what matters in the novel, not merely when Myers is revealing to us what goes on inside the mind of the character which is legitimate, but also when external actions being presented. It is this emphasis on the thought process that leads to a greater abstraction in the entire novel, with very little attempt made by the novelist to concretise human experience through incidents. This aspect of his art will be dealt with in greater detail later on when Myers's status as a novelist will be assessed.

The encounter between Daniyal and Rajah Amar is very significant in view of the light it throws on the moral and ethical preoccupations of Myers as a writer. In fact, Daniyal and his Pleasance of Arts also form the second stage in the growth of Prince Jali. Myers has satirised Bloomsbury through the camp of Daniyal. Amar's exposure to the camp clarifies for him issues like 'civilization', 'aestheticism' and also brings him face to face with evil. It is the aestheticism of Bloomsbury that Myers found extremely distasteful, an aestheticism that tended to ignore the moral basis of experience entirely. The novelist's views are faithfully expressed in the character of Rajah Amar.

While Amar is in the Pleasance, he finds Daniyal's "whole presence and personality ...... infinitely displeasing" and wonders whether he can ever side with him in his attempts to succeed Akbar. It is here that he becomes aware of the importance people give to appearance in their lives—another major theme of the novel. It is this posturing and posing that Amar consciously fights all his life. For Myers, this tendency of valuing appearances is the main obstacle in establishing proper and meaningful relationships between people. Personal relationships are indeed very precious for human beings. Falsity in appearances amounts to immorality, for it discourages genuineness in men and undermines the true value of their character. The truth of his preferences is borne out by the people who inhabit the Pleasance of Arts. Apart from their aesthetic pretension for all that goes in the name of art, there is no innate worth in them. They are, like Bloomsbury, anti-traditional in their attitudes and have "repudiated entirely customary morals, convention and traditional wisdom."[16] Daniyal's camp followers are basically self-regarding individuals without any sense of responsibility. This offers a variation on Rajah Amar's decision to renounce life.

The decision of Amar must bring up the question of responsibility of the individual to his wife, family and the world in which he lives, even though he believes that "when a spiritual call was sufficiently urgent, all mundane considerations became of secondary importance." (p. 490.) He thinks that he can keep his worldly affairs and spiritual quest separate but he is soon to realise that such thinking is a mistake. Apart from the political decision that he should make, the disturbing news of his wife's love for Hari Khan contributes to the continuation of the hold of the material world over him. Cracks begin to develop in his spiritual make-up. There are moments when contact with the world results in "a depressing sense of isolation" in him. And he feels:

> There is no current of human sympathy flowing between myself and the rest of mankind. I still hold firm to my decisions—but not easily, not without doubts. Once more the fascination of Being uncoils like Kundalini within me.

> Life's energies and desires fascinate me — not as temptations but as mysteries. (p. 505.)

Note the appropriateness of the Kundalini image that reveals Myers's intimate knowledge of the Hindu Tantric tradition.

Rajah Amar's conflicts get more intense and disturbing and while he is in such a state, Gokal, his spiritual adviser, asks him to postpone his decision to retire from the world in view of the uncertain political situation, and also because Sita has hardly any regard for Daniyal. Gokal finds in Rajah Amar a disparity between his character and philosophy. And so in his decision to suport Daniyal, Gokal believes that Amar is acting contrary to his own impulses. He wants Amar to obey his instincts in determining his attitude towards Daniyal. But Amar thinks that Daniyal "offers Mobarek a very useful figurehead" and hence needs to be supported even though "he is completely trivial." But he refuses to see Daniyal, the way Gokal does, as "wicked." Trivial-mindedness, for Myers, is the cardinal sin, for it produces evil. In this state of mind, an individual refuses to go beyond trivial interests. He has "an inverted sense of values, in which all that is of true significance is ignored and all that is trivial is exalted."[17] And so his actions were logically the result of "a cruel and malicious desire to cause suffering to anyone, without personal discrimination."[18] Thus we see how triviality inexorably leads to evil.

Thus convinced, Gokal, asks Rajah Amar to fight for Salim. But he refuses, saying that "Right action ... always demands a recognition of what is practicable." To this, Gokal says he is wrong, for 'the world is such that no man has the right to think he knows what is practicable." He continues,

> Man is under obligation to act — under a psychological necessity that is also a spiritual obligation. And somehow in his action he must reconcile the pursuit of his own small, definite, and rightful ends with the working out of an inscrutable purpose. He must not forswear his intimate knowledge that he is the chief instrument of the *supernatural* energy determining whatever in time shall come to pass. (p. 549.)

This view of Gokal the Brahmin, is very close to how a Karmayogin thinks and acts. He has two motives "(1) atmasuddhi, which means 'purifying the self' or 'cleansing the heart', and (2) subserving the purposes of God (Isvara) — a fact which, by the way, implies a mixture of teaching here.'"[19] And it is combination of these two motives that is suggested in the concept of Right action by Gokal.

Rajah Amar's reply to this exhortation is simple, but it is surely a case of self-deception: "The action that lies before me now is to pay my respects to Daniyal. That done, I shall return." (p. 549.) And in the camp, Amar is beset with restlessness from the very beginning. He is uneasy, stiff in the presence of Daniyal. All his doubts regarding the Prince's true nature are set to rest in that terrible scene where Daniyal tramples a cat to death. Myers's forte does not lie in the description of concrete situations but here is a remarkable exception to the general rule:

> At last with a nod he [Daniyal] dismissed his interlocutor, and, still keeping his balls dancing in the air, advanced slowly towards the waiting group. All remained where they were; but the white cat, which had got up from Gunevati's lap, was yawning and stretching itself. It now came running across the floor, and, on reaching Daniyal, rubbed itself against his legs, causing him to miss one of the coloured balls. Than it threw itself down on the ground in front of him, lying on its back, and with a mew invited him to play with it. But Daniyal had frowned when the ball dropped, and now, lifting the sole of his right foot, he placed it on the cat's head. Then with a swift and smiling glance at his spectators he slowly pressed his foot down. One after another the bones in the cat's head could be heard to crack, and, when this sound came, the Prince's eyes glanced for one smiling second into those of Gunevati. The cat's paws were beating the air; its body rose swiftly in an arc and then collapsed in spasms; a little pool of blood spread out upon the floor. (pp. 564-65.)

After witnessing this blood curdling killing, Rajah Amar "finally recognizes Daniyal as not only trivial but also an agent of evil."[20] This recognition prompts Amar to instinctively react to Daniyal. He tries to kill him but instead, he himself is knocked down. Myers apparently intended this as a struggle between 'Good' and 'Evil', though 'Good' here seems to have suffered a temporary setback. The final movement in Amar's life that leads to his renunciation receives adequate treatment at the hands of the novelist, and not otherwise as alleged by D.W. Harding, who thinks that Amar is simply "packed off among the pilgrims,"²¹ at the end.

As a result of his injury, Amar goes blind and passes through a torrid time for nearly two months, afraid that he might go mad. Then there is a storm and "when the turmoil was at its height, peace came to Amar." (p. 606.) He feels relaxed and overcomes his pride, jealousy and anger. He realises that the

> long-imagined moment was arriving at last; and it was as though his blindness were actually showing him the way.... Sight was a distraction that he could well dispense with; its absence was likely to prove more precious than its possession. Blindness was the tunnel that was to lead him out into the perfect daylight of Nirvana. (pp. 607-8.)
>
> He clung to the truth of appearances as something equal to the truth of what underlay them. There were two deserts: one that was a glory for the eye, another that it was weariness to trudge. Deep in his heart he cherished the belief that some day the near and the far would meet. (p. 8.)
>
> How could that mystic *There* ever become a *Here?* It could not—without changing. It existed only in its thereness. No one ever got there—unless, perhaps, in the impossible Heaven of the Christians. (p. 219.)

It is significant that Myers should have chosen the same words 'the near' and 'the far' for the title of the four novels when it was published as tetralogy in 1940. The most comprehensive explanation of the significance of the title is given by Bantock which, though long, deserves to be quoted:

> The 'near' is ever present with its frequent irrelevances, in whose coils we are caught; the 'far' seems to recede, as we seek it. Yet the far exists—'there' is a state which can be attained and in which appearance and reality can coalesce in true human actuality; though all too frequently the ultimate appearance—reality is as remote and as hard of access as Jali is to find it in his life's pilgrimage ...The opposition between the phenomenal world of the immediate present in all its potential beauty and yet its transience, its corruption, and frequent underlying evil, and the more remote and detached states of mind to attain which invol-

ves discipline and sacrifices, a freedom from Maya, is then one of the themes of the book; the 'appearances' of the world are shown to contain many inadequacies when brought into contact with deeper spiritual 'realities.'[26]

In brief, all that is stated above is what constitutes Prince Jali's life and his quest. When we see him at the opening of the novel, he is a boy of twelve who is haunted by the spectre of loneliness and sense of separateness. For him, the world "was a place of mystery and terror.... all threatened by evil." (p. 12.) He has, of course, problems of identity. Instead of belonging to a particular religion, he is "ready to acknowledge every known god as well as others of his own imagining." (p. 16.) He is an extremely sensitive, precocious young boy who believes he was different from others especially "in being full of fear." Generally he felt that the others were "utterly different", and this makes him "feel so lonely." Jali broods with terror over the actual experiencing of life. While in Agra, Jali was "resolved to shirk nothing, to welcome every experience." He realises that

And it is only then that he joins a band of pilgrims on their way to Ceylon. In their company, "he was filled with a deep peace, and at the centre of his peace there glowed a quiet exultation." (p. 610.)

In Rajah Amar, Myers created a character who is very close to his idea of human goodness. He is a man of noble character, fine impulses, absolute integrity who has chosen the Buddhist path of renunciation. He also has to undergo the process of learning, before he realises that the personal and the political cannot be so easily separated as he had earlier innocently assumed and that the individual has a social responsibility to carry out. Amar represents the fastidious in its conflict with the trivial, a recurrent theme in Myers's novels as pointed out by G.H. Bantock.[22]

In portraying Rajah Amar, Myers drew on Buddhism because he intended to project the conflicts of a man who always differentiated between the spiritual and the material, that is to say, the call of the spirit and that of wordly affairs. Amar stands for 'Good' in life which is engaged in an eternal struggle with 'Evil'. And his major aim in life lies in Becoming, which is why he chooses the path of renunciation. Myers perhaps had to turn to India to present authentically the life of the spirit in an individual. For the Hindu, as well as the Buddhist, "the spiritual is the basic element of human nature."[23] And it was again

Buddha who "taught only what is necessary for overcoming evil whose prevalence, is according to him, the chief characteristic of life."[24] We also know that "Buddha's theory strikes a mean between two extreme courses, e.g., believing neither in Being nor in non-Being, but in Becoming; believing neither in chance nor in necessity exclusively, but in conditioned happening."[25] Thus we see that, Buddhism was eminently suited to depict the kind of dilemma present in an individual like Rajah Amar.

It is difficult to think of a protagonist who dominates the novel, but in terms of a single individual who unifies the entire action, we have Prince Jali. *The Near and the Far* begins and ends with Prince Jali on the balcony of a palace in Agra. His problem is how best he can relate himself to the world in which he lives and overcome his sense of isolation. And towards this end is directed his individual development. His problem is one of reconciling reality with appearances:

> people had to choose between *seeing* and *being.* The more of reality you saw, the less of being you possessed. He ... *saw* things as they really were, and *was,* in consequence, practically nothing at all. (p. 224)

He is, no doubt fascinated by "the essential secrecy of the human mind." He comes to see that people around him were all playacting and that they project a mask behind which their true personalities are hidden. He grows to learn that unless one breaks through these masks one cannot achieve true meeting with his fellowmen. Jali learns, to his sorrow that both Buddhism and Christianity fail to resolve the problems of his inner life. But he notices in Gokal's utterances, "a spirit of infinite refreshment" and thinks that

> Gokal ... might actually both *be* and *see*: in him vision might be combined with power. (p. 228.)

There are three distinct stages in Prince Jali's growth. The first stage is his life with Gunevati, a Vamachari, the second, his experiences at the Pleasance of Arts and finally his meeting with the Guru. 'How to live?' has been Jali's almost obsessive preoccupation all along. When he looks around, in vain, for answers to his ceaseless questionings, he meets Gunevati and thinks that he has found the key to his problems in her irrational rules of living and her obsession with religion and sex. After being initiated into Gunevati's world, Jali enjoys a brief period of pure bliss. He even believes that he has "discovered the necessary bond between himself and the rest of mankind."

(p. 237.) Even if it is a momentary feeling, it is without doubt, Gunevati's outlook that "had brought him out of isolation into communion with the kindly race of man." (p. 237.) He discovers that her interests resided

> in the body, in sex; and sex and religion were one. This position established Gunevati very firmly on life's bedrock ... She lived in her body, and her body was her present sufficiency. (p. 238.)

She lives in the here and now. For her, the present moment is all-sufficient. And her living only in the body, has naturally simplified her existence, and it is this that Jali envies in her, thinking of the doubts of his own inner self.

Prince Jali's reflections are all *stated* in the form of a monologue absolutely without any drama in them. They continue almost endlessly, page after page, to the point of getting monotonously repetitive and the reader looks, almost in vain, for something different in terms of novel writing. Even where the incident could have been described, with greater success from the point of view of form, Myers prefers to record only the mental process of the response to the incident as apprehended by Jali. The result is we do not *see* the real encounter between Gunevati and Jali — there are, however, a few exceptions — but only read the effects of the meeting as stated by Jali through his wordy and mental exercises.

It does not take long before Jali, in spite of the intense excitement of his days with Gunevati, comes to recognise that

> his old problems, instead of disappearing, had only changed their shape. The trouble was that at bottom he remained exactly the same..... he was quite unable to *feel* and *accept* the world as she felt and accepted it; that, he saw, would never be within his power ... although her purely intellectual deficiencies did not particularly vex him, he was unable to accept with the same equanimity her lack of moral taste. (p. 240.)

Jali is too sensitive, too discriminating to be lost in Gunevati's world for ever. He now realises that the change in him is only superficial. The merely physical cannot satisfactorily meet the demands of his inner cravings and hence he finds it impossible to identify himself with Gunevati's outlook on life. Even where he is prepared to overlook her limitations of intellect, her total neglect of moral taste amounts to a serious limitations character. To continue to live by being totally oblivious of the moral side of life is despicable for Jali. And so is it for Myers. He could never divorce the problem of living from its moral responsibilities. This accounts for the continuous moral discriminations that Myers makes when he is dealing with characters and their attitude to life.

Just as triviality is shown to lead to evil in Daniyal, simple animality in Gunevati is also capable of producing evil. Myers sees a close connection between the problem of evil and the problem of sex. The choice of Gunevati for this representation of a woman who is an incarnation of sex is appropriate, for she was "a Vamachari, a Follower of the Left-Hand Way." (p. 251.) As in the case of Amar, we see Myers making creative use of the Indian religion; here it is the Hindu Tantric tradition, to portray pure sensuality in women. Vamacharis are one of the three best known Sakti sects. Sakti cult is the worship of force personified as a goddess and subordinately in all women. The Vamacharis follow the teaching of the Tantric literature. They worship great Sakti, or power of Nature, Jaganmata or Jagadamba, the mighty mysterious force, whose function is to direct and control two quite distinct operations: namely first, the working of the natural opposites and passions, whether for the support of the body by eating and drinking or for the propagation of living organisms through sexual cohabitation; secondly the acquisition of supernatural faculties *(sidhi)*, whether for a man's own individual exaltation or for the annihilation of his opponents. To put it more succinctly, they believe in the five M's — *makarapanchakam: matsya, mamsa, madya, maithuna, mudra* — fish, flesh, wine, copulation and gestures.[27]

Gunevati is a truly typical representative of Vamacharis. In other words, she stands for a certain attitude to life and is definitely not someone who "represents the mysterious forces that he [Myers] sees as being the heart of India."[28] She is indeed a mysterious girl for Jali, till he is able to understand her fully. But this mystery cannot be equated with India, since in Myers, "the core of the problem seems always to be the age-old dualism between spirit and flesh. No one can decide whether it is best to cleanse the spirit by asceticism and complete withdrawal from the world, or to try to reach the unknown through the gateway of the senses."[29] And in one like Gunevati, Myers is examining the role of sex in the life of a human being. With his knowledge of Indian religions, he could not have chosen a better school of religious thought than the Vamacharis to portray this particular aspect of life.

The second stage of Jali's development is to do with his encounter with Daniyal and his Pleasance of Arts. On meeting Ali, his cousin, who is member of the camp, Jali becomes aware of his limitations. All these years, life and its meaning had engrossed him so much that he had not developed a personal taste, an aesthetic judgement of his own. Hence, he begins to read, compose verse, and finds all this "exciting in a new and delightful way." And so he most enthusiastically pursues the glorious freedom of the mind that would, hopefully, lead him towards perfect Beauty.

But to Jali's disappointment, the camp he moves into is as much conventional as any school, for here is no independent thinking and the novelty of thought is valued merely for its newness and nothing else. It has only a 'shock' value. Jali finds the camp informed by frivolous character. He finds out that

> in the Pleasance of the Arts, everyone was, so to speak, *somebody*. Here you might come across people of every variety — except one, the commonplace. Dull, conventional people — people who weren't lit by the divine spark, had no chance of gaining admission here ... Originality of mind, intellectual merit, poetic fire, these alone counted with him [Daniyal]; and on this basis all were equal ... Pedantry bored him; he liked to be amused; the art which he recognized as Art had to be forever young and new and gay. (pp. 309-10).

The powerful irony in the passage is evident, so also is Myers's satire directed against Bloomsbury. While witnessing a play by Daniyal in the camp, he is deeply disillusioned, for it is nothing more than "a string of ... vulgarities and ineptitudes." (p. 315.) In spite of this, he is prepared to go on like this for some more time. But at the end of it all, he confesses :

> How tired he was of deceits and trickeries! Whether at home or at the Camp, he was always acting a part. His true self seemed to be incapable of honest relationships: it was condemned by some deep defect of nature to everlasting treachery. (p. 365.)

One might feel Jali has made hardly any progress since his early days at Agra, for he still finds himself acting a part. But he has, of course, learnt a great deal after he left Agra. As he learnt from Gunevati of the insufficiency of the body and that animality could lead to evil, in the Pleasance of Arts Jali finds that aestheticism without any moral basis leads to drabness, triviality and boredom and that out of triviality comes evil.

While staying with Rajah Bhoj and Lakshmi, he meets Guru Bhupendra who lives in his dell close by. This constitutes the final phase in Jali's growth from adolescence towards maturity. The Guru clarifies his problems, answers his questions and resolves his doubts. As a result, we see Jali at the end of the novel, sure of himself and of his place in the world. It is the ability to look at life from various points of view, that renders Jali's search not only very convincing but also makes it modern. In the last stage, there occur two important events in his life. These are his meetings with Rajah Bhoj and Lakshmi, and Mohan and Damayanti.

The palace of Bhoj and Lakshmi is located in a lonely place, "a spot unconnected in time and space with the rest of the material world" where they live a life of "privileged seclusion. (p. 657.) After living with them for sometime, Jali discovers that Bhoj and Lakshmi

> '... have to regard themselves as superior beings and to persuade the rest of mankind to regard them as such. But — are they really superior beings? And don't they enormously over-estimate their culture, their graces, the value they add to human life as a whole?' (pp. 734-35.)

And he further confesses :

> '...It seems to me that at the palace I belonged to a little group of people who, while apparently living lives of dignity, self-discipline, and public-spiritedness, were really living in an ignoble cause. I feel that in all of them the intelligence of the heart has been suffocated, so that their secret lives have become self-defensive, mean and calculating.' (p. 735.)

Finally Jali comes to understand that it is because of this "cult of 'first-rateness'" that they care more for self-decoration and attach such an exaggerated value to appearances. But it is Damayanti who with her sure moral sense is able to account for the life-style of Bhoj. She tells Jali that "these people are afraid of appearing second-rate. They are afraid of each other. That is at the root of the trouble." (p. 736) Once again it comes to the same thing. That is how this posturing, in the final analysis, destroys the innate goodness in men.

Now Jali goes over to Hawa Ghar to live with Mohan and Damayanti. Even on the first glimpse that he has of Damayanti, he finds her "a picture of quickness, lightness, and spontaneity." (pp. 670-71) When he sees her first at Hawa Ghar near the water pool which has a large statue of Vishnu, he is filled with a strange feeling of satisfaction because of the beauty and tranquility of the scene. Something remarkable happens to him. While savouring these moments of unalloyed happiness, he plays on his flute, "a wandering disconsolate sequence of notes which to his imagination were the voice of a grey wind sweeping over icy plains." And then

> 'Play that again!' she said, and he rejoiced to feel her eyes, large and dark in the half-light, fixed intently upon him. He was weaving a spell about her, he was contributing magic of his own to these moments of divine enchantment. With an intensity unknown to him ever before he was aware of the world around him — branch-entangled gleamings left behind by the sun, a cool upwelling from the low-hung moon, small bird-sounds, leafy silences, scents — now cold, now warm — breathed up from the water and the stone. All this he felt, all this he *was*.
>
> *Tat tvam asi.* (p. 705.)

This is indeed a momentous occasion for Jali. Here is a profound experience which is described by Myers. Jali is most acutely aware of the world of nature around him and has a communion with these natural objects, and feels he is one with them. What is interesting from the point of the present study, is Myers's use of the Upanishadic phrase *Tat tvam asi.* In the Chandogya Upanishad, Svetaketu questions his father Uddalaka about the true nature of Brahman or the Absolute Self, and the father answers:

> in the beginning there was Existence alone — One only, without a second. He, the one, thought to himself; Let me be many, let me grow forth. Thus out of himself he projected the universe; and having projected out of himself the universe, he entered into every being. All that is has its self in him alone. Of all things he is the subtle es-

sence. He is the truth. He is the Self. And that, Svetaketu,
THAT ART THOU *(Tat tvam asi).* [30]

In other words, Jali is said to have discovered that "the eternal is in one's self. The Real which is the inmost of all things, is the essence of one's own soul."[31] It would also mean that he has recognised the spiritual truth that "the Absolute is not conceived here objectively — as merely inferred from outer phenomena; but as revealing itself within us."[32]

Theoretically, it is not beyond the bounds of the plausible. But how is it realised in terms of fictional art ? It is nothing short of a revelatory moment in Jail's life. And how does it come about? No doubt, the deep serenity of the atmosphere, the idol of Vishnu, the nearness to Damayanti all contribute to bring about this state of mind in him. Despite all this, the reader is left with a feeling that this is simply not adequate to the profundity that underlies the conception of *Tat tvam asi* as it is envisioned in the Chandogya Upanishad. It is likely that one views the Sanskrit phrase as being merely tagged onto the passage, for it does not seem to emerge out of the context under pressure of events. However admirable his intentions are, Myers has failed to realise the true significance of the Upanishadic concept in terms of his art. It is just a case of Myers's art being unable to rise to the level of his thematic preoccupations.

Jali's predilections continue to be seen in his conversations with both Damayanti and the Guru. And he learns that the Guru is against false appearances that force a man to hide his true self behind a mask. He is a believer in the essential goodness of human nature and hence he refuses to make any discriminations between people. He is for candour in human relationship. This wisdom in the Guru's words sets Jali's doubts about the falsity in men at rest forever.

Jali has one final and extraordinary meeting with the Guru at Hawa Ghar before he leaves for Agra to join his mother, and then proceeds to Vidyapur to take over the reins of his kingdom. He now experiences something that is very akin to what he had undergone while he was with Damayanti beside the pool of Vishnu. He knew that

> something within him was loosened, and that his spirit went forth. With the Guru's it went forth into freedom — to mix in the black leafiness of the trees, and mount to the grow- ing light of the stars, and sail in the dusky, placid air. And it looked down upon the sleeping god in the pool. In

his mind there was a memory. He was reminded of something that had happened to him before. And as he returned to the solitude of himself, he found that he had moved, and was leaning his head against the Guru's knees, and held his hand, as he had done in the dungeon at Daulatpur. (p. 940.)

Once again, Jali has the conviction of having seen into the nature of things. Myers does not use *Tat tvam asi* on this occasion, but instead offers us its prose equivalent in the words of the Guru that immediately follow the above description:

'My son ... this is the heart of the mystery. We go forth, we meet, and in the meeting we are as one. At one also with all life.' (p. 940.)

The Guru takes the Vedantic position when he speaks of "the greatness and melancholy of man's estate:"

'...although we know that we are Spirit, and that all Spirit is one, yet by an unalterable rhythm of our being we swing out from the world of communion into the world of separated things.' (pp. 940-41.)

And the Upanishadic *Tat tvam asi* also provides the basis for universal love. "We should do unto others as we do to ourselves because they are ourselves — a view which places the golden rule of morality on the surest of foundations."[33] But it is because of the deficiencies of human and the resultant ignorance, that we move into a divided world and fail to see the oneness of things.

And immediately comes Jali's question :

'How to hold fast?...How — in the world of separation — to hold fast?'

The Guru replies:

'One must cling to the memory. One must remember and one must act. The knowledge gained in communion, and ripened in solitude, must pour its life into the world through action. Thus only will you and the world about you live.' (p. 941.)

It is a mixture of Jungian psychology and the Indian concept of action. The central point of the teaching of the *Gita* is *Karmayoga* or activism. And the knowledge that the Guru speaks of will teach man to be unselfish, and this can be identified with the message of the *Gita* that "we ought to engage ourselves in our work as members of a social order in the usual way, and yet banish from our mind all thought of deriving any personal benefit therefrom."[34] That is why, the Guru wants a man to always return from his solitude, his communion. He is, to put it differently, preaching not "renunciation *of* action, but renunciation *in* action."[35]

The place that a man has in the world in which he lives is very important for the Guru. He should belong to it and struggle towards achieving proper relationships. That is the reason why he dreads "spiritual separation", for that would mean one "cannot get to the Centre. He cannot reach his fellowmen." Jali asks, "Must one reach the Centre?" The Guru answers:

> 'One must. All communion is through the Centre. When the relation of man is not through the Centre, it corrupts and destroys itself. This you already know.' (p. 942)

The Centre can be interpreted as the Divine. According to the Guru, the key to right action is to act in close relation to the divine purpose. Man should not lose sight of the Centre. He must not become a victim of the phenomenal world. He has to learn to act according to the dictates of his inner spirit *(Atman)*, the Spirit that has experienced communion with the world. Only through such action born out of this awareness can one establish the right relationship with another person.

Jali's search has now come to its conclusive end. All his doubts have been resolved so that he can now get on with the problem of living in real earnestness. He should not only live but also learn to act. He will remember that "Spirit is the world's master." (p.943.) Man is not a mere speck in the universe, a helpless being, but the great instrument of divine destiny. It is Jali's destiny to live a full life on this earth with his fellow beings and this is the awareness he has of his place in the world at the end. In a sense, he is reborn, for he is convinced that "there was a correspondence between outward things and the inner landscape of his mind." (p. 947.) The Near and the Far have met and it is most appropriate that this revelation should have come to Prince Jali at Hawa Ghar, for it is only while living here that he encountered the real world.

The character of the Guru is fascinating since it shows Myers's considerable knowledge of Indian religious thought. Though he mouths the views of the existential philosopher Martin Buber, he is essentially Indian in his outlook on life. According to Myers, he had certain reasons for creating the character of the Guru:

> My intention was to portray a good man (There are many in the world all the time, but only knaves and fools are portrayed as a rule). And a good man exhales an atmosphere of serenity.[36]

The Guru's "dress was a white dhoti that left his arms free. He looked strong and wiry; he had an air both of alertness and repose." (p. 626.) In him, we see the typical paradoxical combination of the active and the serene that characterises great Indian saints. There is in the Guru both tranquility and a desire to act. Talking of his life, he tells Hari that it is

> '...like the peeling of an onion. One skin after another of self-deception and pretence do I strip off. In the process my eyes water and my vanity smarts.' (p. 632.)

This suggests that he is in the process of one's journey towards attaining self-perfection.

The Guru, in the Indian tradition, has renounced his ego. M. Hiriyanna tells us that "the prime object of upanishadic discipline is the removal of aham-kara, which is the basis of all evil; and vairagya is the name given to that attitude towards the world which results from the successful eradication of the narrow selfish impulses for which it stands."[37] And now he has taken up in all earnestness the work of ameliorating the conditions of the untouchables, helping the struggles of the poor and the oppressed. Because of this emphasis on the service to humanity, and in his belief in the essential goodness of human nature, M.K.Naik takes this view:

> A distinctively un-Indian feature of the Guru's thought would seem to be this, that his *weltanshauung* appears to be ethical rather than metaphysical. His quest is not essentially religious, but secular. How best to live in this world, and not how to attain salvation is his chief quest. If, as Albert Schweitzer notes, the chief difference between Indian thought and modern European thought is that the former is dominated by 'the idea of ... world and life negation,' and the latter by the principle of 'world and life affirmation,' the Guru's thought would appear to be charac-

teristically Western, at least in this respect.[38]

It is true that the emphasis in the Guru's life is on the ethical and the secular, but M.K.Naik's contention that such an emphasis is un-Indian is not wholly true. Schweitzer, despite his sympathetic understanding of Indian thought, has certainly simplified the differences between the East and the West in his assertion that they occupy two contrary positions. His main arguments have been rejected in a brilliantly sustained manner by S.Radhakrishnan in his book, *Eastern Religions and Western Thought*. Radhakrishnan proves beyond doubt that the emphasis on the ethical, and the concern with "how best to live in this world," was as much a preoccupation with the Hindu as his spiritual quest. We have on the authority of the *Gita* that "man [should] continue to work even in this perfected state, there being nothing in outer activity which is incompatible with inner peace."[39]

The asceticism that characterises the life of the Guru is typically Indian. What is most striking in his later life is his simple living habits and the life of seclusion. This does not mean that he has withdrawn into his own private world since he is ever willing and anxious to help the poor and the distressed, and also offer wise counsel to those who have personal problems, both social and spiritual. As M. Hiriyanna remarks, "the two elements common to all Indian thought [are] the pursuit of *moksa* as the final ideal and the ascetic spirit of the discipline recommended for its attainment."[40] But in the novel, Myers has not paid adequate attention "to the pursuit of *moksa*" and to that extent the portraiture of the Guru as an Indian saint is incomplete, and M.K. Naik's contention is partly right. However, it is his preoccupation with the problem of living and his belief in the life of action that puts him in line with great Indians like Swami Vivekananda and Mahatma Gandhi whose emphasis was rather more on this world. It was Vivekananda who learnt from his master Ramakrishna that one should not be wholly lost in the life of contemplation, but get back to the actual world. He was for a "man-making religion" since he believed that the best way to reach God was by serving man. Vivekananda asserted :

> I am not a believer in God or even in Ramakrishna. I am a believer in those who adore service to humanity. It is those people who accept service to humanity whom I worship.[41]

He believed that social service and transformation of the human individual is the real goal of religion. So did Mahatma Gandhi. And the Guru both in his words and deeds, comes closer to these ideals. We see in the life of the Guru the enactment of profound faith in the belief of "religion as experience, religion as toleration of others, religion as service of man, for which Swami Vivekananda stood."[42]

If this is one aspect of the Guru's character, there is also another in which we see him, that is in the role of spiritual adviser to Jali, Mohan, Damayanti, Akbar and Hari Khan. It is in this role of phycoanalyst, as D.W. Harding[43] calls him, that we see him drawing upon his inner reserves of wisdom to clarify the doubts of these individuals in their personal crises. It is evident from the novel, that Myers uses him as his mouthpiece to express his views on various issues that troubled him in his own deep disillusionment with the world in which he lived. It is the innate goodness of the Guru and his unshakeable faith in man that leaves a memorable impression on the mind of the reader. In addition, we see him echoing mainly the opinions of Martin Buber, the existential philosopher.

The Guru sees candour as constituting the real basis for any ideal relationship between persons. He offers it to Hari as the universal panacea for all men in their dealings with others. This conception of human relationship, Myers owed almost entirely to Martin Buber. Buber in his book, *I and Thou*, urged man to live in an I-and-Thou relationship with God and the universe, a personal, reverential relationship, rather than the more common I-and-It relationship which the excessive analysis of rationalist philosophers had created. He wrote, "Each of us is encased in an armour which we soon, out of familiarity, no longer notice."[44] In the latter situation, a man treats other men, the universe, and indeed the concept of God, as objects to be manipulated, rather than as a totality that includes the man in which there are reverential relationships. Buber also said, "The primary word 'I-Thou' can only be spoken with the whole being. The primary word 'I-It' can never be spoken with the whole being."[45] It is only the 'I-Thou' conception in the relationship between man and man that leads to man's humanity to man, and existence of mutual respect and compassion, and beyond this to a love for all God's creatures.

In his advice to others, the Guru's sagelike wisdom is very pronounced. The following statements, a random selection from among his numerous generalisation on life and human nature, make this clear:

> One has to be very simple or very saintly to live in the

present. (p. 940.)

I believe in the essential goodness of human nature. (p. 791.)

Intention must never be adulterated; nor does it admit of degrees. A terrible purity of intention is demanded of man. (p. 902.)

My theories amount to nothing more than that every man has the right to be treated as a person ... and not merely as a member of a category or class. (p. 791.)

[In men] the most powerful of appetites is the craving for consideration; and the most powerful of fears is the fear of losing consideration. (p. 759.)

As a matter of fact, these generalisations, however impressive in themselves, point to a failings in Myers the novelist. It is difficult to really conceive the Guru as a character in a novel. Even the development from the earlier days of his life of self-deception, to the later life of maturity and greater poise, is revealed only through his confession to Hari. And the memorable statemernts are all uttered by the Guru in his conversation with other characters. But the interaction between characters that one is familiar with in a novel is conspicuous by its absence in *The Near and the Far*. On the other hand, different persons like Jali, Mohan, Damayanti and Hari Khan seek the guidance of the Guru to dispel their numerous doubts. The Guru, thanks to his deep insight into man and his nature, answers them to the great satisfaction of each one of them. He is at best, to again use D.W.Harding's phrase, "a psychoanalyst" who clarifies and interprets and *not* a character in the real sense of the term. The amount of clarification and interpretation done by the Guru far exceeds the thinking done by the other characters in these encounters, thus upsetting the delicate balance that is required in a successful novel.

In spite of these limitations in the characterisation of the Guru, Myers can be said to have created in him a truly Indian saint who believes in asceticism and service to mankind mainly through action. However, it should be added, that in spite of the Vedantic stance that we notice in some of his speeches, he is much too closer to Martin Buber's philosophy to be considered entirely Indian.

It would now be rewarding to turn to the various references in the novel to Indian thought, to examin the extent of Mayers's familiarity with Indian philosophy.

When Rajah Amar breaks the news of his decision to retire from the world, Sita is deeply saddened. She understands his decision, but yet she finds it strange, viewing it as she does from the point of view of the Westerner. She confides her feelings to Gokal, the brahmin. In their discussion, we have the meeting the Western and the Eastern ideals. To her queries he says :

> 'In our country, as you know, men often do this thing. At a certain age, after a man has discharged his duty as a husband, father and citizen, he responds to another call.'

Sita is not satisfied, for she believes that the best way to serve God is by living in this world. Gokal answers :

> ' ... The *Upanishad* says: "In darkness are they who worship only the world, but in greater darkness they who worship the infinite alone. He who accepts both, saves himself from death by the knowledge of the former, and attains immortality by the knowledge of the latter"... Where we differ from you is in our recognition of the value of holiness. In our minds the relation of man to man is secondary, right conduct following naturally when the relation of man to God is made perfect. Moreover, there is no greater benefit that a man can confer upon his fellows than the example of his own spiritual achievement ...'(p. 90.)

This is a correct restatement of the Indian position. To overcome one's selfish impulses one has to go through "a long course of training through the three *asramas* or disciplinary stages—those of the religious student (brahmacharya) the householder (grahasthya), and the anchorite (vanaprastha). As the very word *asrama* ('toil') means, they are stages of strife when selfishness is slowly but steadily rooted out."[46] The Upanishadic statement is from the Isa Upanishad, "Into deep darkness fall those who follow the immanent. Into deeper darkness fall those who follow the transcendent."[47] It isn't either-or, but man shall pursue both simultaneously to make each of them meaningful. Myers seems to tell the West through Gokal:

> ' ... I think that you of the Western world should consider carefully whether you have not made an error in idealizing the will to live. Life! The enrichment of life! The intensification of life! The prolongation of life into eternity!

...'(p. 90.)

This indeed constitutes the vital difference between the West and the East. As S. Radhakrishnan has pointed out, even the

> ...religious man in the West believes in life, affirms life, and throws himself with joy and resolution into the tasks of life ... the Western man is engaged in the vindication of personal worth; he directs all his energies to our joys and sorrows, our troubles and fears, our plans and confidences.[48]

Even after all these patient efforts by Gokal to convince Sita, she reiterates:

> ' ... I, for my part, shall always affirm what Amar denies. Between us there is a gulf.'

Gokal again clarifies perceptively:

> 'The gulf lies not between those who affirm and those who deny, but between those who affirm and those who ignore... I believe that between your affirmations and our denials there is, in reality, little more than a long difference of mental habit. Fundamentally your mind and Amar's are similar in type; you both raise the same problems and the answers you give are the same in essence, if their substance is not the same. You advocate life's intensification', Amar its extinguishment; but you both recognise imperfection and you both aim at perfection. Your goal is the same whatever names you give it.'
> (p. 91.)

Once again Gokal's masterly understanding of the Western and Eastern positions contrasts with the simple stand taken by Sita. It is not simply the case of two opposites as suggested by her. Gokal is right, for the West does not deny but tends to ignore the spirit. However, both the West and the East recognise the prevalence of imperfection in life and strive towards perfection. And only the means are different. Elsewhere Gokal maintains that "the tendency of Christianity was to exalt the ideal of social duty at the expense of the ideal of self-illumination." (p. 177.) This is another important difference between the two attitudes. In the words of S. Radhakrishnan, "World and life affirmation results in social service, whilst the other [Hindu] takes no interest in a world which it dismisses as a stage play or at best a puzzling pilgrimage through time to eternity."[49]

There are other references to Hindu ideals as well in the novel. For instance, Rajah Amar, very rightly, considers Karma as "the noblest institution of our race." He remarks:

> ' ... there is a distinction between causation in dead matter, causation in the organic world, and causation in the animate world, where the operation of moral law is superimposed upon the natural. This is Karma; it is the chief force in the universe in as much as it controls life's gradual progress towards final deliverance.' (p. 122.)

This is faithful interpretation of the law of karma which "signifies that nothing can happen without a sufficient cause in the moral as in the physical world — that each life with all its pains and pleasures is the necessary result of the actions of past lives and becomes in its turn the cause, through its own activities, of future births."[50] In other words, we see that law of karma is the general moral law which governs not only the life and destiny of all individual beings, but even the order and arrangement of the physical world. As Emerson has remarked in his essay on 'Compensation', there is no contingency in Nature.

When asked by Hari Khan as to what constitutes Reality, Mabun Das answers in the traditional Hindu mode:

> ' ... By reality I mean Maya — the phenomenal world, Illusion, if you please to call it so. But for us illusion alone exists; we live in it; it is our life; let us accept it! Hari Khan, if there is a God, it is our Hindoo God — Shiva, the dancing God — Shiva, the sportive God, who out of the super-abundance of his energies has created the world for his play. Do not be depressed. After Akbar another will arise. Individuals are nothing. Shiva dances on!' (p. 170.)

Here is the reference to the creation of the world which constitutes the Reality. Creation is a necessary part of God's being. And the analogy of the play (lila) "suggest(s) the free overflow of the divine into the universe. It does not mean that there is nothing real or significant going on all the time."[51] The dance of Shiva has been closely identified with the process of cosmic creation. As Coomaraswamy has pointed out, the essential significance of Shiva's dance is that, its Rhythmic play is "the source of all Movement within the Cosmos."[52]

Then there is the brief appearance of a yogi who believes that "spirit and flesh are one." He belongs to the Sakti school as is clearly evident in the following speech:

> '... The true religion of a man is that which he lives, — and that which all men live is the religion of Creativity, the religion of sex. Knowingly or unknowingly all men worship Woman, and all women worship Man. To understand this in its simplicity is to grasp the truth; to grasp truth is to be in contact with reality; and to be in contact with reality is power.' (p. 511.)

Myers's insight into Hinduism and its intricacies is proved beyond doubt in a passage wherein both Hari Khan and Rajah Amar attempt a critical view of the religion:

> ... Hinduism in general, however, appealed to him [Hari Khan] as the broadest and most elastic of all religious systems. He was attracted by its independence of dogma, the smallness of its demands upon blind faith. But these attractions also constituted its weakness, lending point to the criticism made by Amar that Hinduism was not a religion but simply religiousness itself. Upon the spiritual substance it imposed no form, to the urge it gave no certain direction; and although among the uneducated it borrowed shape from the myths, superstitions, and customs, with which the common mind was already richly stocked, in an unencumbered intelligence it remained fluid and colourless, as rarefied, indeed, as any brainspun metaphysics. (pp. 112-13.)

But for a more impressive and elaborate restatement of the tenets of Hinduism, we should consider at great length, the meeting of Rajah Amar and Smith, a travelling Englishman in India. They discuss the Greek, Christian and Hindu view of life in detail. It is a veritable symposium on these religions with both Amar and Smith arguing their positions with uncompromising rigour. In their discussion on the Western and Indian views of life, it is easy to see on whose side the sympathies of the novelist lies. And this sympathy for the Hindu view of life offers a clue to Myers's setting the novel in India, for he was undoubtedly fascinated by the Indian mind as opposed to Western thinking.

Rajah Amar finds Smith "friendly, uncertain and inquiring." Smith did "conceive the dominant note of India to be religion." (p. 423.) But his sympathies are with the Greeks, for they had discovered "the difficult art of enjoying the best things of life." Amar knows that they had achieved this "at the cost of ignoring the universe." In other words, they had eschewed metaphysics. And in doing this, according to Smith, "they were not unwise" and this helped them to live "wisely and happily, shut in from the abyss." Amar is shocked by the superficiality of Smith which makes him value the ignorance of the Greeks.

Smith, of course, knows that "the Hindu does ... really believe that the true life is a spiritual life." (p. 426.) The difference according to Amar, between the Greek and the Indian is that the latter "be he an illiterate Hindu peasant or an erudite Buddhist recluse, lives in an unceasing consciousness of the immensities around him." The Greeks are "boyish and immature" in evolving "a small but exquisite culture, at the price of ignoring the immensities in the midst of which men live." Amar asserts that "to ignore metaphysical problems is not to abolish them; and in a sense it may be said that every man who thinks at all is, willy-nilly, a metaphysician." (p. 428.)

Interestingly, Amar, an Indian finds Christ closer to him than Socrates. It is the other way round for Smith who values reason more than intuitions. Amar finds that the "Christian conception of God as a loving father ... is a beautiful one ... Christianity gives brotherhood to men, and value to every human life." In spite of his being a Buddhist, he values "the freshness, true hope, true tenderness, the courage, of Christianity." (p. 429.) The true similarities between different religions undoubtedly touch a sympathetic chord in the heart of a sensitve individual like Rajah Amar.

But this does not happen in Smith, for he is not only an agnostic but also a rigid materialist. And as Amar knows, the European "is generally imbued with a sense of the value and reality of phenomenal world in and for itself." (p. 430.) Hence, for someone like Smith, the life of an individual begins in birth and ends in death and consequently he finds" no higher significance to which to relate it" as does the Indian. Amar is aware that even a sensitive woman like his wife Sita, would sympathise with one like Smith because she too believes that "man is at the centre of the universe." Even "she cannot understand the Indian way of placing the Absolute at the centre, and regarding the whole history of mankind from first to last as nothing but a ripple upon the surface of that Supreme Mind." (p. 431.) Myers has here successfully captured the essential difference between the Indian and the Western way of viewing man in relation to his universe.

Amar, midway through his long conversations with Smith tries to assess him as a man. He finds, that though Smith has sensitiveness and sensibility, his nature is "in love with ease and superficiality." At this juncture, one should recall the basic similarities we find between Smith and Daniyal. Both of them are men who dwell in the trivial and derive great satisfaction from it in their lives. While it is Reason for the former, it is Art for the latter. And both of them were equally detestable for Myers. That is why he has Amar commenting on Smith thus, apparently with his own approval:

> It is well that people like Smith should exist, and it is perhaps inevitable that they should exaggerate their own importance, but it is also well that society should not give them even the importance they deserve. A world that honoured them would be a dacaying one. (p. 432.)

Such men who are "inimical to religion in general" have no place in a civilized community. And this accounts for Myers's bitter attack on Smith.

But then the purpose of bringing in a character like Smith into the novel is not merely "to attack the West"[53] by contrasting it with the positive aspects of Indian religion. It is not a simple black and white contrast as it would have certainly been if it were an attempt to only malign the West. This meeting assumes significance in view of Rajah Amar's decision to renounce life. He very frankly admits the influence of Smith on him at this critical juncture in his life:

> Contact with the Western mind, as represented by Smith, has had a disturbing effect upon me. It shows me too well how, from every other angle except that at which we Indians stand, my present intention soon to withdraw from the world must appear selfish, and this moment singularly ill-chosen. India is on the verge of civil war; I am needed in my capacity of ruler; my wife and son require guidance; and my best friend — the man upon whom I rely to give them guidance — is in danger of falling into disgrace. (p. 431.)

Here the West does play a positive role in spite of its "disturbing effect" on Amar. It leads him into an introspective mood wherein he is forced to take a second look at his decision to retire from active life. All this while he has never been bothered about the correctness of his decision. But now he realises, when viewed from the Western perspective, that it "must appear selfish." This would mean, that the West makes him aware of his social obligations which he had tended to compeletely ignore while looking upon his decision solely from the Indian viewpoint. He discovers, thanks to the West, that he cannot keep his personal desires and political responsibilities separate. And hence, he puts off his plans for the present.

Their conversations continues, and Smith is "determined to make out that between the European and the Hindu there is a profound difference in spiritual outlook." He argues that "while the European believes that life in this world is, or should be, a good in itself, the Indian has always held it to be an evil, from the everlasting recurrence of which he aspires to escape." This differentiation reads as though it is straight out of Albert Schwitzer's book on Indian thought. It is far too simplistic to be taken seriously. But Amar believes "this is only looking at the surface of things" and goes on to give his own analysis of Hinduism. He believes that

> ... the Hindu, in common with all men, instinctively clings to life, and instinctively seeks pleasure and happiness while alive. It is only in his capacity as a thinker that he proclaims life evil. (p. 435.)

Even this position is not entirely accurate, since for the Hindu life is never evil but it becomes so only when one is ignorant of the Absolute Principle that governs the universe. Whereas for the Buddhist, in sharp contrast, life is evil and transitory. Amar's view of Hinduism is apparently coloured by his own Buddhist convictions. The Hindu is, despite his unworldiness, very much concerned with living in the immediate present. But his ultimate concern is with personal salvation or attainment of *moksa*. And hence the material, in the final analysis, is subservient to the spiritual for the Hindu.

In contrast, "Why does the European fail in detachment?" asks Amar and locates the reason for such a failure in the climatic conditions:

> In a cold, even in a temperate climate, bodily exertion is pleasanter and more natural than in the tropics, and, unlike exertion in the tropics, it produces an agreeable

> fatigue and an increased capacity for exertion. A habit of body and mind is thus set up which directs a man's attention outwards and attaches his thoughts to material things. (p.435.)

For once, one suspects Rajah Amar is not being Indian in his response, since this is more a Western way of looking at things. It is true that there is the emphasis on the material ends of life in the West. Religion is treated as a means for procuring worldly peace and prosperity in this life and escaping hell and winning heaven in the next. But to treat Western materialism as purely the result of natural climatic conditions is to simplify this complex issue. This closely approximates to the West's attempt to explain the Indian reality and the Indian character, in terms of the heat and dust of the tropical land. This is perhaps the only instance in the entire novel where Myers's western upbringing interferes in his attempt at understanding the Indian mind.

Amar continues his comparison to assert that the Indian "recognizes that life is appetition, and that appetition is unrest, anxiety, pain and sorrow" and that the real difference between the East and West "is not one of religiousness but of spiritual insight." He perceptively remarks, that the preoccupation with material things has developed the quality of practical reason in the West and that Christianity has developed their hearts. And so he tells Smith rightly, that "it is now time that you developed the spirit that is in you." (p. 436.) This is a very important advice as

> it is a fact of history that civilizations which are based on truly religious forces such as endurance, suffering, passive resistance, understanding, tolerance are long-lived, while those which take their stand exclusively of humanist elements like active reason, power, aggression, progress, make for a brilliant display but are short-lived.[54]

Now the conversation between the two takes a slightly different turn. They move on to religious and aesthetic experiences. Smith believes that the religious is different from the aesthetic, in that the former isolates man and the latter unifies him with his fellow men. Smith asserts: "I see no reason why man should 'worship' anything ... So long as men aspire after goodness, truth and beauty, that is enough." The limitations of an agnostic and humanist like Smith is evident in this statement. The Indian point of view is given expression by Amar:

> 'It is through his moral, rational, and aesthetic intuitions that man apprehends certain goods, but the apprehension of the spiritual order of the universe is apprehended by the spiritual sense, and by that faculty alone.' (p. 441.)

To this, we have the stereotyped response of Smith that because of this preoccupation with the spiritual, the Indian attitude towards life is pessimistic and it has sadly retarded India's "material and social development." Rajah Amar retaliates by saying that "the European's concentration upon the mechanism of civilization" has not brought him any nearer to happiness.

For Rajah Amar, the means of evaluating art is not merely through the aesthetic sense since the greatness of a work of art is inextricably linked to the spiritual truth it communicates. And as such, he rejects Smith's attempt to identify the aesthetic sense with the spiritual, because the former is at the service of the latter. Myers shares Amar's predilections and this is discernible in his rejection of a writer like Proust. Smith's view is also seen to correspond closely with that of Daniyal and his followers. It is this "spiritual vulgarity" in Smith that disturbs Amar. They witness, as a matter of fact, "an insignificant and tawdry entertainment" given by a party of strolling players. Smith watching this play is unable to "see in what respects it was commonplace and merely bad" due to his aesthetic judgement being divorced from moral grounds. And in praising the play, Amar believes that Smith "is certainly wanting in intellectual honesty."(p. 438.)

Amar's disenchantment with Smith is complete in the latter's reaction to the killing of a man by Fazul, an Arab, the horseman of Shaik Mobarek. Actually, the dead man had mocked Fazul at his prayers. Smith, with his faith in goodwill and tolerance as the cures for all the world's ills, cannot comprehend the unequalled and fanatical faith in God which springs out of the splendid aridity of the desert. Indeed Smith opposes Fazul's God directed fanaticism, with his own fanatical scepticism, for there is always a certain intensity of envy and hatred in the unbeliever's attitude to the believer. It is interesting that Amar, though a Buddhist who does not believe in God is able to comprehend and even respect the primitive faith of Fazul. Looking at Smith's behaviour, Amar is now convinced of his rather distasteful pettiness of mind and spirit.

This meeting between Rajah Amar and Smith forms a significant part of the novel. Bantock regards this meeting as an incident "imposed on the structure of the book rather than growing inevitably out of it."[55] There is no doubt that as, D.W.Harding[56] points out, Smith's introduction in the novel is a little too sudden. But he disappears soon afterwards never to appear again in the novel after being present in only 27 pages in a novel of 950 pages. Despite the suddenness and the brevity of his appearance, it should be evident from what has gone before, that his meeting with Amar is of central importance in the novel and more so from the viewpoint of the present study.

The Eastern and Western views of life are examined without any bias and rancour by Myers. And that his sympathies should almost lie wholly, perhaps justifiably, with the Indian position speaks of Myers's fascination for Hinduism in particular and Indian thought in general. It is the Spiritual as opposed to the Material, the Religious and Moral as opposed to the Aesthetic and Vulgar that forms the basis of the differences between Amar and Smith. In such a conflict, for a novelist like Myers with his moral and ethical preoccupations, there was hardly any choice. Smith is an aesthete and materialist besides being superficial and fanatic as well. The East-West encounter can be related in the novel to the relationship between Rajah Amar and Sita and the discussion between Gokal and Sita. Myer's knowledge of Indian religious thought is seen to be both adequate and comprehensive for the purposes of his art. It is not coloured by the western outlook, except for one occasion which has been already referred to. From the above thematic analysis of the novel, and the detailed discussion of the significant meeting between Rajah Amar and Smith, it is evident that India as a religious idea operates in a central way in the novel, *The Near and the Far*.

III

After discussing the significance of the role of Indian religion and thought in the novel, we should now turn to Myers's representation of the historical India, that is, India of Akbar's time during the sixteenth century. This can be rewardingly examined by considering *The Near and the Far* as a historical novel. Despite Myers's plea that this is not a historical novel, we may attempt to establish that it is a kind of 'mixed' historical novel, for it is a curious combination of both the classical and the romantic conventions of the genre. As a matter of fact, *The Times* in its obituary notice of Myers on 10 April 1944, wrote: "In 1929 the growing taste for historical novels ensured success for *The Near and the Far*."[57] Myers insists that fact and fancy are inextricably mixed in the work, and this is seen in the liberty he has taken in the names of some of the characters and with regard to some historical situations. But basically, the historical outline of the novel corresponds closely to the historical events of the sixteenth century India, which goes to show that the novelist paid more attention to the historical reality of India than he actually professed in his prefaces.

In a consideration of *The Near and the Far* as a historical novel, the major problem one encounters is about the use of history by Myers. In other words, the question is what is the function of history in relation to the theme of the novel. To answer this, it is useful to refer to certain theoretical problems relating to the genre of the historical novel. The historical novel uses the past in a meaningful way to illumine the present. Conventionally, the past events highlight the significance of a chosen aspect of life that the novelist wants to convey in his work. It is good to remember that a historical novel is never a mere transcript of historical events, for then it would degenerate into a historical tract. The novelist takes certain liberties with the facts available to him but when he is a little over-indulgent with his liberties, the work borders on romance. Otherwise, historical authenticity is maintained by a thorough fidelity to the basic history.

As Georg Lukács maintains,

> The historical novel ... has to *demonstrate* by *artistic* means that historical circumstances and characters existed in precisely such and such a way.[58]

His book *The Historical Novel* is helpful in understanding the genre in all its complexities. According to him,

> What matters therefore in the historical novel is not the retelling of great historical events, but the poetic awakening of the people who figured in those events. What matters is that we should re-experience the social and human motives which led men to think, feel and act just as they did in historical reality. And it is a law of literary portrayal which first appears paradoxical, but then quite obvious,

> that in order to bring out those social and human motives of behaviour, the outwardly insignificant events, the smaller (from without) relationships are better suited than the great monumental dramas of world history...[59]

These features characterise the work of Sir Walter Scott. And in his historical novels, according to Lukács, the great historical figures are only minor characters in the story. But Scott

> does not stylize these figures, nor place them upon a Romantic pedestal; he portrays them, as human beings with virtues and weaknesses, good and bad qualities. And yet they never create a petty impression.[60]

That is to say, the great historical figures are never idealised in the classical historical novels. And then the historical necessity in Scott's novels is of a very severe kind and this necessity

> is no other-worldly fate divorced from men; it is the complex interaction of concrete historical circumstances in their process of transformation, in their interaction with the concrete human beings, who have grown up in these circumstances, have been very variously influenced by them, and who act in an individual way according to their personal passions.[61]

When the above definition by Lukács is used in this attempt to examine *The Near and the Far* as a historical novel, we find its validity in view of Myers's own intention in writing this novel.

Myers does not attempt to convey "great historical events" of Akbar's India but only creates a poetic picture of people like Akbar, Salim, Daniyal, Shaik Mobarek, Abul Fazl who figured in the major political events of the day. He has given social and human motivations to some characters, especially Akbar, Salim and Daniyal. But he does not always rely, as Scott does, on "outwardly insignificant events" and "smaller relationships" to bring out these motivations. It is in the choice of great historical figures to be only minor characters in the novel that Myers comes very close to the practice of Scott as a historical novelist. For in *The Near and the Far*, we have Akbar, the great emperor, who is portrayed convincingly as a minor character. And as Myers himself claimed, he is "the only person drawn with any regard for historical truth."[62] As in Scott, Akbar emerges not as a romanticized figure but as a *real* human being with all the qualities in him portrayed to give him the appearance of a rounded character.

Finally, the sense of historical necessity in Myers. As in the classical historical novel, we have the complex interaction of concrete historical circumstances with concrete human beings. We notice this predominantly in the characters of Rajah Amar, Prince Jali and Hari Khan who are the major figures that dominate the novel. In all of them, we see how the historical circumstances effect their individual character, while they no doubt also act according to their own inner motives. This is especially true of Amar. He tries to act "in an individual way according to [his] personal passions" but then discovers that the forces of history can never be ignored. In the context of the novel, Rajah Amar is seen making up his mind to give up his Kingship and retire to a monastery in the true Buddhist tradition. He really believed that this personal decision of his had nothing to do with the political realities of the times. To put it differently, he was trying to ignore this concrete interaction of the historical and the personal forces. But then he discovers that this is not possible and hence, the delay in the execution of his decision. It is this process of discovery that constitutes the major part of Amar's characterisation. Thus we realise in the character of Rajah Amar that the individual and historical destinies are intimately connected as in a classical historical novel of the Scott tradition.

There is also another major tradition in the historical novel, that of the romantic writers. Novelists like Flaubert and Conrad Ferdinand Meyer place the action in a far off, exotic land to escape from the present day reality. And according to Lukács,

> ... the *innermost conflicts* of [their] heroes do not grow out of the real historical conditions of the given period, out of the popular life of the period. Instead they are specially modern conflicts of passion and conscience in an individual artificially isolated by capitalist life ...[63]

Meyer's purposes of using the form of the historical novel seem to faintly echo Myers's own intentions in his choice of setting his novel in India:

> 'I use the form of the historical *Novelle* simply and solely to express my experiences and my personal feelings. I prefer it to the "period novel", because it gives me a better mask and puts the reader at a greater distances...'[64]

For the romantic historical novelist, the need to go to the historical past is not to establish a connection between history and the present as in Scott, but only to repudiate the present. And hence, for them,

> ... the representation of historical subjects is simply a question of costume and decoration, simply a means for expressing their subjectivity more fully than ... a contemporary subject would permit.[65]

That would mean, it is only the strangeness of history which holds attraction to them. The well-known positivist sociologist and aesthetician, Guyau, speaks of this relationship with clarity:

> There are various ways of escaping the *trivial*, of embellishing reality for ourselves without falsifying it; and these ways consitute a kind of idealism which is also available to naturalism. They consist above all in the distancing of things or events, whether in time or in space ...[66]

It is of particular interest that Guyau makes no distinction between the temporal and spatial distancing of the artistic subject. As Lukács comments, "What is essential for him is the embellishing effect of the picturesque, the unfamiliar [and] the exotic."[67] That is the reason, why, for the romantic "away" is more important than "where" in their longing to get away from the present. And so in the portrayal of a spatially of temporally remote, exotic world as in Flaubert's case, the intention is "not to investigate the social-historical character of such a world, but to achieve pictorial effect."[68]

When viewed from the perspective of the above mentioned characteristics of the romantic historical novel, *The Near and the Far* no doubt appears closer to the classical genre. However, one cannot but point out certain differences, even though there are significant parallels, between Myers and writers like Flaubert and Meyer. For instance, in Myers, the innermost conflicts of his heroes are a direct product of the historical conditions unlike in the latter novelists. His characters are not artificially isolated in India but then their conflicts are essentially modern, that is, they have a contemporary relevance. Also if Meyer was using the form to give him a mask, Myers's intention was to go into the past to achieve greater distancing not from the reader but from the present itself. The use of the past in Myers does not involve a total repudiation of the present as in the romantic writers, but in his desire to go so far back in time seems to bring him closer to them.

Myers also thought of India as a picturesque and decorative background:

> ... But take India in the reign of Akbar: enough and not too much, is at once outlined on the canvas. You see, I imagine, a vague picture of emperors and elephants, white marble palaces, trees and so on — nothing very precise, put plenty of fine, confused colouring for a background.[69]

As in the case of a novelist of the romantic genre, he seems like one who wants to get away from the present. But there has fallen a shadow between his actual intentions and the completed work as we have it. It is abundantly clear, as seen in the preceding pages, that India is present not merely as a pictorial background but has important thematic significance within the novel. Hence we discern in Myers, the "where" is as significant as the "away". Finally, one can remark that in his desire to get away from the present, Myers resembles Flaubert and Meyer, but the importance that the "where" has in the novel brings him closer to the Scott tradition. And it is because of this combination, that *The Near and the Far* can be rightly described as a curious mixture of both the classical and the romantic historical novels.

After establishing the fact that *The Near and the Far* is a historical novel, it is imperative to assess the picture of Sixteenth century India in a study of this nature. How far is this depiction of India authentic? Does the image of India that emerges from the novel fully tally with the image of the historical India? In the main, the portrait of Akbar will be examined since Myers himself has in his preface to *The Pool of Vishnu* confessed:

> I have a fair measure of justification for my picture of Akbar. I look upon my Akbar as a plausible, although sketchy, reconstruction of the personage very incompletely presented to us in history.[70]

The confidence of Myers is obviously recognisable because even his supposed limitations in the portraiture of Akbar are related to history.

As remarked earlier, Akbar, the chief historical figure, occupies the position of a minor character. True to the Scott tradition, Myers has pictured Akbar's character in all its complexity revealing the different facets of his personality. The strategy adopted by the novelist is fairly simple. There are some objective descriptions of Akbar but it is the views of others about the sovereign that predominate. To begin with, Akbar's physical appearance will be discussed. We see him through the eyes of Prince Jali and Salim. These descriptions can be compared with the historical accounts available to determine the accuracy of Myers's picture. Here is Akbar as seen by his son, Salim:

> 'In his august personal appearance, my father is of middle height, but inclining to be tall ... he is lion-bodied, with a broad chest, and his hands and arms long ... His august voice is very loud, and in speaking and explaining has peculiar richness...'(p. 36.)

Akbar's mode of dressing is referred to by Jali in his meeting with him:

> ... He wore a tunic of silk ...His trousers were of white sarsanet caught up at the ankle with strings of pearls. A small turban fitted right to his head in a mode halfway between the Moslem and the Hindoo. It was decorated with rubies and diamonds...(p. 771.)

It is indeed amazing how strikingly similar Myers's descriptions are to those of the historian, Vincent Smith:

> Akbar ... was a man of moderate stature ... strongly built, neither too slight nor too stout, broad-chested, narrow-waisted, and long-armed ... The eyes sparkled brightly and were 'vibrant like the sea in sunshine' ... His very loud voice was credited with 'a peculiar richness' ... On his head Akbar wore a small tightly rolled turban, made so as to combine Hindu with Mussalman modes. The head-dress was enriched by pearls and other gems of inestimable value ...[71]

The various references to Akbar's character made by others in the novel also bear a very close correspondence to the historical account. His addiction to opium, the divine revelation he had in his thirty-sixth year, his great interest in religious matters, his devotion to work, his fits of anger are all included in the portrait of the emperor that we have in the novel. There are also perceptive remarks made by others about Akbar's real nature. Narsingh views Akbar as a combination of "the soldier, the administrator, the statesman, [and] the despot." (p. 34.) He also believes that Akbar "had never learnt how to deal with his children or with God" which was, as a matter of fact, the real problem for the emperor. Gokal refuses to condemn Akbar for his decision to impose Din Ilahi on his subjects because "ordinary canons do not apply to Men of Destiny."(p. 88.) He regards him "a mystic rather than a thinker" (p. 89.) Mabun considers the emperor as "a practical visionary; he keeps much more in touch with actuality." (p. 471.) The Guru refuses to believe that Akbar is "a conscious hypocrite." There is an interesting comment made by him on Akbar's failures in life. He believes that Akbar

> 'knows how to acquire power, but not how to use it. And even his power over others is of a very unsatisfactory kind. Consider how completely he has failed to establish his New Religion! Consider how he has failed with his sons! And, indeed, with himself.' (p. 640).

But he also remarks that

> '... Akbar has got great strength of character: that is just my point. He follows his own natural bent: he drinks, he gives himself up to fits of religious mysticism, he forgets his audience not merely for hours but even for days at a time. On the whole, he lives the life determined by his fundamental character — not merely one imposed upon him by vanity ruling through the will.'(p. 760.)

In fact, it is perhaps the Guru who makes the correct assessment of Akbar the man and the emperor. Once again, we notice that Akbar's portrait, in spite of its close approximation to the historical account, fails to convince the reader as a character in fiction. Throughout the novel, we have other persons reporting on Akbar's nature and there is only one concrete encounter with him in terms of fictional art. The meeting of the Guru with him is indeed a memorable scene. But apart from that, we never see him in action and that is the reason for the artistic failure of Myers. Finally, a reference to the famous reconciliatory meeting between Akbar and Salim. Myers in his preface to *The Pool of Vishnu* says:

> I cannot take credit for having invented the extraordinary incident of the box on the ear. It is to be found in Indian history books.[72]

We have the following description in the novel of this meeting that is said to have taken place in 1604 at Agra:

> ... Although his arm was still round Salim's shoulders, his face inflamed with rage, was that of a fiend ... Akbar was not standing opposite Salim and glaring at him — and Salim's face wore a sheepish, apprehensive smile. Then suddenly there was a lightning movement, and the hall echoed to a resounding smack. Salim staggered back against the wall, completely dazed by a stinging box on the ear. Again there was a brief, appalling silence, and then Akbar proceeded to overwhelm his son with a flood of contemptuous abuse. 'To think', he shouted, 'that a child of mine should play such a fool's part! With seventy thousand good men behind you you cringing upto me like a starved and beaten dog! Well, I am going to treat you as you deserve' ...Salim was hurried down a short passage leading to a Turkish bath. (pp. 784-85.)

Compare this with the account of Vincent Smith:

> He was received publicly in a certain gallery or verandah with every appearance of cordiality and affection. Suddenly as he prostrated himself reverently, Akbar seized him by the hand and drew him into an inner apartment. The emperor, inflamed by intense passion, then administered several violent slaps on his face, showering upon him bitter reproaches for his unfilial conduct, and mocking him because, when he had 70,000 horsemen at call, he had been fool and coward enough to cast himself at his father's feet as a suppliant. After that scene Akbar, who professed to regard the prince as a patient requiring medical treatment, directed to cure his vitiated tastes, ordered that he should be kept in close custody in a bath-room ...[73]

The close parallels make it clear that Myers was very well read in Indian history. More significantly he does not show the bias, often found in British historians, towards Muslims since as a novelist, he takes a critical look at the character of Akbar.

In addition to the above parallels, there are numerous accurate references to historical facts in the novel, like the great hall that Akbar built where religious debates took place (p. 35.); disaffection among orthodox muslims because of Akbar's less than devout attitude towards Islam (p. 35.); the inscription on the arch of the Gate of Victory at Fatehpur-Sikri (p. 89.); the founding of the new religion Din Ilahi and the oath one had to pronounce while joining it (p. 421.); the way Akbar conducted his court (pp. 684-90.) and the portrait of Abul Fazl (p. 787.) All these certainly give the lie to Myers's contention that his work is not a historical novel. Myers occupies an unique place among British writers who have written on India, since for an authentic fictional image of the Sixteenth century Mughal India, one has nowhere else to turn but to his novel, *The Near and the Far*, though there is a far less satisfactory picture of the times in Flora Annie Steel's novel, *A Prince of Dreamers*, (1908).

IV

The nature of the image of India in *The Near and the Far* needs to be exmined in some more detail. In addition to the creative use of Indian religion and philosophy and historical circumstances, there is another important aspect of the Indian reality present in the novel. It is this aspect which contributes to the creation of a real and recognisable India. That is to mean, the evocation of the physical image of India in the novel. It might seem rather strange, that one should discuss the picture of the land and its people when the writer in question had never set his eyes on the country. The choice of Myers in this study was precisely because of this singularly unique position he occupies among all those Western writers who have written on India.

Hence, an attempt will be made to see how far Myers is successful in his imaginative comprehension of India. We have references in the novel to the Indian landscape, dress, food habits and social conventions that help Myers in his depiction of India. And the characters are recognisably Indian and it is this Indianness that determines their behaviour and attitudes to life. What is remarkable is that all the descriptions relating to these essentially Indian features are mostly concrete and realistic, though, one must add that there are occasions when Myers is rather vague. This, of course, is understandable given his limitations.

We have quite a few descriptions of the Indian landscape in the work. Here are two typical ones:

> Our way ran along a dyke under the spur of the hill that

runs steeply up on the south of Kathiapur and just out for two or three miles into the plain. The country in front of us as far as the eye could see was flat and green — green with the delicate colouring of young crops. For a quarter of an hour we went an thus, then the hill came to an abrupt end, and the new view that opened out took me entirely by surprise. In this direction, the plain became a desert. Right up to the distant southern horizon there was nothing but hard, pebbly sand. And a hot dry wind came off this sand, — a wind that was delicious to me after the enervating air of Kathiapur. (pp. 500-1.)

Nearly every evening at home he would climb up into the tower to gaze upon it. Beyond the roofs, beyond the green of irrigated fields, beyond the glistening palms and the dark clumps of citrus, cypress, and mango — beyond the little world that he knew, there stretched that other world which his eye alone could reach. (p. 7.)

These two descriptions do not have the stamp of India on them. It could have been a picture of any tropical country. For that reason, M.K. Naik[74] is very critical of Myers and compares his descriptions with those of Raja Rao and E.M.Forster and finds them wanting. This comparison would have been quite fair, had Myers, like Forster and Raja Rao, intended such a precision in his pictures. Instead of criticising him for what he did not set out to do, Naik might consider how through these descriptions, Myers is able to create a vague though adequate image of the landscape of India. However, there are moments when he seems to succeed to a greater degree as in this presentation of the early morning scene:

... It seemed long ago since the thin, nasal call of the muezzins had floated through the air, but the creak of an occasional ox-cart still rose from the long, powdery roads below, and he could still hear the familiar croaking of the dusty crows preparing to roost.(p. 10.)

Myers's description of a Hindu temple makes interesting reading:

... a small dilapidated Hindu shrine that stood by itself in the midst of the wood. You could hardly call it a temple, for it was so small, but it had its own enclosure which was separated from the jungle by a low mud wall; and it had a

group of sacred fig trees at the back of it. In days long ago
its squant sun-baked walls must have been gay with paint,
but the colours had nearly all peeled off. The low, round,
whitewashed dome sheltered an altar upon which stood a
primitive lingan. So it was really a temple, although a very
humble one; it still was the home of a god. (p. 230.)

If these details do not make for precision—as a matter of fact, they
do—we have Myers's knowledge of the Hindu tradition of the worship
of Shiva that is quite astounding:

Fresh offerings of marigolds and bilva leaves appeared
nearly every day upon the altar ...(p. 230.)

The mention of bilva leaves at a shrine dedicated to Siva should do the
novelist great credit. There are other references to Hindu gods as
well:

... a shrine to Ganpati. The god of luck! (p. 14.)

... a lie is easily atoned for by a little offering to Saraswati.
(p. 16.)

The universe was full of terrifying and destructive forces.
There was Kali... (p. 18.)

These clearly reveal Myers's unerring aquaintance with the Hindu
pantheon of gods and goddesses.

And now to the people themselves. Notice, for instance, the dress
of men and women. Here is Rajah Amar's apparel:

It put a flush upon his white tunic and touched with a faint
glitter his only ornaments, a jewelled sword-belt and the
aigrette clasp on his turban. (p. 9.)

His wife Sita wore a dress that was

rose-coloured, with a fringe of silver, and a veil of pale
lilac draped her head and shoulders. (p. 9.)

It is, however, the portrait of Gunevati that is very picturesque:

She was wearing cherry-coloured silks, and on her arms
and bosom were silver bangles and precious stones. She
glowed like an idol against the dark forest shades ... In
those fine clothes and with that look in her eyes her proper
place was, in truth, the harem of some royal prince—a

> harem where she could recline all day upon cushions of
> golden tissue, breathing an air of sandal-wood and musk.
> (p. 274.)

He is good in observing minute details like when he writes that Damayanti "began to apply kohl to her eyelashes" (p. 886.) or while he describes Gunevati's reactions to the persistent questioning of Hari about who she is:

> Playing with the folds of her dress, fingering the braids of
> her hair, she gave answers that told him nothing. She was
> as baffling as a stubborn child. (p. 65.)

He has been able to capture this essentially Indian feminine trait accurately. Indeed, neither a Narayan nor a Raja Rao could do better than this, in portraying the Indian woman. Myers is also aware of the subtle differences in the behaviour of Indian women who belong to different regions of the country. The vehement and tempestuous outbursts of Lalita, who belongs to the North Western province elicits the following acceptable generalisation from the novelist, if we can forgive him the outlandish name Lalita for a North-Western frontier woman:

> These mid-Asian women have a quality of independence,
> self- assertion and violence, which contrasts strongly with
> the age-long submissiveness of the Hindu. (p. 475.)

We also have valid generalisations about the country itself. The all too powerful influence of India on people is referred to in this one:

> Men cannot live in this country without becoming what the
> country wills. (p. 17.)

And this one is quite true though there have been occasional exceptions:

> India has always been full of holy men preaching the
> religion of freedom and equality, but without producing
> any *practical* results. (p. 725.)

What is obviously surprising is Myers's awareness of the social and cultural realities of India, especially the terrible status of the untouchables and also their relationship with the upper castes. While Gokal, the brahmin in walking in grief, he encounters

> ... the gaze of two large brown eyes that were staring at him

> in innocent amazement. It was a little, low-caste lad of ten, who was lost in wonder at the sight of a venerable brahmin stumbling along with a face bathed in tears. (p. 51.)

This is indeed realistic, considering the hierarchieal nature of the Indian society and the social convention that an untouchable should not cross the path of a brahmin. There is another incident where the low caste colony is attacked for defiling the water streams used by the upper castes. The picture as seen by Jali is shockingly authentic:

> ... Only a few of the huts had been burnt, the others having escaped owing to the absence of wind. But the dirt, squalor, and destitution were beyond belief. Before these wretched homes, men, women, and children were standing about apathetically; it was evident that they were without the spirit to resume the business of living. Riding past them, he came to a group in which something seemed to be going on, and, looking down over the heads of the crowd, he saw a little old man kneeling beside one of those who had received a beating. The back of the victim showed fearful lacerations, and others in the same plight were squatting near by, awaiting their turn for treatment. (p. 681.)

Such a scene is almost an everyday occurrence in the India of today. There is no spirit left in the untouchables and the sheer apathy in them, to their condition is what characterises their situation in life. It is this depiction of the utterly helpless attitude of the low castes that makes for the sureness of touch in Myers's handling of such a scene.

And then there are numerous significant details that contribute to the solidity of the picture of India that emerges from the novel. Myers's acute perception is evident, for instance, in this little detail as observed by Amar:

> I led the way out of the house. Her palanquin-bearers had gathered some friends about them, and by the light of their lanterns were playing a betting-game by the roadside. They got up, spat into their hands, and made ready. (p. 477.)

There are scenes of Daniyal slicing a mango on his plate; Prince Jali cutting water-melons and Hari Khan drinking arrack. In addition, there are abundant references to the flora and fauna of India — Khas-

khas grass, orange, pepper tree, jasmine [once wrongly spelt as "jessamine" (p. 131.)] marigolds, bilva leaves, pipal boughs, water lilies, rhododendrons, tamarind, rice, cardamom; peacocks, kokila-bird, bul-bul, snakes, pigeons, kites, crows, cat-bears, monkeys, lions, elephants and bear cubs.

The influence of the setting on the novelist's use of language is hardly noticed in *The Near and the Far*. What we have is, only an occasional mention of Hindustani words. Interestingly, it is found when the characters swear. Salim swears "by Shaitan"; Guru and Hari swear by Rama; Gokal's servant "salaamed" Amar and the peasants cry, "Ahi! ahi!" Sometimes, Myers uses Indian terms such as *upacharas* (of the vamacharis), *vina, rishis,* and *baniya,* all in italics.

In spite of such overwhelming evidence of facts that have contributed to the creation of a genuine Indian atmosphere in the novel, there have been criticisms of Myers's deviations from the actual India. No doubt, a few of the things that occur in the novel seem anachronistic. Dantawat ramarks, "Not a penny left." (p. 551.) But we may say that the expression is still current among educated Indians of today. Some others are plainly incredible like Damayanti telling her friend Ratnivara: "Well, tell him that I am naked in the water, but that he can come, if he likes." (p. 811.) Even some of the names sound very strange. Hari Khan is a name literally out of the blue. M.K.Naik is very critical of Myers for this lapse and thinks that "the fact that he marries Ambissa, the sister of Rajah Amar who is a Buddhist show(s) that Myers assumed Hari Khan to have been a Hindu."[75] But, at this point, it should be recalled that Myers believed that his picture of India was made up of both fact and fancy. And so, he occasionally gets fanciful, hence these deviations. However, in this instance, Naik is ignoring the historical facts. Hari Khan is indeed a Muslim,[76] and is meant by the novelist to be so, and his marriage to Ambissa does not make him a Hindu. The practice of a Muslim marrying a Rajput was not all that uncommon during the time of Akbar, for the emperor himself had taken a Rajput wife. And the son born to Hari Khan and Ambissa is known by the name of Ali. Similarly, Naik is critical of Rajah Chandre's name. In his anxiety to point out this lapse in Myers, he ignores that the name has been correctly spelt as Chandra elsewhere in the novel (p. 575.).

Both M.K. Naik and K. Viswantham[77] are also critical of certain behaviour patterns in some of the characters in the novel. For instance, Jali's continuing to like Hari Khan in spite of his knowledge that he is his mother's lover, and Rajah Amar not fighting a duel with

Hari Khan when he discovers that he is in love with Sita. Such criticisms are the result of a notion that there is a standard Indian behaviour and that there cannot be possibly any deviations. Life in India or anywhere else for that matter is not such a simple phenomenon. Beside, in any novel, the writer has the licence to make departures but the basis for them should be found within the novel and not outside it. In these two cases, the critics bring in their understanding of Indian behaviour from outside the novel entirely ignoring its framework.

In the first case, we see Jali obsessed by the question of his relationship with the world. He finds the worlds of his father and mother very strange. Because of his inability to comprehend their lives clearly and his belief that he has not understood his own world, he is convinced that he has no right to interfere with their preferences—here it is his mother's preference for a man like Hari Khan. In the second case, Rajah Amar is, no doubt, disturbed by the news of the amorous relationship between his wife and Hari Khan. If he had fought a duel as demanded by K. Viswanatham, it would have gone against the very grain of his character. On the contrary, like a true Buddhist who has made up his mind to renounce life, he tells Gokal that Sita is free to do whatever she likes after his departure, even marry again. So we find that Myers has given adequate motives within the novel to Jali and Amar for their actions.

Even when Myers tampers with some historical facts, as in the case of transforming the Muslim saint Salim Chisti into the Hindu Guru, Bhupendra, it has an artistic function in the scheme of the novel. A Hindu saint can easily take on the burden of being Myers's mouthpiece and fulfil the novelist's philosophic intentions. And so in the ultimate analysis, it can be said on the evidence of having considered *The Near and the Far* as a historical novel, and then accounted for its authenticity as an Indian novel, that Myers is perhaps the only English novelist who has explored, within the limitations of his fictional art, India both as an idea and as a country in terms of its history.

V

Though this study mainly attempt to discover the image of India in Myers's works, it cannot entirely ignore a consideration of Myers as a novelist. This is particularly imperative in view of the disitinctive nature of his genius. Whether such a genius was suited to meet the demands made by the novel form is the question for which an answer should be sought. The major problem that one encounters in the novel, *The Near and the Far* is that of the genre. It can be viewed as a philosophical novel, a psychological novel, a historical novel and even as a novel of ideas. That is why Gai Eaton remarked that, the novel is "neither fish, flesh or fowl."[78] And this accounts for the confusion in the mind of the reader while responding to this work. But it could perhaps be said with some certainty that if there is one particular genre that would describe *The Near and the Far* accurately, it is the philosophical novel.

There are certain general features that characterise a novel irrespective of the genre to which it belongs. In a novel, more than other literary forms, the emphasis is on the presentation of experience in all its totality. The individual experience is invariably related to and is also the outcome of social reality. That is to mean, the interaction of the individual and the society occupies a central position in a novel. Hence, the portrayal of the external world is as important as the depiction of individual feelings in a fictional work. Then there are the relationships between various individuals where significant interactions take place. So, in a novel, we notice a close connection between incidents, characters and the theme. In a philosophical novel, we expect the philosophy to generate credible and adequate events and characters which in turn reinforce or vitalize the abstract and general conceptions present in the work. And hence we will have to assess *The Near and the Far* as a novel which tries to synthesise and balance these two elements — the abstract and the concrete.

From a reading of *The Near and the Far,* it is evident that Myers did not have the technical interest in the novel form that one normally associates with great novelists. His concern was more with the ethical and moral preoccupations about life that were to be expressed in his novels. It should be kept in mind, that the mode of expression *did* receive some attention from Myers but not as much as it does at the hands of a serious novelist. However, his themes are so compellingly relevant that they demand recognition. He shares with the writers in the great tradition of the English novel, "a vital capacity for experience, a kind of reverent openness before life, and a marked moral intensity."[79]

And it is this that has made critics like F.R.Leavis, and D.W. Harding ignore his technical limitations and recognise his significance as a writer. F.R. Leavis believes that *"The Root and the Flower* is a very remarkable novel. Anyone seriously interested in literature is likely to have found the first reading a memorable experience and to have found also that repeated re-readings have not exhausted the interest."[80] Harding puts it more succinctly when he remarks that "it is the maturity of his interests and outlook that gives Myers his primary appeal."[81]

In the tetralogy, *The Near and the Far,* the first three parts that appeared together under the title *The Root and the Flower* is more successful as a novel than the fourth part, *The Pool of Vishnu.* In the first three parts, there is seen a fairly close relation between the character, action and setting which in turn contributes to the thematic development. No doubt, the focus in his novels, in the main, on two characters, Rajah Amar and Prince Jali. In portraying these characters and their development, Myers seems to conspicuously rely, unlike other major novelists, more on their mental process. As a result, the inner life of the characters is greatly highlighted. But it is also not that the external world is lost sight of completely. For instance, in the life of Rajah Amar, there is a clear interaction between his life and the prevalent political situation. The political struggle between Salim and Daniyal to succeed Akbar is convincingly presented. We see both of them as persons and we also have the delineation of their strengths and weaknesses as possible future rulers in the views expressed by their supporters and detractors alike, namely those of Mabun Das, Shaik Mobarek, Gokal and Hari Khan. This contributes to the solidity of the picture of the external world which in turn makes Amar's personal crisis so much more real. Amar, no doubt, acts according to his ethical preoccupations that befits a Buddhist, but this is, like in all great works of fiction, not divorced from his conduct in the world of men. And so we see how other individuals and external events delay his personal decision to retire from active life. In other words, Amar's character is realistically portrayed as in other great novels.

In Prince Jali's character development, there are three clearly marked stages. In the first, he comes into contact with Gunevati who "represents a deeper animalism"[82] latently present in all human beings. Her character is credibly sketched by Myers, specially because she is seen as a follower of the Vamacharis. But it is the particular relationship that Jali enjoys with her that troubles the reader: the main reason being his age, Jali is hardly is twelve years old. Moreover, if it is the physical nature of the relationship that disturbs the reader, he is also confronted by another problem, that of the narrative method. What predominates in Jali's character is the "retrospective interpretation of adolescence."[83] We read pages and pages without anything really happening. What we have is a narrative that is essentially reflective in nature, and the absence of concrete situations produces a feeing of monotony. Myers uses "the quasi-musings, half soliloquy from a character and half author's comment"[84] to trace the inner thought process of Jali. His encounter with Daniyal and the Pleasance of Arts is convincing but once again his reflections on the camp seem to be too mature for his age.

But it is in third stage that we have serious difficulties. In his numerous meetings with the Guru who clarifies his various doubts, the relationship between the two is seen to be very different from what we normally find in a novel. In fiction, we always get the impact of one character on another. This is seen, for example, in the interaction between Gunevati and Jali. But here, "the to – and fro – of relationship in direct physio-psychological contact"[85] is conspicuous by its absence. The Guru, thanks to his wisdom, makes a series of valid generalisations about life. But, despite their validity, they do not emerge in the novel either as a result of his meetings with different people or because of the nature of the world in which he lives. That is to say, the Guru is not presented as *character* in a novel but more as an *interpreter* of life. The only notable exception is his personal meeting with Akbar which is one of the memorable scenes in the novel.

And so, in conclusion, it can be said that Jali's character is not very successful as a picture of adolescence, though very convincing as a picture of the mental development of an individual. But, we may ask that since he is only about twelve years old at the beginning of the novel and not more than fourteen at the end, isn't Jali invested with greater significance for a boy of his age? This, of course, offers a clue to Myers's interests. On being questioned on this point by K. Viswanatham, Bantock wrote to him, "... In fact he [Jali] behaves in a rather more mature manner than his chronological age would seem to make possible. I do not think Myers was particularly interested in the minutiae of novel writing and he was quite capable of this sort of confussion."[86] True, Myers was more interested in dealing with "the problem of the sensitive individual's feeling of isolation"[87] in the character of Jali. And in doing full justice to this problem, he overlooks, what perhaps constituted for him minor irritants, like the question of the age of a character. On accounts of this, the high degree of realism that one expects to find in a novel is glaringly absent in *The Near and the Far*. That is why, Jali's quest in the novel appears to be "the concern of late adolescence and early manhood, rather than childhood"[88] as his age would warrant us to believe.

Another feature of Myers's writing is that he depends more on statement than enactment to convey truths about life. He prefers to *state* things when it would have undoubtedly been more dramatic had he presented them as incidents in concrete terms. The result is that we have innumerable generalised descriptions in the course of the novel. This has led to a greater abstraction which makes the reader of a work of fiction rather uneasy. This is not to suggest that there are no attempts made by the novelist to concretise experiences through particular situations. But they seem to progressively decrease and almost disappear entirely in *The Pool of Vishnu*. This is felt all the more keenly because of the predominantly reflective tone of the novel. One simple illustration of his generalised description should make this point clear. This is the moment when Jali is displeased with his cousin Ali and a scene with dramatic potential is given up in preference to a tamer account of it :

> But he was boiling with rage, and Ali's curiosity offered him his chance. He set about teasing his questioner with hints and partial disclosures, and then, when he saw that nothing could annoy him more than the naked truth, he looked Ali mockingly in the face and made a bare-faced avowal. (pp. 330-31.)

It is also true that Myers was more interested in ideas. We have the feeling on many occasions that in Myers, ideas precede characters so much so, that critics like Marchesa Iris Origo[89] and Leavis[90] regard him as a writer who uses the novel as a vehicle for his ideas. This should not be taken to mean that he wrote the novel of ideas of the Huxleyan kind. Curiously, Myers himself was aware of his limitations and felt that "the novel form forces one rather into unfairness ... The most one can hope to do in a book of this kind is to be 'suggestive' — a compromise between philosophy and fiction, it was foredoomed from the start to great defects."[91] As a matter of fact, he has pinned down his failure very rightly to his inability to coalesce art and philosophy in his novel. Abstract thinking in the novel to a very considerable degree mostly in *The Pool of Vishnu* is undigested by art. And it is this inability of Myers which has made Leavis view him as one who "is not primarily a novelist."[92] But as remarked earlier on, Leavis rated his work very high in view of his serious moral concerns. No doubt, Leavis was concessive to Myers, a favour he seldom showed to any other writer. He always believed that a great writer, while exploring the possibilities of life also explored the possibilities of art. This did happen in Myers, but not to the extent seen in the truly great writers. His mind revelled in abstractions and perhaps was more suited to philosophy than to writing fiction.

It should, however, be added that Myers was endowed with remarkable powers of description. Whether he is describing persons like Akbar and Gunevati, or the Indian landscape, or a storm as seen from the castle of Sesodia, he is equally effective. Descriptions of Daniyal trampling the cat to death and the vision of the tongueless mouth of Gunevati are indeed brilliant. Since such descriptions are too few and far between in such a long novel as *The Near and the Far,* Bantock asserts that "he was never interested in his descriptions; and despite the praise they have received that all too often become little more than backcloths."[93] He also believed that "the 'spirit of place' that Lawrence had so profoundly, is beyond the scope of Myers,"[94] though this is not wholly true, for India emerges as a living presence in the novel. The pulse of Indian life, a little faint perhaps, is well captured by Myers. The landscape is Indian, the characters that inhabit this landscape are recognizably Indian in their habits, conventions and attitudes towards life. India is not merely a colourful backcloth in this novel as is the case in his other novels. We see the setting impinge on the consciousness of the characters and affect their personalities. The 'spirit of the place' is captured mainly through the assimilation of Indian philosophy and religion in addition to the various references to the country as has been dealt with in great detail in the foregoing pages. Myers's concern with the problems of living in the modern world is probed in greater detail in *The Near and the Far* with India providing answers to the numerous questions raised in such an exploration. The backdrop gets totally merged into the action.

Why did Myers choose to set the novel in India? On the evidence of the preceding pages, it is beyond doubt that India cannot be referred to as a mere device for achieving detachment as he claims in his prefaces. And yet again, Bantock perceptively provides the answer:

> ...Concern for eastern ideas is, of course, one of the marks of the eclecticism of our age; with the decay of Christian

dogmatic beliefs we have sought consolation in what at best must be an inadequate comprehension — because we are not 'of' the culture — of other religious approaches. This eclecticism points, perhaps, to one more aspect of our decaying moral order; it makes the particularly 'subjective' emphasis of Myers just mentioned more than usually difficult to transcend because there is no assured moral or religious tradition within which the writer can work. His own personal integrity inevitably bears too heavy a burden because there is no body of vital ideas and beliefs in the society of our time on which he can depend.[95]

Myers, profoundly dissatisfied with the decaying moral order of his times had to turn back both in space and time to the India of the Sixteenth century. It was perhaps appropriate, for Akbar too was in search of new religion that would answer to the inner spiritual needs of man. In Rajah Amar, Myers found that the Budhdhist doctrine provided the solution to the problem of social responsibility in an individual. And in projecting Jali's mental growth, he relies on Indian religion and thought to a great degree in addition to the philodophy of Martin Buber.

In conclusion, it should be reiterated that Myers was successful in portraying the Mughal India of the Sixteenth century mainly because he relied extensively on using India as an idea and also as a pictorial setting. The latter helped him evoke the country in all its vividness. This made the world of India real and the people living in it unerringly Indian. This, in turn, created the necessary atmosphere for the former, that is, India as an idea to function artistically within the novel. It is in Indian religion and philosophy that the idea of India is preserved. Physical accounts of the country might vary but the essence of India is timeless and can only be captured through an awareness and understanding of Indian thought. Myers brought his wide reading of Indian Philosophical systems to good use in *The Near and the Far* and realised this truth. And in this he found the key to unlock the mystery that lay at the heart of India, a key that was denied to most Western writers who wrote on India.

Notes

1. G.H.Bantock, "L.H.Myers and Bloomsbury" in *The Pelican Guide to English Literature,* ed. Boris Ford (1961; rpt. Harmondsworth: Penguin Books, 1970), VII. p. 271.
2. L.H.Myers, *The Root and the Flower* (London: Jonathan Cape, 1935), p. 6.
3. L.H.Myers, Quoted in *The Pelican Guide to English Literaeture,* ed. Boris Ford, VII. p. 7.
4. G.H.Bantock "L.H.Myers and Bloomsbury," *The Pelican Guide,* VII, p. 272.
5. Ibid.
6. D.W.Harding "The Work of L.H.Myers," *Scrutiny,* III, No. 1. (June 1934), p. 44
7. Ibid., p. 49.
8. L.H.Myers, *The Near and the Far* (1943; rpt. London: The Reprint Society, 1956), p. 5. Subsequent quotations referred to in the text are from this edition.
9. Myers, *The Root and the Flower,* p.5.
10. A.J.Greenberger, *The British Image of India: A Study in Literature of Imperialism 1880-1960* (London: Oxford University Press, 1969), p. 85.
11. D.W.Harding, "The Work of L.H.Myers," *Scrutiny,* p. 50.
12. G.H.Bantock, "L.H.Myers and Bloomsbury," *The Pelican Guide,* VII, p. 273.
13. Quoted by S. Radhakrishnan, *Our Heritage* (New Delhi: Orient Paperbacks, 1973), p. 65.
14. Quoted by S. Radhakrishnan, *Our Heritage,* pp. 64-65.
15. Ibid., p. 66.
16. Keynes, Quoted in G.H.Bantock, "L.H.Myers and Bloomsbury", *The Pelican Guide,* VII, p. 276.
17. Gai Eaton, *The Richest Vein: Eastern Tradition and Modern Thought* (London: Faber & Faber Ltd., 1949), p. 159.
18. D.W.Harding, *"The Root and the Flower", Scrutiny,* IV, No. 1 (June 1935), p. 8
19. M.Hiriyanna, *Outlines of Indian Philosophy,* p. 125.
20. D.W. Harding, *The Root and the Flower,* Scrutiny, p. 80.
21. D.W.Harding, "A Statement of Positives: *The Pool of Vishnu", Scrutiny,* IX, No. 2 (September 1940), p. 161.
22. Bantock, "L.H.Myers and Bloomsbury", *The Pelican Guide,* VII, p. 273.
23. S.Radhakrishnan, *Eastern Religions and Western Thought.* p. 77.
24. M.Hiriyanna, *Outlines of Indian Philosophy,* p. 137.
25. Ibid., p. 151.
26. G.H.Bantock, L.H.Myers: A Critical Study (London: Jonathan Cape, 1956), pp. 44-45.

27. A.L.Bashan, *The Wonder that was India* (1954; rpt. Calcutta: Rupa & Co., 1982), p. 340.
28. A.J.Greenberger, *The British Image of India*, p. 113.
29. Margaret Rudd, "L.H.Myers and 'The Near and the Far'", *Mandrake*, (1953), p. 203.
30. Swami Prabhavananda and Frederick Manchester, trans., *The Upanishads: Breath of the Eternal* (1948; rpt. New York: Mentor Books, 1957), pp. 68-69.
31. S.Radhakrishnan, *Religion and Culture* (New Delhi: Orient Paperbacks, 1968), p. 110.
32. M.Hiriyanna, *Outlines of Indian Philosophy*, p. 375.
33. Ibid., p. 381.
34. Ibid., p. 120.
35. Ibid., p. 121.
36. Letter to Gai Eaton, 21 May 1943, quoted in G.H.Bantock, *L.H.Myers: A Critical Study*, p. 134.
37. M.Hiriyanna, *Outlines of Indian Philosophy*, p. 75.
38. M.K.Naik, "John Bull and the Idol in the Pool: India in L.H.Myers's *The Pool of Vishnu*," in *The Image of India in Western Creative Writing*, ed. M.K.Naik, S.K.Desai and S.T.Kallapur, (Dharwar: Karnatak University and Macmillan India Limited, 1971), p. 199.
39. M.Hiriyanna, *Outlines of Indian Philosophy*, p. 127.
40. Ibid., p. 24.
41. Quoted in S. Radhakrishnan, *Our Heritage*, p. 89.
42. S.Radhakrishnan, *Our Heritage*, p. 94.
43. D.W.Harding, "A Statement of Positives: *The Pool of Vishnu*," p. 163.
44. Martin Buber, quoted in *100 Great Thinkers*, ed. Jay E.Greene (1967; rpt. New York: Pocket Books, 1969), p. 552.
45. Martin Buber, quoted in John Macquarrie, *Existentialism* (1973; rpt. Harmondsworth: Penguin Books, 1976), p. 108.
46. M.Hiriyanna, *Outlines of Indian Philosophy*, p. 75.
47. Juan Mascaro, trans., *The Upanishads* (1965; rpt. Harmondsworth: Penguin Books, 1973), p. 49.
48. S.Radhakrishnan, *Eastern Religions and Western Thought*, p. 66.
49. Ibid., p. 65.
50. M.Hiriyanna, *Outlines of Indian Philosophy*, p. 79.
51. S.Radhakrishnan, *Eastern Religions and Western Thought*, pp. 92-93.
52. Ananda K.Coomaraswamy, *The Dance of Shiva* (1918; rpt. New Delhi: Sagar Publications, 1968), p. 76.
53. A.J.Greenberger, *The British Image of India*, p. 85.
54. S.Radhakrishnan, *Eastern Religions and Western Thought*, p. 254.
55. G.H.Bantock, *L.H.Myers: A Critical Study*, p. 77.
56. D.W.Harding, "The Root and the Flower", **Scrutiny**, p. 80.
57. Quoted in Ronald Bottrall, "L.H.Myers", *A Revieiw of English Literature*, 2 (April 1961), p. 52.
58. Georg Lukács, *The Historical Novel* (1962; rpt. Harmondsworth: Penguin Books, 1969), p. 45.
59. Ibid., p. 44.
60. Ibid., p. 47.

61. Ibid., p. 64.
62. L.H.Myers, *The Pool of Vishnu* (London: Jonathan Cape, 1940), p. 10.
63. Lukács, p. 269.
64. Quoted in Lukács, p. 269.
65. Likács, p. 277.
66. Quoted in Lukács, Ibid.
67. Lukács, p. 277.
68. Ibid., p. 279.
69. Myers, *The Root and the Flower*, p. 5.
70. Myers, *The Pool of Vishnu*, p. 10.
71. Vincent A.Smith, *Akbar The Great Mogul, 1542-1605* (1892; rpt. London: Oxford University Press, 1927), pp. 333-34.
72. Myers, *The Pool of Vishnu*, p. 10.
73. Vincent Smith, *Akbar The Great Mogul*, p. 319.
74. M.K.Naik, pp. 192-94.
75. Ibid., p. 189.
76. For instance, Iqbal Narayan, a former Vice-Chancellor of Benares Hindu University, is a Hindu.
77. K.Viswanatham, *India in English Fiction* (Waltair: Andhra University Press, 1971), pp. 173-74.
78. Gai Eaton, *The Richest Vein*, p. 149.
79. F.R.Leavis, *The Great Tradition* (1948; rpt. Harmondsworth: Penguin Books, 1972), p. 18.
80. Ibid., p. 15. f.n.
81. D.W.Harding, "The Work of L.H.Myers," p. 49.
82. G.H.Bantock, p. 49.
83. D.W.Harding, "The Work of L.H.Myers," *Scrutiny*, p. 54.
84. Ibid., p. 55.
85. G.H.Bantock, p. 110.
86. Quoted in K.Viswanatham, *India in English Fiction*, p. 194.
87. G.H.Bantock, p. 2.
88. Ibid., p. 70.
89. "He regarded his novels merely as a vehicle for his *ideas* — and was *not* interested in the novel-form in itseilf — or even in most of his characters, except as a peg to the ideas they represented" — Marchesa Iris Origo to G.H.Bantock in *L.H.Myers: A Critical Study*. p. 131.
90. "Myers hasn't the great novelist's technical interest in method and presentment; he slips very easily into using the novel as a vehicle." — F.R.Leavis in *The Great Tradition*, p. 15, f.n.
91. Letter to Olaf Stapledon, 19 Oct 1934, in G.H.Bantock, *L.H.Myers: A Critical Study*, p. 133.
92. F.R.Leavis, *The Great Tradition*, p. 15. f.n.
93. G.H.Bantock, p. 110.
94. *Ibid.*
95. *Ibid.*, pp. 87-88.

Chapter - 4
Raja Rao

Raja Rao born in 1909 at Hassan had his early education at Hyderabad and Aligarh. He went to France for his higher studies and was educated at the Universities of Montepellier and Paris. He spent a number of years in India in the 40's and 50's until he finally went to America in 1961 where he has since been teaching Indian Philosophy in the University of Texas at Austin. During his various visits to India, Raja Rao came under the influence of Gandhi, Sri Aurobindo, Ramana Maharishi and Pandit Taranath with most of whom he spent considerable stretches of time in their ashramas. The climax to his spiritual quest was his meeting with Sri Atmananda Guru at Trivandrum in 1943. Like the true Guru, he clarified Raja Rao's metaphysical doubts and revealed to him the path of self-knowledge. Raja Rao has been visiting India regularly, almost every year, to replenish his spiritual roots.

It is this profound awareness of his Indian heritage along with his being an expatriate that gives Raja Rao an unique place among Indian writers in English. His own conception of literature as a spiritual discipline is important. Here is his elaborate statement in this regard:

> For me literature is *sadhana* (spiritual discipline) — not a profession but a vocation... my writing is mainly the consequence of metaphysical life, what I mean by *sadhana*. I had this conflict in me — should a man be a writer first and then a man, secondarily, or a man first and a writer afterwards? And by man I mean the metaphysical entity. So the idea of literature as anything but a spiritual experience ... is outside my perspective. I really think that only through dedication to the absolute or metaphysical principle can one be fully creative... Literature as *sadhana* is the best life for a writer. The Indian tradition which links the word with the Absolute *(sabdabrahman)* has clearly shown the

various ways by which one can approach literature, without the confusions that arise in the mind of the Western writer viewing life as an intellectual adventure. Basically, the Indian outlook follows a deeply satisfying, richly rewarding and profoundly metaphysical path...[1]

The entire corpus of his writings has to be viewed in the light of this manifesto.

A chronological study of Raja Rao's works reveals a clear pattern in his portrayal of India. The image of India which is concrete to start with, grows gradually into an image that is almost entirely ideational. As a writer of fiction, Raja Rao began in his early twenties, with short stories which culminated in the novel *Kanthapura*. Then followed a long gap of over twenty years before his second novel *The Serpent and the Rope* was published in 1960, soon followed by *The Cat and Shakespeare* in 1965. At the same time a French translation of *Comrade Kirillov* was published while the original English version came out as late as 1976.

It is now a cliché to speak of India as a country of villages but the cliché has a very important truth in it and Raja Rao was deeply aware of this. As one who knows his village with the intimacy of an insider, he is able to create in his short stories an authentic image of rural India, evoking the Indian village with all its myths, superstitions and rituals with tremendous power. Significantly, in *The Cow of the Barricades*, his first collection of nine short stories, all except one, are set in rural India.

'Javni',[2] the first story in the volume, has an epigraph from the Kannada saint-poet *Kanakadasa*:

> Caste and caste and caste, you say,
> What caste has he who knoweth God?

Ramu the narrator of the story through whose eyes we see Javni informs that she is,

> past forty, a little wrinkled beneath the lips and with strange, rapturous eyes. Her hair was turning white, her breasts were fallen and her bare, broad forehead showed pain and widowhood. (p. 3.)

From the moment he sees her, Ramu is drawn to her completely. He learns from her of her life of suffering and misery which she has endured with touching devotion to Talakamma, the goddess of the village. She is glad that she has served with loyalty all the revenue inspectors of Malkad and her only source of happiness is her brother's child.

There is no doubt a certain amount of idealizing in the portrayal of Javni, but it is in Ramu's response that the story is lifted to a higher plane, thus avoiding simplification. Though Javni is "almost a mother" to Ramu's sister, she is made to eat in the byre in total darkness unable to see what she is eating. This is, of course, because of her low caste. What is, however, realistic is the way Javni herself reacts to this abominable practice without any protest or any touch of regret, and certainly not with any self-pity. But in the response of the narrator to this inhuman practice, we hear the voice of protest of a modern progressive individual. Ramu the sensitive being feels most acutely for her plight:

> I heard an owl hoot somewhere, and far, far away, somewhere too far and too distant for my rude ears to hear, the world wept its silent suffering plaints. Had not the Lord said: 'Whenever there is misery and ignorance, I come?' Oh, when will that day come, and when will the Conch of Knowledge blow?
>
> I had nothing to say. My heart beat fast. And, closing my eyes, I sank into the primal flood, the moving fount of Being. Man, I love thee.
>
> Javni sat and ate. The mechanical mastication of the rice seemed to represent her life, her whole existence. (pp.11-12.)

Raja Rao could not have thought of a more apt symbol than the "mechanical mastication of the rice" to illustrate her dreary life. Writing at a time of social and political upheaval in the country he is committed to winning attention to the plight of one like Javni. And when the time to leave Malkad approaches, Javni is so grief-stricken that she is seen weeping for one whole week. The story avoids the pitfalls of sentimentality as Ramu looks upon Javni as an integral part of the world — the sky, the tree and the river — around him even though "she seemed so small, so insignificant."

What makes the story a truly moving account of the life of a low caste Indian village woman is the author's keen awareness of Javni's actual living conditions and his ability to portray them without recourse to either sentimentality or idealization.

As in 'Javni', Raja Rao is concerned with the traditional Indian society in his portrayal of a widow belonging to the upper caste in the story, 'Akkayya'. The tragedy of Akkayya is presented with "the Charles Lamb kind of humour and pathos."[3] While her "horoscope foretold a most brilliant marriage," she is destined to be a widow, for she loses her husband when she is only eight or nine years old. And the rest of her life is one long poignant story "as though she were born with a vessel at her waist and a broom in her hand." (p. 79.) Her stepson sends her back to her house making false accusations and she is, of course, not wanted by her brothers. The only redeeming fact of her life is that "God always supplied her with orphan children" and she lovingly looks after them thus fulfilling her dormant instinct of motherhood. But "the thwarted life of Akkayya which is not allowed to run its natural course avenges on itself with cannibalistic self-destruction."[4] It is indeed a terrible disease that she is afflicted with: "She stinks like a manure-pit." When she finally dies, the utter inhumanity of the reactions of the close relatives is shocking:

> 'Could they not have had the sense to hide it from us for *the* six months? What a nuisance!'
>
> 'Idiots!' howled my father.
>
> 'Perfect idiots,' spat my stepmother.
>
> 'Who is Akkayya?' asked my little sister.
>
> 'A grandmother whom you have never seen, and thank heavens you will never see,' said my stepmother and walked away into the kitchen.
>
> We duly bathed, changed our clothing, and after dinner we went to the cinema. (p. 95.)

None of them, including her three brothers are inclined to perform her obsequies. At last, one of her brothers in an act of kindness or rather as brotherly duty gives a brahmin a few rupees to perform the 'necessary' ceremonies by himself though one is not sure whether "the Brahmin did it." But Raja Rao concludes the story most touchingly: "Anyway, here I have written the story of Akkayya, maybe her only funeral ceremony." (p. 96.)

The value of such a story lies in Raja Rao's ability to dramatise the continuous changes in traditional Indian society. He is able to perceive the breakdown of the stable family system that was once the pride of our culture, and in doing so, his sympathies are obviously with the poor victim of cruel neglect, Akkayya. And that this has been brought out in the story effectively without resorting to melodrama is a sure sign of his maturity as an artist, even while he was in his early twenties. While in 'Javni', the plight of the widow results in the narrator explicitly criticising the caste system, no such comment is necessary here, for Akkayya's own life is a living testimony to the cruelty and inhumanity present within one's family. In both these stories, Raja Rao is reacting passionately against the signs of decadence, injustice and brutality in our culture.

The life of a bania couple Motilal and Beti Bai is the stuff of the story, 'The Little Gram Shop'. Motilal, "the wretched bania... poor as a cur in a pariah street" ends up as a rich money-lender whose greed is proverbial. It is ironical, however, that at the height of his prosperity he should be run over by a motor car when he has almost gone mad because one of his borrowers has disappeared. The life of the bania couple is appalling with all its dirt and squalor. Beti Bai is sadistically abused by her husband and her suffering inevitably brings to mind the character of Akkayya. But her life has its little compensations as well. "These were the gifts of religion and the simple folk's innate sense of art, in actual living."[5] There is the green parrot in the cage, her "only solace," her strange affection for the narrator Ananda to whom she would give a "handful of salted grams with such trust and tenderness." She dies of plague at the end, and only the parrot survives adding a poignant touch to the realistic portrayal of a domestic tragedy in 'The Little Gram Shop'.

In this collection, there are two stories, 'Companions and Kanakapala, Protector of Gold', both serpent legends. "The serpent is a friend or an enemy" is how one of them begins, though in both the serpent is a friend.

The snake is called Kanakapala because it is the protector of gold, the gold saved for pious use by Vision Rangappa. But his evil minded descendents cast their wicked eye on the gold. Brothers kill a brother — and a sister abets in the crime. But gold eludes them, because Kanakapala the snake

> went round and round the god and goddess, once, twice, thrice, and curling himself at the foot of the Divine couple, swallowed his tail and died. (p. 68.)

The story concludes, "For is it not sad, a snake loves death better than undutiful life?" (p. 68.) But this leaves a curse on the people of Vision-House that no woman in their family would bear a child, and this will go on till they are seven times dead and seven times reborn. This is a typical *sthalapurana* told in the racy and vigorous style of the folk tale. As Raja Rao remarks in his foreword to *Kanthapura,* "there is no village in India, however mean, that has not a rich sthala-purana."[6]

'Companions,' is another snake legend where again the snake is a friend that helps Moti Khan in his self-realization, and is indeed the means of his redemption. These two stories have "the elements of a folk legends or myth: a dream vision, a curse, a quest, fulfilment and finally something tangible (a tomb, or a temple) as testimony to the truth of the legend."[7] In other words, these stories recount the legendary associations of a specific locality, namely Kashipura and a place near Agra.

'A Client' is the only story that was originally written in Kannada. Curiously, the story is set in Bangalore, the capital of Karnataka whereas all the other stories are set in villages. However, it is only the setting that is different, for the story is of a village boy Ramu who has come to Bangalore for his college education. His encounter with Hosakere Nanjundayya, the marriage broker, makes fascinating reading. Ramu, hardly nineteen, unwilling at first, is initially gently persuaded, then coaxed and finally trapped by the clever and scheming Nanjundayya. He is a superb actor endowed with the great ability of displaying various emotions all with a single purpose — to trap the innocent, gullible young boy. Here is a true presentation of the much abused social convention prevalent even now in this part of the country.

The remaining three stories in the collection 'Narsiga, In Khandesh' and 'The Cow of the Barricades', have the freedom struggle for their theme. The thirties was a period of great political activity and the contemporary writers naturally reacted to these events in their works. The youthful Raja Rao, himself caught up in the movement for independence, has artistically captured the spirit of the times in these stories.

'Narsiga' like the other stories in the collection is a typically Indian story of an orphan shepherd boy of the same name. He is taken by the kind Master to his Ashram where he lives looking after a flock of sheep. The story dramatises the tremendous impact of Gandhi on the people of India and shows how even someone like Narsiga is deeply affected by his example. Raja Rao is able to capture brilliantly the mythopoeic consciousness operating in a village peasant boy. For instance, when he rides the sheep his mythical imagination establishes a parallel between him and the gods of the Hindu pantheon who have animals as their vehicles:

> Now he would be Shiva, the Serpent-garlanded, and the knotted grass became the serpent and the long-horned goat the bull. And now he would ride on Rama's chariot of flowers, a bael flower at the sheep's tail, and two others behind its ears. (p. 100.)

And in the ashram, which has the resonance of Raja Rao's own stay at the ashram of Pandit Taranath, Narsiga gets to know from the Master's wife that Gandhi,

> is a great man. They say he is an incarnation of God, that is why everybody touches his feet, even Brahmins ...
> (p. 105.)

It is from the teacher at the ashram that he learns about the citizen's duty to love his country. And especially for an orphan like him, the concept of motherhood has far greater significance and his love for his country assumes deeply religious overtones. The teacher tells Narsiga that the

> red man rules us. He takes away all our gold, and all our food, and he allows the peasants to starve and the children to die milkless. He has put the Mother into prison. (p. 112.)

He is a subtle teacher who knows what touches the tender chords of a simple village orphan. Of course, this has its immediate implications for Narsiga, since Gandhi who fought for the country was put in prison by the Redman. And precisely for that reason his message, "Tell the truth, and love everyone" leaves a deep impression on his mind. But what he did, in reality, was to wave long sticks and throw stones towards the redman's trains. The same evening he gets "a fever such as he had never seen." Such is the writer's insight into adolescent psychology that the boy could see that cause and effect are closely linked. Narsiga prays to Gandhi in penitence:

> 'Saint Gandhi,' he said, beating his cheeks to ask forgiveness, 'pardon me, O Saint. You are great. You are next only to God. You are by the Mother. Saint, I shall never hate the redman again. Take away the devil from me,

Saint. Saint, I fall at thy feet and kiss them. O Saint! (pp. 115-16.)

We are told that the "Saint seemed to take him in his arms and pat him in his arms as the Mother did." In his mind the figures of the Mother and Gandhi have coalesced successfully.

Hence Narsiga's rejoicing over Gandhi's release from prison is wild:

'Uncle, He, Uncle Sampanna! The Mahatma is released. Leave the fields and rejoice. The Mahatma, you know, is going to fly in the air today like Goddess Sita when she was going back from Lanka with her husband Rama. He is going to fly in the air in a chariot of flowers drawn by four horses, four white horses. He is going to pass by our home, Sampanna, what do you say to that, he? (pp. 116-17.)

It should be said to the credit of the writer that with his intimate knowledge of the village, he is able to faithfully depict the response of the delighted Narsiga. The boy's mind, as is evident, to us by now, has mixed historical fact and myth and this comes so naturally to him. So deeply has the epic permeated Indian consciousness that illiteracy is no bar — a point which proclaims the culture of the masses.

It is interesting to note that a similar mythical parallel is established in *Kanthapura* as well:

They say the Mahatma will go to the Red-man's country and he will get us Swaraj. He will bring us Swaraj, the Mahatma. And we shall all be happy. And Rama will come back from exile, and Sita will be with him, for Ravana will be slain and Sita freed, and he will come back with Sita on his right in a chariot of the air, and brother Bharata will go to meet them with the worshipped sandal of the Master on his head. And as they enter Ayodhya there will be a rain of flowers.[8]

The comparison has an extended meaning here, in that the idea of Rama Rajya is introduced. It is in this context that one is surprised to read Meenakshi Mukherjee's interpretation that "Narsiga can romanticise the independence movement and the person responsible for it mainly because he is not directly involved in it."[9] In the first place, Narsiga is not romanticising the Independnce movement nor is Achakka in the novel *Kanthapura*. Both of them are involved in their own way, though it is only peripheral in terms of actual participation in Narsiga's case. They are able to, thanks to their peasant sensibility and folk imagination, transform a living person into a mythical hero. If there is a truly authentic response to the Independence movement as seen in our villages, it is found in 'Narsiga' and *Kanthapura*, again a tribute to Raja Rao's understanding of his country. The response is not one of romanticising reality, as Meenakshi Mukherjee suggests, but one of mythifying reality. However, she is right in pointing out that the language achieves "a deliberately stylised and archaic effect"[10] through the repetition of this mythical parallel three times in the last two pages.

The story's most memorable quality can certainly be traced to the writer's own complete involvement in the freedom struggle, that enables him to render the Gandhian movement in terms of art in a story like 'Narsiga'. Whether he succeeds in doing so in the title story, 'The Cow of the Barricades' is a debatable issue. It is no doubt an ambi- tious work, for Raja Rao is trying to do so many things in little over eight pages, which makes it the shortest story in the collection. Gauri, the cow is both an actual animal and symbol of India in bondage. Whether Raja Rao is able to achieve the delicate balance between fact and fancy without straining the credibility of the reader needs to be examined. Gauri is 'a stange creature' who visits the ashram of the Master every Tuesday and eats only the handful of grain given by him. To a question as to who this cow is, the Master "smiled with unquenchable love and fun" and said:

> 'She may be my baton-armed mother-in-law. Though she may be the mother of one of you. Perhaps she is the great Mother's vehicle.' (p. 175.)

A certain playfulness is evident in his answer, but it is clear even at this point in the story that this is no ordinary cow. True to its role in the Hindu tradition, merchants, students, young girls, widows and the childless offer prayers to her, seeking fulfilment of their desires. The idealisation reaches its climatic point in the following description:

> And Gauri was no doubt a fervent soul who had sought the paths of this world to be born a sage in the next, for she was so compassionate and true. (p. 175.)

And then comes the information of her having nibbled at the hair of the Mahatma also in addition to that of the Master.

The Indian Independence movement is also described in some detail, especially the passive resistance and the boycott of British goods as suggested by Gandhi. But the mill workers go beyond this, erect a number of barricades and so become masters of the town. The Master tries to dissuade them in the name of the Mahatma, but without success. And now the cow came every evening to the Master and

> she looked very sad, and somebody had even seen a tear, clear as a drop of the Ganges, run down her cheeks, for she was of compassion infinite and pure. (p. 177.)

It is the people's decision that saddens the cow, besides the emotional bond of sympathy between the cow and the Master. The likening of the tear drop to the Ganges seems a rather forced attempt to further elevate the cow to a symbolic plane.

But the people move out of the town and the battle lines are drawn. Here, comes the test for the young writer and he seems to be unsure of himself and hence we fail to see on whose side he is, whether on the side of the workers who are for confrontation with the redman, or on the side of the Master who resigns his Presidentship and goes away and sits in

> meditation and rose into worlds from which come light and love, in order that the city might be saved from bloodshed. (p. 179.)

While reading the story, one has a feeling that there is an approval of both the stands by Raja Rao.

Now comes Gauri striding into the town and is soon up on top of the barricades. Even the soldiers on seeing "the cow and its looks and the tear, clear as a drop of the Ganges" are moved to shout: "Victory to the Mahatma: Mahatma Gandhiji ki Jai!" along with the crowd. Seeing this, the redman fires a shot at Gauri's head and the following description once again points out the inability of the writer to resist easy and simplified glorification of the cow:

> But they said blood did not gush out of the head but only between the forelegs, from the thickness of her breast. (p. 181.)

Years have elapsed and there is peace now. A metal statue of Gauri has been erected at the same place where she fell. The Master says

> 'Gauri is waiting in the Middle Heavens to be born. She

will be reborn when India sorrows again before she is free.' (p. 182.)

It should be clear from the foregoing summary of the short story, that the author's main purpose was to bring out the Mahatma's faith in the fullness of love. In order to achieve this, he has sacrificed all the essential requirements of good art and resorted to sheer manipulation. No doubt the choice of the animal, the cow, gives certain inherent advantages to the writer, for traditionally the cow stands for motherhood, kindness, non-violence and also enjoys a divine status among the Hindus. Hence, to assign the cow some of these attributes as Raja Rao does in this story, is both logical and natural. But the conclusion "is not sufficiently grounded in the narrative that precedes."[11] In his eagerness to give the cow a mythical status, Raja Rao strains both our credibility and conviction since the animal from the beginning to the end of the story is so unique that there is hardly any quality associated with it which is not out of the ordinary. By loading Gauri with such heavy symbolism, he has failed to achieve the right relation, that every artist should, between the realistic and the symbolic levels of meaning.

'In Khandesh' also uses the independence movement for its theme but not in a central way as in 'Narsiga' and 'The Cow of the Barricades'. It stands apart from the rest of the stories in the collection by its technical virtuosity and innovativeness, while the other stories have a deceptively charming simplicity about them. The language of the story relies on the use of symbols and metaphors and is therefore highly evocative. The technique is the stream of consciousness method that had been successfully used by writers like James Joyce and Virginia Woolf only a few years earlier. It is through this mode, that Raja Rao describes the inner workings of the mind of Dattopant. He couldn't have thought of a more effective opening for the tale, the drum beatings as they are heard by Dattopant lying sleepily on his bed:

> 'Tom-Tom... Tom-tom... Tira-tira... Tira-tira... Tira- tira... Tom-tom... Listen, villagers, listen! Assemble ye all after midday meal... Tom-tom... Tom-tom... Tira-tira... Tira-tira... Everyone... All... Important business... Important... Tom-tom... Tira-tira... Tom-tom... Tom-tom...' (p. 142.)

This is the impressionistic technique but since the drum beats are heard that way in actual life, the choice of the technique is so ideal that it does not seem forced. In India, the drumbeats have various associations ranging from public announcements to marriage processions and to funeral marches. But curiously, for one like Dattopant it has only ominous forebodings about death. Added to this, he hears the owl hoot. Instinctively he exclaims, "Ram, Ram." The ominous quality is sustained brilliantly by Raja Rao through a change in the image:

> Then the owl changed into sheep, the sheep grew long, twisted horns and became a buffalo. A black rider sat on it, a looped serpent in one hand. The buffalo put its nuzzle on Dattopant, licked his flesh, sniffed — then with a dart flung into the depths of the raging clouds and was lost. Dattopant too was lost. A noose was round his neck. The black rider was dragging him ... dragging him ... where? Oh, that eye-shutting abysm! ... 'Ram Ram', 'Ram Ram', he yelled in his sleep. 'Ram Ram, Ram Ram.' (p. 143.)

The awesome fear of death in Dattopant is well brought out through this vivid description of the God of Death, *Yama*. And then he wakes up to hear the drumbeats again proclaiming some important business. He thinks of the various possibilities and finally gets up to go to the ravines for his morning ablutions. The description of the landscape of Khandesh is brilliantly evocative:

> In Khandesh the earth is black. Black and grey as the buffalo, and twisted like an endless line of loamy pythons, wriggling and stretching beneath the awful beat of the sun. Between a python and a python is a crevice deep as hell's depths, and black and greedy and forbidding as demon's mouths ... Field on field is nothing but pythons and abysms — crocodiles waiting for their prey, vermin searching for a carcass. Then, suddenly, there is a yawning ravine in the endless immensity of the python-world, the chief python of pythons, with his venoms flowing in red and blue and white ... The blood of the earth mingles with the pus of the skies — to bear cotton. (pp. 146-47.)

Such a description could only come from one who is sensitive to his surroundings. Being an Indian Raja Rao enjoys the added advantage of being an insider, and hence the striking quality of the picture. What is significant in such a picture, is his ability to go beyond the merely realistic. What would otherwise have been a straightforward description of cotton trees in a lesser writer, assumes subtler shades of meaning in Raja Rao:

> Rows and rows of cotton. Thin, unmoving, bone-like plants, with little skulls in their hands that split and crackle with the heat of the sun. Like the purity of the soul in their substance, within the twists and holes of the skull. But within their purity is the hidden venom — venom again! Black seeds, small knob-like seeds, sitting beside one another as though in clasped conspiracy. (pp. 147-48.)

The fate that awaits Dattopant is prophetically stated in a brief but powerful paragraph:

> The sun will hit him on the head, the earth maul him by the legs, the red man eat all his soul — and within the black and blue of the ravines, the white venom will flow to the end of time. The trains of the redman rush towards the city.
> (p. 148.)

On his return to the village, talking to his friends and the Patel, Dattopant learns of the arrival of the Viceroy in a train, and that they should all stand with their backs to it.

The next day, they are near the ravines and when they stand beside the railway line, there is heavy rain accompanied by whirlwind and lightning. And here we have an impressive rendering of the mind of Dattopant as it records "images, thoughts and sounds"[12]:

> Curtains follow curtains. It is like a prison-house — the storm. Walls of curtain that tear with a breath ... Curtain again... Hard, gory, smeared with black blood. Clutter-clutter ... clutter-clutter ... Like a leopard the rain scratches on the back, brusque, roaring, satisfied ... Puddles soft as goat's flesh, but sticky and dogged. Then the eruption of lightning — a whole world of trembling glory ...
> (pp. 162-63.)

And as he rushes forward, he is crushed by the ballast train that heralds the Viceroy's special. Perhaps the redeeming feature of his death is that he dies ceremoniously dressed in coat, turban and kummerbund. His death "must have been an act of grace from God which comes to even the undeserving"[13] and not "an empty gesture in the diseased milieu of colonial oppression"[14] as suggested by Janet

Powers Gemmil. In terms of the locale, this tale is set in Maharashtra while the rest of the tales in the collection are set in Karnataka, then known as Mysore.

Though *The Cow of the Barricades* is a product of the formative period in Raja Rao's literary career, the stories reveal remarkable maturity. Each of them is a finished piece, the sole exception being, rather ironically, the title story in the collection. In view of this, it is hard to agree with Meenakshi Mukherjee's assessment that "these tales do not have the cohesion of structure one expects in a short story: they exist merely as vehicles for the manipulation of the symbol."[15] As a matter of fact, it is only the symbol of the cow that is manipulated, whereas Javni and Akkayya, even though symbols of suffering women in Hindu society, are women in flesh and blood with a warmth of human feeling that touches the sympathetic chords in the hearts of the readers. Mere symbols divested of human emotions cannot evoke such a response in readers. If the stories were just vehicles for manipulating symbols, they would not have had a credible narrative flow that operates successfully at the realistic level. In these stories, the movement is from the realistic to the symbolic and hence, the charge of manipulation must fail. Raja Rao is aware that the experience he is mediating in these stories is specifically Indian, and hence should find its own suitable form. Most of these tales have the structure of a conventional short story, while stories like 'Companions' and 'The True Story of Kanakapala, Protector of Gold' have the folk tale structure as they recount legends, 'In Khandesh' is modern in its technique.

Lastly, we may consider Raja Rao's creative use of the English language. As the publisher's note says, "through the medium of the English language the author seeks to communicate Indian modes of feeling and expression." (p. vi.) And in this endeavour Raja Rao achieves astonishing success for a first collection of short stories. Here are some representative illustrations of the various ways in which he has made use of English for artistic purposes.

The peculiar method of identifying people with either their house or their profession is achieved by compounding words:

> eight-verandahed-house Chowdayya ... Cardamom- field Venkatesha. (p. 60.)
>
> Dasappa of the oil-shop, Sundarappa of the stream-fed-field. (p. 67.)

Even a tree is located and its identity established in a similar way:

> the pipal tree where-the-fisherman-Kodi-hanged-himself-the-other-day. (p. 4.)

For terms of abuse, literal translations from Kannada are employed:

> You donkey-whore! (p. 90.); You donkey's widow. (p. 5.)

Similes specifically Indian, constitute the major portion in Raja Rao's Indianisation of the English language. Descriptions of the nature and character of people:

> Javni, she is good like a cow. (p. 7.)
>
> He (Moti Lal) lived, sister, like a sacred bull of the street which wanders wild and eats what it finds. (pp. 25-26.)
>
> They looked hale and strong as exhibition bulls. (p. 67.)
>
> Oh! to have had a father with a heart pure as the morning lotus ... (p. 61.)
>
> Akkayya was as pure a thing as the jasmine in the temple garden. (p. 80.)
>
> Nanjundayya went grey as a plantain flower. (p.133.)

The beauty of woman:

> bride(s), some beautiful as new-opened guavas, and others tender as April mangoes ... (p. 55.)
>
> (women whose) breasts are pointed like young mangoes ... (p. 168.)

Translations of certain characteristic expressions in Kannada are also used by Raja Rao to suggest annoyance and irritation:

> Oh, shut up! and don't bother me with all your *Ramayana* (p. 74.)
>
> Why don't you shut up ... and not pour out all your vedantic knowledge? (p. 5.)

or fear:

> But he was afraid Motilal would catch him, and break his 32 teeth. (p. 33.)

or satisfaction:

> I would poison these two brothers, and, drinking half a seer or warm milk with undisturbed contentment, I would go and drown myself in the river, happy ... very happy. (p.68.)

Forms of address and exclamations are literally reproduced:

> mai-mai; hoye-hoye; Ayyo... ayyo... ayyo

Certain onomatopoeic sounds are used for naturalistic effects. The sound of the hookah:

> *gud, gud, gud* (p. 30.)

or the sound of the drum beat:

> *Tom-tom, Tira-Tira* (p. 142.)

Or the sound of the vultures:

> *Grhita, grhita, grhita* (p. 146.)

All these bear ample testimony both to Raja Rao's knowledge of the Indian scene and his genius at linguistic and stylistic experimentation. It is worth reminding ourselves that these stories were written by a young man who was only in his 20's. Two examples should illustrate his intimate knowledge of the Indian villager's way of comprehending reality. How does the Indian villager speak of time? Certainly not in terms of dates and months in a calendar year. Asked by Ramu as to how long she has been with his sister's family, Javni, replies:

> 'How long? How long have I been with this family? What do I know? But let me see. The harvest was over and we were husking the grains when they came.' (p. 7.)

And to the question about how many revenue inspectors she has served, her answer is once again characteristically Indian:

> 'How many? Now let me see.' Here she counted upon her fingers, one by one, remembering them by how many children they had, what sort of wives they had, their caste, their native place, or even how good they had been in giving her two saris, or four-anna tip or a sack of rice. (p. 8.)

But Raja Rao's greatness lies not merely in his Indianising the English language, for he is able to use standard English with telling effect. Note his description of the slow passage of time:

> The morning slowly rolled along, and the afternoon too creaked heavily away, and yet nothing had happened.
> (p. 38.)

Or his description of a stormy rain:

> All of a sudden a whirlwind rose over the fields. It seemed as though the earth vomited, spurting and flooding to the very skies. Round and swift and it swept, brushed over the sands, swirled over the trees, and rushed into the air — and fell with a groaning, rasping cough. The stones on the railway lines glittered hot and bitter. Their glitter seemed the glitter of fangs. The clouds began to heap up. They roared. They grunted. And thunder shot against thunder. Then all of a sudden there was a commnotion in the heavens, and lightning flew across the air, splitting a tree. The tree caught fire and burst into flame. The flame of sunshine danced with the flame of lightning ... And rain pelted against the earth. (p. 161.)

It is this fine ability of Raja Rao to fully extend the English language to convey what is essentially an Indian experience even in these early stories of his, that sets him apart from his contemporaries like Mulk Raj Anand and R.K.Narayan. And he is able to realise this without either doing great violence to the language or sounding artificial or resorting to a kind of Babu English. Whereas the latter sometimes happens in Anand, Narayan deliberately employs a neutral style.

It is not surprising that these stories, because of their faithful evocation of the land and its people performing different roles, occupy a significant place in Indian Fiction in English. For one desirous of knowing rural Indian life with all its beliefs, superstitions and legends in its true native flavour, all in admirable English, there is no better book than *The Cow of the Barricades*. These stories present "lyrical slices of Indian life"[16] in a most memorable manner.

To discover the image of India in the fictional works of Raja Rao, an analysis of his works from the chronological point of view seems best suited, for it reveals, as in the case of many writers, the growth of mind of the artist. What makes such a study fascinating is not merely the growing maturity of the works but that the conception of India assumes subtle and complex shades of meaning. As in the short stories, the image that emerges from his novel *Kanthapura*[17] is that of rural India. While there are any number of Indian writers in English who have used the village as the setting for their works, it is undoubtedly Raja Rao who has given us in *Kanthapura* a fully rounded picture of village life which has not been excelled for its verisimilitude.

In his foreword to the novel, Raja Rao speaks of every Indian village having its own legendary history. And it is this legendary history of Kanthapura that he has tried to recount in the novel. In a sense, it could be said that the form of the work is determined by this intention of the writer. The choice of the narrator and the narrative mode further emphasize this. Achakka, the old grandmother figure is the narrator and she narrates the story of the village: "episode follows episode" and we have "one interminable tale." The reader is directly addressed by the narrator at the very beginning of the novel, "our village — I don't think you have ever heard about it" and later at regular intervals: "what do you think?"; "A real grand marriage, I tell you.", This also sustains the illusion that the reader is part of an imaginary audience to whom the grandmother is narrating the sad tale of her village, Kanthapura. Such a mode makes for intimacy and greater effectiveness.

Achakka the narrator is a brahmin and in most of Raja Rao's short stories and all his novels, the 'point of view' is provided by the brahminical consciousness. In *Kanthapura* it is wholly tradition-bound and rather naive at times, and yet it enables Raja Rao "to mingle fact and myth in an effective manner"[18] and in doing so the reader's acceptance is won without much difficulty. This mixing of fact and myth is the basic feature of all *sthala puranas*. By choosing one like Achakka, Raja Rao has a narrator "who can assimilate all facts into a mythical structure, for whom no fact becomes really significant unless it can be identified as part of a myth."[19] Obviously Achakka's method reminds one of the oral tradition of story telling. She is given enough latitude by the novelist to assume omniscience while describing scenes which she could not have possibly witnessed. And finally, the language and the style of the novel is determined by the choice of an illiterate woman like Achakka for its narrator. As a matter of fact, the rightness of such a choice was the first crucial step in determining the success of the novel. In the light of such overwhelming reasons for the choice of Achakka, it is surprising to read M.K. Naik's remark that since Raja

Rao worked on the novel in the room of the queen in a castle in the French Alps, "the gracious spirit of the French queen seems to have induced the author to make a grandmother his narrator in the novel."[20]

Kanthapura dramatises the powerful impact of the Gandhian movement on a South Indian village in the thirties, and we see how the village is shaken to its core with the result that, at the end of the novel it is left with none of its original inhabitants. The village is evoked with tremendous power by Raja Rao through the Jamesian 'solidity of specification'. All the little and significant details are there and we have a concretely realised picture of the village. Along with it is evoked the spirit of the place as well. Kanthapura like all our villages has a hill, the Tippur Hill, and Himavathy river and presiding deity, Goddess Kenchamma, who is invoked by the people on every occasion, both happy and sad. Thanks to our rigid caste system, the Indian villages are strongly stratified into various quarters—each quarter for a particular caste. So too this village has a Brahmin quarter, a Pariah quarter, a Potter's quarter, a Weaver's quarter and a Sudra quarter. The names of important houses and people complete the physical picture of the village.

The novel has in it "three strands of experience ... the religious, the social and the political."[21] The close connection between these three levels of experience in an Indian has always disturbed the Western observers of India. While they conjure up India as a land of sadhus, mystics and magicians and dub the country sprititual, they do not realise that for the Indian the spiritual is never divorced from the material reality. The manner the Indian makes the leap from the material to the spiritual with such ease has always baffled the pragmatic western man. And such an attitude is best exemplified in the life of the Indian villagers that is depicted in this novel.

The setting up of the Kanthapuriswari temple in Kanthapura, with which the novel's action begins, is a good exmaple of the "fine fusion of the social and religious impulses and how they integrate and nourish one another in the Indian people."[22] When Moorthy finds the "half-sunk linga", it is consecrated and all the boys get together and put up a temple, which becomes the nerve centre of the village where Sankara Jayanthi is performed by a reading of the *Sankara-Vijaya*, followed by harikathas and other ceremonies. The multifarious activities of the temple become clear as the novel progresses. The willing participation of the various people in a religious activity shows how close knit is the village community. When postmaster Suryanarayana suggests that "somebody will offer a dinner for each day of the month," Bhatta says, "let the first be mine," Agent Nanjundia says, "The second mine" and Pandit Venkatesha insisted "the third must be mine" and others willingly join. What is striking is the spontaneity of their response and the feeling of oneness among the people. It is this sense of community that makes not only for the setting up of the temple but for a number of festivals to be held throughout the year. That is why Moorthy is the successful organiser of varioius religious functions. Then we have a harikatha by the famous Jayaramachar. Initially, there is resistance among the orthodox to listen to a harikatha on an ordinary mortal, for they have been fed all these years on the stories of Gods. But Jayaramachar is no ordinary harikatha man. He knows the mind of his audience and is able to present the life story of Gandhi in a most appealing manner. This particular harikatha on the life of Gandhi is of central significance to the theme as well as the technique of the novel and hence needs to be quoted in full:

> In the great Heavens, Brahma the Self-created One was lying on his serpent, when the sage Valmiki entered, announced by the two doorkeepers. 'Oh, learned sire, what brings you into this distant world?' asked Brahma, and, offering the sage a seat beside him, fell at his feet. 'Rise up, O God of Gods! I have come to bring you sinister news. Far down on the earth you chose as your chief daughter Bharatha, the goddess of wisdom and well-being. You gave her the sage-loved Himalayas on the north and the seven surging seas to the south, and you gave her the Ganges to meditate on, the Godavery to live by, and the pure Cauvery to drink in. You gave her the riches of gold and diamonds, and you gave her kings such as the world has never seen! Asoka, who loved his enemies and killed no animal; Chandragupta, who had the nine jewels of Wisdom at his court; and Dharmaraya and Vikramaditya and Akbar, and many a noble king. And you gave her, too, sages radiating wisdom to the eight cardinal points of the earth, Krishna and Buddha, Sankara and Ramanuja. But, O Brahma! you who sent us the Prince propagators of the Holy Law and Sages that smote the darkness of Ignorance, you have forgotten us so long that men have come from

across the areas and the oceans to trample on our wisdom and to spit on virtue itself. They have come to bind us and to whip us, to make our women die milkless and our men die ignorant. O Brahma! deign to send us one of your gods so that he may incarnate on Earth and bring back light and plenty to your enslaved daughter ...', 'O Sage—pronounced Brahma, 'is it greater for you to ask or for me to say "Yea"? Siva himself will forthwith go and incarnate on the Earth and free my beloved daughter from her enforced slavery. Pray seat yourself, and the messengers of Heaven shall fly to Kailas and Siva be informed of it.'

And lo! when the Sage was still partaking of the pleasures Brahma offered him in hospitality, there was born in a family in Gujarat a son such as the world has never beheld. As soon as he came forth, the four wide walls began to shine like the kingdom of the Sun, and hardly was he in the cradle than he began to lisp the language of wisdom. You remember how Krishna, when he was but a babe of four, had begun to fight against demons and had killed the serpent Kali. So too our Mohandas began to fight against the enemies of the country. And as he grew up, and after he was duly shaven for the hair ceremony, he began to go out into the villages and assemble people and talk to them, and his voice was so pure, his forehead so brilliant with wisdom, that men followed him, more and more men followed him as they did Krishna the flute-player, and so he goes from village to village to slay the serpent of the foreign rule. Fight, says he, but harm no soul. Love all, says he, Hindu, Mohomedan, Christian or Pariah, for all are equal before God. Don't be attached to riches, says he, for riches create passions, and passions create attachment, and attachment hides the face of Truth. Truth must you tell, he says, for Truth is God, and verily, it is the only God I know. And he says too, spin every day. Spin and weave every day, for our Mother is in tattered weeds and a poor mother needs clothes to cover her sores. If you spin, he says, the money that goes to the Red-man will stay within your country and the mother can feed the goodless and the milkless and the clotheless. He is a saint, the Mahatma, a wise man and a soft man, and, a saint. You know how he fasts and prays. And even his enemies fall at his feet. You know once there was an ignorant Pathan who thought the Mahatma was a covetous man and wanted to kill him. He had a sword beneath his shirt as he stood waiting in the dark for the Mahatma to come out of a lacture-hall. The Mahatma comes and the man lifts up his sword. But the Mahatma puts his hands on the wicked man's shoulders and says, 'Brother, what do you want of me?' And the man falls at the feet of the Mahatma and kisses them, and from that day onwards there was never a soul more devoted than he. And the serpent that crossed the thighs of the Mahatma, a huge serpent too ... (pp. 18-19)

As the novel has the impact of Gandhian ideology on an Indian village for its theme, Raja Rao could not have thought of a more effective method to introduce Gandhi to the people of Kanthapura. India, its rich tradition and all its past glories are evoked with references to her great emperors, sages and philosophers. This is done as it is important for the people to realise what they have lost now, in being enslaved by the British who have come from across the seas. And so the Gods go to Brahma with a request to free Mother India from her enforced slavery and He sends Shiva to the earth to be born as Gandhi. His principles are stated briefly. He says, "Love all ... Truth must you tell ... for Truth is God." The Gandhian dictum, that one should spin daily is also mentioned and there is also a concrete illustration of his faith that one can win over anyone through love by a reference to the anecdote of a Pathan. In short, Gandhi is firmly established in the minds of the people as "a saint, the Mahatma, a wise man and a soft man, and, a saint." Where any speechmaking or any other form of intellectual persuasion would have failed, a recourse to traditional means like the harikatha is shown to succeed.

Raja Rao is here exploiting nothing new but only a well-known and time-honoured device. Gandhi by being portrayed as an avatar of Shiva becomes a mythological figure and hence the freedom struggle is presented as a modern myth. The spirit of nationalism is thus infused into the minds of the people of Kanthapura, literate and illiterate, and the rest of the novel is an enactment of how their lives are affected being seized of this spirit.

In employing the device of Harikatha as "political education as well as entertainment,"[23] Raja Rao has also overcome a minor irritant involved in the depiction of Gandhi as a character in fiction. While some novelists like R.K.Narayan, Mulk Raj Anand, K.Nagarajan and K.A.Abbas have introduced Gandhi as a real person in their novels with little or no success, Raja Rao prefers to avoid a direct portrayal of Gandhi in *Kanthapura* as well as in his other stories, 'Narsiga' and 'The Cow of the Barricades.' Paradoxically however, he is able to present the spirit of Gandhi with greater success by resorting to mythification. And this spirit of Gandhi, in spite of (or is it because of?) his unseen presence, pervades the entire novel.

The unseen, however, needs to be experienced by the villagers. It is obvious that for a myth to endure there has to be a close relationship between the mythical and the factual. The Gandhian myth is realised in living terms through the character of Moorthy. The word 'Moorthy, in Kannada means the image and he is the image of Gandhi in Kanthapura. One who takes on the mantle of Gandhi has to be inevitably idealised by the novelist to a considerable degree. And so is Moorthy, for we are introduced to him at the very beginning as

> Corner-House Moorthy, who had gone through life like a noble cow, quiet, generous, serene, deferent and brahmanic, a very prince, I tell you. (p. 11.)

His own conversion to Gandhism is marked by two important events. A college-going young man with a bright future ahead of him, Moorthy has a vision of the Mahatma. He hears him say, "There is but one force in life and that is Truth, and there is but one love in life and that is the love of mankind, and there is but one God in life and that is the God of all" (p. 43.) and Moorthy is so overcome by the surge of emotion within him that he falls at the feet of Gandhi and is told by him to give up foreign clothes and foreign education and work among the dumb millions in the villages. While saying this, Gandhi pats him on his back and "through that touch was revealed to him as the day is revealed to the night the sheathless being of his soul."(p. 44.) Thus Moorthy returns to his village Kanthapura as a Gandhi man.

As far as the techniques of the vision is concerned, we see that Raja Rao is once again able to avoid the dangers of romanticisation by not attempting to describe the conversion of Moorthy through a real meeting with Gandhi. Instead, by resorting to fantasy, he has been able to achieve both the necessary detachment and credibility.

The arrest of Jayaramachar after his harikatha on Gandhi marks the beginning of the Gandhian movement in Kanthapura. It is because of Moorthy's organizing ability and his capacity to convince the uneducated villagers of the need to drive the British out, the movement gathers momentum. The value of freedom, the uses of the spinning wheel are all brought home to the villagers, by him, in homely terms that make for easy comprehension.

It is actually, after the first brush with the authority at the Skeffington estate that Moorthy decides on his fast, an act of self-purification, before beginning the 'Don't-touch-the-Government Campaign.' Moorthy, after the three day fast, is convinced that he "would send out love where there was hatred and compassion, where there was misery." (p. 79). Raja Rao has convincingly dramatised the inner change in Moorthy which leads to the emergence of a new and spiritually enlightened Moorthy.

He now begins the campaign against the government in right earnest going first to the village Patel Rangegowda, to convince him of the need to start a Congress group in Kanthapura and seek his co-operation. From there, he goes to the different quarters in the village and finally to the Pariah quarter to see Rachanna. Even though Moorthy has been idealized by the novelist, this scene offers a true test for the artist in Raja Rao. No doubt after his fast, Moorthy has realised that he should love all fellowmen despite the differences in caste, creed etc. But he is shown to be, in spite of this realization, a brahmin at heart in his attitudes, and hence the struggle in him. Rachanna is not at home and his wife asks Moorthy to come in. And for him

> this is something new, and with one foot to the back and one foot to the fore, he stands *trembling and undecided*, and then suddenly hurries up the steps and crosses the threshold and squats on the earthen floor. (p. 83)
>
> (emphasis mine)

With fine psychological insight, Raja Rao shows how there is that momentary hesitation in Moorthy, and then he quickly overcomes it to enter the pariah house. This handling of the scene indicates the sureness of touch in the writer:

> Rachanna's wife quickly sweeps a corner, and spreads for him a wattle mat, but Moorthy, confused, blurts out, 'No, no, no, no,' and he looks this side and that and thinks surely there is a carcass in the backyard, and it's surely being

> skinned, and he smells the stench of hide and the stench of pickled pigs, and the roof seems to shake, and all the gods and all the manes of heaven seem to cry out against him, and his hands steal mechanically to the holy thread, and holding it, he feels he would like to say, 'Hari-om, Hari-om,' But Rachanna's wife has come back with a little milk in shining brass tumbler, and placing it on the floor with stretched hands, she says, 'Accept this from this poor hussy:' and slips back behind the corn-bins; and Moorthy says, 'I've just taken coffee, Lingamma ...' but she interrupts him and says, 'Touch it, Moorthappa, touch it only as though it were offered to the gods, and we shall be sanctified'; and Moorthy, with many a trembling prayer, touches the tumbler and brings it to his lips, and taking one sip, lays it aside. (p. 83.)

All this is extremely credible and there is hardly a false note in the depiction of Moorthy's behaviour. When he gets back to Rangamma's house he takes a bath and drinks a spoonful of Ganges water and

> he feels a fresher breath flowing through him, and lest anyone should ask about his new adventure he goes to the riverside after dinner to sit and think and pray. (p. 85.)

The final word on this episode is allowed to the narrator who remarks, "After all a brahmin is a brahmin, sister!" (p. 85) This is what really saves Moorthy from being totally idealized which would in turn have made him far less convincing as a human being. This scene is a real triumph for the writer. In the light of this evidence it is amusing to read Haydn Moore Williams's remark that, "Moorthy is less a human being than a paradigm of the freedom struggle, a localized miniature version of the Mahatma."[24] D.S.Maini shares a similar view, for he too believes that "Moorthy is by no means a fictional character. In fact, he in developed more as a Gandhian principle than as an individual."[25] And then there is Narsingh Srivastava who takes an extreme view in suggesting that in Moorthy, Raja Rao "is creating an extraordinary character acting his extraordinary part at a critical time of national resurgence ... We would never like him to be perfectly life-like because he is destined to be above the ordinary course of life."[26] But he fails to appreciate that one of the pre-requisites for a writer in creating exceptional characters in a fictional work is to be able to render them, at the same time, as recognizable human beings. If a character is too extraordinary in nature, he might fail to move us since he would then lack certain primary human attributes.

Raja Rao avoids both these dangers by presenting Moorthy as an individual who is an idealistic and devout follower of Gandhi and his ideals, so much so that he is regarded by the villagers as, 'He is our Gandhi' and 'He is the saint of our village.' In portraying the character of Moorthy, Raja Rao is operating within the Indian philosophical tradition. He is aware that for the Indian, the highest goal in life is *moksha* or Self-realization. And to achieve this, three ways are open to the individual — those of *Karma* (action), *jnana* (knowledge) and *bhakti* (devotion). We notice a progression in the novels of Raja Rao since in *Kanthapura*, the path chosen is the path of Action. The two later novels, *The Serpent and the Rope* and *The Cat and Shakespeare* follow the path of Knowledge and Devotion respectively.

So Moorthy chooses the path of action. He is indeed a true *nishkamakarmin*, a believer in Selfless Action. He is no doubt a visionary but also a man of action as well. Moorthy exemplifies here, the attitude to life expounded in the *Bhagavadgita*. While portraying an Indian, it is perhaps only an insider like Raja Rao who can present him as an individual who is a true representative of the Indian genius. No doubt, at times even an outsider like Kipling was able to portray a character like Puran Bhagat so admirably because he had grasped the Indian nuances of life with both sympathy and understanding. However, such instances are very rare in the Englishman's response to India and its people.

In spite of Moorthy the idealist at the helm of affairs, Raja Rao is aware of the resistance in Kanthapura to the freedom struggle. Such is his integrity as an artist and it is a considerable achievement for a writer who was still in his late twenties. In a highly tradition-bound milieu that exists in an Indian village, conservative elements are bound to resist any change that would effect their lives. And so we have Bhatta, Waterfall Venkamma, Patwari Nanjundia, Temple Nanjappa, Schoolmaster Devarayya and others that form the group which opposes the movement and refuses to take any part in it. As a result, the Gandhian movement is referred to variously as "Gandhi Vagabondage," "Oh this Gandhi! Would he were destroyed!" It is this awareness of the novelist that prevents *Kanthapura* from being reduced to a thesis novel. [27]

The people in addition to the land form here the major constituents of the image of India. To probe into Raja Rao's portrayal of Indians, the best illustration would undoubtedly be the creation of Bhatta. It is a typical from-rags-to-riches story. Bhatta who began his life with "a loincloth at his waist and a copper pot in his hand" was extremely efficient in performing any function whether it be marriages or obsequies. He "is very learned in his art" but he is shown to be an inconsiderate husband. He marries again after the death of his wife and is the recipient of a handsome dowry. And we notice the priest gradually turning into a moneylender and finally he is "no more a pontifical brahmin" but a landowner, a fine example of T.S.Eliot's 'Cultural Élite' wanting to be the 'Governing Élite.' And as world history has demonstrated time and again, it is always the vested interests that most vigorously resist any change that would ultimately endanger their own position in society. That is why, Bhatta "would have nothing to do with these Gandhi bhajans" in Kanthapura. It is he who gets Moorthy excommunicated by the Swami for his "pariah business" which eventually results in the death of Narasamma. No doubt, he finally goes to Kashi to wash off his sins, but it is not this act of his which redeems him in our eyes and makes his character fully rounded. He too has a better side in him. "Clever fellow this Bhatta" is justifiable in view of the business acumen in his financial dealings that singularly accounts for his prosperity. He never charges more interest than Subba Chetty or Rama Chetty, the traditional moneylenders of Kanthapura. And more importantly he had sent 'our Fig-tree-House Ramu' to the city for higher studies in spite of his being only a distant relation of his. Bhatta had said to him:

> 'If you will bring a name to Kanthapura—that is my only recompense. And if by Kenchamma's grace you get rich and become a Collector you will think of this poor Bhatta and send him the money— with no interest, of course, my son, for I have given it in the name of God. If not, may the Gods keep you safe and fit ...' (p. 33.)

And the narrator adds, "I tell you, he was not a bad man, was Bhatta." Raja Rao, like all true artists, is capable of a portrayal free from any bias or rancour. A lesser writer might have been tempted to turn Bhatta into an unredeemed villain. Such a character study contributes in no small measure to the authenticity of the village life described in *Kanthapura*, for credible human beings help make the locale credible as well.

In a book dealing with the freedom struggle, the image of India will not be complete without a portrayal of the English. Whereas we notice the point of view of the coloniser in writers like Kipling and Forster, here in Raja Rao we have that of the colonised. How far does his belonging to the subject race affect Raja Rao's portrayal of the English is worth considering in some detail. We have a very vivid account of the life at the Skeffington Coffee Estate. After establishing its locale, we have references to the labourers from the neighbouring states of Tamil Nadu and Andhra who come to the estate seeking better prospects, 'a four-anna bit for a man and a two-anna bit for a woman." Their march is described vividly:

> armies of coolies marched past the Kenchamma Temple half- naked, starving, spitting, weeping, vomitting, coughing, shivering, squeaking, shouting, moaning coolies.
> (p. 55.)

We are told of the Hunter Sahib "who used his hunter and his hand to reap the first fruits of his plantation." The maistri, instructed by Hunter Sahib, tells the coolies that

> if you work well you will get sweets and if you work badly, you will get beaten — that is the law of the place. (p. 57)

Haydn Moore Williams alleges that the "British 'masters' are all cardboard cut-out figures. They never emerge as real with genuine conflicts and dilemmas."[28] He also views the freedom struggle as dramatised by Raja Rao in the novel, rather simplistically as a fight between good and evil.

We see that Raja Rao has understandably chosen to dramatise the independence movement from the *Indian* point of view and not from that of the British. Hence the focus of attention in such a novel will be on the Indian characters and at least some of them will have to be rounded. The English will either be 'flat' characters or caricatures or to use Williams's phrase, "cardboard cut-out figures." The right question to be raised in this context, however, is whether Raja Rao has been unfair in his treatment of the English characters. This is hardly the kind of novel to project the "genuine conflicts and dilemmas" of the English. While portraying Hunter Sahib and his cruelties, Raja Rao brings out the superstitions of the coolies who refuse to take the quinine pills given by the Sahib but resort to various vows to cure malaria. The Sahib's righteous indignation at this is recorded by the novelist. After the death of Hunter Sahib, there is his nephew now to manage the estate. Raja Rao makes an interesting distinction between the two:

> He is not a bad man, the new Sahib. He does not beat like his old uncle, nor does he refuse to advance money. But he will have this woman and that woman, this daughter and that wife, and everyday a new one and never the same two within a week. (p. 66.)

Of course, the exploitation of the poor coolies continues but in different forms, all of them eventually crushing them into utter submission. But the point to note is that Raja Rao is not interested in painting the English characters all in black.

He has also given us the British view of our struggle for Swaraj. As pointed out earlier, the opposition within the Indians has been duly recognised and accommodated within the scheme of the novel. The British point of view, is rather curiously, put forward by an Indian, a lean, tall man in durbar turban and filigree shawl, and he wears gold-cased *rudrakshi* beads at his neck:

> ... I am a toothless old man and I have seen many a change pass before me, and may I say this: All this is very good, but if the white men shall leave us tomorrow it will not be Ramarajya we shall have, but the rule of the ten-headed Ravana. What did we have, pray, before the British came — disorder, corruption, and egoism; disorder, corruption and egoism; I say ... and the British came and they came to protect us, our bones and our dharma. I say dharma and I mean it. For hath not the Lord said in the Gita, whensoever there is ignorance and corruption I come, for I, says Krishna, am the defender of dharma, and the British came to protect our dharma ... When the British rule disappears there be neither brahmin nor pariah, vaisya nor sudra — nay, neither Mohamedan nor Christian, and our eternal dharma will be squashed like a louse in a child's hair. My young brothers, let not such confusion of castes anger our manes, and let the religion of Vasistha and Manu, Sankara and Vidyaranya go unmuddied to the Self-created one ...' (p. 101.)

This is the conservative Indian voice speaking through the old man.

The coloniser always saw himself as the instrument that established peace, order and rule of law in the colonies. It is the typical imperialist's position that is being reiterated by the old brahmin. The choice of the brahmin decides on the mode of defending the English. He, being an orthodox brahmin, offers a vigorous plea for the continuation of the British rule by suggesting that the English are the protectors of Hinduism in all its purity.

Thus, it has to be said in fairness to Raja Rao that however brief his references to the British position, and however few are the British characters in the novel, he is largely free from either bias or prejudice. That is to say, the political situation has not in the least affected his artistic integrity.

Moorthy the little Gandhi of Kanthapura is shown to succeed in initiating a mass movement. The men and women of Kanthapura profess and practise Gandhian ideals like truth and non-violence. They refuse to pay taxes to the British Government and also picket toddy booths. The last one-third of the novel is taken by the detailed descriptions of these activities, the enthusiasm of the people, the brutal attacks by the police which finally leave the villagers shattered, the village so desolate that "there's neither man nor mosquito in Kanthapura." Now the question remains, what have the poor people of Kanthapura gained through this experience when they are materially ruined and are forced to settle down in a nearby village, Kashipura. The answer comes from Achakka:

> No, sister, no, nothing can ever be the same again. You will say we have lost this, you will say we have lost that. Kenchamma forgive us, but there is something that has entered our hearts, an abundance like the Himavathy on Gauri's night ...(p. 199.)

As Meenakshi Mukherjee observes, "there is very little lasting regret because some abundance has entered their hearts and they look forward to Ram Rajya. The hope is collective while the loss has been individual."[29] There is also perhaps an implicit comment that this movement succeeded in *unifying* a fragmented society. Such is the passionate devotion to the cause of freedom in these people, that at the height of the struggle the people of Kanthapura "seemed to feel they were of one caste, one breath." (p. 140.)

After one reads the novel,

> One is left in no doubt of the novelist's valuation: the lot of

the poor and the low continues the same regardless of who rules—the Redman or Gandhiman. Such is the pattern of the whole novel—parallel streams of life and ambivalent attitudes persist and deepen the tension and the end is left unresolved.[30]

Thomas A. Vogler writing in another context speaks of two ways of reading a novel. He asserts that a novel can be either read as "an articulation leading to fuller understanding of a problem's complexities or as the assertion of an answer to the problem."[31] Raja Rao is not attempting in *Kanthapura*, to locate an answer to the problem of freedom for the country but only trying to understand it in all its complexities.

And finally to Raja Rao's use of the English language to convey a distinctively different sensibility that is essentially Indian. His foreword to the novel, a memorable piece, will continue to be the manifesto of Indian writers in English. What has been so admirably stated in it, has been realised in terms of art in the novel *Kanthapura* so completely that there is hardly any work in the entire body of Indian fiction in English that would stand favourable comparison. Critics have exhaustively illustrated this achievement and hence a few examples should suffice.

Kanthapura is one long, interminable tale that is told in a breathless fashion. There are no chapter divisions and this contributes to the forward surging movement of the novel. The long, meandering sentences, capture the basic speech rhythm of Kannada in an 'alien' language like English. For one unfamiliar with Kannada, the entire narrative will convincingly sound Indian and this is one singularly important factor that contributes to the authenticity of the image of India in *Kanthapura*. The near perfect fusion between the theme and technique is the signal achievement of Raja Rao.

The names of the villagers with epithets refer to either their houses or nature or profession or physical features: 'Corner-House Moorthy,' 'Front-House Akkamma,' 'Waterfall Venkamma,' 'Patel Rangegowda,' 'Patwari Nanjundia,' 'Pock-marked Sidda,' 'Bent Legged Chandrayya.' This is indeed the traditional Indian way of recognising people and particularising them as individual human beings. The same method is used to describe the names of cattle: 'the Whity, the Blochy, and the One-horned one'.

Here are a few similes which have specifically local term of reference:

the sky became blue as a marriage shawl. (p. 63.)

> Narasamma was growing thin as a bamboo and shrivelled like banana trunk. (p. 53.)

Literal translations of Kannada proverbs are used:

> the sinner may go to the ocean but the water will touch only his knees. (p. 108.)

And there are expressions peculiar to the Indian cultural context, rendered into English. The happiness of the villagers is described as "their mouths touching the ears with delight" and displeasure is expressed as in "he will get a jolly fine marriage-welcome with my broom-stick." Another good example is the way one enquires about another's welfare. The English 'How are you?' and 'Fine, thank you' will sound patently false in our situation, and so Raja Rao simply translates the Kannada reply into English as "Like this. As usual." (p. 34.) It is so typically Indian and sounds just right.

These representative examples illustrate the remarkable success achieved by Raja Rao in portraying a microcosmic Indian village, Kanthapura caught up in the throes of the great movement for Independence. The historic movement is captured so convincingly, that one is left wondering as to how a young man in his late twenties could have produced such an outstanding work, because Raja Rao with his own passionate involvement in the Independence struggle might have written a totally idealised, one-sided account of the freedom struggle. But he remarks in a letter to M.K.Naik:

> I wrote *Kanthapura* in a thirteenth century castle in the French Alps belonging to the Dauphins of France and I slept and worked on the novel in the room of the Queen.[32]

The clue to the achievement of Raja Rao lies in this fact. He gained both the necessary detachment and perspective to view the entire movement dispassionately as a result of this geographical distance from the Indian locale in which the novel was set. And so he is able to successfully register the various responses of individuals and groups of people to the historical event to give a fully rounded and aesthetically satisfying account in *Kanthapura*.

We have in *Kanthapura*, the image of an Indian village with all its socio-political realities given due importance. The descriptions of the Kartik festival, Vaisakh season, marriage ceremony are all given in minute particularities, and the circumstantial reality is powerfully evoked to present a solid picture of Kanthapura, which could in turn be any Indian village. As Gandhi said, "India lives in her villages", and no one can conceive India without its villages. The real India is still found in the villages and not in the cities where the traditional mores of life have been deeply disturbed by the industrialisation so that they have become standardised, characterless, a fate, no doubt, shared by all the cities of the modern world. And it is this real India that is depicted in terms of fictional art in *Kanthapura*.

For anyone wanting to know the Indian village, whether he is a foreigner or a modern city educated Indian who has lost contact with his roots, *Kanthapura* is the only one of its kind available in the English language. In spite of such overwhelming evidence to the contrary, it is surprising to read even a sensitive critic like Meenakshi Mukherjee remark that "no major novel has yet emerged on the theme of this great national upsurge."[33] Not only is *Kanthapura* a major work, but is undoubtedly one of the few classics in contemporary Indian fiction in English.

When we move from *Kanthapura* to *The Serpent and the Rope*[34] in our search for the image of India, we enter an area that is at once complex and challenging. It has been described as a metaphysical novel, a novel of ideas, and even as a work that cannot be called a novel. This is nothing new, for anything unique in literature has evoked, at least initially, hostile reactions. First critical responses to the Metaphysical poets, Hopkins's poetry and Joyce's fiction can be cited as examples. Gradually, however, these hostile responses have given way to those of acceptance and finally to an even enthusiastic recognition of the uniqueness of their achievement. Raja Rao does make certain departures from the novel form but whether such a departure is a logical offshoot of the newness of experience to be mediated is a point for consideration. A novel which has for its theme the growth towards self-knowledge of a brahmin intellectual, Ramaswamy, who is given to interminable philosophical reflections, intellectual pursuits and metaphysical discussions, certainly demands a more fluid novel form than what Raja Rao had employed for his first novel, *Kanthapura*. In communicating the genuinely Indian experience of Ramaswamy, Raja Rao has created a novel that can perhaps, with justification, take on the label, "Indian." That is to mean, *The Serpent and the Rope* is *different* from other Indian novels in English which are primarily Indian in theme but more often Western in technique. While Mulk Raj Anand employs the European Realistic novel to convey his view of life, R.K.Narayan finds the Comic-ironic mode of Jane Austen suitable to describe his vision of life. Raja Rao, on the other hand, creates a work that is Indian both in its theme and technique. However, this does not rule out the presence of certain western influence in the novel.

The Serpent and the Rope is the most ambitious of all Raja Rao's works. Even his detractors are agreed on this point, for the various intertwining themes give the novel a complexity that is perhaps almost wholly absent in any other Indian English novel. The protagonist of the novel, Ramaswamy is a Vedantin and an avowed believer in the non-dualistic philosophy of Sri Sankara of the 9th century. This determines his attitudes towards people, places and his own life. In marrying a French woman Madeleine, the author portrays the encounter between the East and the West, in which generalisations about the two races are made and there is also an implied judgement and evaluation of the two different ways of life. The relationship of Ramaswamy and Savithri posited by the novelist as the ideal one between a man and a woman is offered not merely as a contrast to the Ramaswamy-Madeleine relationship but rather as a corrective.

In trying to discover the image of India in the novel, we should first take critical look at the brahmanical consciousness operating in the narrator who is also the protagonist of the novel. Once this operative consciousness is established, everything else — his marriage to Madeleine, his relation with Savithri and his view of India — falls into its proper place. By choosing the first person narrative, Raja Rao has made Ramaswamy the central consciousness in the novel, through whom we observe everything else. It is this brahminical point of view that determines the nature of the image of India in the novel.

In the ensuing pages, an attempt will be made to define the truly brahminical sensibility as seen in a foreign educated intellectual like Ramaswamy. And this in turn should also enable us to identify whether Raja Rao had idealized the brahmin or not and whether he is aware of the degeneration that has set in the brahmin of recent times. In that case, it should be examined how far irony is used as an operative principle. The novel opens with,

> I was born a Brahmin—that is devoted to Truth and all that.

and curiously enough has a reference to the brahmin on the last page of the novel as well:

> A Brahmin is he who knows Brahman. That is one definition. There is another, a roguish definition. A Brahmin is he who loves a good banquet. (p. 406.)

One sees the ideal and perhaps the actual in both instances. The ideal is tempered with irony and this makes for a healthy attitude in the writer who is not given to merely romanticising the position of the Brahmin. As a matter of actual fact, the roguish definition has long enjoyed a proverbial status. Such ironical references are scattered throughout the novel but whether there is a sustained ironical perspective is doubtful despite the opinion to the contrary.[35]

Ramaswamy says he is "a good Brahmin" and that he "even knew grammar and the Brahma Sutras, read the Upanishads at the age of four, was given the holy thread at seven." (p. 5) This is perhaps not too credible and S.Nagarajan wonders rightly whether "Raja Rao does not slip up"[36] here. And thanks to his education and his sojourns to France and England, he describes himself aptly as a "European brahmin." As referred to earlier, he is a believer in Advaita Vedanta and this is synonymous with India for him. That is why, he asserts that "Duality is anti-Indian; the non-dual affirms the Truth." (p. 41.) He declares, "The Brahmin, the Vedantin, has such arrogance." (p. 79.) And one might as well ask whether Ramaswamy is himself free from this arrogance, for he does confess in his first meeting with Savithri:

> the fact that I was a Brahmin by birth and a South Indian seemed to have given me a natural superiority. (p. 31.)

Later he tells her in that famous scene in his London hotel room, that "a Brahmin is necessary to educate you all, kings, queens, peasants and merchants." (p. 212.) The feeling of superiority persists till the very end as when he says, "A Brahmin can touch anything, he is so high – the higher the freer." (p. 400.) This superiority is further made clear when he uses the Brahmin as the ideal for truth, virtue and all that which makes for the highest excellence. And that is why, when he finds the English during the spiring of 1953, on the eve of the coronation, very courteous and without any "triumphant arrogance," he observes: "They have grown more Brahminical."(p. 346.)

While these observations have more to do with the intellectual side of the brahmin, even the physical emphasis gets its due. Being a brahmin, he is endowed with very sensitive olfactory organs and that is the reason why he prefers to travel by train for "the bus is all right, but all this smell, and this rubbing against one another." (p. 339.) This expresses itself in his uneasiness when he cannot stand the bad odours that emanate from Madeleine's body during her forty-one day fast. While this is perhaps understandable, what is rather amusing is that even in one of his dreams he sees Georges teaching Shakespeare and the students laughing and they were all Indians and he adds, "They smelt bad and they all seemed sons of princess." (p. 302) There is another variation of this obsession when he meets an Italian girl in a café in Paris and gives her some money and takes her address but never goes to see her, for he remarks: "I needed the smell of camphor, and the yellow of turmeric on the limbs." (p. 219) Even in his food habits, his brahminical taste comes through:

> Oh, it was so wonderful to have *rasam* with assafoetida in it, and chutney with coconut and coriander leaf! (p. 27)

All these details establish for the reader the person of Ramaswamy, as one who is uncompromisingly Brahminical in his tastes, attitudes and view of life.

And now to the ironical references about brahmins. Curiously enough, they are all carefully linked with the fall of the brahmin from his exalted spiritual status — the fall is due to his material desires, a sure sign of his decadence as Raja Rao seems to suggest. At Benares, when the brahmin priests refuse to perform the ceremonies on the ground that Ramaswamy has been to Europe and married a French woman, Little Mother gives more money and the irony is scathing, "just fifty silver rupees made everything holy." That is the reason why Rama says: "I would rather have thrown the rupees to the begging monkeys than to the Brahmins." (p. 11) Then during Saroja's wedding, the brahmins fawn on Ramaswamy and "showed their thirty two teeth," for they "know there would be nothing lacking in honour and silver." (p. 256) If their servility is the target of Raja Rao here, he does not spare the brahmin for his enormous appetite either:

> There are Brahmins, imagine, that do three funerals a day
> ... you know from their belchings and rounded bellies much food has already gone into them. (p. 191.)

But it is only the following ironical statement about the brahmin which is significant because it goes beyond the traditional criticism of brahmins that is seen in the preceding references:

> The Brahmins sold India through the backdoor — remem-

ber Devagiri — and the Muslims came in through the front. Purnayya sold the secrets of Tippu Sultan and the British entered through the main gateway of Seringapatam. Truth that is without courage can only be the virtue of slave or widow. (p. 350.)

This betrayal is "motivated, it appears, by the sordid ambition of the cultural élite to be the governing élite without the necessary courage to equal the ambition."[37] Surely, this is a perceptive insight of Raja Rao into one of the causes for the downfall of the brahmin but it should be reiterated that this is the only instance we have in the entire novel. And so it can be said that irony is only incidental to the novel and a consistent use of it is absent in the work. In view of this, one is forced to add that the overwhelming impression we have in the novel is the glorification of the brahmin as personified in the character of Ramaswamy, who is also the narrator in the novel. Thus, the novel is completely coloured by the point of view of one who is almost wholly proud of his rich brahminical heritage.

Ramaswamy's individual search is closely related to his being a brahmin. He having lost his mother at a young age has persistently experienced the feelings of an orphan:

> I was born an orphan, and have remained one. I have wandered the world and have sobbed in hotel rooms and in trains, have looked at the cold mountains and sobbed, for I had no mother. One day, and that was when I was twenty-two, I sat in a hotel — it was in the Pyrennes — and I sobbed, for I knew I would never see my mother again. (p. 6.)

This is indeed most moving for his "poignancy is personal and metaphysical."[38] There were a series of deaths in the family culminating with that of his father. And from the beginning, he has feelings that point to an acute consciousness of absence within him:

> Something had just missed me in life, some deep *absence* grew in me, like a coconut on a young tree, that no love or learning could fulfil ... I was anxious about something, anxious with an anxiety that had no beginning, and so no maturity. (p. 26.)

This persists even in England:

... I knew no peace. All was an absence, like the space over the bare trees and the Cam. (p. 194.)

The traditional Indian view regards life as a pilgrimage and so does Ramaswamy, the true Indian, an integral aspect of Raja Rao's image of India. The two Indian ways of life are commonly described as the *pravritti-marga* or 'the path of active life' and *nivritti marga* or 'the path of renunciation.' Ramaswamy opts for the former since that *is* the way for one like him. And while Moorthy of *Kanthapura* chose the way of action (*Karma marga*), Ramaswamy, befitting an intellectual, chooses the way of knowledge (*Jnana marga*) to achieve self-knowledge. The first articulation that life is a pilgrimage comes very early in the novel: "Life is a pilgrimage, I know, but a pilgrimage to where—and of what?" (p. 26.) And it recurs at regular intervals: "I felt what I always know I am, a pilgrim" (p. 166.); "life is one long pilgrimage." (p. 191.) The anguish of the first cry persists throughout: "Lord, how can one ever get out of oneself!"(p. 83.) The climax is reached when we read this in his diary:

Yes, I say to myself, 'I must leave this world, I must leave, leave this world.' But Lord, where shall I go, where? How can one can go anywhere? How can one go from oneself? (p. 339.)

And soon after he, "a holy vagabond" who had "wandered, like a sacred cow" in various countries *realises* that he needs a Guru:

... For now I know the name of Him to whom I have to go, though I have always known Him without knowing His name. So to Travancore I will go ... (p. 404.)

All the deeper philosophical truths related to the Advaitic view of life are brought out with understanding by the novelist. What is it to live on this earth and what is the mission of one's life are the basic questions that confront every Indian. In Ramaswamy, all these are asked with a sense of urgency that reveals to us his sensitivity and his deep awareness of his roots, both cultural and philosophical. Being an intellectual, he can articulate this awareness in a highly convincing manner. And being an Advaitin, he asserts

There can be only two attitudes to life. Either you believe the world exists and so—you. Or you believe that you exist—and so the world. There is no compromise possible

... The first is the Marxist's position — the second is the
Vedantin's — and they are irreconcilable. (p. 333)

He is also aware that "the meaning of life is *lila*, play" and that "not achievement but self-recognition is pure significance." (p. 215.) What constitutes a real journey for a true brahmin is stated beautifully in the following passage:

> For the going inward is the true birth. He is indeed the Brahmin who turns the crest inward, even if you are a pandit great as Jagannatha Bhatta or learned in logic as Kapila-charya, the true life, the true Brahminhood commences when you recognize yourself in your eternity. At some moment you must stop life and look into it. Marriage or maternity, pain or the intimacy of success — love — may dip you into yourself ... (pp. 215-16.)

And the novel is the 'dramatisation' of this inward journey of Ramaswamy. The word dramatisation is used in a restricted sense because while some ideas are *enacted*, some others are merely *stated*. This aspect of the novel will receive a detailed treatment in the discussion of the form of the novel.

There are two important constituents of Ramaswamy's journey — his marriage with Madeleine and his relationship with Savithri. These are of central importance in his life since both take him closer, in different ways, to an awareness of his own Self and the ultimate meaning of existence that constitutes the search for a brahmin like him. First, let us consider his marriage with Madeleine. Since Raja Rao has made Ramaswamy the narrator, everything in the novel is seen through his eyes. His marriage with Madeleine and the reasons for its eventual failure are all available to us only through the reflections, statements and observations of Ramaswamy, i.e., we see this complex relationship entirely from his point of view. If the reader gives a complete and unqualified assent to Ramaswamy's views, he is bound to identify his own response with him. However sympathetic Ramaswamy is towards Madeleine and her limitations, he is ultimately judging her from his own predilections. Hence, an attempt should be made to view Madeleine's own individual role in this relationship. To put it differently, her standpoint should also be taken into account before any final judgement is passed on her marriage with Ramaswamy. This advantage is only given to the reader. In a novel that employs such a narrative scheme, the reader should pay special attention to a tendency often noticed in the narrator to gloss over his limitations and also to any possible discrepencies that may exist between his words and deeds. And only then can one be truly fair to Madeleine's position in this coming together of two nationalities.

The marriage of Ramaswamy and Madeleine is the natural culmination of their interest in each other at various levels — physical, intellectual and philosophic. Madeleine has a kind of obsession with purity and touch — possibly the result of her interest in Cathars — and also an ascetic streak that finds a kindred soul in Ramaswamy who also values them for he is uncompromisingly brahminical. He is an Indian, and being French "she loved India, for India was a cause to love." (p. 32.) And also "everything good for [her] has only come from India." (p. 68.) Both of them sincerely strive for a successful marriage. And in their marriage, "two contrary world-views, two contrary epistemologies, come together, and the novel is a study of that encounter."[39] These differences are evident to both of them and she articulates it most beautifully in one of her letters to him:

> Your impersonal approach was strange to me, you yourself so impersonal... you people are sentimental about the invisible, we about the visible... (pp. 36-37.)

Ramaswamy, while aware of the difference, is seemingly more at ease since for him "the world... was as you made it." (p. 55.) And then he knows that "to wed a woman you must wed her God" (p. 84.) and reiterates again that the "God of Woman must be the God of her Man." (p. 113.) At this juncture, a very important episode of the toe-rings should be critically examined in some detail, because it is now that the first signs of the cracks in their marriage appear and reasons can be sought in this episode for its eventual failure.

Ramaswamy who has come to India on hearing of his father's illness is able to renew his Indian awareness through his pilgrimages to Benares, Hardwar and other holy places. Little Mother gives him two little toe-rings of his mother to be given to Madeleine and his response is clear: "I felt at last I was going to make Madeleine mine." (p. 53.) But due to the delay in his flight, he arrives late and feels that "things were not going too well." (p. 60.) He gives her the sari that was a gift from Saroja and Madeleine is naturally disappointed, for she expected it to be from him. As a Frenchwoman, she wishes it to be from her husband and seems to value less a gift from her sister-in-law. It is in these little details, that the cultural incompatibility between the two emerges to the surface. And when they try to make conversation, she asks him whether he hated the Europeans while he was in India, again a question that is unwarranted, Rama replies frankly:

> "Hate them? You know the Englishman is more loved in India than foreigner has ever been. We forget evil easily. Naturally we love the good."

And Madeleine is provoked to retort:

> "So that the pariah may have his separate well, and the woman slave for men." (p. 62.)

Ramaswamy is upset by this "bitterness" in her, while we realise that her remark is not without its basis in truth. But the damage has been done. And he feels that "something has happened... to everything." Madeleine understandably queries:

> "I have failed your gods?"

His response is crucial:

> "No", I said, looking at her; and for some un-understandable reason I added, "you've failed me." (p. 66)

How far is this justifiable in the context of the given situation is the question. Is it a failure only on the part of Madeleine and is Ramaswamy entirely free from blame? The onus is on her, if we go by *his* remark. And it is true that Madeleine has perhaps needlessly provoked him. This certainly prevents Ramaswamy giving her the toe-rings. But after a few days, he wants to put the past behind him and decides, "Yes, I would be happy with Madeleine." (p. 104) but even here he sees the suitcases in a corner and shuts them away in a cupboard. Much later while in London, he remarks, "the toe-rings remained in my trunk and I knew no peace." (p. 194) And finally in the Radha-Krishna episode, he puts them on to Savithri's toes:

> The toe-rings were the precise size for her. Little Mother was right: for Madeleine they would have been too big.
> (p. 212)

That he finds in Savithri a woman who can legitimately wear the toe-rings because she is deeply Indian is a perfectly valid decision of his. His decision not to give the toe-rings to Madeleine is also partly determined by his renewed awareness of *the* Indian woman born out of observing the burgeoning of Saroja into womanhood during his visit to India. This awareness makes him realise what he actually missed in one like Madeleine.

One of Ramaswamy's generalisations about their relationships and its validity with reference to the actual incidents in the novel throws new light on his judgement. He remarks, "Madeleine had never participated in my superstitions, though I had in hers." (p. 54) But, what actually follows in the novel amounts to a flat denial of this remark as Madeleine's involvement with his superstitions is both sincere and total. Like Ramaswamy, she takes the huge flat stone near their garden for Nandi bull and offers it grass and flowers. On seeing this Ramaswamy frankly confesses, "the Hindu in me used to be so happy." (p. 55) And when their neighbour starts hammering away at the rock, her reaction is quite genuine: "My heart bled as though something terrible was going to happen." (p. 239) On her plea, the neighbour Scarlatti relents and the bull is saved. And rather curiously, the bull seemed to communicate both happy and sad news to her that Ramaswamy is sure that "in some past life Madeleine must have been an Indian woman." (p. 241) So we see that Madeleine makes genuine attempts to share her husband's superstitions in order to come closer to him.

But the point to be reckoned in their marriage is that Madeleine is sadly unable to go beyond these little gestures. For instance, when Ramaswamy leaves for India on hearing of his father's illness, he would have very much liked to take Madeleine along with him to India. He admits,

> to me Madeleine's presence would have meant the daughter-in-law coming home, the division of family responsibility; truly it would have been "the crossing of the threshold." I almost felt that, if she came, Father could not die, he would not die. How, when the first daughter-in-law came home, could the father die? (p. 56)

But Madeleine does not go to India.

On the other hand, Ramaswamy, in spite of his Indianness is able to relate himself very convincingly with the members of Madeleine's family—Oncle Charles, Tante Zoubie and Catherine. He can feel that "Oncle Charles in the house was like an elder brother" (p. 88) and has such love and affection for Catherine that she tells him, "You are my godfather of happiness." (p. 227) Even Little Mother without ever having seen Madeleine takes interest in her welfare and prays for her as well.

The differences that come to the surface on Ramaswamy's return from India are accentuated further through his meetings with Savithri. She makes him aware of what Madeleine is not, and also of what he has been missing in his married life. But it is not correct to suggest "conscious of the growing rift, Ramaswamy and Madeleine desperately seek and find temporary fulfilment in sex."[40] Their relationship has a beautiful physical side to it but that is never seen by them as the only basis for their living together. The final break comes with the death of their second child, an event that occurs while Ramaswamy is away in India for Saroja's marriage. On his return to France, he finds rather ominously that "Life had changed everywhere."(p. 298) And surely enough he sees change in his wife's life style. She has now become deeply ascetic and follows Buddhist rituals like fasting, counting of beads and chanting of mantras. What has driven her to this state is the premature death of the second child.

Her involvement in Buddhism should be discussed at some length. As a teacher of history, she was interested in tracing the origin of the Holy Grail in the Cathars and she puts forward a theory that the Holy Grail was originally a Buddhist relic that later came to the West via Persia. But soon she abandons her work on the Holy Grail and turns to Buddhism, for she is fascinated by its "intellectual virility and the deep compassion of the Buddha." (p. 115) And this interest in Buddhism had, as Rama says, given her "a step, a conscious foothold in India." (p. 244) After all, she herself had written to Ramaswamy that "India is infectious, mysterious, and infectious." (p. 40) No doubt, after the child's death, she begins to practise a more ritualistic form of Buddhism and moves away from him, that is, only physically. He might say: "There was a clear, pure space between us. Something had happened to Madeleine." (p. 312) But what is very credible and convincing is the thoroughness with which she takes on this new role, once again typical of westerner. This elicits a sincere response from Ramaswamy: "You are more of a Brahmin than I." (p. 313) There is no irony here, for he says again a little later that, "she's more of an Indian than me. She already knows more about Buddhism than I do." (p. 343.)

But this conversion brings in many notable changes in Madeleine. She grows happier, her classes become brilliant, her colleagues, her headmistress and even the inspectors are all praise for her work, and she is their Simon Weil. Rama remarks, "Even I received a little of this veneration; they thought I was the noble cause of this transformation of Madeleine." (p. 315.) Her face shines with "a glow of truth between her eyes" and Ramaswamy acknowledges that she "looked a saint: I worshipped her." (p. 326.) At the same time, she grows sentimental about crushed pansies, wounded centipedes and caterpillars. Ramaswamy with his intellectual awareness can say that "her insight into Buddhism was more psychic... than religious." (p. 312.) But Madeleine has made up her mind, her path has been chosen, the path of renunciation of the flesh. However, her concern for Ramaswamy needs to be examined here. Her attention to little details that constitute the duties of a wife has been earlier expressed by Ramaswamy:

> There was nothing I needed which she did not know beforehand, and bring to me: my medicine after lunch, my handkerchief when I started on a walk, my pencil, duly sharpened and laid on my notebook. (p. 77.)

But now it assumes more significant overtones. She undertakes a forty one-day fast to pray for his health telling him, "you must, must be cured." (p. 322.) And she also tells him later of what she has been praying for, in his absence:

> "... I have prayed night after night, as you said Emperor Baber prayed for his son Humayun, that I be taken away in your place. You are young, you are a man, you have yet to live. When I knew you first you were such a sprightly, vivacious being. It is I who brought all this on you. I am only a log of flesh, and anyone can take my place. But you, you are the head of the family." (p. 331.)

What is clear here is that her conversion to Buddhism is not something that is solely intellectual which does not take into account human considerations, though one suspects a slight touch of cynicism in the last two sentences. She, on occasions, sounds cruel as when Ramaswamy confronts her on his return from London. She asks him:

"Why did you come?"
"To see you?"
"You cannot see anything but the eighteen aggregates"
"But eighteen aggregates can see eighteen aggregates", I said, laughing.

"Then it is no business of mine," she said, and started

counting beads.(p. 387.)

This cruelty has to be seen in relation to her conversion to Buddhism. No doubt, the beginnings of her interest in Buddhism were sincere but towards the end they certainly take a rather debased form of worship, ritual and fasting. And when she accuses Ramaswamy of being the major cause for the change in her, "it's you who have brought me all this," (p. 314.) she is being more than unfair to him. And at the end, she writes to Catherine expressing her desire to divorce Ramaswamy for he

> "... must marry someone younger from his own country.
> He will be happy with an Indian woman, I have no doubt..."
> (p. 394.)

In this case, it is rather difficult to sympathise with Madeleine, for we would have expected her to talk it over with Ramaswamy in a responsible, adult manner. It is, however, true that the death of their two children has driven her to regard her marriage as a total failure.

An attempt to pin down the reasons for the failure of their marriage will be made after a brief consideration of Rama's relationship with Savithri. Like his marriage with Madeleine, Rama's meeting Savithri forms an important step in his growth towards self-knowledge. Savithri is the daughter of a Rajah of a small princely state, studying in Cambridge and later marries Pratap, a civil servant. She is westernized, given to smoking, dancing boogie-woogie and singing jazz. But as Rama finds out she is truly Indian deep down, strongly aware of her roots, and it is not for nothing that the novelist has given her the name of Savithri, a name that has rich associations from the Vedic times for every Indian. This superficial exterior is something typical of India, as Raja Rao has himself suggested in a brilliant image:

> The crust is so superficial — it lies about everywhere but
> you can remove it, even with a babulthorn. (p. 30.)

For Ramaswamy the brahmin, the true match, the marriage of true minds lies with one like Savithri and not Madeleine. Because she with her 'peacock-gold choli,' saree of 'colour of the sky' and a large kumkum on her head, a black bead chin around her neck and her ability to sing songs of Mira is the woman with whom he can strike a perfect relationship from the moment he meets her. After all, it is good to remember that the lack of all these in Madeleine bothered Rama intensely for his ideal woman is:

> Auspicious, so auspicious—with kumkum, coconut and choli piece, bangles on the arm, the necklace of black beads—is life. (p. 56.)

But when we examine Savithri as a character in fiction, we see how she is created for us by Raja Rao with the help of various details which are abstract generalisations and do not help to create the figure of Savithri in flesh and blood. All that Ramaswamy expected in a woman is found in her. She is the very epitome of Indian womanhood. Notice both her attributes and their effect on him:

> Her presence never said anything, but her absence spoke. (p. 31.)

> For Savithri life was a game, a song. (p. 122.)

> ... one knew she had some wisdom of herself that made her voice so intimate, so sustaining and so pure. (p. 134.)

> With Savithri truth and tact were but one instinctive experience. (p. 142.)

> ... to know Savithri was to sake into the truth of life, to be remembered—unto God (p. 169.)

> She became the awareness behind my awareness, the leap of my understanding. I lost the world and she became it. (p. 169.)

> Savithri proved that I could be I. (p. 170.)

> Savithri had such a reverence for things—were she picking up a spoon, or holding your pen in hand to write an address... (p. 175.)

> She wanted to surrender to Truth—and be *free*. (p. 187.)

> Savithri is a saint. (p. 187.)

> She is whole and simple wherever she is... (p. 289.)

There are many more of such references to Savithri. She is only an idealised conception of woman and not so much a *real* person. She is to be taken only as a symbol, and is offered almost as a foil to Madeleine by the novelist.

Ramaswamy justifies even her smoking, though it is offensive to his brahminical sensibility, as her capacity to be 'never un-at-home anywhere!' Apart from his visit to India, it is his meeting with Savithri that accounts for the fissures in his marriage with Madeleine. This becomes evident when specific instances in the novel where Ramaswamy makes a comparison between Savithri and Madeleine are scrutinised. The first time is when Savithri visits them. As she enters their villa she,

> threw open the window and looked out and said, "Oh, it's so beautiful here, look at that Moon of Shiva!" And she added, "Just like in Nainital." As she went up the steps to the landing above, she felt it was a palace — and so did we. We make objects — objects do not make us. Madeleine could no more have made it a palace than I a home. For Madeleine it was a villa, and I always felt I was her guest. (p. 124.)

It is this innate instinct of Savithri to see things Indian everywhere that unites her with Ramaswamy. On the contrary, Madeleine, being a Frenchwoman is unable to do this. But it is important to remember, that this not only points to a limitation in her but it must count as a deficiency in Ramaswamy's scheme of values as well. And then he had always said *namaskara* to her and never kissed goodbye in public. For that matter, he says

> Even to take Madeleine's arm in public seemed a desecration to me. But with Savithri it was different. Why, I wondered, why indeed... (p. 244.)

Ramaswamy the narrator, evades a direct answer to this question but it is all there most implicitly. With a Hindu woman like Savithri, he is totally uninhibited. The third instance is when he is in India for Saroja's marriage; he receives a long letter from Madeleine so full of protestations of love and affection for him. She declares, "I can love no one but you." (p. 260.) But even such a sincere letter evokes no kind response in him, and he feels actually angry though he adds, "may be it was for Saroja." Soon comes a cable from Savithri which says simply, "Be happy for me. In your joy is my freedom. And greetings to Saroja." This means so much for Rama that he decides to make the marriage a success, and "make the whole world happy."(p. 262.)

These three instances act as pointers to the relative positions of importance that Savithri and Madeleine occupy in Ramaswamy's life. We see that Rama assigns to Savithri, a far too significant a place in his life but this point is being emphasised only to counter the general trend of critical opinions that view Madeleine as the main culprit for the failure of their marriage. Rama's comparative assessment of the two women is best expressed in his own words:

> With Madeleine everything was explanation. With Savithri it was recognition. (p. 340.)

In understanding the relationship between Rama and Savithri, we see clearly another major reason for the failure of the Ramaswamy-Madeleine marriage. There is also between Rama and Madeleine a basic metaphysical difference in their view of the Self in spite of their emotional and intellectual bonds. That is why, Rama repeatedly refers to what the sage Yagnavalkya had said to Maitreyi:

> For whose sake, verity, does a husband love his wife? Not for the sake of his wife, but verily for the sake of the Self in her. (p. 24)

Their two different world-views constitute a fundamental hurdle to achieve a successful marriage for we see that "throughout the novel Rama is constantly seeking sameness, unity and the impersonal (these are Vedantic ideals) while Madeleine seeks the opposite: the personal, difference, other people as real."[41]

Actually, it is this philosophical position that explains the behaviour of each towards the other. While Ramaswamy because of his Vedantic view of life is able to see the sameness of things whether he is in India, France or England, Madeleine is bound by the personal and refuses to go beyond it. That is the reason why Ramaswamy has a sense of belonging wherever he lives, despite his profound feelings of loneliness and he is able to relate himself to people around him and establish a meaningful relationship with them as seen in his attachment to Oncle Charles, Tante Zoubie and Catherine. However true Madeleine's love is for Ramaswamy, she is unable to think of herself as a member of his family in India. Indeed, the family is the anchor that sustains individuals and when it is absent they have to perforce depend on each other. Even this does not happen in their case, for we notice Madeleine in her conversion to Buddhism moving away from Ramaswamy and such a marriage has to inevitably perish.

In the Ramaswamy-Madeleine marriage, Raja Rao has portrayed, taking into account all the complexities inherent in such a relationship, the coming together of an Indian and a Frenchwoman. His treatment makes for a probing that depicts them not merely as individuals but as representatives of cultures, ways of life, philosophical positions that are different. Despite the various factors that have contributed to the failure of their marriage, Raja Rao, as an Indian novelist has been very fair to Madeleine. Paradoxically, it is she who emerges as perhaps the most convincing character in the novel. She is as truly French as Ramaswamy is Indian in her reactions. That her involvement with Buddhism should ultimately degenerate into the level of rituals is a fine insight of Raja Rao. The western interest in India has more often than not ended up this way giving birth to numerous cults. In Ramaswamy, on the other hand, we have the presentation of an Indian who is aware of his *Indianness*. And it is through characters like Ramaswamy, that Raja Rao is able to give us a convincing image of India, for real people help make the locale authentic.

In this encounter of two individuals belonging to different nationalities, a cultural confrontation is also involved. Raja Rao has objectively portrayed both the French and Indian cultures in the novel. But in such a portrayal, evaluation of the cultures become inescapable. One suspects that the Indian culture is placed on a pedestal as exemplified in the character of Ramaswamy. However legitimate his feelings are, there is an air of superiority that is directly the consequence of his being a brahmin, a heir to a five thousand year old civilization. Hence his remark that

> Brahmins are like race horses; they are either good at their job, or they're sent to the vet to be shot. They are never sent to the common butchery; they could not be. (p. 334.)

In contrast to this, Madeleine tells Rama, "After all, we Europeans have been civilized only for a thousand years." (p. 116.) And after her meeting with Savithri, she tells him, "It's three thousand years of civilization that produces a thing like her." (p. 142.) Madeleine's tone is matter of fact, the tone betraying the approval of such a value judgement by the novelist. To take another example, talking of his own understanding of Buddhism in contrast to Madeleine, he remarks:

> "... I feel the word *dukka* almost with the entrails dropping into my hand, whereas for her it is mere sorrow. *Dukka* is the very tragedy of creation, the sorrow of the sorrow that *sorrow* is." (p. 80.)

Though this is not wholly untrue, the superiority of Ramaswamy is beyond question. Then we have Dr. Seraphin who is all praise for Ramaswamy because he is the ideal patient that any doctor can ever hope to get. He says:

> "... In his country it must be so easy to be a doctor. It must all come from their age-old civilization. Not like the cattle we have to deal with here... (p. 329.)

One last example should suffice to drive home this point. His guide, Professor Robin-Bessaignac signs Rama's papers and confesses of his "feeling that I had brought light to him and not he to me." Lest one should accuse Ramaswamy of being vain, we have his guide telling him clearly, "You have the wisdom of the ages—you're not barbarian like us." (p. 223.) All these references are sure to make a sensitive reader wonder whether Ramaswamy's pride in his being a brahmin and an Indian does not smack of racial arrogance. Had Raja Rao used the third person narrative, these remarks would have sounded less offensive.

The Serpent and the Rope has God's plenty to offer in terms of the presentation of various aspects of Indian life. To avoid labouring the obvious, only two aspects—marriage and family life—will be dealt with in some detail. There are of course many marriages in the novel apart from that of Ramaswamy and Madeleine. We have Ramaswamy's father's three marriages; his sister Saroja's marriage with Subramanya Sastri; Lakshmi's unhappy marriage with Captain Sham Sunder; Savithri's with stump Pratap; Catherine's with Georges and Tante Zoubie's with Oncle Charles. All of them in different ways are measured against the wisdom of Yagnyavalkya who had propounded that "Not for the husband's sake is the husband dear but for the Self's sake" and found to be wanting because "the desire to possess is the attribute of the self steeped in ignorance."[42] It is only Savithri's love for Ramaswamy that has successfully transcended the petty self into a recognition of the Self, the Absolute in personal relationships. This perhaps constitutes the ideal marriage of true minds in the novel.

If the philosophical basis of marriage receives profound treatment at the hands of the novelist, we also have a wonderful picture of an Indian marriage—of Saroja—in the novel. Observe, for instance, the elaborate preparations for the marriage:

> Men and women came in and out to decide whether this

> sari was good or the other, peacock-blue one; whether the opposite party should be given Dharmavaram saris or only cotton Kanchi ones—"And the gold sovereign will do the rest.!" The cooks, fat-bellied, belching, bejewelled, snuff in their palms and money tucked away at their waists, came in to ask if one needed a thousand laddus or a thousand two hundred, and whether the laddus would be for the second day or the third and whether milk had been ordered for the Khir, and saffron, almond and sugar. The house began to fill increasingly with neighbours making pappadams, the Brahmins came and showed their thirty two teeth, knowing that now the Master of the House was come—"And from London too," they said between themselves—there would be nothing lacking in honour and silver. The bamboos for the pandal began to arrive too. (pp. 255-56.)

All the bustle that marks the Indian wedding house is faithfully captured by Raja Rao with the help of significant details. Such a description could have come only from an insider. And a marriage in the Indian family is not merely a ritual that brings together two people but is also an occasion for all the relations, near and far, to meet and renew their acquaintances:

> Of course Uncle Seetharamu was there, and my cousins Seetha, Parvathi, Papa, Lakshmidevi, Nanja, Sita, Cauvery, Anandi, Venkatalakshmi, Bhagirathi and Savithri (This Savithri was a lean and haggard thing, having borne four children in succession, year after year; her belly was round and her breasts interminate.) Father's cousins Ramachandra and Lakshminarayana were there too, gay with laughter and spontaneous pun. Sanskrit, Kannada, Urdu, Telugu, English, were full of contradictory significances, so a word in this language meant something to me and something quite different to you, and so you laughed. (p. 256.)

Indian marriages are so full of gaiety, fun and laughter and all this comes through in the novel.

A few more illustrations should conclusively point to the remarkable evocative quality in Raja Rao's writings. Notice the atmosphere under the wedding pandal:

> All the women were gathered under the pandal, and there was a smell of camphor, Lucknow perfumes and betel leaves; the shine of white teeth, the splendour of black and gold saris, the magnificence of earrings, neckbands, nosedrops, diamond-marks on the forehead — an innocent joy which showed that man was made for natural happiness. (p. 264.)

Or in the inner courtyard of the house:

> What blues and greens of saris, what diamonds, rubies and sapphires were seen to glint. And by the tulasi Saroja was drying her spread hair on the fire-basket while the women were busy annointing her with henna and turmeric. Mango leaves and silver pots were to be seen all over the veranda... (p. 268.)

Or after the wedding is over:

> But the whole house seemed empty now. The women had all gone to the other-House. Carpets were deranged, flower garlands were withering in corners, children were asleep on half-open beds, and smells of incence and children's urine wandered everywhere, with no one to smell them. (p. 270.)

Any more comment would certainly be superfluous.

In one of the numerous *upakathas* (subsidiary stories) present in the novel, we have the story of Iswara Bhatta's pilgrimage to Benares. As he sets out, he carries his seven year old daughter on his shoulders and the manner in which he gets her married to an ascetic is uniquely Indian:

> And when he had approached the ascetic and offered many courtesies, Iswara Bhatta said, 'Venerable sir, you are lonely. I have a daughter to marry. Please become my son-in-law.' And the venerable ascetic said, 'What may I do with a wife? I have all my five austerities to perform.' To this Iswara Bhatta made answer 'No, Venerable Sir, it is meet for a man to marry and found family and health, that sacrifice may be made. Aye, Sir fulfil the duties of a householder.' And the venerable man said, 'So be it, so be

it,' whereupon Iswara Bhatta took tulasi lead and water and gave the daughter unto the venerable ascetic. Then he said, 'I go. Be happy, Daughter and Son-in-law,' and running towards the setting sun, he went. (p. 251.)

It is these experiences that fall outside the ken of Anglo-Indian novelists. What would have surely come for an ironical treatment at their hands is rendered convincingly by one who is rooted in the Indian culture. And then there is also the ritual marriage of Ramaswamy and Savithri in his room at Kensington. Even though Savithri marries Pratap, there is a higher relationship with Rama who "though only potentially, represented the highest Self, that which she was in quest of, from life to life."[43] But still she was Savithri and not Radha as Ramaswamy was not yet Krishna. And hence we have only a symbolic union in the novel.

Family is a very important institution in the Indian society for "the family, rather than the individual, was looked on as the unit of the social system."[44] Within the family, human relationships play a very significant role and this has been very well delineated by Raja Rao. We have Ramaswamy's deep attachment for his father. The father, a mathematician, was sad that his son did not follow his area of study, but was happy that Ramaswamy chose to work on Albigensian heresy "for he thought India should be made more real to the European." When Rama marries Madeleine, his reaction is mixed. He is unhappy for she "could not sing at an *arathi;* but before the world he boasted of his intellectual daughter-in-law." (p. 17.) Rama who found it hard to know his father and love him while he was alive understands him only after his death. Even though Little Mother is his stepmother, Ramaswamy is able to find in her his lost mother, for she loved him very dearly. And there is the wonderful relation between a brother and a sister as seen in Ramaswamy and Saroja. It is she who makes him aware of the sensibilities of a Brahmin girl and also of the blossoming of womanhood in a young girl. She is so close to her brother that she can only confide with him. It is again her love for him that finally makes her yield to marrying Subramanya Sastri. It is these relationships that help make the presentation of Indian family life real and credible.

It is true that joint family "is a microcosm of the profoundly pluralistic nature of Indian culture in all its manifestations."[45] There is a strong feeling of connectedness among the members of a family in India. This incisively brought out in Ramaswamy's reflections:

Living in the intimacy of my own family—where every gesture, idiosyncrasy or mole-mark was traced back to some cousin, aunt or grandfather; where there were such subtle understandings of half-said things, of acts that were respected or condemned according to the degree of stature, age or sex of one another—gave a feeling of complex oneness, from which one could never get out save by death, and even after that one would get into it again in the next life, and so on till the wheel of existence was ended.

And he goes on to illustrate it with a few instances:

"Father scratched his leg just there, at the arch of his foot, with the second finger, just like you," Sukumari remarked one evening. "Look, Rama, look!" Little Mother said; "Sridhara has a mole under his right arm, just where you have..." One night, when Little Mother was telling me a story, I went to sleep saying, "Yes, yes, Hum-hum," and everybody laughed, for I was snoring. "Just like his grandmother," said Aunt Sata, who had joined us. (p. 277.)

There are innumerable references to India scattered all through the novel. India is a major preoccupation of Raja Rao and this is nowhere more evident than in this novel. References to the Indian landscape are no doubt present as in the description of India as a

beloved land of many mountains and cliffs, of cedars and deodhars, of elephants and tigers, of pigeons that sing and owls that hoot. (p. 388.)

But more importantly, observe Ramaswamy's love for the land of his birth. For instance, what it is for Rama to be an Indian:

It is beautiful to live, beautiful and sacred to live and be an Indian in India. (p. 302.)

And this feeling towards the land gets more and more sentimental and romantic. This can be accounted for by Raja Rao's living away from his country. It is the expatriate's love for his country that degenerates, at times, into pure jingoism:

India was wonderful to me. It was like a juice that one is supposed to drink to conquer a kingdom or to reach the deathless-juice of rare jasmine or golden myrobalam...

(p. 15.)

For an advaitin like Ramaswamy, India is contiguous with time and space. That is why, he can assert, "India is everybody's: India is in everybody." (p. 193.) He later tells Madeleine:

> "Can you understand that all things merge, all thoughts and perceptions, in knowledge? It is in knowledge that you know a thing, not in seeing or hearing... That is India. *Jnanam* is India." (pp. 331-32.)

Hence, for Ramaswamy India is not merely the brahminical India but more significantly is synonymous with Sankara's *Shuddadvaita,* the philosophy of pure non-dualism. And for one who holds such a view

> India is not a country like France is, or like England; India is an idea, a metaphysic. (p. 376.)

Raja Rao's presentation of India as an idea needs to be examined. In some cases, he progresses from the concrete to the abstract:

> The whole of the Gangetic plain is one song of saintly sorrow, as though Truth began where sorrow was accepted, and India began where Truth was acknowledged. So sorrow is our river, sorrow our earth, but the green of our trees and the white of our mountains are the affirmation that Truth is possible; that when the cycle of birth and death is over, we can proclaim ourselves the Truth. Truth is the Himalaya, and Ganges Humanity. (p. 35.)

Also consider a description of the Himalayas:

> The Himalaya was like Lord Shiva himself, distant, inscrutable, and yet very intimate there where you do not exist. He was like space made articulate, not before you but behind you, behind what is behind and which is behind one; it led you back through abrupt silences to the recesses of your own familiar but unrecognized self. The Himalaya made the peasant and the Brahmin feel big, not with any earthly ambition, but with the bigness, the stature of the impersonal, the stature of one who knows the deepest sleep. For in the deepest sleep, as every pilgrim knows, one is wide awake, awake to oneself. And the Himalaya was that sleep made knowledge. (p. 42.)

This is not the Raja Rao of *Kanthapura* who evoked India through the accumulation of concrete details. Here, there is no pictorial description of the Himalayas but only the true significance of these mountains, that is "space made articulate" and "sleep made knowledge." These mountains along with the river Ganges are external manifestations of Truth, Humanity and Knowledge all of which constitute the idea of India. And so, "India has no history for Truth cannot have history." (p. 102.) "India is outside history" (p. 247.) also because there "the past and the present are for ever knit into one whole experience." (p. 19.) Rama reiterates again that India for him is "not a country, not a historical presence among nations, but a hypostatic presence." (p. 193.)

It is hence logical that one like Rama should ignore the historical presence of India. On his arrival at Santa Cruz for Saroja's wedding,

> It was India I wanted to see, the India of my inner being. Just as I could now see *antarakasi*, the 'inner Benares,' India for me became no land — not these trees, this sun, this earth; not those ladle hands and skeletal legs of bourgeois and coolie; not even the new pride of the uniformed Indian official, who seemed almost to say, 'Don't you see, I am Indian now, and I represent the Republic of India' — but something other, more centred, widespread, humble; as though the gods had peopled the land with themselves, as the trees had forested the country, rivers flowed and named themselves, birds winged themselves higher and yet higher, touched the clouds and soared beyond, calling to each other over the valleys by their names. The India of Brahma and Prajapathi; of Varuna, Mithra and Aryaman; of Indra, of Krishna, Shiva and Parvathi; of Rama, Harischandra and Yagnyavalkya; this India was a continuity I felt, not in time but in space... (p. 246.)

The realities of actual living in India do not seem to interest him, for he is so wholly preoccupied with the timeless and eternal India. This has apparently disturbed some critics of Raja Rao, notably D.S.Maini among them, since they believe that a writer cannot be oblivious of the harsh and unpleasant truths of life. To be fair to Raja Rao, it should be said that he is aware of these facts of life but he deliberately plays down this India in favour of a timeless conception of the country. He is conscious of the independent India.

> ... where the new crude Congressman and the old vulgar aristocracy mingled for the building of a magnificent India. But it would never be my India, it could never be Savithri's India. It would in fact be nobody's India, till someone sat and remembered what India was. (p. 375.)

His concern is for the immaculate India and hence for him the real India almost ceases to exist. Despite what the corrupt politician might do to this country, Raja Rao the expatriate is absolutely certain that his India which is the essence of Truth will always continue to survive. Note his rhetorical question:

> India would never be made by our politicians and professors of political science, but by these isolate existences of India, in which India is rememorated, *experienced* and communicated; beyond history, as tradition, as the Truth. Anybody can have the geographic — even the political — India; it matters little. But this India of Coomaraswamy, who will take it away, I ask you, who? Not Tamerlane or even Joseph Stalin. (p. 352.)

Such an attitude has to be viewed in its proper perspective by taking into account the central concerns of Raja Rao. For him, man is more a metaphysical being, one who is involved in a pilgrimage, which is a quest for truth. Without such a quest, man's life ceases to have any meaning. Of course, this metaphysical search has to be undertaken here and now while taking on all the responsibilities of being a member of a household and a large family. He has to pass through different stages in his growth towards Self-knowledge. Such is the life of the protagonist that is depicted in the novel. But it is the ultimate reality that is truly significant for the novelist and everything else becomes subsidiary to this quest of man. In view of this position of Raja Rao's, we see him assert that "Truth is metaphysical and not moral.":

> I hated this moral India. True, Indian morality was based on an ultimate metaphysic. Harischandra told the truth; and lost his Kingdom and his wife, but he found the Truth. (p. 349.)

What is being emphasised at this point is, that Raja Rao's near-rejection of contemporary India is consistent with his own view of life. The implications of such a view of life will be considered in some detail at the end of the chapter.

Ramaswamy as an Advaitin is able to perceive fundamental oneness among all things. That is the reason why he never feels out of place anywhere and also has an inclusive view of the world. He carries his India, as it were, with him wherever he goes. While going to meet Savithri in Paris, he remarks: "I was going to meet the Himalayas. The Ganges flowed everywhere." (p. 118.) For him, 'the Mediterranean is an Indian sea, a Brahminic ocean." (p. 385.) And "Mother Rhone, sister to Ganga, flowed on the other side." (p. 385.) This attitude is most emphatically stated by him towards the end of the novel:

> India is the Kingdom of God, and it is within you. India is wheresoever you see, hear, touch, taste, smell. India is where you dip into yourself, and the eighteen aggregates are dissolved. (p. 389.)

While all these references are to India as an idea, the novel is not entirely bereft of allusions to India as a geographical entity. These allusions deal mostly with the present day India and hence help us in our search for Raja Rao's attitudes. Industrial India has no place in Raja Rao's world. Bombay is "a barbaric city" and "had no right to exist." Curiously, even in such a place he makes an exception as far as the Hindu area is concerned since there "you almost felt you were back in Benares." (p. 44.) Furthermore, Raja Rao with his brahminical sensibility makes a clear cut distinction between North and South India and shows a distinct preference for the latter. For him, "the whole of the North, but for the Ganges, was one desolation of dirt."(p. 27.) Little Mother tells Saroja on her return from the trip to the North:

> "Say what you will, Saroja, the Northerners haven't the sensibility of living such as we have. You can see married women without kumkum on their faces, or men spitting on the floor. And as for dirt, well, the less said the better. It is something, Saroja, to be born a Brahmin." (p. 48.)

Ramaswamy wonders:

> I could not understand these Northerners going from strict purdah to this extreme modernism with unholy haste. We in the South were more sober, and very distant. We lived by tradition—shameful though it might look. We did not mind quoting Sankaracharya in law courts or marrying our girls in the old way, even if they had gone abroad.

(pp. 31-32.)

And even Savithri, herself a Northerner, writes to Rama, "we in the North are new to civilization" (p. 107.) and "Your South still has so much beauty, wisdom and purity." (p. 347.) The only complimentary reference to the North comes from Rama and it is significant that it should be about Savithri. He tells Lakshmi in London that,

> "... You and I, who come from the South, we know too much: We shall never have such innocence. Savithri is a saint." (p. 187.)

This really means no change of attitude in Ramaswamy, for the person in question is Savithri who is always associated with all that is holy, good and innocent. When such is the evidence, it is quite amusing to read R.K. Kaul[46] suggesting that the views of the characters are not necessarily shared by Raja Rao. As a matter of actual fact, this propensity to glorify the brahminical South is a positive outcome of his thematic concerns as seen in the novel.

At this point, it would be rewarding to briefly examine Raja Rao's evocations of France and England in the novel. Ramaswamy grows lyrical over France. It seems to be,

> a rolling garden of carrots and turnips, of plane trees that made diagonal approaches to river and castle, and of long, white roads that went to the infinity of the three seas. (p. 52.)

And Paris,

> somehow is not a city: it is an area in oneself, a Concorde in one's being, where the river flows by you with an intimacy that seems to say the divine is not in the visible architecture of the Orangerie or the presence of the Pont des Arts, but where the trees would end; and even when the lorries have trundled over the cobbled streets—with potato and onion, geese, lard, margarine and cows' flesh; oranges, birds, Roquefort... (p. 51.)

In these descriptions it is evident that the novelist is not merely trying to evoke France and Paris in concrete terms but, more importantly, sees them in their inner essence.

Raja Rao adopts another mode to establish the spirit of the place as when he describes Montpalais in terms of its history, myths and legends. In a similar vein, he rhetorically questions:

> Does he who sets foot on the soil of France know he treads where Saint Louis trod, walks where Henry IV rode, goes where the great Mistral walked? Or that he looks at Mont Sainte- Victoire which Cezanne made famous, in violet and silver, in Venetian green and in mud-red? Or that Peguy walked eighty–eight kilometers from Paris to Chartres, to carry the homage of the country of Beaune to the Queen of France? (p. 124.)

Here is an outsider's view of France that can easily pass for that of an insider. Such is Raja Rao's sympathy, understanding and intellectual awareness of a country, not his own.

Similarly, Ramaswamy goes into raptures over the river Cam:

> The Cam had flowers floating on it, and boats and the laughter of the very young. The Cam seemed never to have grown old, even though the buildings were so aged, for the Cam like us men and women flows right in herself, outside of history. Who, after all, could write the history of the Cam, for she was certainly there before man came to the British Isle, and she will be there even if the whole of England join the European Continent... The Cam is silent and self- reflective. It teaches you that history is made by others and not by oneself. Trinity may have a bridge over the Cam, but the Cam has no bridge... The Cam is a river that lives on giving dreams. (pp. 167-68.)

Also, observe his reflections on the Thames:

> What an imperial river the Thames is — her colour may be dark or brown, but she flows with a majesty, with a maturity of her own knowledge of herself, as though she grew the tall towers beside her, and buildings rose in her image ... the landowner is eminently good. He is so warm, he is indeed the first citizen of the world. The mist in Thames is pearly, as if Queen Elizabeth the First had squandered her riches and feminity on ships of gold, and Oberon had played on his pipe, so worlds, gardens, fairies and grottoes were created, empires were built and lost, men shouted heroic things to one another and died, but somewhere was one woman, golden, round, imperial, al-

> ways lay by her young man, his hand over her left breast, his lips touching hers in rich recompense. There's holiness in happiness, and Shakespeare was holy because Elizabeth was happy. (pp. 198-99.)

Apart from the exquisitely lyrical quality of the descriptions that contributes to the rich evocation of the Cam and the Thames, it is again the ability of Raja Rao to look at them in their totality—the fact, as well as its different associations—historical, political and literary that gives the pictures a wholeness, a rare achievement indeed for an outsider. In addition, there is also the wonderful picture of the pub life in England.

Along with these evocations, we have minor but recognizable portraits of the peoples of France and England. All these go to show how a gifted novelist without any political axe to grind, is able to give an authentic image of a country other than his own. This comes as a sharp contrast to the failure of the vast majority of Anglo-Indian novelists to portray India successfully.

One of the important aspects of this study is to consider how far the fictional techniques of these three writers is determined by their attitude to Indian actuality and the spirit of India. While Raja Rao employed the folk-narrative mode in *Kanthapura* to depict the life of an Indian village caught in the freedom movement of the 30's, in *The Serpent and the Rope,* he was trying to achieve something very different and perhaps more ambitious, for he is telling the story of Ramaswamy, a South Indian brahmin intellectual profoundly aware of his Indian roots. His life, a pilgrimage, as he repeatedly terms it, is so completely Indian in its spiritual and metaphysical sense that Raja Rao had to, like all great writers, evolve a form that could accommodate this new experience. He evolves in *The Serpent and the Rope,* a truly Indian novel-form without entirely ignoring the western notions of the novel.

It would be appropriate to begin with the objection raised by David McCutchion in his review of the novel. He asks "is this a novel at all?" because in his view, in *The Serpent and the Rope,*

> All the central concerns of the western novel are absent—social relations, psychological motivation, characterisation, judgement, a passion for the concrete.[47]

That a perceptive critic like David McCutchion chooses to view the novel from an accepted, traditional point of view brings home the truth in the cliché, that habits die hard even among literary critics. The dominant strain in the novel is reflective and meditative, but to suggest, as McCutchion does, that all the features of the Western novel are absent in *The Serpent and the Rope* is to ignore the rich content of life in the novel.

Social relations, for instance, are not entirely absent in the novel: the joint family system prevalent in India receives considerable attention at the hands of Raja Rao. We see how after his father's death, Ramaswamy has to assume the headship of the family and how, in his absence, Little Mother takes on this role. All the intricacies of this position are clearly brought home to us in the responsibilities, obligations and duties as evident in Ramaswamy performing the last rites of his father, and then the marriage of his sister, Saroja. Also consider his relation with the peasants of his village, Hariharapura. The spontaneous show of affection, reverence and pride in the peasants towards him speak of the enduring ties that exist between him and his tenants. However, this, is not to assert that social relations between individuals are depicted as extensively as, say, in a novel of Dickens.

Psychological motivation is imperative in a work where we have relationships between human beings and it is this motivation which provides the thrust for both their actions and growth. To indicate that in this novel such a psychological motivation is absent is to betray basic ignorance of the complexities involved in a marriage, especially between two persons of different races. A thorough delineation of the Ramaswamy-Madeleine marriage that we have in the novel would not have been possible without Raja Rao paying adequate attention to the psychological motivations in the two. The crisis in their relationship is shown to be motivated entirely by the impact of the death of the second child on Madeleine. Unlike most characters in fiction, Rama's growth is conditioned by his metaphysical search but this search is, without any doubt, motivated and assisted by his encounters with the two women, Savithri and Madeleine.

In a novel with a host of characters, the author cannot escape from what is normally described as 'characterisation.' Raja Rao's major characters are Ramaswamy and Madeleine and in his portrayal of these two, the emphasis falls mainly on their inner conflicts and inner problems. The inner being receives all the attention and this is quite legitimate keeping in view the central concerns of the novelist. But this is not to suggest that he ignores the exterior, for we know what Ramaswamy looks like, and we are even told of how Madeleine's hair smells.

Georges is another rounded character though persons like Little Mother, Saroja, Oncle Charles, Tante Zoubie are all 'flat' characters. Only because there is a different conception of 'characterisation', the novel cannot be said to have ignored characterisation as a technique.

The next objection is that in the novel there is no judgement. Whatever may be the form that a novelist employs, he can never escape from judging his characters unless he is a writer without a sense of responsibility and a creative conscience. Raja Rao is not merely presenting Madeleine and Savithri as women but is judging them from his own standpoint — the brahminic and the advaitic — and finds the former wanting. Though there are references to other religions, most notably Buddhism among them, it is the world view of the advaita philosophy that is upheld in the novel.

The final point, that a passion for the concrete is absent in Raja Rao, is perhaps the most valid of all McCutchion's objections. While a novelist's major concern is to render the abstract into concrete in terms of specific particularities and localised details, Raja Rao moves from the concrete to the abstract. This is initially very disturbing to the reader but he gets accustomed to it once he gets past the early pages of the novel. But even Raja Rao presents India through accumulation of concrete details. However, in addition to this conventional manner, he also evokes the land through associations of abstract ideas. To choose a specific illustration,[48] talking of the Himalayas, Raja Rao does not give a description in concrete terms but goes on to speak at length on the essential and timeless significance of these Indian mountains. He sees them not as physical and geographical entities but as external manifestations of Truth, Humanity and Knowledge, i.e., in terms of abstractions.

Though one is convinced that *The Serpent and the Rope* is not a Western novel in the widely-understood sense of the term, a detailed rebuttal of McCutchion's view became necessary to drive home the point, often ignored by critics, that the novel *does* contain all the essential features of a Western novel. But it is in his conception of social relations and characterisation that Raja Rao is different both from his Western and Indian counterparts. For him, the relation between the 'I' and the Absolute is more significant than all the known social relations. His conception of characterisation is primarily a portrayal of the inner self of a character. And the preference for the abstract is a direct result of his philosophical preoccupations that makes him view the world as *Maya* or illusion. It is these unique characteristics that make the novel seem, from the western viewpoint, a work that "has a loose almost formless structure, plotless and very nearly actionless." [49]

The clue to the form of the novel is given by Raja Rao himself in his assertion that, "the Indian novel can only be epic in form and metaphysical in nature. It can only have story within story to show all stories are only parables."[50] And in *The Serpent and the Rope* we have an admirable attempt made by Raja Rao to create an Indian novel that is true to his own conception. And as M.K.Naik succinctly points out, "Indian epics like the later puranas, are a medley of narration, history, description, and philosophical and religious discourse."[51] Ramaswamy the narrator observes at one point in the novel:

> I am not telling a story here, I am writing the sad and uneven chronicle of a life, my life, with no art or decoration, but with the "objectivity," the discipline of the "historical sciences," for by taste and tradition I am only a historian. (p. 231.)

He is a historian by "taste and tradition" and his historical account is rooted in actual facts while the history of the *Puranas* is mythical. The historian's method is evident when he visits Hyderabad and recounts the legend associated with the place. It was the King of Golconda who lured Lakshmi, the Goddess of Wealth, into residing in the city for all the times and that is why the city is called Bhagyanagar after Bhagyavathi, another name for Lakshmi. And he adds that "Hyderabad is but a vulgar homonym." (p. 248.)

As in both the Indian epics and puranas, numerous legends and stories abound in the novel. We have the *Katha* (main story) — that of Ramaswamy — and number of Upakathas (subsidiary stories). There are stories of Satyakama and Budumekaye (pp. 119-21); of Iswara Bhatta and his family (pp. 249-55); of Radha, Krishna and Durvasa (pp. 380-82); of the good man who tried to cover the whole earth with leather to protect himself from the scorching heat of the sun (pp. 336-38); of Jagannatha Bhatta and Shahajahan's daughter (pp. 177-78); of Tristan and Iseult; of Buddha and Vasista (p. 236) and of Yagnyavalkya and Maitreyi (p. 24.) and many, many more. These stories must not be seen entirely in terms of the Jamesian conception of an organically structured novel to determine their significance. In actual fact, all these stories like, reflections from a prism, tangentially illumine the main theme of the novel, the ultimate nature of reality.

Apart from the usual dialogues that are found in any novel, we have in *The Serpent and the Rope* dialogues where profoundly philosophical issues are discussed in the form of questions and answers so characteristic of our Upanishads. Ramaswamy and Savithri attempt a definition of Truth in this mode (pp. 130-31) and in another place he and Georges try to define Knowledge. (pp. 108-12.) In both these instances, Ramaswamy invokes the assistance of the Upanishadic sages. Here is another example of Raja Rao using the ancient Indian method in his novel.

A dialogue slightly different in nature between Rama and Madeleine before their break up, should be quoted in full since it throws important light on Raja Rao's method:

"What is it separated us, Rama?"
"India".
"India? But I am a Buddhist."
"That is why Buddhism left India. India is *impitoyable*."
"But one can become a Buddhist?"
"Yes, and a Christian and a Muslim as well."
"Then?"
"One can never be converted to Hinduism."
"You mean one can only be born a Brahmin?"
"That is — an Indian," I added, as an explanation of India.
"Your India, then, Rama, is in time and space?"
"No. It is contiguous with time and space, but is anywhere, everywhere."
"I don't understand."
"It stands, as it were, vertical to space and time and is present at all points."
"This is too mystical even for me."
"Would you understand if I were to say, 'Love is not a feeling; it is, you might say, a stateless state, the whole condition of oneself'?"
"I don't. But suppose I did?"
"Can you understand that all things merge, all thoughts and perceptions, in knowledge? It is in knowledge that you know a thing, not in seeing or hearing."

"Yes"

"That is India. *Jnanam* is India"

"But that is the place of the Guru — of Buddha?"

> "Well, for me India is the Guru of the world, or she is not India. The sages have no history, no biography—who knows anything about a Yagnyavalkya or a Bharadvaja? Nobody. But some petty King of Bundelkhand has a panegyric addressed to him, and even this is somewhat impersonal. We know more of king Harsha than we do of Sankara. India has, I always repeat, no history. To integrate India into history—is like trying to marry Madeleine. It may be sincere, but it is not history. History, if anything, is the acceptance of human sincerity. But Truth transcends sincerity; Truth is *in* sincerity and *in* insincerity—beyond both. And *that* again is India. (pp. 331-32)

Before commenting on this passage, it would be helpful to examine the reservations expressed by C.D.Narasimhaiah who feels that "it sounds a little unnatural for Ramaswamy and Madeleine to be engaged in dry intellectual discussion when the relationship has already strained between them."[52] What is however disturbing is the conviction with which he goes on to assert that the,

> entire conversation is meant to illuminate the main theme, but is not organic to the action of the story, does not arise from it inevitably, inexorably, and can therefore be cut out without injury to the main action—which would be very unfortunate considering how important it is. But had it been incorporated into the structure of the novel without letting it stand outside the narrative, its value would have been inestimable.[53]

To recapitulate a little on this situation, Ramaswamy and Madeleine have almost reached a deadend in their married life. Madeleine after her conversion to Buddhism, is more and more convinced of the failure of their marriage though this conviction does not in the least lesson her love and concern for Ramaswamy. On the other hand, he is most unhappy with the change that has come over Madeleine and is unable to understand it despite his sincere efforts. It is at this critical juncture in their lives, that she questions him as to what is it that separated them. She has always had the highest regard for Ramaswamy who, as a brahmin and an Indian, is for her a true repository of wisdom. That is the reason why she poses this question to him and it is the natural culmination to the differences between them. And now follows this long, intellectual dialogue between the two. It is not as if this is the first time that they indulge in such conversation since as two intellectuals we have seen them earlier give expression to their inner conflicts and dilemmas. This answer of Ramaswamy pinpoints the reason for their separation as being the difference inherent in the two cultures. For him, Madeleine's conversion to Buddhism, as she had unfortunately assumed, does not bring her closer to India. As emphasized earlier on, Ramaswamy could only marry an Indian and none else. The entire passage is of central importance to an understanding of their relationship and hence organically connected to the theme of the novel.

C.D.Narasimhaiah is aware of the importance of the passage, but believes quite contrary to the facts of the situation, that it does not emerge out of the context of the novel. Now what is important is to remember that the conversation between Ramaswamy and Madeleine does not stop there. It continues with Ramaswamy going on to speak of the Marxist's view of the world that "the world exists and so—you" and of the Vedantin's that "you exist—and so the world." (p. 333.) Madeleine who is not perhaps totally convinced by Ramaswamy's earlier answer wants to know the position of Buddhism in view of these two attitudes to life. He tells her that "to have compassion ... presupposes the existence of the world." (p. 333.) He states it in unequivocal terms a little later:

> " ... The Buddhists say the world, the perception is *real*, 'Sarvam-Kshanikam,' that everything is minutous the moment we see it. The Vedantin says the perception is real, yes; but that reality is 'my self.' And that difference is big enough to drive the Buddhism of Gautama outside our frontiers." (p. 334.)

Even then Madeleine would like to be left to her poetic world of Buddhism. As a further clarification of these two different attitudes towards reality, he enacts the difference through the metaphor of the serpent and the rope:

> "The world is either unreal or real—the serpent or the rope. There is no in-between-the-two—and all that's in-between is poetry, is sainthood. You might go on saying all the time, "No, no it's the rope,' and stand in the serpent. And looking at the rope from the serpent is to see paradises, saints, avataras, gods, heroes, universes. For

wheresoever you go, you see only with the serpent's eyes whether you call it duality or modified duality, you invent a belvedere to heaven, you look at the rope from the posture of the serpent, you feel you are the serpent — you are — the rope is. But in true fact, with whatever eyes you see there is no serpent, there never was a serpent. You gave your own eyes to the falling evening and cried, '*Ayyo*: Oh! It's the serpent!' You run and roll and lament, and have compassion for fear of pain, others' or your own. You see the serpent and in fear you feel you are it, the serpent, the saint. One — the Guru — brings you the lantern; the road is seen, the long, white road, going with the statutory stars. 'It's only the rope.' He shows it to you. And you touch your eyes and *know* there never was a serpent. Where was it, where I ask you? The poet who saw the rope as serpent became the serpent, and so a saint. Now, the saint is shown that his sainthood was identification, not realization. The actual, the real has no name. The rope is no rope to itself."

"Then what is it?"

"The rope. Not as opposed to the serpent, but the rope just *is* — and therefore there is no world."

"But there can be a Beatrice?" she implored.

"Yes", I said, after a long while. "Yes, where I am not. When I can love the self in Maitreyi, I can be Yagnyavalkya."

"Find then, my friend, an Indian Maitreyi. Let me be the woman of the marches." (pp. 335-336.)

This is the climax to this long dialogue that runs on for almost five pages. As Ramaswamy himself puts it, "the battle at last had ended."

Hence the passage quoted by C.D.Narasimhaiah cannot be read in isolation, but has to be taken in its entirety in the context of their attempt to intellectually comprehend the reasons for the "catastrophe" that their marriage eventually turned out to be. When viewed in this manner, the entire passage has a thematic relation to the theme of the novel even in the Jamesian sense.

The passage quoted above in full, is again significant from the point of view of Raja Rao's mode of writing. *The Serpent and the Rope* is "a wise combination"[54] of altogether two different modes — the aphoristic and that of enactment. The central concept of Sankara's Advaita philosophy is not stated but it is most poetically enacted by the novelist in an artistically satisfying manner in the passage. Another example of such a mode illustrates this point further. To Madeleine's query, whether "is it possible always to speak the truth?", Ramaswamy replies in the negative because for him "truth is a question of perspective." And this intellectual belief of his is rendered through enactment:

> "...We're all like men and women and children at a wrestling match or a holy procession: the tall father sees the wrestler hit or the God bejewelled, and the son says, 'Papa, why is it you laugh, what did you see?' And he has to take the child on his shoulder and tell him the name of the Muslim wrestler from North India or of the Goddess whose Lord is awaiting Her at the temple door. But in either case the child, being higher than his father now, sees differently. Nobody can see at the level of your eye — and so nobody can speak the real truth. Not even the scientist."
> (p. 129.)

And there are many more examples scattered throughout the novel. The enactment is achieved, as in this case, through stories that are illustrative in nature. But it should be conceded that there is no attempt by Raja Rao to balance the two modes in a consistent manner to the satisfaction of critics fed entirely on the western novel. And surely enough, the critic turns a blind eye to "the embarrassing amount of enactment"[55] in the novel and concludes in the manner of D.S.Maini that "one of the weaknesses of *The Serpent and The Rope* is that Raja Rao fails to fully dramatise the ideas swarming in his mind."[56] Such is the rigidity of the critical canons employed by some critics of Raja Rao.

The aphoristic mode has inevitably come in for harsher criticism. While David McCutchion believes that Raja Rao "is given to pretentious aphorisms ('affection is just a spot in the geography of the mind'),"[57] D.S.Maini is convinced that "in this novel, aphorisms and epigrams are, generally speaking more a rhetorical device than earned and felt truths."[58] The assumption here is once again typically western oriented. That is, all aphorisms should be the logical outcome of what has gone before or they ought to be the climactic statement in any given situation. Interestingly, Raja Rao shares these assumptions to some extent though not entirely. McCutchion's own example can be examined to see how pretentious are Raja Rao's aphorisms. It is while in Benares as Ramaswamy goes down the river with Little Mother, with Sridhara on her lap that he "could so clearly picture Madeleine." He can visualise her sitting by the window in their Villa Sainte-Anne and then his mind traverses through the period of time they would spend together on vacation. There is a deeply felt inner longing in Ramaswamy for Madeleine and his feelings are epigrammatically expressed in the aphorism: "Affection is just a spot in the geography of the mind."(p. 18.) It is anything but pretentious since it is a natural conclusion to his yearning with thousands of geographical miles separating them. Let us take another example. He is still in Benares, the city which is for him, 'eternal.' It is now evening, naturally illuminated because of the burning funeral pyres on the ghats. Little Mother recites Sankara's *Nirvana-Astakam* and Rama joins her in singing hymns of Sankara. Something inexplicable happens to him and he is moved to tears not by sorrow but by happiness. And he makes the equation, "Holiness is happiness. Happiness is holiness."(p. 22.) an equation that has the force of a discovered truth for Ramaswamy in the given situation. These apart, there are those that do not emerge as the culmination of his feelings but are merely stated by the novelist such as, "Truth must be simple, natural and sweet" (p. 81.), "Holiness is wheresoever love is." (p. 385.) This is an integral part of Raja Rao's fictional mode. The validity of these numerous aphorisms is justified by either their direct or tangential reference to the various themes in the novel.

As in a *purana* that has almost an encyclopaedic sweep, in *The Serpent and the Rope* we have innumerable subjects discussed either briefly or in some detail. Such are communism, monarchy, nazism, imperialism, law, sanskrit, catholicism and a host of others. *The Serpent and the Rope* can also be regarded as a novel of ideas in view of the preponderance of ideas in it. But it should be observed that a fair balance between ideas and events that we notice in a good novel of this genre is not always achieved by Raja Rao. However, it should be obvious by now that for one attempting to innovate an Indian novel, such a balance was outside his artistic intentions. And so we see that though he achieves this balance in a number of instances, by and large the ideas predominate over the events.

And apparently it is this predominance of ideas that has disturbed every reader. C.D.Narasimhaiah expresses deep "reservations especially in regard to the considerable chunks of metaphysical disquisition scattered through the book" but he offers a solution as well when he suggests that "fortunately ... one can cut them out without injuring the organic structure of the novel."[59] If the choice of Achakka in *Kanthapura* made for a very homely kind of writing, in *The Serpent and the Rope* the choice of Ramaswamy, an intellectual and a brilliant scholar with a natural preference for philosophical speculations, makes for a speculative and meditative strain in the novel which accounts for the "considerable chunks of metaphysical disquisition." Once the reader gets used to the new experience of reading a novel like this and makes the necessary mental adjustments, he is sure to comprehend the various strands of experience present in the novel. This is not to belittle the difficulties involved in reading *The Serpent and the Rope*. It will become amenable to critical analysis once the reader is able to discover how the novel "sets up its own unique rhetorical structure."[60] It will be seen that this structure is similar to the one found in our epics and *puranas*, a point forcefully made with illustrations by M.K.Naik.[61] But the most satisfying formulation with regard to the form of the novel comes from G.S.Amur:

> The novel derives its structure from a dialectic between two levels of presentation, one operating horizontally and dealing with events in time and space and the other operating vertically through a celebration of truths transcending these dimensions.[62]

Thus in *The Serpent and the Rope*, we have a truly Indian novel which need not be subjected to the Jamesian canons of criticism of the novel, and evaluated solely from the standpoint of western criticism. Even David McCutchion for all his reservations, concedes that

> Raja Rao's book makes no attempt at half-way solutions taking the 'best' of both worlds: its sensibility and values are uncompromisingly Indian absorbing all experience from the point of one who seeks Brahman.[63]

It is a tribute to the artistic integrity of Raja Rao that he refuses to compromise and make a concession to his readers in his undertaking to produce an Indian novel. This he has been able to achieve by extending the frontiers of the fictional form through an intelligent use of traditional Indian literary forms such as epics, puranas, and Upanishads. He has made us aware of the rich possibilities of the novel form in the twentieth century for which we owe him a debt of gratitude.

Now we may cast a glance at the way the author has used the English language to convey the distinctly Indian experience in *The Serpent and the Rope*. The departures from Standard English are not as numerous and startling as in *Kanthapura*, for in this novel the narrator is a English educated intellectual. Even then Indian English expressions are frequently seen in the novel. Take for instance, Indian terms of reference in conveying feelings and emotions:

> It seemed as though happiness was near at hand, could be cut from a tree like a jackfruit, like a *bel*. (p. 366.)

> Lakshmi had such a heavy sadness, like a sari she had wetted and pressed under her feet, and forgotten in the corner of the courtyard to rot. (p. 294.)

There are also many typical Indian expressions:

> What could you do with Tante Zoubie's tongue — it was like that. "You can't stitch it with a gunnybag needle." (p. 93.)

> Milk would flow in the house and the cattle would fill the courtyard with holiness. (p. 47.)

> When a Mysore peasant woman sees a rainbow, she exclaims, 'There, there! It must be the wedding of the dog and the jackal.' (p. 141.)

> "Ah, till the *tali* is tied all is sweetness; afterwards it's the festival of the bitter neem leaf."(p. 275.)

But for a more creative expression of Indian sensibility in English language, two illustrations should point to Raja Rao's genius. The first one is the "strange sensation" that Ramaswamy feels on observing Saroja becoming a woman:

> ...Saroja's presence now obsessed me sometimes, like one of those nights with the perfume of magnolia. Rich and green seemed the sap as it rose, and it had a night of its own and a day ... I was intoxicated with Saroja's presence, like a deer could be before a waterfall, or an elephant before a mountain peak; something primordial or awakening in a creature, and I felt that maturity in a girl was like the new moon or the change of equinox, it had polar affinities. There was, something of the smell of musk, of the oyster when the pearl is still within, of the deep silent sea

before the monsoon breaks. There was, too, a feeling of a temple sanctuary, and I could now understand why primitive peoples took the first blood of menstruation for the better harvesting of their fields. And why the Indians have such beautiful names to their woman, and told us how Malavika when she poured water made the asoka flower, or Shakuntala the karnikar blossom. What a deep and reverential mystery womanhood is. I could bow before Saroja and call her Queen. (pp. 49-50.)

The second is a description of the pregnant woman in her mother's home.

... Just as bottled champagne remembers its own springtime, the grandmother-to-be goes through a new motherhood, and absolves the pain of her own child. She offers her big, round daughter cashew nuts and paprika, Bengal-gram payasam and hot tamarind chutney; she makes brinjal curry for the evening, with Marathabuds, coriander and cardamom; and once in three days there is onion curry, smelling from the kitchen to the mat on the floor. The pregnant daughter eats almost where she lies, and when she is taken into the lying-in-room, how wonderful to hear the child cry — a long, broken-glass sound, but happy, new, reviving — the limbs become renewed, fresh, whole; the stomach feels vacant, and the nostrils are filled with the smell of garlic and betel nut ... (pp. 241-42.)

It is this capacity to convey an experience through phrases, figures of speech and images that are typically Indian which accounts for the authentic Indian ring about them. Interestingly, when Ramaswamy visits his village Hariharapura, we are once again back in the world of *Kanthapura* and are witness to Raja Rao's sureness of control over his material. This is seen even while he describes an emotion in terms of an image that is not Indian but French as in Ramaswamy's response to the news of his father's illness:

Despite my lack of love for father, tears came to my throat; I felt the beginnings of my biological presence on the earth disappear one by one. Not that he was my father, I felt; but like the wine in the cellars of champagne that ferments when spring comes to the vineyard outside, and sinks and bubbles back at the fall of autumn, the sap in me, the continuity in me, was being strained, was being broken. (p. 56.)

And now back to Ramaswamy's search for the meaning of his life. It is carried out not in abstract terms, but through his relationships with Savithri and Madeleine and his growing awareness of his Indian roots. At the end of it all comes this realisation, after a painful search:

> "...No, not a God but a Guru is what I need. 'Oh Lord, my Guru, my Lord..." (p. 402.)
>
> For now I know the name of Him to whom I have to go, though I have always known Him without knowing His name. So to Travancore I will go. (p. 404.)

In his quest for self-knowledge, he discovers that it is only through the spiritual guidance of the Guru that the true nature of the Self can be understood. And for an Advaitin like Ramaswamy, knowledge of the Self is not distinct from the knowledge of Brahman. And Raja Rao refers to this in one of his letters to M.K.Naik:

> ... Man's life here in *Samsara* is an august mission to find the Absolute. The Absolute according to the Indian tradition being incarnate in the Guru. [64]

It is this "august mission" of man that Raja Rao has presented in the life of Ramaswamy in *The Serpent and the Rope*. It is only an ignorance of this metaphysical position, that makes David McCutchion suggest that in the novel, "there is no development, it moves to no conclusion, ends where it beings."[65] The same inability to comprehend the conclusion of the novel is evident in Ahmed Ali who in an otherwise perceptive essay, remarks that Ramaswamy "has no longer any desire to return, not even to the Guru, the teacher, the knower of the path and saviour – in short to Salvation."[66] He believes that Ramaswamy gives up all this "in tired hopelessness to relax in the plush chairs with his chocolate."[67]

S.C.Harrex, a sympathetic Australian critic, rightly takes objection to this view, but even he can only speak of the chocolate drinking as "a toast to Rama's new life, and the novelist's toast to his work and vision."[68] Ramswamy's choice is made at the end of the novel and he looks forward eagerly to his visit to Travancore. If he still drinks chocolate, it is not done as a toast to this decision of his. And if he gets back to plush chairs at the end, he is not giving up his decision to go to his Guru. These two views come from a mistaken notion of what is now commonly and conveniently regarded as Indian spirituality. In India, the Spiritual and the Metaphysical have never been at the expense of the Material and the Mundane. The two have their unique place in the Indian view of life though a higher significance is assigned very rightly to the former, but a preoccupation with higher truths does not come in the way of actual living in the present. This is more explicitly stated in *The Cat and Shakespeare* by Govindan Nair:

> To live is not difficult,
> sir, for flesh is the form of
> existence, and man in his journey to
> the ultimate knows that
> to yield to the flesh is to grow grain.[69]

And so there is nothing wrong in the way the novel ends. On the contrary, it is a positive triumph for Raja Rao since he is able to suggest that despite Ramaswamy's newly discovered awareness of the meaning of his existence, life must go on.

In conclusion, it must be reasserted that, for a truly authentic image of India as an idea, one has nowhere else to turn but to the novel *The Serpent and the Rope*. The philosophical idea that forms the basis for Rama's view of Life, as has already been suggested, is provided by Sankara's *Advaita* philosophy. And for Ramaswamy who is aware of the other view that objects do exist as objects, makes it supremely clear in the course of the novel that objects exist only in so far as the individual is able to perceive them. His preference for the Advaitic view of the world is reiterated throughout the novel with uncompromising vigour since he is totally convinced of the incompleteness of Christianity, Buddhism, and various other religions and philosophical views of the world. When *The Serpent and the Rope* is both a statement and enactment of this faith in *Adwaita* vedanta, it is curious to read Meenakshi Mukherjee point out that the novel presents the two modes of apprehending reality "but does not come to definite preference of one over the other."[70] For Raja Rao, Advaita is synonymous with India and his deep reverence for India is unmistakable. Hence, for Ramaswamy, "India is the Guru of the World." (p. 332.) This view is supported by both Savithri who says "India still has the most ancient civilization on earth" (p. 189.) and Madeleine who believes that "from India all must look young." (p. 308.) It is this unanimous view of the major characters that is fully endorsed by the novelist which gives us in *The Serpent and the Rope* a truly exalted image of India.

In the novel, we have "the finest and fullest possible expression of a profound Indian sensibility"[71] and "the form is as truly Indian as its sensibility."[72] If one finds the real Indian village in *Kanthapura*, it is the essence of India that one discovers in *The Serpent and the Rope*.

The Cat and Shakespeare is a continuation of the philosophical preoccupations of Raja Rao since it forms along with *Kanthapura* and *The Serpent and the Rope*, "a philosophical trilogy."[73] In this novel also, Raja Rao is concerned with the quest for the Ultimate Reality. While in his first two novels, the paths chosen for this purpose were those of *karma* (action) and *jnana* (knowledge), here it is *bhakti* and *prapatti* (Devotion and Surrender to the Divine Principle). While Sankara's Advaitic philosophy determined the world view presented in *The Serpent and the Rope*, it is Ramanuja's Visistadvaita of the Tenkalai school that forms the basis for the view of life delineated in *The Cat and Shakespeare*.

Ramakrishna Pai, a thirty three year old Saraswath Brahmin married to Saroja, father of Usha and Vithal and a divisional clerk, is the narrator. He is the uninitiated and his search for the Ultimate Reality is presented in the course of the novel. His neighbour, Govindan Nair, a second division clerk in the ration shop, is his spiritual mentor or Guru. Here, the success of Raja Rao in portraying the characters of the initiated and the uninitiated needs to be examined.

Ramakrishna Pai is obsessed with a desire to build a three storied house, a very human desire to possess a roof of one's own, as we say in peasant India. The house in which Pai lives is known as Kamala Bhavan. The house "was new and it was white. It had ochre bands on it — almost as on a temple." (pp. 5-6.) There is a garden across the wall which he has never seen, for the wall is symbolic of *Maya* or the world of appearances. He is the ordinary man who is totally steeped in *samsara*, of life here and now. Raja Rao never undermines the importance of this mundane reality and we see it established convincingly in Pai's life whether be it his unhappy marriage with Saroja, his concern for his daughter Usha, or his suffering from British boils, his love for his mistress, Shanta and his child growing in her or his wish to own a house. That he is totally submerged in his own ego is clear as when he says:

> I worship nothing (no, not even money, although it will make the three stories possible), and I don't think I care for anything. (p. 23.)

But he has moments of awareness as when he remarks: "In life we search for truth but live in the illusion of permanence." (p. 30.) And when Govindan Nair's son is down with high fever, he tells Pai that "Usha is the cause of Sridhar's illness." (p. 65.) Pai is naturally troubled and he reflects:

> "Was I responsible for Usha's birth? Was I? Was Usha responsible for Sridhar's illness? So I am the sole responsible person. Lord, where shall I go now? For I am cause." (p. 66.)

And then follows the central question: "How mysterious life is. Does one know anything?" How does one understand the nature of death and the mysteries of life? Pai cannot go beyond the cause and effect equation when he is confronted with any problem. That is the reason why he can articulate in these terms when Sridhar dies:

> Famine is the cause of death. Wars are the cause of murder. Imperialism is the cause of slavery. Sri Krishna is the cause of Mahatma Gandhi. Lord, how can man be free from birth and death? Why should death come to our door? (p. 67.)

He is so totally preoccupied with the actual world that he cannot see beyond the world of appearance. Hence his confession:

> ... I read *The Hindu* too much, that is the trouble with me, and I cannot understand. What can *Malayalarajyam* say, except what its correspondents see? (p. 99.)

In contrast to Ramakrishna Pai, we have the character of Govindan Nair, easily the most fascinating creation in all of Raja Rao's works. In the words of Ayyappa Paniker,[74] he is the 'Perceiver–Benefactor' while Pai is the 'Narrator- Beneficiary' in the novel. Before proceeding any further, it would be especially useful to have in mind, Raja Rao's own formulation about such a character:

> How does a being behave after he has been revealed the impersonal principle or the truth? He is a-logical, not illogical, his action is impersonal but full of love, which is not dramatic but simple. He is also one who sees many meanings in one act and it is *this* that the a-logicality confirms the condition of being beyond cause and effect. So there are three levels, as it were — the logical life sequence the a-logical meaning of the logical life sequence and the reality which is beyond logic and a-logic.[75]

Raja Rao is attempting to create in the character of Govindan Nair one who has seen the truth of life. His moment of mystical illumination is not presented to us, but it is only his behaviour after that moment that we see in the novel.

Govindan Nair "Knew everything for he was so concerned with everything." That he is an Advaitin is apparent when we learn that "to him all the world is just what he does. He does and so the world comes into being." To him, "nothing is particular, a chair means all chairs, a knife means all knives, a clerk means all the clerks." To him, "the whole world was one living organism." Hence, "for him all gestures, all words have absolute meaning." As Pai remarks, "he must twist a thing into essence and spread it out." That is Govindan Nair's method and so "he has an explanation ... for everything." These are not mere formulations, for they are satisfyingly enacted for us in artistic terms in the novel. How has he come to achieve this state of mind? Nair himself states this explicitly:

> "...The kitten is being carried by the cat. We would all be kittens carried by the cat ... Ah, the kitten when its neck is held by its mother, does it know anything else but the joy of being held by its mother? You see the elongated thin hairy thing dangling, and you think, poor kid, it must suffer to be so held. But I say the kitten is the safest thing in the world, the kitten held in the mouth of the mother cat. Could one have been born without a mother? Modern inventions do not so much need a father. But a mother — I tell you, without Mother the world is not. So allow her to fondle you and to hold you. I often think how noble it is to see the world, the legs dangling straight, the eyes steady, and the mouth of the mother at the neck. Beautiful ...Let the mother cat hold you by the neck..." (pp. 10-12.)

As Raja Rao makes it clear,

> "the cat represents the impersonal principle. The cat is the she-cat or the female cat. It is a being of compassion."[76]

The Cat image also represents the Feminine Principle. In terms of Indian philosophy this position is that of Ramanuja, the celebrated philosopher of the 12th century who propounded his philosophy of *Visistadvaita* (modified non-dualism) in which he emphasised the path of *Bhakti* and *Prapatti* in man's quest for the Ultimate Reality. In the words of Swami Prabhavananda:

> God as the controller of the universe is absolutely good and the redeemer of all beings. Evil and suffering ... are caused by the individual's Karmas. Karmas — good or evil deeds — create happiness or misery; but by Karmas alone man cannot redeem himself, only the grace of God can save him; God is therefore the saviour. In his infinite love, his absolute goodness, he is forever merciful, for he even becomes flesh in human form to redeem the prodigal and to rejoice in the ecstasy of communion with his devotee.[77]

But man's relationship with God was interpreted in two different ways by the two later day schools, called the Vadakalais and the Tenkalais. The difference between them is clarified by P.N. Srinivasachari:

> The *Tenkalai* School ... interprets prapatti not as a yoga or human endeavour, but a mere faith in the grace of God ... The *Tenkalai* denial of human initiative as a requisite condition of redemption leads to the predication of arbitrariness and favouritism in the divine will. The denial by the other school ... the *Vadakalai* school of the absoluteness of the divine grace, or the free flow of divine *daya*, without even a *Vyaja*, affirms the primacy and priority of human freedom. This school ... employs the analogy of the young monkey clinging to the mother for protection to illustrate the *mumuksh* seeking refuge at the feet of the *saranya* or saviour. The Tenkalai school maintains the opposite view, as it coheres with mystic experience and illustrates it by the analogy of the cat carrying the kitten in its mouth or the *marjaranyaya*, as contrasted with the *markatanyaya* of the Vadakalais.[78]

Govindan Nair's position as is evident from this, corresponds to that of the Tenkalais. All his actions in the novel consistently conform to this view. For an ordinary clerk in the ration office, he has extremely wide range of interests. He has knowledge of law, agriculture, philosophy, poetry, sanskrit, enfield guns and many more varied disciplines. Though a Nair, he is able to "explain to the Brahmin what Brahman is." He can cross the wall, with effortless ease:

> What a will-o'-the-wisp of a wall it is, going from nowhere; tile-covered, bulging, and obstreperous, it seems like the

> sound heard and not the word understood. It runs just a little above my window, half an inch higher, and on the other side it dips and rises, running about on its wild, vicarious course.(p. 13.)

Since he has transcended his ego, he is able to achieve this leap from the world of appearances to the Real world like the Cat effortlessly. He is a very friendly neighbour to Pai ever willing to help him. Apart from the many little acts of kindness, Nair willingly pays the first instalment of seven thousand rupees to Pai for the purchases of the house in which he lives. The philosophical basis for such an attitude in Nair is clearly stated by Pai :

> Everybody is half-brother to you, man and thing. So why worry? That seemed the principle on which Govindan Nair worked: I am, so you are my brother. (p. 36.)

He becomes half-brother to mankind. For him, "Life is a riddle that can be solved with a riddle." He believes that the world is connected. Hence his logic :

> The ration shop is meant to fight famine, and famine is there because there is war, and war because of the British, and the British because of whom? Danes, Normans, etc., say the textbooks. But actually who cares? If you fight the British in the ration shop, you solve the British problem. (p. 37.)

This is the typical Indian attitude that takes a cyclical view of history in sharp contrast to the linear view of history of the western man. Govindan Nair believes that "the unknown alone resolves the unknown" and so his advice, "work and be merry." He religiously follows his own advice and that is the secret of his happiness even though he is only a clerk in a ration office earning forty five rupees a month. Since he issues ration cards, he is engaged in a noble task which is to do with *giving,* an important aspect of Indian life. And so he can reason that,

> " ... He who gives is a prince. I give rations or rather ration cards, so I give food. I am a prince..." (p. 33.)

Govindan Nair views everything around him in an admirably inclusive manner. It is "both-and' and never 'either-or'". Hence, for him life is a 'lila' that encompasses in it both the realities—the Ultimate Reality and the Mundane. It is because of this knowledge that he can face all experiences with equanimity. When his son Sridhar dies, he takes it in his stride as he recognizes it as part of the phenomenal reality. Actually, he has gone beyond Samsara and in it has "complete fulfilment, not the denial of life."[80] It is this awareness, which prompts him to offer Abraham the position of the boss on the death of Bhootalinga Iyer.

It is indeed very appropriate that Ramakrishna Pai should consider such a man as Govindan Nair as "my guide." In the words of Raja Rao, "poor Pai is only an Arjuna and Govindan Nair is Sree Krishna. One is the 'man-man', the other is 'man-beyond man!"[81] The uninitiated Pai is finally led to Self-Realisation, by following the cat across the wall when he sees a beautiful vision :

> I found a garden all rosy and gentle. There were bowers and many sweet-smelling herbs, there were pools and many orchids that smelled from a distance. There were old men with beards as long as their knees, and they talked to no one. Young men were in green turbans and others, children and women, sang or danced to no tune but to the tune of trees. Snakes lived there in plenty, and the mongoose roamed all about the garden. (p. 114.)

Here is the vision of life in all its harmony that accommodates opposites effortlessly. He hears "very lovely music" and is "breathless." As he climbed the staircase, he says, "I looked in and saw everything" and what follows is his moment of illumination :

> I saw nose (not the nose) and eyes seeing eyes seeing, I saw ears curved to make sound visible, and face and limbs rising in perfection of perfection, for form was it. I saw yet knew not its name but heard it as sound, I saw truth not as fact but as ignition. I could walk into fire and be cool, I could sing and be silent, I could hold myself and yet not be there. I saw feet. They made flowers on stamps and the curved hands of children. I smelled a breath that was of nowhere but rising in my nostrils sank back into me, and found death was at my door. I woke up and found death had passed by telling me I had no business to be there. Then where was I? Death said it had died. I had killed death. When you see death as death, you kill it. When you say, I am so and so, and you say, I am such and such, you

have killed yourself. I remain over, having killed myself. (pp. 115-16.)

Ramakrishna Pai here acheives the transcendence of his ego, the sole hurdle to his perception of the Ultimate Reality. In the words of M.K. Naik, this vision "presents the divine principle as perfection incarnate, absolute Good and infinite Love as both immanent and transcendent; and shows how the ego into which the self degenerates in the world must die when one surrenders oneself to the Absolute, and recovers the true Self which is an eternal mode of it."[82] In a similar way, we are earlier told how salvation comes to even a hunter as a consequence of accidently dropping bilva leaves on the idol of the Shiva. This is because "it's not the way you worship that is important but what you adore."

In terms of the image of India, the novel *The Cat and Shakespeare* is a further extension of the image presented in *The Serpent and the Rope*. The image has grown more ideational even though the concrete details are very much present. At one level, the novel faithfully evokes the life of Kerala through the suggestive use of significant details. Regarding contemporary India, we are told that "in the new India plans are never so difficult, the new is made with plans." True indeed, for we have our interminable five-year plans. The yielding of the old order to the new is prophesied:

> Sit C.P. will go and Gandhi-raj will come. In Gandhi-raj everybody will have a house. (p. 118.)

But in actuality, we learn that "Governments are notoriously mismanaged." And, of course, "Doctors are expensive — even government doctors. They don't take fees, but they like gifts." To delineate the actual world, that is the material reality, Raja Rao could not have thought of a more appropriate symbol than that of the ration shop :

> Life is like that. Life is a ration shop. The scale weighs everything according to the ration card. (p. 48.)

> And rationing is one of the grandest inventions of man. You stamp paper with figures and you feed stomachs on numbers. (p. 11.)

The ration shop is, of course, not free of mismanagement and corruption. There are the missing files reportedly eaten away by rats and "two rupees a ration card is the official black-market price, if you want to know." And sometimes the printers deliberately repeated a number and sold the duplicate to hotel servants for ten rupees. As Govindan Nair remarks: "If not, tell me how are the hotels to thrive? Once again, Sir, It's a matter of starvation." The ration office is the holiest of places as argued by Nair in his own typical-logical-fashion:

> "Sir, it is holy because we feed the starving. That which feeds the starving is holy. That which feeds the thirsty is sacred. So the Ganges is sacred. That is why we worship the cow. This shop, this office is a very Kamadhenu. We give what others want." (p. 78.)

Corruption in men as seen in the employees of the ration shop is suggested in subtler ways by Raja Rao. Of John, it is said:

> He built a house, that is John did. He built a modest little, house. He said it was done from the proceeds of his wife's property sale. Her grandmother had just died. Everybody has a grandmother, you now. (p. 27.)

Then there is Velayudhan Nair's wife :

> When you see her at a cinema, [she] has an array of gold bangles on her hands. She inherited some money from her aunt. We all have aunts; why don't we inherit? (p. 43.)

The ration shop and the goings on there establish for us a solid and real world. Raja Rao even in a novel like *The Cat and Shakespeare* wherein he is essentially concerned with the quest for Ultimate Reality does not ignore the normal everyday world its realities. Raja Rao is not without his digs at 'social' India. But in his case, he transcends the social in the attempt to apprehend the Ultimate Reality. The novel works on two levels throughout — the realistic and the metaphysical, each illuminating the other. For one like Raja Rao, each of them in isolation would be meaningless, indeed they both acquire a value through mutual dependence. This is a point quite conveniently ignored by his detractors like D.S.Maini who accuses Raja Rao of having "missed the entire beat and pulse of today's India."[83]

As a novel, *The Cat and Shakespeare* is without doubt, an exceptionally remarkable work. It has a teasing complexity about it, for Raja Rao has packed "infinite riches" into a work that runs to a little over 100 pages. The difficulty is pronounced because he deliberately reduces the narrative to its barest minimum, and concentrates more on the symbolic design of the work. It is called "a tale of modern India." In the words of the novelist, it is "a new version of an old story."[84] The old story, as old as the Vedas, is to do with man's eternal search for the Ultimate. Only the setting and the characters are modern.

We have a clue to the form of *The Cat and Shakespeare* in Raja Rao's description of the novel as "an allegory, a poem or a fable."[85] The mode employed is both comic and symbolic. As in the traditional fable, in the novel we have a cat in flesh and blood. It symbolises the Divine Principle in its feminine aspect, and related to it, is the Cat-Kitten philosophy of Govindan Nair, a man who has discovered the impersonal principle in life. He is seen as a friend, a rogue, a clown, a sage, a philosopher, all rolled into one. Two scenes, one in the ration office and the other in the court stand out, for they dramatise his ability to win reverence to the cat for she is the Mother. All his actions are seen to be a-logical. Once this is grasped by the reader, the novel's meaning becomes clear. The novelist's real triumph lies in his choice of the narrator, Ramarishna Pai, who is the uninitiated. He is so deeply rooted in reality that Raja Rao has found in him, "the best perspective to fictionalize a philosophy that would otherwise sound too abstract and out of reach."[86]

As in *The Serpent and the Rope*, we have here also a combination of concept and enactment, though it should be pointed out that the former dominates over the latter. This is inevitable in an allegorical work of this kind. Added to this, the limited canvas imposes its own restrictions. Whereas the earlier novel was more detailed and analytical in its approach, this work is suggestive and aphoristic. At some places in the novel, the echoes of the Upanishadic dialogues are discernible. Notice, for a good illustration, the dialogue between Govindan Nair and Lakshmi in the brothel:

"Are you happy?" asked Govindan Nair.
"Are you?" she asked.
"Can't you see I am happy?"
"Where does it come from?"
"Where does water come from?"
"From the tap?"
"And the water in the tap?"
"From the lake?"
"And the water in the lake?"

"From the sky."
"And the water in the sky?"
"From the ocean?"
"And the water in the ocean?"
"From the rivers."
"And the river waters?"
"They make the lakes."
"And the tap water?"
"Is river water."
"And so?"
"Water comes from water," she said. (p. 50.)

If the shattering logic of this conversation is convincing, there is another kind of logic present in the novel that is equally credible. When Usha calls Ramakrishna Pai, Father, he reflects:

> As if I were able to be cause of anything. For father simply means cause of her. And the cause of cause, what is it? Is it not she? Could there be a father without a daughter? What would Usha be without me? What would this house be if I did not own it? Is it not possible not to own it and yet it would somehow be mine? Air I own not, and yet I breathe. I breathe myself. Do I own I? (p. 64.)

Whst Raja Rao does here, is to concretise the philosophical abstractions through the symbolic mode. The philosophy of Devotion and Surrender to Divine Principle is enacted through the Cat-Kitten relationship and more significantly and meaningfully in life of Govindhan Nair himself. Similarly the wall, the garden, the ration shop, the house with three stories are all concrete equivalents of philosophical truths about existence. A natural consequence of such a mode is in "words becoming images, images fusing into myths, myths manifesting as symbols, and all organizing the material of the novel into a rich and complex presentation."[87]

In conclusion, it should be reiterated that *The Cat and Shakespeare* constitutes a fitting climax to Raja Rao's philosophical preoccupations that began with his novel *Kanthapura*. With this novel, he has now completely rendered it terms cf fictional art all the three paths to Self-Realization enshrined in Indian philosophy. The novel is a brilliant restatement of the Visistadvaita Philosophy of Ramanuja. Unlike *The Serpent and the Rope*, there is no attempt to overtly celebrate India in this novel. On the other hand, *The Cat and Shakespeare* presents the image of India both as an idea and as a locale in a succinct manner.

Raja Rao's next novel, *Comrade Kirillov,* originally written in English was first published in its French version in 1965. The English edition came out as late as 1976. This novel, even though outside his "Philosophical trilogy" is important since it presents the image of a modern Indian intellectual. In the portrayal of Comrade Kirillov, we see the predilection of an Indian, who is subject to contrary pulls between his emotional impulses on the one hand and his intellectual beliefs on the other. The novel is also significant, because of a more satisfying view of Hinduism present in it. And finally, in terms of the form, this is probably the only work wherein Raja Rao has consistently used irony as a structural principle.

As in his other novels, the novelist employs a narrator in *Comrade Kirillov.*[88] He is R., a young reporter for *The Hindu,* "a Gandhian, and a Vedantin and an Indian." He is also a South Indian brahmin like the other narrators — Achakka, Ramaswamy and Ramakrishna Pai. We have a dual perspective on the fascinating personality of Kirillov, — one is that of the narrator R. and the other is provided by his wife Irene's diary which is present as a sort of postscript at the end of the novel. This dual focus helps Raja Rao in creating a perfectly convincing portrait of Kirillov.

Comrade Kirillov, actually known as Padmanabha Iyer, is a South Indian brahmin who has an "ancient and enigmatic face." He is "learned, uninnocent, and brilliant of mind" and is "essentially and throughly honest." As a member of the theosophical society, he goes to California. As Kirillov is a genuine intellectual, he is far from being complacent in his theosophical comforts and begins to sincerely think of his India:

> Was this indeed the India that had to be? Where aerial chariots, pulled by heavenly horses and bedecked with many unearthly precious stones, should move, the thin-legged Indian drove his miserable bullock, its sides flagging for want of fodder, and its bones speaking of the chemistry of death .. (p. 10.)

The sharp contrast between the ideal and the actual, profoundly disturbs Kirillov. He reflects on the existing social conditions:

> The humiliation of man is awful, especially if you have

seen the way an untouchable has to leap the fence to let your brahminic presence pass by, or the niggardly twist of dhoti on a ploughing peasant, or the brutal bamboo of ancestral masters. (p. 11.)

What is significant is that these darker aspects of Hinduism that were either glossed over or entirely ignored as in *The Serpent and the Rope*, find expression in this novel. In spite of the pitiable condition of the vast masses of people, the new India seems to be all smooth sailing for the university educated Indian:

> In new India the University degree spoke the stars and threw into darkness the horoscope of the ancients. Marriage became a commodity, and European clothes the new Uniform. Success waited at your garden-gate, and the British came and took you away in a landau and four to a comfortable sub- collectorship. (p. 12.)

Raja Rao's suggestive use of irony cannot be missed. This awareness of his and her people leads Kirillov to serious thinking. He learns German, French and Russian languages. He reads a lot, mainly socialist books and has realised that "the only hope for humanity was better living wages, more muscular ways of thought." The theosophist in him gives way to a new ideology, that of communism since he is convinced that the Russian Revolution "was the only historic revelation of the modern world." Russia is the answer to the Indian's problems, for he is convinced that,

> The Messiah was not only born—he worked, and his land was called the Union of the Soviet Socialist Republics, and maybe a new Ganges flowed there, and man there had all the prismatic colours of the prophetic world. Besides, it was built on reason and the stream-engine. (p. 15.)

Even this conviction of Kirillov is not without a tinge of irony. But then Padmanabha Iyer became Comrade Kirillov and he "found in communism a joyous knowledge for the neophyte." And as a diehard communist he is certain that,

> The predictability of events in the dialectical calendar far surpassed the accuracy of the Indian astrologer. The deft astrological hands could play humbug, but the figure of statistics never does. (pp. 20-21.)

These remarks assume an ironical overtone in view of the realignment of historical forces that take place during the Second World War referred to later in the novel.

It is a well acknowledged truth that of all the political ideoligies in the world, communism has been most successful in winning total loyalty and commitment from its votaries. Kirillov is no exception to this and during the communist phase of his life, he rejects the political India entirely. That is why, he believes that "he was finished with Gandhi and all that." And he is of the view that,

> India lies a coward under the steel of British occupation.
> Nehru's neophyte speeches are only for nightingales.
> (p. 24.)

If these were his political views brought about by his conversion to communism, it has also resulted in a recognisable change of his personality :

> Marxism had given a strange ascetic incision to his brahminic manners and his sweetness had that unction, the theological compassion, of a catholic priest. (p. 30.)

The inner changes in his personality find an objective correlative in the necktie he wears, a tie that has become an indivisible part of his individual self. The tie "was his boon companion, his poetry, his sole possession ." Here are two descriptions of the tie:

> His necktie had such a praterplusparenthetical curve, as though much concrete philosophy had gone into its making, and it revealed a soul so ambivalent that I could not gaze on its self-aware turpitudes without human compassion. (p. 25.)

> The indrawnness of his nature gave a prominent curve to his chest, which in turn gave that peculiar parabola to his necktie, as though man in his destiny had shaped his garment to his thought and had given a certain twist of psyche; this particular intensity of approach from the thick neck to the narrow waist, where within the folds of the shirt, this greygreen stretch of respectable cloth found its umbilical end. (p. 30.)

The tie is indeed a powerful symbol of his deeply obsessive faith in communism. This faith also "hangs around his neck and on his heart very much like his tie and without which he probably cannot exist,"[89]

For that reason, the narrator imagines Kirillov whispering to the tie night after night :

> "You, you, my noble, secret friend, you lie in the faithfulness of my scholarly solitude. O, go not away from my habitation, for what shall my destiny be without your contiguous presence ..." (p. 32.)

Kirillov has written a book, "Mahatma Gandhi — A Marxist Interpretation," in which the entire Gandhian ideology is attacked rather bitterly since it runs contrary to Marxist dialectics. For example, observe his assessment of Gandhian non-violence :

> Non-violence was a biological lie. Man was born to fight — fighting is an instrument of Darwinian evolution, which made dialectics possible. (p. 34.)

This is a typical ideological approach to a problem that refuses to take into account local conditions behind such a faith in non-violence. Kirillov launches a tirade against Gandhi in his conversation with R., calling him "a kleptomaniac," "an ungrown adult." He adds :

> " ... Your Gandhian morality, fattening itself on the *marwari*-capitalist, and speaking a brother-brother language! It is nothing but the plainest of vulgarity. A decadent society, changing from feudal to the capitalist order, especially when it wants to throw over imperialist slavery, seeks moral and mystical accompaniment for its inevitable fight ... Mahatma Gandhi should have been born in the Middle Ages, and he should not have bothered us with his theology in this rational age of ours." (p. 37.)

A scientific belief in the laws of cause and effect that every Marxist professes is responsible for taking such a one-sided view of the freedom struggle in India. The implied criticism of Raja Rao is surely to suggest how any blind allegiance solely to the intellect can be so misleading. For Kirillov, it is not through "this I-love-you, I-love-you-brother business" that India will be able to secure her independence but only when the great masses of the working classes and landless labour "rise in historical inevitability." According to him, communism will bring into India :

> "A state of Society where no man will be master of another, and where a man like you will sit on some lone

> hilltop and write beautiful books, instead of wandering in search of metaphysical will-of-the-wisps, and a cup of coffee, or listening to nonsense from men like me ..." (p. 39.)

Once again, Raja Rao's irony directed against Kirillov and probably the narrator also, is very evident.

The narrowness of Kirillov's truth in the communist doctrine has inevitably led to an atrophy of mind. The novelist's implicit irony of his view of the world is clearly discernible in these two remarks :

> " ... I know only one God, and that is the common man. I know only one morality, and that is a classless society ..." (p. 39.)

> "Anonymous my name ... Logic my religion, Communism my mother land." (p. 71.)

For him man is anonymous. He is merely "a biological number." An ideology that glorifies the party and the society at the expense of the individual is certainly not admirabale as Kirillov would have us believe. Such a complete surrender to reason will undoubtedly end in situations that border on the ridiculous. Consider the reactions of a communist like Kirillov, to his wife having a child not his own :

> His wife may have deserted him, but when she returns and the baby is born — somebody else's baby — how he still rushes to the midwife in wild joy: "Sister, sister, I have a baby — that is, my wife has a baby, and it is not mine, but just as well mine because my wife has borne it. Birth is a biological phenomenon, the sperm just a question of numbered genes ..." (p. 49.)

A more explicit criticism of communism is made by exposing its inherent anomalies that are conveniently ignored by Kirillov even as he states them ;

> If the biology of selective killing were understood, humanity might yet attain the clean apex of history. There, you build the point of the pyramid, and under it through the mystic cave door you bring in processional, all the treasurers of the three worlds. You have all the desert in golden perspective, and the Nile flows in chartered movements to a mellow sea ... Death, the Moscow deaths, were the antiseptics of history — you kill for the beauty of your

eyes. (p. 46.)

And for one like Kirillov, the material ends of life are all that matter since we see him, on occasions, express opinions rather naive :

> "Kalidasa and all that is perfect. But Kalidasa does not produce lentils, nor Bharathrihari milk ..." (p. 83.)

One can also recognise a certain ambivalence in his attitude. He finds, perhaps as a truly accomplished Indian, these great writers "perfect" but as a communist he seems to be more concerned with their material value, a wrong thing to look for in great art. Such an ambivalence is a little more explicit in his impressions of India:

> Kirillov was an Indian, and he had peculiar reactions which no dialectic could clarify. He could almost speak of India as though he were talking of a venerable old lady in a fairy tale who had nothing but goodness in her heart, and who was made of morning dew and mountain honey. (p. 52.)

Here is the first direct reference to the theme of the novel — an Oriental caught under the onslaught of an Occidental ideology. Kirillov's Indianness has given him "peculiar reactions" which fall outside all dialectics. It is this Indianness that now and again breaks through the veneer of his communism. Once this conflict is recognised, his seemingly contradictory attitudes can be viewed in their proper perspective. That is how, for instance, his remarks about Gandhi are to be regarded. While he was severely critical of Gandhi earlier, there is a mixed response now :

> He could not bear a word said against Mahatma Gandhi (though he could sometimes say more severe things than even Churchill might ever about the saintly Indian leader). (p. 58.)

Here are clear signs of conversion in Kirillov. Or wouldn't it be more appropriate to call it a reconversion ? Stalin asks the Indians to fight along the British during the Second World War. For Kirillov :

> If Stalin had asked Indian to side with the British, Stalin had a definite, logical construction on which to base his conclusions. (p. 60.)

And this inner conversion results in Comrade Kirillov becoming once more Mr. Padmanabhan Kirillov and "his skin shone as on the first day of creation." The lid of his communist ideology is thrown open to let his Indian self emerge once again to the surface. It is not that his ideological fervour is in any degree lessened, but that his consciousness of being an Indian is reawakened with the result that there is now a new flowering of his personality. He still believes that the working classes and the poor peasants form the best hope for India, though in his view, "we are not ready for a revolution, and we can afford to wait."

There is a perceptible change in the man, even in his physical appearance:

> His eyes had grown sharper, but a strange, abundant sweetness flowed from his nervous, rich face and his gentle hands.

The narrator adds :

> I had never known Kirillov himself more Indian, and, either out of pride before Irene or for patriotism, he started speaking Hindusthani with me. (pp. 70-71.)

Kirillov spoke Hindustani badly since he was a South Indian, but even then he insisted on speaking the language for that is the national language of free India. Such is his national pride. And now Kirillov speaks of his visit to India made after a gap of twenty-five years. He is not too happy with the social conditions prevailing in his motherland. He finds "rank and riceless poverty in the villages." His analysis of the character of Nehru is brilliantly incisive. According to him, Nehru

> " ... is such a well-meaning, Utopian liberal, sitting crosswise on the hedge between socialism and liberalism. The great danger is his infinite charm. He has the sensibility of a poet, and his intellect, never very brilliant in its initiative, takes Shelleyan wings to Kashmiri heights where, seated on a green *maidan,* your lunch spread on a carpet, you can have a fine meal, simple but fair. He can talk to you of everything under the sun, and his sincerity is unquestionable ..." (p. 75.)

The man who had earlier blindly rejected the classics since they had no material significance for him, now reacts very differently :

> "... But one thing I felt sorry for when I was in India — the neglect of our classics. I forgot my politics for a time and jumped into the classics. It was such a joy to go back to

Uttarrama Charita, and to Kalidasa ..." (p. 75.)

This is the assertion of his Indian self in Kirillov. He, in fact, challenges the narrator that he would recite four sanskrit verses for each one uttered by him. Even Irene and his young son Kamal have learnt to recite Sanskrit verses. Kirillov's new position with regard to his country is clarified again by the narrator :

> ... he loved India with a noble, delicate, *un-reasoned* love. He loved her poetry as few among the so-called educated ones in India had — he loved the intricacies, the permutations, the magnitude of the Sanskrit verse. To hear him recite Sanskrit verse was like listening to a Pandit from Tanjore. His sincerity, his enthusiasm, his learning, were all alike — of one sovereign made. (pp. 86-87.) (emphasis mine)

This is an insight almost impossible for an outsider, and even to many an insider, for that matter. Kirillov also believes

> that from the airplane to the latest theories of democracy, passing through medicine and mathematics, all had one, and only one, origin — Holy India. (p. 79.)

However, lest one should have the impression that Kirillov and his India are all idealised, there is Raja Rao's controlling irony that forestalls any such opinion. Examine, as an illustration, Kirillov's view of the Hindu :

> Indeed, the most reactionary force in world politics today — far more poisonous than Chiang Kai Shek — is your Hindu. He and his metaphysical myths, his Karma and his caste, his I-will-not-eat-this, and I-will-not-touch-that, his superior feelings and his impotence — his decadence is the foulest our earth has to bear. (p. 83.)

This is more complex, for there is a double-edged irony that operates here. On the one hand, the decadent Hindu is being attacked, while on the other, Kirillov's own fanatical loyalty to his communist doctrines is not spared by the novelist. Raja Rao's irony cuts both ways.

Asked by the narrator about the state of Indian politics today, Kirillov replies :

> "A good masala ... You have ginger and cinnamon, coriander and chilli, and if your taste be too elegant, you

can have what we call Marathabuds and mountain cardamom. You have every opinion you want." (p. 81.)

Raja Rao could not have made a more appropriate comparison than a "masala" which was truly the political state of the country soon after independence. It is this ability of Raja Rao to concretise life, even an ideological situation, in terms of uniquely Indian images that is quite remarkable.

The paradox of being a communist and an Indian at the same time is crystallised in the character of Kirillov. However, strong and insistent may be one's conviction in any political ideology, even communism, he will find it doubly difficult to suppress the powerful pulls of his Indianness. Such is the hold of this ancient culture with its rich tradition on its people. This paradox is beautifully summed up in the narrator's retort to Kirillov :

> "You brag about progress and remain a vegetarian. You brag about Islam and Communism and call your son Kamal Dev instead of calling him Stephanovich, or Electricity, as in the earlier days of the revolution. And when you wake up in the morning in your bed, I am sure you remember your mother's instructions: Open your hands, and say the verse, *hasta-kamale,* etc. You are an old hyprocrite, I am sure, and an unrepentant one." (pp. 85-86.)

The first part ends with Kirillov willing to go to Benares with Irene and their two children in holy pilgrimage. There is no doubt as to what would finally happen to Kirillov for,

> Kirillov was an Indian — and his Indianhood would break through every communist chain. (p. 91.)

Communism might still come in the guise of a devil or Mara and tempt Kirillov in "fearful fascination" :

> "Here be the Urals for your Iron, here the Dnieper for your bounty, here the Song of Marshal Stalin for your slumber, and here the Lenin Institute of Agronomy for your rice fileds."

But then Kirillov, the true Indian that he is, would surely reject outright such a deceptive temptation:

> "Go, go, Mara ... I know of your doings. I know the dialec-

tic of Feurbach, and the *State and the Revolution* of Lenin. Marx has been suppressed by hagiography, and Lenin is in his tomb. Go, you many-mouthed, many-armed, you multiple monster, Mara!" (p. 92.)

However, the novel does not end here, since we now have Irene's diary. As suggested earlier, this offers another perspective on the character of Kirillov since who else should know a man better than his own wife. This diary offers a complementary view of Kirillov's personality already made clear to us. All the different facets of his individual self, like his communism, his love for India and his attitude to Gandhi are clarified to us, thus helping the novelist in giving a fully rounded picture of Kirillov.

Irene states in her very first entry, that Kirillov "lives on grave tensions", and adds as though in an after-thought, that she "should have said tensions and explanations." In fact, the earlier account has been a dramatisation of precisely this tension within the mind of Kirillov. She then goes on to state Kirillov's inwardness with Sanskrit aesthetics, especially Bharatrihari's *Sphotavada*. Her diary entry of April 17 reveals the ambivalence in his reaction to Gandhi. When he is filled with national pride, he considers Gandhi as "the greatest of the epoch, with Lenin," but as he finds Gandhi's philosophy of life at variance with his own intellectual position, he calls him "that old puritan humbug" or "that fine, moral hypocrite." Irene can see through this contradiction in Kirillov which is caused by his "Marxist baggage." She has understood him and hence can tell him :

> "You old hypocrite .. At heart Gandhi is your God. You tremble when you speak of him sometimes. I once saw even a tear, one long tear, it was there when you spoke of Gandhi to S." (p. 101.)

But Kirillov is not to be so easily outdone and he defines tears as "chemical reactions to remembered conditioned reflexes" in his own sound logical manner. Irene rightly regards this as nonsense for she knew,

> he cannot bear any European, bourgeois, or even communist, speak against the Congress or Gandhi. Curious this in so clear a head. Even I become an enemy — I say to him — when India is not described as all virtue. (pp. 101-2.)

What is considered as "curious" by a European woman like Irne is only natural in a modern Indian intellectual. That is what Raja Rao is suggesting throughout the novel, *Comrade Kirillov*. Though Irene is unable to understand his hardcore Indianness, she chooses to call him "racially arrogant," a judgement she has never revealed to him.

Irene's own attitude to India also deserves to be examined in some detail. Though she is herself a communist, she speaks of her enthusiasm for her husband's country:

> India—it is that which called me first, long before Marx ever spoke to me. (p. 106.)

It is this enthusiam that led her to marry Kirillov.

> Irene like(s) Orthodoxy—Communist or Indian. Both are satisfactory, and equally valid. (p. 109.)

And hence she believes that she "probably love (d) P. because he is so truly and inescapably orthodox." However, she has serious misgivings about both her relation with Kirillov and her attitude towards India. She is convinced that only her mother understood her and not even Kirillov.

> P. has such infinite love, but he completely lacks understanding. Is it the difference of race? Will I never understand Kamal wholly? I hope I shall never have to settle in India. I have grown afraid of India. P. is completely an Indian. Will I ever recognize him there? Will his people accept me? I am such a bourgeois—I want the approval of my father-in-law and mother-in-law. No, no I will not go to India. I almost begin to hate it. (p. 112.)

And when Kirillov leaves for India, she is happy that she is not going to India. She confesses: "I never told him the whole truth. India is now my enemy." In the marriage of Irene and Kirillov, we have an encounter between two races. Irene with her European and Slav sensibility believes that there is a cultural barrier between them. Though she recognises his infinite love for her, she is frightened by his Indianness which is only a manifestation of her own inability to sympathise with her husband's way of life. This is the limitation of Irene even though she considers it a "joy in life to have met this dear, this deeply sensitive, this magnanimous soul." On the other hand, Kirillov was attracted to Irene mainly because of her loyalty to communism. There is no doubt some irony in the description of his love for Irene :

> Kirillov really loved Irene. She had the red blood, the red

> hair, the passionate index finger, and dialectics had drained her lust into irate channels. Her comradely duty was to be faithful to this man, and fight for the Party. (pp. 54-55.)

The irony is directed more against Kirillov's love of communism than his love for Irene.

Granting her fear of India, Irene is no doubt prophetic in her apprehension that India,

> will eat up P. His Indianness will rise once he touches the soil of his land, and all this Occidental veneer will scuttle into European hatred. He hates Europe, does P. And yet he speaks of internationalism. (p. 113.)

That is the reason why she calls him "a strange mixture." As readers, with the dual perspective on Kirillov available to us, we know it is not that Kirillov begins to hate Europe after he lands in India but that he rediscovers his own roots which he had grown oblivious of due to his total allegiance to communism. Ramaswamy of *The Serpent and the Rope* is similar to Kirillov but in a different way. For him, Hinduism and Christianity, India and the West are not irreconcilable.

Irene's understanding of Kirillov's personality is total, for she is able to perceive his divided self. She knows that he hates the Muslims and the British deep down but will defend them because of his Marxist faith. She is certain that Kirillov "will fight for them — even die for them. But on his deathbed he will say Rama-Rama." This is indeed an impeccable insight of Raja Rao. And now follows probably the most convincing explanation of Kirillov's character that we have in the entire novel:

> There is a certain honestly of mind that is the grossest dishonesty of being. There lies Marxist danger especially among an ancient people like the Indians. (p. 119.)

The primary reason for the divided mind of Kirillov is the constant struggle between his honesty of mind and his honesty of being. While the former is responsible for his total commitment to Marxism, the latter accounts for the assertions of his Hindu self. He is justifiably called an "inverted brahmin" by Irene, for while the spiritual predominates over the material in the brahmin, the Marxist attaches overriding importance to the material. The novel *Comrade Kirillov* is saved from a simplified conclusion, as Raja Rao lets Kirillov go to

Moscow at the end. Thus it is the teasing ambivalence in the character of Kirillov that leaves a lasting impression in the minds of the readers.

It should be reiterated that Raja Rao has dramatised in Kirillov the profound truth that "Communism — an ideology of occidental origin can win the mind of an oriental traditionalist but not his heart; producing inevitably a dilemma of the divided consciousness."[90] This "dilemma of the divided consciousness" is no doubt common to all modern intellectuals but is most acutely experienced by a sensitive Indian since the conflict between the traditional values and modernist thought is violently intense in a tradition-bound culture such as in India. It is common experience in India to find Indians mouthing radical, revolutionary and progressive ideals in their intellectual conversations and writings, but acting most conservatively in their day-to-day living. Raja Rao has successfully presented such a predicament in *Comrade Kirillov* giving us in the process a truly authentic image of a modern Indian intellectual, perhaps the only such portrait in Indian-English fiction.

Finally, a brief reference to the three stories that were published along with his earlier stories in a new collection entitled *The Policeman and the Rose* in 1978. The stories are 'Nimka', 'India — A Fable' and 'The Policeman and the Rose.' Each is very different, in terms of form, from the earlier stories as they belong to the later phase of the author. In all these three stories, the narrative is kept to the barest minimum, for the treatment is essentially poetic and symbolic. Raja Rao works more through associations that reveal to the reader new layers of meanings present in the story. While such a mode is successful in both 'Nimka' and 'India-A Fable', it leads to complete obscurity in the title story, 'The Policeman and the Rose.' This happens because "the policeman remains a private symbol"[91] and the reader finds it hard to unravel the meaning of the story even after repeated readings.

'Nimka' is a tragic story — probably the greatest story ever written by an Indian in English — of a beautiful, white Russian girl. She "has green mongoloid eyes, and a soft lolling tongue that contains rounded sweetness." Her exceptional beauty is described thus:

> Nimtotchka was good, very good, and of a simple true beauty, as though you cannot efface it even were you to cut her face with many crosses. Her beauty had certainty, it had a rare equilibrium, and a naughtiness that was feminine and very innocent.[92]

Raja Rao achieves the leap from the physical to the transcendental with the ease of a great artist when he suggests that Nimka's beauty

> projected a quality of assurance that you were good, even were you bad, for this beauty could not be bad, so you had to be good. It was beauty — it always will be, and you cannot take it, and as such you cannot soil yourselves. How could you, for when you contemplate beauty, you end in contemplation ... (p. 99.)

No doubt, the narrator, a young Indian student at the Sorbonne loves her. He used to narrate to her some text from the *Ramayana* or the *Mahabharata*. It is however the story of Nala and Damayanti and their exile that deeply moved her as in her mind "she made a link between the Smolny Courtyard and the palace of Damayanti."

Being a Russian, a photograph of Tolstoy decorates the wall of her little house. When the narrator reads Tolstoy's letter to Mahatma Gandhi, her recognition of the cause of India results in the following reaction:

> so Tolstoy was right and India was right, and since she was right and India was right, and since she could not put up a picture of me on the wall, she put up Mahatma Gandhi's. (p. 100.)

Michel, a friend of the Indian student is also in love with Nimka thus giving rise to the proverbial triangular relationship. But the inability of the Indian to win her hand is suggested in a brilliantly aphoristic manner:

> The Indian is too simple in his depth — if there's no concierge and the cat, there's no goodness. Success is sin. Gandhi is poverty. The Maharaja is proof of truth. Truth is unnaked. Love is unsaid. So, Nimotchka fell in love with Michel. (p. 101.)

Each short sentence has a profound truth to communicate about the Indian. It all points to the genius of Raja Rao that manifests itself in the ability to compress complex thought processes in such a memorable style.

But Nimka could not marry Michel either, for "he had kissed her" or the Indian because he was "too far, too distant and different." What now follows is an account of her tragic life. First, her unhappy marriage to a Russian count, elder to her by twenty years, who deserts her.

Then there is her son Boris for whose sake she even became a mannequin. But he goes to Russia as a soldier never to return, and her life of misery is complete. To add greater pathos to her story comes the news that "Mahatma Gandhi was shot, and Nimka knew that was the price of righteousness." After all, we had been told earlier that "The good is what had distinction, and the bad what is successful." The story *enacts* the significance of this important truth about life. And now Gandhi's picture has gone up above Nimka's bed since,

> He knows, does Mahatma Gandhi, the pinching pain of mankind. With every scrub of the floor, and with every cry of the child in the street, there's a voice that responds, and that is Mahatma Gandhi's. Mahatma Gandhi, said Nimka to me yesterday, is not a man, he is not a saint, he is a country. (p. 103.)

But nothing can break the spirit of Nimka since,

> Virtue is the woman's privilege, man is the undiscoverable. Nimka was not sad. Her heart contained an intimacy of sorrow that was almost Kin of joy. She was warm, of course, and spoke beautifully. Her French accent had that silvery touch of the Slavs that makes the language almost sing.

And the story ends thus :

> Nimka asked nothing of life. She asked nothing of me. When I said goodbye, she did not say when shall I see you again? She knew the life that has ended is eternal. When you are shot you become immortal. (p. 103.)

That she has achieved this transcendence in life is entirely in keeping with her character. Even though 'Nimka' is "a very European story,"[93] Raja Rao successfully assimilates into it the symbol of Gandhi and the Indian tale of Nala and Damayanti of the *Mahabharata*.

'India — A Fable', as the title suggests, is not only a fable but also a fantasy. The western response to India has been mainly one of either romanticising or mystifying the land and its culture. In this story, such a stock response to India is made rather curiously by Pierrot, "a child of five or six, pink-skinned and clear-eyed." Pierrot is seen in a Luxembourg Park dragging along a wooden camel. The conversation opens like this:

'Where are you going? I asked.

'To the oasis of Arabia,' he said, and stopped. (p. 104.)

While the narrator's question is on the factual plane, the boy's answer is on the level of fantasy, and this juxtaposition between the two levels constitutes the technique of the story. It "mixes fact and fancy: fact melt into fancy and fancy crystallises as fact and when the line that divides the two disappears, the teasing begins."[94]

Pierrot, in his mind's eye, has pictured Arabia as a land "where there is a lot of sand, and a prince who rides a horse of gold." It is also the land of the camels and oases. He imagines there is a wedding of Prince Rudolfe. On meeting the narrator and seeing faces in the golden buttons of his sherwani, he becomes curious. Pierrot learns that his name is Raja, meaning a prince and that he comes from India, which is "far, very far." And the Arabia of his fantasy is transformed imperceptibly into a fantasy of India wherein he sees the narrator as the prince with goddesses, one on his right and one on his left. They are,

> 'ladies with four arms and a golden crown on their heads, and the water of the Ganges, all sweet with perfumes, runs at their feet.'

There are two weddings,

> 'One for the wedding of the night, and one for the wedding of the day. One who is dark as the bee, and the other who is blonde as butter. One is like dreaming. The other like waking up.' (p. 108.)

The fantasy is conclusively pictured by the little boy's mind:

> ' ... We are far, far away, fifteen days by steamship. There are no sands. There are no camels. There are forests — and then, there are elephants. Then, there's the Ganges...' (p. 110.)

And at the Medici fountain, looking at the water, he remarks:

> 'Look, there, that's your country. How beautiful it is. Now it's the hour of the wedding.' (p. 111.)

The story concludes with Pierrot now seeing faces in the golden buttons of his navy suit and saying:

> 'I am a maharaja. I ride the elephant. The wedding is over.' (p. 112.)

In the mind of the boy, one fantasy thus yields to another pointing out to perhaps the basic truth stated in the epigraph to the story, that there is a fundamental unity that lies beneath all things of the world.

To consider Raja Rao's achievement as a novelist and the overall image of India that emerges from his fictional works is a critical endeavour that is both challenging and difficult. The image of India present in his fictional works is fascinatingly diverse, faithfully reflecting the diversity and the seeming contradictions of India. We have the image of rural as well as urban India, with life as it is lived in our villages and towns portrayed with a vividness and an evocative power that is seldom equalled by other Indian novelists. But the image of India is not merely visual and physical, because there is more significantly, the presence of the image of India as an idea in his works. This is the natural consequence of his absolute faith in the Indian philosophy of non-dualism, which resulted in non-dualism being synonymous with India for him. And so, an exploration into India can only be metaphysical since for him "Truth is metaphysical and not moral."[95] In a writer who is concerned with the metaphysical aspects of reality, problems of a very fundamental nature are invariably considered, and we see Raja Rao portraying in his works the essence of India in the form of philosophical abstractions and metaphysical speculations. And so the image of India that predominates in his fictional works is that of the essential and timeless India.

In his first phase when he was in his twenties, two works, *The Cow of the Barricades* and *Kanthapura* appeared. These were the natural outcome of his social and political preoccupations. In them, we have the depiction of an image of India that highlights the life in Indian villages with all the nuances of its legends, superstitions and myths accommodated in an artistically satisfying manner. The political theme predominates *Kanthapura* without ignoring the social and religious aspects of Indian life. Despite the extraordinary novelty of his linguistic experiments in the novel, both these works are modelled on the western notions of the short story and novel without, in any way, affecting their 'Indianness' which constitutes their central significance.

Then after nearly two decades of creative hibernation, followed his two novels *The Serpent and the Rope* and *The Cat and Shakespeare*. During this period, Raja Rao was himself engaged in a spiritual quest that finally led him to Sri Atmananda Guru at Trivandrum in 1943. He learnt from him that the *Advaita* philosophy of Sankara provided the answer to man's search for the meaning of life and his self-knowledge.

It is this non-dualistic philosophy that constitutes the basis for his vision of life found in these novels. While Ramaswamy is an *advaitin* in the absolute sense of the term, Govindan Nair is a *visistadvaitin* who has already achieved transcendence in his life. Has Raja Rao been able to subsume into his advaitic view of the world all the various strands of experience present in the two novels? This question assumes crucial relevance since in the advaitic view of the world which perceives oneness beneath the surface of all things, no conflict is ever possible. And one cannot visualise any kind of fiction without any conflict.

In *The Serpent and the Rope*, Ramaswamy is portrayed as one who is consistently *advaitin* in his view of life. But Raja Rao has dramatised for us, in the novel, his search for the meaning of life. This search is to be carried out in the here and now, that is in the phenomenal world through his relationships with Madeleine and Savithri. And so there is the cultural conflict that reveals to Ramaswamy what he has sorely missed in life by marrying a Frenchwoman like Madeleine. Savithri, no doubt, acts as an agent in this discovery of his. At the end of the novel, we see him realise the need for a Guru, a spiritual teacher who only can save him from the brink of disaster. Whereas in *The Cat and Shakespeare*, there is Govindan Nair who has perceived the impersonal principle in life and assists a lesser mortal like Ramakrishna Pai to overcome his human dilemmas and conflicts and ultimately achieve the transcendence of his ego. We see that an absolute faith in the advaitic view of life does not act as a hindrance to the artistic realisation of India in Raja Rao because he is concerned in both the novels with human beings who are in the quest for the Ultimate Reality. As a matter of actual fact, it is this philosophical position that enables him to achieve transcendence which in turn makes it possible for him to take an objective and sympathetic view of both France and England and their peoples. That is why, even as a representative of the ruled race, he can triumphantly celebrate the coronation of the Queen of England which is the celebration of the Feminine Principle, an integral aspect of his adavitic standpoint.

As regards the image of India, unlike in the earlier works, in these two novels, especially in *The Serpent and the Rope*, it is the result not so much of accumulation of concrete details but of abstract ideas as has been pointed out earlier. And so we note quite clearly that the concrete image of India in *The Cow of the Barricades* and *Kanthapura* grows more ideational when we come to his later works, *The Serpent and the Rope* and *The Cat and Shakespeare*. But as far as his attitude to contemporary India is concerned, the later two novels offer a sharp contrast. In *The Serpent and the Rope*, Raja Rao with his pronounced preference for the ideal and the eternal India seems to ignore the contemporary India. This indifference can be accounted for by his belief that our present degradation is born of our unawareness of the timeless India. However, the social and material concerns are present though subsumed by the spiritual quest. But Raja Rao's works defy easy generalisation about his view of India since in *The Cat and Shakespeare* there is no shying away from the unpleasant realities of Indian life. He is acutely aware of the rampant corruption as seen in the ration office, government hospital and the police department. His satire against such an evil is powerfully felt in the novel. Even in *Comrade Kirillov*, he gives us a more comprehensive view of Hinduism since its decadence and seamier sides are highlighted along with its mighty hold on Indians.

Raja Rao's complex attitude towards India that formulates the various images of the country and its people in his fictional works can be clarified further by considering him as a writer in exile. He confessed in an interview to R. Parthasarathy:

> "Whether I am in Paris, London, New York or Austin, Texas, I don't think my life changes. By force of circumstance, purely accidental and sentimental, I have lived abroad. My roots are in this country. That is why I come here every year and spend as much time as I can. I live abroad but I am chained to my country."[96]

It is this awareness of his roots that makes him an insider, in spite of his being an exile. Terry Eagleton speaking of the predicament of the exiles suggests very perceptively that,

> great art is produced, not from the simple availability of an alternative, but from the subtle and involuted tensions between the remembered and the real, the potential and the actual, integration and dispossession, and exile and involvement.[97]

It is this very tension that is much in evidence in Raja Rao's works and we realise how, being an expatriate writer, he gains the necessary detachment and probably a better perspective to write about his country. Such a detachment must entirely account for the remarkable success he achieved in *Kanthapura*, a work that could have easily degenerated into a thesis novel considering his age and his involvement in the nationalist movement.

But then something quite contrary to this might also happen because of this distancing in space and time. Derek Walcott remarks in a similar context:

> The further we move from home, the more strongly rooted the particular becomes, the more distinctive and describable those things that are true to their time and place. Whether they are the indigenous components of a novel, a play or a recipe.[98]

In Raja Rao's case even this is very valid, for we see how his own awareness of his country and its traditions were heightened as a consequence of his exile. To use a phrase of Patrick White's, it is perhaps due "to the stimulus of time remembered."[99] In spite of his exile, the incontrovertible fact remains that Raja Rao is sensitively alive to both the eternal and the actual India, and this awareness has found artistic expression in his fictional works.

Meenakshi Mukherjee presents another view of the effect of staying away from India for such a long period on Raja Rao's work. She believes that "his earlier work was full of fresh perceptions and a first hand response to life"[100] and suggests that they disappear altogether from his later works. She remarks that in

> *The Serpent and the Rope* (1960) and *The Cat and Shakespeare* (1964) this concrete imagery is replaced by general reflections and abstract speculations. The reason for this change in style may be related to the increasingly metaphysical nature of his themes. But another possible reason cannot be ruled out altogether. At the time of writing *The Serpent and the Rope*, Raja Rao had already been an expatriate long enough to have lost touch with the vivid details of landscape and daily life in India that filled the pages of his early volumes."[101]

This is a very interesting point of view put forward by Meenakshi Mukherjee, which she offered as a general truth applicable to all exile writers, in an article[102] published four years later. Such a critical opinion, however plausible it might seem on the face of it, needs to be examined with reference to the novels. Meenakshi Mukherjee states that Raja Rao's natural mode of concretising reality is through the use of specifically Indian images. To prove her point, she offers a few typical examples from *The Cow of the Barricades* and *Kanthapura*:

> the sky ("as blue as a marriage shawl," *Kanthapura*, p. 72.) or women ("some beautiful as new-opened guavas and the others as tender as April mangoes," *The Cow of the Barricades*, p. 58) or young boys ("bright as banana trunks," *Kanthapura*, p. 245.).[103]

Her contention is that such an ability to particularise and concretise reality is not present in the later works. However, here are some illustrations from *The Serpent and the Rope* that give the lie to her view:

> [Grandfather Kittanna] rubbed himself till the body shone as the young of a banana tree.(p. 7.)

> [Little Mother's] bright smile and the song that shone like the copper vessels in the house. (p. 9.)

> I had, wonderful muslin-like dreams, made of purest cotton white, and beneath which shone breasts like the down of doves. (p. 97.)

> the day was as fresh as a pomegranate... (p. 108.)

> my body is parched like a banana skin. (p. 249.)

> "... He's frail as an accacia flower (p. 267.)

> [Madeleine] smelt like a thousand-petalled jasmine, or like the blue lotus. (p. 326.)

The list is by no means exhaustive but enough to make the point. But, no doubt, this mode of perception disappears almost entirely from *The Cat and Shakespeare* but for an occasional example like this:

> How I love the smell of Shantha's body, it's like the inner curve of a jackfruit — pouch and honey of wondrous odors and succulent. (pp. 116-17.)

But the reason for such a disappearance is not due to Raja Rao's stay abroad, as Meenakshi Mukherjee suggests, but because of the different form employed in *The Cat and Shakespeare*. These illustrations should make it clear that, however valid her observations are to other exile writers, they are untenable in Raja Rao's case.

Raja Rao is unique, for his exile has given him both the requisite detachment and a greater need to become intensely aware of his spiritual roots. It would not be out of place to mention here that he makes his pilgrimage to India almost every year. However, it should be pointed out that like in other expatriates, Raja Rao is also susceptible to romanticising his mother country occasionally, as it happens in *The Serpent and the Rope*.

The choice of Raja Rao among Indian novelists in English was made precisely because he touches on almost everything, that other Indian writers have done in fiction—the family, the village, the city, the country, the world and the concerns appropriate to them. Even while he is dealing with the social, material conditions of Indian life, almost always the metaphysical and the spiritual are lurking behind, and therefore *completely* engage the reader's attention. The highest gets the greater attention and becomes a value in relation to routine, ephemeral preoccupations. And this is charactistically Indian and in novel after novel, Raja Rao seeks to bring out this truth of India and Indians—regardless of what they are, whether he is a young half-backed fellow like Moorthy in a small village; an accomplished intellectual like Ramaswamy; a clerk in a ration shop like Govindan Nair or a political ideologue like Padmanabha Iyer. It is this understanding of Indian reality that has enabled Raja Rao to give us images of India in his fictional works that are both authentic and artistically satisfying.

Notes

1. S.V.V., "Face to Face," *The Illustrated Weekly of India* (January 5, 1964), pp. 44-45.
2. Raja Rao, 'Javni', *The Cow of the Barricades* (London:Geoffrey Cumberledge Oxford University Press, 1947). All quotations referred to in the text are from this edition.
3. C.D.Narasimhaiah, *Raja Rao* (New Delhi: Arnold Heinemann, n.d.). p. 7.
4. P.Rama Moorthy, "Death in Raja Rao's 'The Policeman and the Rose' and Witi Ihimaera's 'Pounamu' pounams" in *Commonwealth Literature: Problems of Response,* p. 130.
5. C.D. Narasimhaiah, *Raja Rao*, p. 6.
6. Raja Rao, *Kanthapura* (1938; rpt. New Delhi: Orient Paperbacks, 1971), p. 5.
7. Meenakshi Mukherjee, *The Twice Born Fiction: Themes and Techniques of the Indian Novel in English,* 1971; rpt. New Delhi: Arnold Heinemann, 1974), p. 139.
8. Raja Rao, *Kanthapura,* pp. 200-1.
9. Meenakshi Mukherjee, *The Twice Born Fiction*, p. 42.
10. Ibid., p. 42.
11. C.D. Narasimhaiah, *Raja Rao,* p. 20.
12. Janet Powers Gemmil, 'Raja Rao: Three Tales of Independence' in *World Literature Written in English,* Vol. 15. No. 1 (April 1976), pp. 142-43.
13. C.D. Narasimhaiah, **Raja Rao**, p. 25.
14. J.P.Gemmil, 'Raja Rao: Three Tales of Independence', *WLWE,* p. 135.
15. Meenakshi Mukherjee, 'Raja Rajo's Shorter Fiction' in *Indian Literature,* Vol. X. No. 3. (1967), p. 68.
16. Syd Harrex, *The Fire and the Offering* (Calcutta: Writers Workshop, 1978), II, p. 147.
17. Raja Rao, *Kanthapura* (1938; rpt. New Delhi: Orient Paperbacks, 1971). All quotations referred to in the text are from this edition.
18. Meenakshi Mukherjee, *The Twice Born Fiction*, p. 38.
19. Ibid., p. 142.
20. M.K. Naik, *Raja Rao* (New York: Twayne Publishers, 1972), p. 60.
21. C.D.Narasimhaiah, *Raja Rao,* p. 47.
22. Ibid.
23. Syd Harrex, *The Fire and the Offering,* II, p. 155.
24. Haydn Moore Williams, *Studies in Modern Indian Fiction in English* (Calcutta: Writers Workshop, 1973), II, p. 104.

25. D.S.Maini, 'Raja Rao's Vision, Values and Aesthetic' in *Commonwealth Literature, Problems of Response*, p. 68.
26. Narsingh Srivastava, *The Mind and Art of Raja Rao* (Bareilly: Prakash Book Depot, 1980), pp. 51-52.
27. C.D.Narasimhaiah, *Raja Rao*, p. 44.
28. Haydn Moore Williams, *Studies in Modern Indian Fiction in English*. II, p. 105.
29. Meenakshi Mukherjee, *The Twice Born Fiction*, p. 42.
30. C.D. Narasimhaiah, "The Novels of Raja Rao" in *National Identitfy*, ed. K.L.Goodwin (Melbourne and London: Heinemann, 1970), p. 159.
31. Thomas A. Vogler, "Introduction", *Twentieth Century Interpretations of 'Wuthering Height,: A Collection of Critical Essays*, ed. Thomas A.Vogler (Englewood-Cliffs, N.J.: Prentice-Hall, Inc., 1970), p. 6.
32. Quoted in M.K.Naik, *Raja Rao*, p. 60.
33. Meenakshi Mukherjee, *The Twice Born Fiction*, p. 62.
34. Raja Rao, *The Serpent and the Rope* (1960; Delhi: Orient Paperbacks, 1968). All quotations referred to in the text are from this edition.
35. C.D.Narasimhaiah, *Raja Rao*, p. 87.
36. S.Nagarajan, "An Indian Novel", *Considerations,* ed. Meenakshi Mukherjee (New Delhi: Allied Publishers, 1977), p. 86.
37. C.D. Narasimhaiah, *Raja Rao*, p. 78.
38. Ibid., p. 83.
39. S.Nagarajan, 'An Indian Novel,' in *Considerations*, p. 85.
40. M.K.Naik, *Raja Rao*, p. 82.
41. H.M.Williams, *Studies in Modern Indian Fiction in English*, II, p. 126.
42. C.D.Narasimhaiah, *Raja Rao*, p. 112.
43. Ibid., p. 114.
44. A.L.Basham, *The Wonder that was India*, p. 156.
45. Richard Lannoy, *The Speaking Tree: A Study of Indian Culture & Society* (1971; rpt. London: Oxford University Press, 1975), p. 88.
46. R.K.Kaul, *"The Serpent and the Rope* as a Philosophical Novel," *The Literary Criterion*, Vol. XV. No. 2 (1980), p. 40.
47. David McCutchion, "The Novel as Sastra," *Considerations*, p. 92.
48. *The Serpent and the Rope*, p. 42.
49. H.M.Williams, *Studies in Modern Indian Fiction in English*, II, p. 111.
50. Raja Rao, "India's Search for Self-Expression," *The Times Literary Supplement,* August 10, 1962, Quoted in M.K.Naik, *Raja Rao*. p. 27.
51. M.K.Naik, *Raja Rao*, p. 28.
52. C.D.Narasimhaiah, *Raja Rao*, p. 120.
53. Ibid., p. 121.
54. Ibid., p. 93.
55. Ibid., p. 93.
56. D.S. Maini, "Raja Rao's Vision, Values and Aesthetic" in *Commonwealth Literature: Problems of Response*, p. 76.
57. David McCutchion, p. 96.
58. D.S.Maini, p. 75.
59. C.D.Narasimhaiah, *Raja Rao*, p. 75.
60. D.S.Maini, p. 77.
61. M.K.Naik, *"The Serpent and the Rope:* The Indo-Anglian Novel as Epic

Legend", in *Critical Essays on Indian Writing in English,* pp. 296-302.
62. G.S.Amur, *Images and Impressions* (Jaipur, Panchsheel Prakashan, 1979), p. 1.
63. David McCutchion, p. 91.
64. Quoted in M.K.Naik, *Raja Rao,* p. 87.
65. David McCutchion, p. 96.
66. Ahmed Ali, "Illusion and Reality: The Art and Philosophy of Raja Rao," *The Journal of Commonwealth Literature, No.5, (July 1968), p. 19.*
67. *Ibid., p. 20.*
68. S.C. Harrex, *The Fire and the Offering,* II, p. 190.
69. *The Cat and Shakespeare* (1965; rpt. New Delhi: Orient Paperbacks, 1971), p.. 82. Subsequent quotations referred to in the text are from this edition.
70. Meenakshi Mukherjee, *'The Twice Born Fiction,* p. 94.
71. C.D.Narasimhaiah, *Raja Rao,* p. 75.
72. M.K.Naik, *'The Serpent and the Rope:* The Indo-Anglian Novel as Epic Legend,' p. 297.
73. Narsing Srivastava, *The Mind and Art of Raja Rao,* p. 27.
74. Ayyappa Paniker, "The Frontiers of Fiction: A Study of Raja Rao's *The Cat and Shakespeare"* in The Literary Criterion, XV, 1 (1980), p. 67.
75. Ayyappa Paniker, "A Conversation with Raja Rao on *The Cat and Shakespeare,"* Chandrabhaga, 2 (1979), pp. 14-15.
76. Ayyappa Paniker, "The Frontiers of Fiction: A Study of Raja Rao's *The Cat and Shakespeare,"* p. 64.
77. Swami Prabhavananda, *The Spiritual Heritage of India* (London: George Allen & Unwin, 1962), p. 310.
78. P.N.Srinivasachari, *The Philosophies of Visistadwaita* (Adyar: The Adyar Library, 1943), p. 398.
79. C.D. Narasimhaiah, *Raja Rao,* p. 139.
80. Ayyappa Paniker, "A Conversation with Raja Rao on *The Cat and Shakespeare,"* p. 16.
81. Ibid., p. 15.
82. M.K.Naik, *Raja Rao,* pp. 133-34.
83. D.S.Maini, p. 86.
84. Ayyappa Paniker, 'A Conversation with Raja Rao on *The Cat and Shakespeare,'* p. 15.
85. Ibid., p. 15.
86. Ayyappa Paniker, 'The Frontiers of Fiction: A Study of Raja Rao's *The Cat and Shakespeare,'* p. 67.
87. C.D.Narasimhaiah, **Raja Rao,** p. 131.
88. Raja Rao, *Comrade Kirillov* (New Delhi: Orient Paperbacks, 1976). All quotations referred to in the text are from this edition.
89. Narsing Srivastava, *The Mind and Art of Raja Rao,* p. 94.
90. Ibid., p. 92.
91. C.D.Narasimhaiah, 'Raja Rao: The Short Stories, An Afterword,' *The Policeman and the Rose* (Delhi: Oxford University Press, 1978), p. 136.
92. Raja Rao, 'Nimka,' *The Policeman and the Rose* (Delhi: Oxford University Press, 1978), p. 99. Subsequent quotations referred to in the text are from this edition.
93. C.D. Narasimhaiah, 'An Afterword', *The Policeman and the Rose,* p. 133.

94. Ibid., p. 135.
95. Raja Rao, *The Serpent and the Rope*, p. 350.
96. R.Parthasarathy, "An Interview with Raja Rao," **Span**, Vol. XVIII. No. 9 (September 1977), p. 30.
97. Terry Eagleton, *Exiles and Emigres: Studies in Modern Literature* (London: Chatto and Windus, 1970), p. 18.
98. Quoted in Edward Baugh, "Cuckoo and Culture: *In the Castle of My Skin*," *Ariel*, Vol. 8, No. 3 (July 1977), p. 24.
99. Patrick White, 'The Prodigal Son,' *Australian Letters*, Vol.1, No. 1 (April 1958), p. 38.
100. Meenakshi Mukherjee, *The Twice Born Fiction*, p. 187.
101. Ibid., p. 188.
102. Meenakshi Mukherjee, "Literature of Exile," *ACLALS Bulletin*, Fourth Series, No. 1 (1975), pp. 27-32.
103. Meenakshi Mukherjee, *The Twice Born Fiction*, p. 188.

Chapter - 5
Towards Conclusion

The later half of the twentieth century has seen a tremendous revival of interest in the Raj in England. The numerous novels, travelogues and films that have appeared, are an offshoot of this. Nostalgia for a 'vanished civilization' must partly account for this unusually large output. Incidentally, the most prestigious literary award in England, the Booker McConnell Prize for Fiction has gone three times in the 70's to novels with the Raj theme, *The Siege of Krishnapur* in 1973, *Heat and Dust* in 1975 and *Staying On* in 1977. And the long romance between the British Raj and the exotic East continue to flourish in the early eighties through two of the biggest blockbusters shown on the British Television. *The Far Pavillions* based on M.M.Kaye's novel and *The Jewel in the Crown* adapted from Paul Scott's Indian tetralogy. In addition, films based on *Kim* and *A Passsage to India* were made.

We shall now try to understand the nature of the image of India in the works of two British writers, Rudyard Kipling and L.H.Myers in relation to the main trends evident in Anglo-Indian fiction. As against this, Raja Rao's images of India will be critically examined to see the difference in the reaction between them.

In the British image of India, the first important constituent is the portrayal of the Englishmen. In the entire Anglo-Indian fiction, Englishmen dominate the Indian scene the hence it is their situation in India that receives utmost attention at the hands of the English noveliest. But curiously, a very important aspect of their life in India is almost entirely ignored by all these novelists. Historically speaking, India was indeed a land of promise and opportunity for the British since she "seemed to offer the prospect of aristocratic security at a time when England itself was falling prey to democratic vulgarity."[1] And moreover, "the British in India made claims to social rank ignored at home" and because "one's social claims were only respected within India, there was little temptation to return home."² It is this rank and the various privileges that were associated with it which are conspicuous by their absence in Anglo-Indian fiction. For instance, an average memsahib's servants included the following :

> *bhisti* (water carrier), *mehtar (sweeper), khansamah* (cook), *masalchi* (dishwasher and assistant cook), *ayah* (children's nurse), and *syce* (groom). Besides these, there were *dhobis* (washermen) who washed and ironed the laundry for about ten rupees a month; *darzis* (tailors) who came and set up their machines on the veranda to make dresses and repair clothes; and many others.³

In contrast to the comforts the British enjoyed in England, their life in India was indeed princely :

But the Anglo-Indian noveliest deliberately chose to ignore this aspect of their life as he was more concerned with the sacrifices, hardships and struggles of the British in India. No doubt, all this toil was directed towards saving the soul of the poor native! British civilians are seen, almost always, as very resourceful people who value their work in India more than anything else. Kipling not only emphasised the debilitating effect of work on the British, but suggested in some of his stories like 'William the Conqueror', that work gave them a sense of identity and a meaning to their otherwise dreary existence.

Kipling makes us see that the rulers are not, as often thought of, always heroes. They may be superior, patronising, efficient, but are ironically themselves the greater victims of the system that they have prepetuated in India. This feeling of exile is a dominant strain in Anglo-Indian fiction. Consider a passage in an early novel like *Oakfield*:

> How little people at home know or care, what a quantity of unhappiness is shipped off to this country every month. They talk of the Anglo-Indian empire, and the fortunate young lads who get into that glorious service; but they forget that a life of exile, and as such, to all but the most insensible, more or less a life of pain; they forget, or do not care to know, what a tragedy almost every one of those fortunate lads go through; tragedies not the less painful because they are for the most part dull and unexciting; and often too, unwitnessed and unsympathised with. (Vol. I, p.

101.)

Life in India, for Arnold, is a life in exile, dull, painful, unexciting and tragic. And in a later day novelist like E.M.Forster, this sense of exile is identified as something of an indistinguishable aspect of the Indian reality:

> Unfortunately, India has few important towns. India is the country, fields, fields, then hills, jungle, hills, and more fields. The branch line stops, the road is only practicable for cars to a point, the bullock-carts lumber down the side tracks, paths fray out into the cultivation, and disappear near a splash of red paint. How can the mind take hold of such a country? Generations of invaders have tried, but they remain in exile ... She [India] has never defined. She is not a promise, only an appeal.[4]

Forster would have us believe that what the British experienced in India has been the plight of all the invaders to this country.

There is also the emphasis on their life of loneliness and separateness. They have to live by their code and assiduously cultivate their self-image. Even an anti-Raj writer like George Orwell is aware of this. His hero Flory remarks: "You've got to be a pukka sahib or die, in this country."[5] He further argues that in Burma

> ... you are not free to think for yourself. Your opinion on every subject of any conceivable importance is dictated for you by the pukka sahib's code.[6]

If the coloniser ever attempts to break out of this code, the consequences can be disastrous as in Kipling's 'The Man who would be King.'

In L.H.Myers's *The Near and the Far*, the only Englishman present in the entire novel is a wandering traveller Smith who is an agnostic and a materialist like the modern day western intellectual. Like the typical European, he is "imbued with a sense of the value and reality of phenomenal world in and for itself."[7] Myers uses Smith to represent the Western view of life in contrast to the Indian view as symbolised by Rajah Amar. The Material as opposed to the Spiritual, the Aesthetic and Vulgar as opposed to the Religious and Moral, forms the basis for the difference in the two world views presented by them. Given the kind of moral and ethical preoccupations in Myers, his sympathies naturally lie entirely with the Indian position. This is made clear in Amar's judgement of Smith, something that surely has his own approval:

> ... It is well that people like Smith should exist, and it is perhaps inevitable that they should exaggerate their own importance; but it is also well that society should not give them even the importance they deserve. A world that honoured them would be a decaying one. (p. 432.)

A man like Smith has no place in Myers's ideal civilized community. But ironicaly he is respected in the western world.

Myers's use of the Englishman to point out the serious limitations inherent in western civilization takes place at a philosophical level, the level of ideas. A similar preoccupation is noticed in Orwell on a less profound plane and hence, perhaps, there is greater bitterness in Flory's comments on the modernization of Burma.

> 'Of course I don't deny,' Flory said, 'that we modernize this country in certain ways. We can't help doing so. In fact, before we've finished we'll have wrecked the whole Burmese national culture. But we're not civilizing them, we're only rubbing our dirt onto them. Where's it going to lead, this uprush of modern progress, as you call it? Just to our own dear swinery of gramophones and billycock hats. Sometimes I think that in two hundred years all this—' he weaved a foot towards the horizon—'all this will be gone—forests, villages, monasteries, pagodas all vanished. And instead, pink villas fifty yards apart; all over those hills, as far as you can see, villa after villa, with all the gramophones playing the same tune. And all the forests shaved flat—chewed into wood-pulp for the *News of the World* or sewn up into gramophone cases.'[8]

Such a negative view of western civilization is noticed in some of the novels of Maud Diver and Edward Thompson as well.

Raja Rao's portrayal of Englishmen should receive a brief mention here. In *Kanthapura*, we have the two English sahibs, proprietors of the Skeffington estate, presented in their role of exploiters of the poor coolies. If this is a political treatment of the Englishmen in a political novel, there is an important difference in the various Englishmen and women that appear in *The Serpent and the Rope*. There are short sketches of students at Cambridge like Jack Hollington, Michael Swanston, Stephen and Julietta. And they are all very English in their views, beliefs and attitudes to life which contribute to the authenticity of these characters. Raja Rao the artist is free from any political bias or rancour that one normally associates with British writers on India.

The second constituent of the image of India is the depiction of Indians themselves. Most of the Indians portrayed in Anglo-Indian fiction are two dimensional characters who appear in novel after novel with monotonous regularity. Invariably, they are "the loyal servant, the trusty guide, or the passing salaaming villager."[9] In Kipling's stories a number of such people appear, but what characterises their presentation is that they are treated with love and affection and never with contempt or hostility. A possible reason could be that he liked them, having grown up amidst them. Loyalty was one of the virtues that was highly prized in the Indians, especially the servants. Consider the description of Zyarulla, Eldred Lenox's Pathan servant in Maud Diver:

> Zyarulla, entering soundlessly, set down the *chota hazri* on a small table at his master's elbow without betraying his surprise and concern by so much as the flicker of an eyelash. For not even your immaculate family butler can excel, in dignity and true reserve, a bearer of the old school, whose Sahib stands only second to his God, and who would almost as soon think of defiling his caste as of entering another man's service.[10]

It is this total and unquestionable loyalty that found favour with the Anglo-Indian novelists who in turn idealised them. One recalls at this point, Forster's splendid description of the Punkah-wallah, though the reasons are slightly different.

The natives are portrayed as helpless, weak and ineffective children who look upto the authority of the British to govern them. This stock representation is a recurring feature in Kipling as it is in the entire corpus of English fictional writing on India. Even when the natives are hardy, tribal folk from the frontier districts, there is no change in the children-parent relationship, as is evident from the story, 'The Head of the District.' Such an attitude is prevalent even in a later novel, *Siri Ram Revolutionist* in a description of the Punjabis:

> A strong hardy stock, assertive of their own rights, men of the toughest fibre, innocent of nerves, with little or no physical fear, but helpless as cattle when there was no one

to lead them.[11]

If one expects a more favourable characterisation in the Anti-Raj writers, it turns out to be mere wishful thinking. In *Burmese Days* all the native characters have very little or nothing to redeem them. The one individual who could have won our sympathy is Dr. Veeraswami, but even he is seen in a comic light as he is shown to be a rather clownish defender of the Raj, more royal than the King! In his attitude towards the natives, as Richard Cook suggests, "Orwell could on occasion, be rather more the *pukka sahib* than Kipling, who felt a close kinship and attachment to the native population of India."[12] To take an exmple, Orwell could describe the native butler thus :

> The butler, a dark, stout Dravidian with liquid, yellow-irised eyes like those of a dog.[13]

Kipling, even in his rabidly imperialistic stories as 'His Chance in Life' and 'The Head of the District' never resorts to such non-human comparisons.

Among the Indians, distinctions were made by the Anglo-Indian novelists. That the majority of these writers favoured the Muslims over the Hindus is a well known fact. They found the Muslims tough, reliable and masculine as they were once the conquerors of India like the British. The frontier tribes like the Pathans, Dogras, Gurkhas came to be admired for similar qualities in them as these were also martial races. For instance, in Kipling's famous 'The Ballad of the East and West,' there is a distinct possibility of the two races coming together when they are 'two strong men.' Kamal who strikes a relationship with the Colonel's son is a Pathan. The Hindus as opposed to the Muslims and the tribal folk were considered weak, unreliable and effeminate, and among the Hindus, the Bengalis were treated rather harshly by Anglo-Indian novelists. Kipling is no exception to this though his Hurree Chunder Mookerjee is not seen in an entirely negative light, for he is described as a very resourceful and cunning spy of the British government. An exceptional reference to the Bengali is found in *An Indian Day:* "Every Bengali is a born nurse, and compassion comes naturally to the race."[14]

Eurasians, who are half-Indian are treated unfavourably as well. The British having been responsible for the creation of this class of people suffered from a terrible feeling of guilt and at every opportunity attempted to disown them completely. We have seen the ludicrous character of Michele D'Cruze in Kipling's 'His Chance in Life,' and even Forster resorts to caricature in portraying Mr. Harris, the Eurasian chauffer who "was vexed by the opposite currents in his blood ... and he belonged to no one but himself."[15] Only George Orwell, in spite of the comic portrayal of the two Eurasians Mr. Francis and Mr. Samuel, attempts to understand their tragic plight as is evident in Flory's remark Elizabeth :

> But our attitude towards them is rather beastly. We always talk of them as though they'd sprung up from the ground like mushrooms, with all their faults ready-made. But when all's said and done, we're responsible for their existence.[16]

The western educated Indian is usually the target, not always unjustifiably, of satire in Anglo-Indian fiction. In 'On the City Wall,' Kipling gives us the character of Wali Dad, an unreliable Indian who fails to act in a moment of crisis. Such a portrait is presented in great depth by Edward Thompson in the district collector, Kamalakanta Neogyi, "a man without country or an ethos."[17] He tells of his sad predicament to Hamar, the district magistrate :

> ' ... But for any Indian who's lucky enough to serve the Raj this is part of his bed of thorns — he knows that the vilest bullies and tyrants are his own flesh and blood! ... We get the worst of both worlds, our own and that one of yours in which we serve.'[18]

Thompson has sympathetically characterised this unhappiness of an honest Indian civil servant. He gives a curious twist of irony to Neogyi's plight by creating another Indian, Deogharia, the Commissioner who is unethical and corrupt but has no problems like Neogyi and is awarded K.C.I.E. for his services to the Empire. And Neogyi himself is transferred by Deogharia to a remote and backward district at the end of the novel.

In this category also belong the rulers of the country, the Rajas, some of whom had received western education either in England, or at home through English tutors. For a perceptive statement of their actual position, one should look to L.J.Milne's novel, *The Green Goddess*. The Raja of Rukh was educated at Cambridge. And the

> West had infused itself with him more than he dreamed. Cambridge had made something of a half-caste of the high

> born, absolute ruler of Rukh, an intellectual half-caste. He had studied a few western masters profoundly, he had dabbled, and still dabbled, in abominably many. But your true cosmopolitan is born, not made. He is very sure. Europe had given Rukh's Raja Gogol and Herbert Spencer, Byron and Aristotle, Goethe and Ben Jonson and Macaulay, the philosophies of Greece and England, the cultures of France and Spain, the flairs of Mayfair and Rome, but it had taken away more than it had given, had cramped even more than it had developed.[19]

Ironically, the Raja still prided himself upon the fact that

> Europe had made a superficial but accomplished cosmopolitan of him — he knew that at core he was all Oriental still.[20]

The changes in the Raja are only superficial and he has really failed to bridge the East and the West. And so has Rao Sahib of Baraon in Kipling's *The Bridge-Builders* who is shown to be a monstrous hybrid in his "tweed shooting- suit and seven-hued turban." He has a steam launch but is unable to "understand steam-engines" and regards his own religions ceremonies as "dam-bore." Even his distinctly colourful and idiosyncratic English is well brought out by Kipling. A good illustration of this mode of speech is found in *The Siege of Krishnapur* where we have the Maharaja's son Hari who reads *Blackwood's Magazine,* prefers his native ways but acts like the English lest the westerners think him a backward person. Here, Hari is addressing Fleury, an English visitor to the palace:

> 'Mr. Fleury, dear sir, I am delighted to make your acquaintance. Collector, you know, Hopkin is my very good friend, most interested in advance of science. This English coat, sir, is it very costly? Forgive me asking but I admire the productions of your nation very strongly. May I feel the material? And this timepiece in pocket, a half hunter is it not called? English craftsmen are so skilled I am quite lost in admiration for, you see, here our poor productions are in no wise compared with them. Yes, I see you are looking at my coat which is also of English flannel, though bought in Calcutta, unfortunately, and cut by durzie from bazaar and not by your Saville Rows. Timepiece is purchased in

London and not Calcutta also I think?'²¹

Hari's obsession with English goods, his servility and absence of self-pride are all realised effectively through the use of speech rhythms and syntax that are typical of an imitative Indian. However, that the western educated Indian came in for harsh criticism at the hands of the Anglo-Indian novelist need not unduly disturb us, for this category of Indians were far from being admirable figures. Instead of absorbing the best of both the worlds, they ended up as individuals who had no identity of their own. Such persons are not uncommon in present day India for that matter.

Among the educated Indians, nationalists were an important group. But as Hutchins points out, the

> nationalist movement, to an astonishing extent, drew no response from the British imagination in India. It is almost impossible to find references to nationalist politics in contemporary memoirs. Nationalism was simply ignored, wished out of existence, or dismissed with the presumption that nationalists did not represent the "real" India.²²

Though this is on the whole true, nationalists do appear now and then in Anglo-Indian literature. In Kipling's story, 'The Enlightenments of Pagett, M.P.', Pagett is enlightened about the true nature of Indian nationalism. Orde impresses upon him that the Congress is far from the popular movement that he had come to believe. Dina Nath, the Bengali student nationalist is the butt of Kipling's sharp satire and even the sympathetic Pagett is made to dislike him intensely. Edmund Candler is the only Anglo-Indian novelist who deals with the Indian nationalists in a central way in works such as *Siri Ram Revolutionist* and *Abdication*. In both the novels, Siri Ram and Banarsi Das are depicted as young men who are misled into sacrificing their lives for a hopeless cause. Edmund Candler's attitude is made clear in his description of Siri Ram's character in *Abdication,* the sequel to the earlier novel:

> A weak youth, compact of vanity, yet not devoid of virtue, had become the dupe and scapegoat of the revolutionists, who had dragooned every generous instinct in him and perverted it, and then led him blindfold to the sacrificial stone.²³

Both of them end as failures, a conscious acknowledgement of the noveliest's reluctance to come to terms with a movement that was to give India independence in another twenty five years time. In the words of Benita Parry, "the want of mental and physical stamina, the windy idealism, the courting of failure and disaster, make Banarsi Das and Siri Ram pitiful and ignonimous figures, the powerless tools of contingency."[24] Dinabandhu Tarkachuramani, the new style nationalist is portrayed without any sympathy by Edward Thompson in his novel, *A Farewell to India*. He is regarded as the greatest danger to the security of the British Empire and this should account for the hostile treatment in a novelist who is otherwise exceptionally sympathetic in painting Indian characters. Incidentally, *A Passage to India,* that liberal classic of Indo-British relations has no Indian nationalist in it.

Finally to the fullfledged Indian characters in Anglo-Indian fiction. The preceding discussion of the various types of Indians that appear in this genre makes it markedly clear as to the nature of prejudices in these writers. These prejudices were mainly the outcome of their political viewpoint. They wrote not so much as individuals but as representatives of the ruling race. But when the writer in question is a genius like Kipling or Forster, he is able to transcend these limitations and give us rounded portraits of Indians. In Kipling, there is the moving portrait of Purun Bhagat which gives the lie to Somerset Maugham's assertion that Kipling "seldom spoke of the Hindus with appreciation."[25] Then, there is of course the wonderful creation of Ameera in 'Without Benefit of Clergy' who is seen in a better light than the ordinary British memsahib in her selfless devotion to the Englishman, Holden.

But it is in *Kim*, that Kipling achieves his most notable success. While even the numerous minor characters belonging to various races are depicted with understanding and compassion, the characters of the Lama, Mahbub Ali, Hurree Chunder Mookerjee and the woman of Kulu stand out as extraordinary creations in the entire gamut of English fictional writing on India. The figure of the Lama leaves a lasting impression in the minds of the readers since it is created out of a sense of wonder, awe, respect and humility that Kipling feels towards this noble soul. The Lama emerges from the novel a fully rounded figure since he is shown as one, who pursues his goal with a single minded devotion; who has grown so extremely fond of his *chela* that he not only pays for Kim's education but also suspends the search for his River till Kim can rejoin him; who has his moments of weaknesses like his susceptibility to anger in the encounter with the spies and who can think of his *chela* even in that supreme moment of realizing the desire of his lifetime. Unlike the stock Indian characters, Mahbub Ali and the woman of Kulu are portrayed as individuals who have their frailties, strengths and hence recognizably human.

Outside Kipling, there are a few notable Indians as well. In Thompson's well known Indian trilogy, we have Sadhu Jayananda, once in the ICS but who now lives as a hermit having renounced the world. His prime object now is to attain personal salvation :

> he was dreaming on infinity, withdrawing from existence into union with the *Paramatma,* the Absolute, that unconditioned pulseless Silence over whose surface our brief lives flit and twitter for their imaginary hour.[26]

Even then we see him involved in the nationalist movement and clarifying many of the protagonist Alden's doubts about Indians. In him Thompson has portrayed a wonderful balance between the ideal of renunciation and action. In many ways, he reminds us of Puran Bhagat.

Though Prof. Godbole is more of a caricature, Aziz in *A Passage to India* and Hari Kumar or Harry Coomer in *The Raj Quartet* are portraits in depth, truly modern fictional characters. The question has often been asked as to how representative Aziz is of the Muslims. To raise such an issue is to really beg the question. The point is that his character poses no difficulty in being identified as that of an Indian Muslim. Both E.M.Forster and Paul Scott have given adequate motivations to Aziz and Hari Kumar within the novel to make them both human and Indian. These two entities are not treated as constituting separate sides in an individual but as one integral whole. As a matter of fact, this propensity to make a split between the two, and emphasing only the Indian at the expense of the human has resulted in the stereotyped image of an Indian as one who is childlike,weak, unreliable and far from admirable. This accounts for the fact that there are only a handful of Indian characters who are satisfactorily realised in terms of art in the entire body of Anglo-Indian fiction. Undoubtedly, this points to a major failure in these novelists.

As against this, L.H.Myers's portrayal of Indians in *The Near and the Far* comes as a refreshing contrast. The India of Myers's tetralogy is inhabited only by Indians—except for Sita and Smith—unlike the other Anglo-Indian novels. And the wide variety in the novel is quite astounding, for we have Rajah Amar, a Buddhist; Prince Jali; Hari Khan, a Muslim; Gokal, a Brahmin and the Guru, a Hindu. In addition, there are a host of minor characters like Emperor Akbar, his sons Salim and Daniyal, the Vamacharini Gunevati, Mabun Das, Shaik Mobarek, Narsing, Ali, Raja Bhoj, Lakshmi, Mohan, Damayanti and numerous others. While the Anglo-Indian novelists responded to India as colonisers, Myers was blissfully oblivious of this fact, that is, as a writer. Hence he saw the Indians as human beings and had no colonial framework to judge them. This explains the authenticity in his presentation of Indian characters, all of whom are recognizably Indian in their habits, conventions and attitudes towards life. What gives an added profundity to his Indians is that he provides a philosophical basis for the actions of some of his major characters. Whereas Rajah Amar's life is governed by the Buddhist philosophy, those of Gokal and the Guru to a great extent are determined by the Hindu philosophical standpoint. It needs to be reiterated that the Indian character can only be grasped fully in terms of his religious practices and philosophical views. Myers, though an outsider, achieves a degree of success in his Indian characters given normally to an insider, because of his awareness of this inescapable truth about Indian life.

And in our exploration into the image of India in Anglo-Indian fiction, *The Near and the Far* occupies a unique position, for it is perhaps the only significant novel in which the characters are entirely Indian. While in a overwhelming majority of British writers, for reasons that are predominantly political, we have an India almost without Indians. Even while they had their novels and stories set in India, they were more preoccupied with the problems of the British in India and the interest in the life of Indians was, at best, marginal and peripheral. Rudyard Kipling, Edward Thompson and E.M.Forster are the only exceptions to this preponderent preoccupation.

In contrast to these Anglo-Indian writers and even L.H.Myers, Raja Rao enjoys a distinct advantage in being an insider. As one deeply rooted in India, its philosophy, religion and history, he is able to give us an abundantly wide variety of Indians. After all, as Ramaswamy remarks, "India is large and very diverse." (p. 214.) Raja Rao has been able to encompass this diversity mainly through his shifting locales from the rural to the urban and semi-urban India. That is how, he has succeeded in delineating characters drawn from practically every caste and class in India. His own wide range of interests become apparent in the choice of his protagonists, who are quite different from each other — Moorthy, the college educated idealistic young man; Ramaswamy, the brilliant intellectual and an Advaitin; Govindan Nair, a clerk in the ration shop, but one who has solved the mystery of life and Padmanabha Iyer, a Marxist ideologue who discovers the compelling hold of India on him. Raja Rao's sureness of touch is very much in evidence since there is nowhere even a semblance of a false note in his Indian characters. They are all both recognizably human and Indian. His interest in philosophy has no doubt contributed to the overall enrichment of his Indian characters. It is this added dimension of his characters which gives Raja Rao a special place among Indian-English writers.

The third constituent of the image of India is the outcome of the first two in relation to each other, that is, the relationship between Indians and Englishmen. In the colonial relationship, there was the inevitable distance between the colonised and the coloniser. Added to this, there existed such a wide divergence in the world-views and philosophies of both, that "two races could scarcely be more alien from each other than the English and the Hindus."[27]

Consequently, there is the absence of meaningful contact between the two races, for theirs is a parent-child, teacher-pupil, master-servant relationship. And this absence is faithfully reflected in Anglo-Indian fiction. But the better writers attempt to bring together the two races and explore into the reasons for their failure to establish the right kind of contact. Kipling in his stories reveals how, as long as the political equations between the two peoples exist, there is no possibility of their coming together. But in stories like, Beyond the Pale, Georgie Porgie, Yoked with an Unbeliever and most impressively in Without Benefit of Clergy, he does point to a profound truth that love is a significant emotion that can bridge this gulf, even if it is only as long as love relationship lasts. One of Kipling's characters remarks, "Love knows no caste ...There is neither Shiah nor Sunni, forbidden nor idolater in Love."[28]

Related to the theme of Love is that of sex which appears in *A Passage to India* and *The Raj Quartet*. Sexual assult is central to the structure of both the novels. Paul Scott at the very outset asserts, that the *Quartet* is "the story of a rape, of the events that led upto it and followed it and the place in which it happened."[29] Daphne Manners falls in love with an Indian Hari Kumar to successfully transcend the racial barriers, but is unfortunately raped by a group of unknown Indians. A variation to this is offered in the English superintendent of missionary schools, Edwina Crane being attacked by Indian rioters on the same day. But here there is no rape, for she is only abused and physically attacked resulting in her losing consciousness. In Forster's novel,

Adela Quested also believes that she was molested by Aziz inside the Marbar Caves. But a very important difference between Adela Quested and Daphne Manners is "that neither Dephne's love nor her rape is platonic. She has no hallucinations – her love is real; so is her rape."[30] While the earlier Anglo-Indian novelists had used the sexual assault as an external manifestation of the depravity of Indians as a race, both Scoot and Forster make it a means to highlight the problems encountered in an inter-racial understanding. While Forster criticises the British for their role in this imagined rape, Paul Scot goes beyond mere criticism "to assert that despite the brutality of this attack, an inter-racial love is still desirable and beautiful."[31]

E.M.Forster, among other things, makes it very apparent in the novel that the Indians and the Englishmen can never come together until they meet on equal terms. Elsewhere, he remarked that "never in history did ill-breeding contribute so much towards the dissolution of an Empire."[32] For a very appropriate rendering of racial incompatibility, one should quote Robin Alden's words in *An Indian Day:*

> ' ... I know how vexing they [Indians] are, in ways enough. But *we* never shake free from our herd-morality, any more than they do; and we go on judging them because they're not first-rate Englishmen in dark skins. I suppose it's a question of different ethics. They *hate* many of the virtues that we praise; and we hate many that *they* are keen on. We seem to them incredibly rough and rasping; and they seem to us worms. We're both right – by our own standards.'[33]

Put simply, it is the imperialist ideology that comes in the way of Anglo-Indian relations.

The physical image of India in these writers plays a particularly notable role in creating a solid world that is at once Indian. Of course, the visual forms an important aspect of this physical image. The description of the Indian landscape, its flora and fauna usually constitues the forte of the significant Anglo-Indian novelists. But in some of the lesser writers there is a conscious, more often self-conscious effort to include local colour in the form of these detailed descriptions. And so they tend to be repetitive and tiresome, and quite often have no organic relation to the theme of the novel. Their only function seems to be to add local colour and hence they stick out rather conspicuously in their novels. Borges, the Argentinian writer-critic makes out a brilliant case against exaggerating the significance of local

Towards Conclusion

colour.

> Some days past I have found a curious confirmation of the fact that *what is truly native can and often does dispense with local colour;* I found this confirmation in Gibbon's *Decline and Fall of the Roman Empire.* Gibbon observes that in the Arabian book *par excellence,* in the Koran, there are no camels; I believe if there were any doubt as to the authenticity of the Koran, this absence of camels would be sufficient to prove it is an Arabian work. It was written by Mohammed, and Mohammed, as an Arab, had no reason to know that camels were especially Arabian; for him they were a part of reality, he had no reason to emphasize them; on the other hand, the first thing a falsifier, a tourist, an Arab nationalist would do is have a surfeit of camels, caravans of camels, on every page; but Mohammed, as an Arab, was unconcerned; he knew he could be an Arab without camels.[34] (emphasis mine)

But it has to be kept in mind that only a genius knows how to link the camel to the soil and produce an unsuspected insight. And so not mentioning it does not always necessarily make a virtue.

While in someone like L.H.Myers, the evocations of Indian landscape are rather vague for obvious reasons, in Raja Rao they are brilliantly rendered. And more importantly, he is able to go beyond the merely realistic and give us different layers of meaning. To cite some instances, Benares is evoked with tremendous power by Raja Rao through the use of realistic details. But he also includes comments like these:

> Benares is eternal. There the dead do not die nor the living live. The dead come down to play on the banks of the Ganges, and the living who move about, and even offer riceballs to the manes, live in the illusion of a vast night and a bright city.[35]

Raja Rao is also able to describe the Himalayas in abstract terms. Such an ability clearly lies beyond the ken of an outsider.

In all the descriptive accounts of the physical reality of India, there exists a disquieting feature in the continual emphasis on the fantastic heat, dust, disease and other extreme climatic conditions. Hence, a stereotyped image of India as an unpleasant land recurs in British fictional works on India. This image is a direct result of the stereotyped portrayal of Englishmen in India as hard-working, self-sacrificing people who are toiling in dreadful conditions. Where the adverse weather conditions are not stressed, diseases such as cholera and typhoid are used by the writers to accentuate the problems of the British in India. Added to this, some of them also attribute the indolence, fatalism, sensuousness and deceitfulness in the natives to the Indian climate. Mr. McBryde, the District Superintendent of Police in *A Passage to India* has a theory about climatic zones:

> 'All unfortunate natives are criminals at heart, for the simple reason that they live south of latitude 30 they are not to blame, they have not a dog's chance — we should be like them if we settled here.'[36]

But Forster, who reverses many of the stereotypes of Anglo-Indian fiction in his novel, comments ironically on this theory:

> Born at Karachi, he seemed to contradict his theory, and would sometimes admit as much with a sad, quiet smile.[37]

Interestingly, even an early writer like Kipling despite some of his racial prejudices did not support this climatic theory. In this stand of his, he was going against the spirit of the times which had used even climate to justify imperialism.

How far does the image of India in British represent the whole of India? The image that we derive from these writers represents only a small part of India ignoring altogether large areas of the country. As A.J.Greenberger in his exhaustive survey points out, "all the novels of the early period are set in north-western India — the Punjab, North West Frontier Province, and Himalaya foothills. There are a few cases where the locale is Maharashtra or Burma, but Bengal, Central, and South India are almost completely absent."[38] The major reason is that the British writers lived in these areas and hence wrote about places which they knew intimately. And they "far preferred to set their stories in the jungle, mountains, hill-stations, small villages, or army cantonments rather than in the cities."[39] This also came from their belief that real India was to be found in her villages and probably because it gave them a chance to be exotic as well. Also, the disinclination to portray the western educated Indian made these writers ignore the cities. For example, when Kipling chose to set his stories in Lahore as in "The City of Dreadful Night and On the City Wall, he had to introduce a character like Wali Dad in the latter story. The former is only an impressionistic account of the dreadful heat of Lahore and hence he could dispense with characters altogether. There was a slight change at the beginning of the twentieth century when novelists like Edward Thompson and Dennis Kincaid began writing about Bengal and Bombay respectively. One of the few writers to set his works in South India was Hilton Brown. *Potter's Clay*[40] is a collection of short stories which have their locale in places that are now part of Andhra Pradesh and Tamil Nadu. His novel, *One Virginity*,[41] a much recent work is set in Tiruvellipattanam in Tamil Nadu. *The Near and the Far* has its action in North India, the Mughal India of Akbar's time. Raja Rao, being a South Indian naturally preferred Karnataka and Kerala for his locales, although he goes outside India as well in *The Serpent and the Rope, Comrade Kirillov,* 'Nimka' and 'India' - A Fable.

The most complex and crucial aspect of the image of India, that of its religion and philosophy needs to be looked at. There is no gainsaying that India can be fully comprehended only through these two integral facets of Indian life. Some of the Anglo-Indian novelists have achieved varying degrees of success in this attempt. However, when a final balance-sheet is drawn, failures seem to outnumber the limited success achieved by a few of these writers. India down the ages has not changed despite its coming under the influence of various foreign invaders. In an important sense, it is unchanging and timeless. Maud Diver refers to this in her novel, *Far to Seek:*

> ...ancient and unchanging India; utterly impervious to mere birds of passage from the West.[42]

Kipling points to this in one of his stories :

> All kinds of magic are out of date and done away with except in India, where nothing chances in spite of the shiny, top-scum stuff that people call 'civilization.'[43]

Interestingly, even an insider like Raja Rao regards this 'top-scum stuff' as accretions that can be so easily brushed aside :

> The crust is superficial—it lies about everywhere but you can remove it, even with a babul-thorn.[44]

This constitutes a very important truth about India which is sadly not understood by the British writers who almost always speak of this aspect only to attack it. To this view of India as an unchanging land is related the fatalism it is said to breed in the peoples. In *The Great Amulet*, we read of "the dread note of fatalism – the moral microbe of the East"[45] and "the Asiatics with the phlegm of fatalism."[46] This fatalism, as is to be expected, is seen in a very negative light. For example, in *Siri Ram Revolutionist*, Siri Ram's father Mool Chand is shown to be lacking even in fatherly responsibility because of this fatalism in Indians. When cholera strikes his daughter Shiv Dia, he – incredibly! – deserts her leaving the poor girl to her fate. However, though it is true that fatalism has been the bane of Indians, but the sense of acceptance has also contributed to an inner resilience in the ordinary masses of the country, which has been portryed vividly in *Kanthapura*.

In dealing with the Hindu religion, how did the British writers present Indian Gods, rituals and festivals? Not only does this presentation reveal the extent of their knowledge of India but more significantly brings out their attitude towards these facets of Indian life. It is perhaps in keeping with their predilections that most of these writers chose to deal with the popular forms of Hinduism rather than grapple with its philosophical implications. And hence the emphasis is more on child marriages, suttee, worship of Kali and the Tantric rituals that in turn helps them to line up their heavy artillery against Hindu religion. Even an otherwise perceptive novelist like Edward Thompson makes a simplistic identification between Hindu religion and the worship of Kali.[47] Also consider Flora Annie Steel's comment on these sacrifices in one of her stories. A goat is killed and

> a jet of red, red bubbling blood spurting into the dim light ... Graven by age-long iteration in their limited minds and lives was the dogma that Blood is the Life thereof.[48]

Even the Tantric cult is not spare, for it offers yet another ground for attack on the Hindu religion. In *The Swami's Curse*, F.E.Penny presents an ascetic who

> seeks to kill desire by an unlimited indulgence which brings satiety and extinction of emotion. The indulgence is enjoined by his so-called religion; and his depravity is commanded as a great virtue. It is a meritorious act on the part of the ordinary worshipper to lend his aid to the saddhu in carrying out his excesses.[49]

Towards Conclusion

Flora Annie Steel continues this preoccupation in her novel *The Law of the Threshold* where the Aghoris, an extreme Tantric cult is used to illumine her picture of India. The reason for this persistence in Steel is perceptively suggested by Benita Parry :

> In bringing to the fore a taboo rite particularly hideous to the Western sensibility as the pinnacle of Hindu thought, she paints the heart of secret India as a place of darkness.[50]

Such an attitude was born entirely out of an ignorance of the Tantric cult which has its philosophical basis in that it emphasizes the "identity of the Absolute and the phenomenal world when filtered through the experience of *sadhana*, i.e., contemplative exercises"[51] and that its essence consists of "psycho-experimental speculation."[52] But the Anglo-Indian novelists ignored this in their keenness to project an image of India as the land of darkness.

As a marked departure from this attitude, we have a very creative use of the Tantric cult in *The Near and the Far*. Myers with his intimate knowledge of Indian religion and philosophy knew the actual significance of this cult and its place in Indian thought. He was aware of the Tantric faith in fish, flesh, wine, copulation and gestures and he could not have thought of a more apt faith to represent pure sensuality in women. In Prince Jali's growth towards self-understanding, his encounter with Gunevati marks the first stage. She is "a Vamachari, a Follower of the Left-Hand way." Very soon Jali discovers that

> ... She had no life, no being, no reason, except in sex; and she herself felt it. She was a living bait – a bait of the dark, merciless Kali. (p. 249.)

And he puts an end to this relationships as he realises that he cannot live by ignoring the moral side of life. Myers with his profound sense of moral discriminations sees a close relationship between the problem of sex and problem of evil. So we have here an instance of how a sensitive writer, if he chooses to respond in an unprejudiced manner, can effectively employ Hinduism with rewarding results.

Let us now study some of the typical descriptions of Indian gods, festivals and temples in these writers. The best of them, E.M.Forster and Edward Thompson are truly representative of Anglo-Indian fiction. To begin with, the Indian gods:

> Yesterday ... I walked to the Temple of Ram-whose-

> hands- reach-to-his-kness, not to be confused with the Temple of the Monkey God (Hanuman-who-knocks-down Europeans) ...[53]
>
> A great many gods are on visit and they all get up at 4-30 a.m.— they are not supposed to be asleep during the Festival, which is reasonable considering the din, but to be enjoying themselves. (p. 105.)

Forster's sympathetic understanding of India, so assiduously built up by his critics, begins to seem like a myth in the light of these biased, ironical and crude observations about Indian gods. No one expects, perhaps has no right to expect even, an outsider to respond like an insider to the Indian deities in view of the fundamental differences in the world views between the West and the East. But what one can legitimately hope for is a dispassionate account and not something like what we have here, however strange and remote is the encounter and the resultant experience.

Consider now the description of Gokalashtami that goes on for pages. Here is a significant reference:

> What trouble me is that every detail, almost without exception, is fatuous and in bad taste. The altar is a mess of little objects, stifled with rose leaves, the walls are hung with deplorable oleographs, the chandeliers, draperies— everything bad. (p. 106.)

Soon comes an admission of another kind :

> There is no dignity, no taste, no form, and though I am dressed as a Hindu I shall never become one. (p. 107.)

Forster's total disillusionment with the Gokalashtami festival is not difficult to sympathise with, but his confession of his inability to be a Hindu is unwarranted, to say the least. To dress him up in Hindu clothes is part of the Indian hospitality and also perhaps intended to make him feel less like a stranger in these alien surroundings. And so one can conclude that Forster comes out only a shade better in his response to the Indian festival in relation to his reaction to the gods. The irony of it is that these reactions come from one who is very much aware that "everything in India takes a religious tinge." (p. 138.)

To cite another such instance, note how Findlay, a very considerate missionary at that, reacts to the Vaishnava festival :

Towards Conclusion 323

> ... an all-night and all-day clash of cymbals and imbecile skipping and calling of the names of Radha Govinda.[54]

> ... the unclean ecstasies of Vaishnava worship, where men swayed in meaningless excitement and danced through days and nights till they fell in swoon.[55]

Forster's influence on Thompson cannot be entirely ruled out .

In comparison with Forster and Edward Thompson, L.H.Myers has no problems of this kind as his novel is set not only in India but the characters are almsot all Indian. We have references to Indian gods such as Ganpati, Saraswati and Kali and to a Hindu shrine with a Shiva linga in it. But these are all objective descriptions and not subjective responses to alien gods as in the first two novelists. This is not to rule out a more honest and subjective account of the Indian reality by an English writer. Kipling could never be ironical or sarcastic of Indian gods and festivals even when they troubled his emprical mind. Such was his generosity and compassion. In *The Razor's Edge,* there is a description of the goings on inside the famous Madura temple that deserves to be quoted in full :

> ... At nightfall it [the temple] was packed with people. Men, women and children. The men, stripped to the waist, wore dhoties, and their foreheads, and often their chests and arms, were thickly smeared with the white ash of burnt cow dung. You saw them making obeisance at one shrine or another and sometimes lying full length on the ground, face downwards, in the ritual attitude of prostration. They prayed and recited litanies. They called to one another, heatedly argued with one another. There was an ungodly row, and yet in some mysterious way God seemed to be near and living.[56]

Here, Somerest Maugham is able to give us a very precise picture of an Indian temple. Actually, in this case there is plenty of scope for irony and criticism but Maugham avoids this, for his purpose seems to be to see India on its own terms and not judge it from any predetermined standpoint, however valuable and inevitable it might be. Also, he does not suffer from a feeling of superiority.

Let us consider a description of a minor festival like Sankara Jayanthi in Raja Rao's *Kanthapura* to set out the essential differences in the response of the insider and the outsider :

... Then came Postmaster Suryanarayana and said, 'Brother, why not start a *Sankara-Jayanthi?* I have the texts. We shall read the *Sankara-Vijaya* every day and somebody will offer a dinner for each day of the month.' 'Let the first be mine,' said Bhatta. 'The second mine,' said Agent Nanjundia. 'The third must be mine,' insisted Pandit Venkateshia. 'And the fourth and fifth are mine' said Rangamma. 'And if there is no one coming forward for the other days, let it always be mine,' she said. Good, dear Rangamma! She had enough money to do it, and she was alone. And so the *Sankara-Jayanthi* was started that very day. We hastily pushed rice on the leaves of the young and came back for the evening prayers. There used to be a bhajan. Trumpet Lingayya with his silver trumpet was always there, and once the music was over, we stayed till the camphor was lit, and throwing a last glance at the god, we went home to sleep, with the god's face framed within our eyes. It was beautiful, I tell you — day after day we spent as though the whole village was having a marriage party. (pp. 13-14.)

For the villagers of *Kanthapura,* religion is "not a compartmentalized business but a socialising and integrating factor, generating a sense of participation, an insistence on duty which here, paradoxically sounds like a privilege, because of the strong impulse to share, celebrate and rejoice collectively which is characteristic of a homogeneous peasant community and therefore a value to cherish."[57] Unfortunately, this sense of community and the feeling of oneness in an organic society found in an Indian village is not taken cognizance of by the Anglo-Indian novelist who merely skims the surface of Indian life.

When even the major Anglo-Indian writers lack the necessary artistic detachment in their view of Hindu religion, the less said the better about the minor novelists. And it comes as no surprise that they should all conveniently ignore Hindu philosophy since they have failed in giving us a convincing and disinterested presentation of even the surface realities of Hinduism. It was precisely because of this reason that L.H.Myers was included in this study, for he is the only English novelist to have successfully made use of Indian religion and philosophical thought to convey his vision of life in his tetralogy, *The Near and the Far.* His major purpose was "to give form to his intuition of the undying conflict that exists between sensitive and cultured individuals and the world of commercial values and social competitiveness"[58] in his novels.

With his strongly ethical and moral preoccupations, he was interested in exploring the spiritual and religious aspects of life. And in such an exploration, Hindu philosophy admirably served his artistic intention. In his "intention ... to portray a good man" who "exhales an atmosphere of serenity,"[59] he found that only an Indian Guru could satisfactorily take on this role. So Myers created in the Guru a truly Indian saint, a Vedantin, who believes in asceticism and service to mankind through action. More significantly through his emphasis on Indian religion and philosophy, Myers uses India as an idea in an artistically satisfying manner. This success is achieved by relating the religious India to historical India, that is, India of Akbar's time during the sixteenth century. Actually, this also helped him to render the world of India in concrete terms.

Like Myers, though on a much smaller scale, Somerset Maugham reveals a comprehensive grasp of Advaita Philosophy in his novel *The Razor's Edge*. It is the story of Larry's unhappy exprience as a pilot in the First World War. The crisis comes when his dear friend Patsy gets killed trying to save him. Then begins his search for the meaning of life. He wants to understand the nature of God, evil and the soul; and his search leads him to India. His Indian experience constitutes the sixth chapter which is of central significance in the novel. As he lands in India, he learns from an Indian: "The East has more to teach the West than the West conceives." He visits Benares, Madurai and finally goes to Shri Ganesha's Ashrama near Trivandrum, where he is

> taught that it is not essential to salvation to retire from the world, but only to renounce the self. He [Shri Ganesha] taught that work done with no selfish interest purifies the mind and that duties are opporunities afforded to man to sink his separate self and become one with the univerisal self. (p. 274.)

After two years in the ashrama, Larry has a mystical experience in the nearby woods. And then "intense sense of peace, joy and assurance" abides with him for the rest of his life. He realises that he cannot

> leave the world and retire to a cloister, but to live in the world and love the objects of the world, not needed for

themselves, but for the Infinite that is in them. (p. 278.)

At the end of the novel, we see Larry give up his regular income and work as a mechanic or a taxi-driver, having achieved spiritual joy and the knowledge of the Absolute. Maugham makes lucid expositions of the conceptions of Maya, Brahman and other tenets of Advaita philosophy in the novel. Maugham did visit India in 1938 and we can locate close parallels between his account of that visit in *A Writer's Notebook*[60] and *The Razor's Edge*. Though the novel is far less satisfying as a work of art, it is significant in view of the nature of this study since Maugham turns to Hindusim like Myers in order to stress the importance of the Spiritual over the Material.

Kipling's understanding of Hinduism is portrayed in depth only in the story, 'The Bridge-Builders.' Apart from showing an intimacy with the Hindu pantheon of gods, he demonstrates, in the course of the story, that for the Indian the empirical world is not merely not illusory in nature but more important, a part of the Ultimate Reality. But in a story like 'The Miracle of Puran Bhagat,' Kipling reveals only a partial knowledge of Hinduism in implicity suggesting that there is no place for action in the life of contemplation chosen by a Hindu. And for his major Indian character, he chose the Buddhist Lama in *Kim*. Apparently, Kipling found the golden mean between the practical and the spiritual in Buddhism.

This brings us to the fascination that the Anglo-Indian writers had towards Buddhism. Even though no one employs the religion in the way Kipling does in *Kim*, we come across numerous favourable references to Buddhism in these novels. Maud Diver refers to "the Middle way, which is the way of Truth."[61] Alice Perrin regarded Buddha as "the greatest reformer, save one, that the world has ever known."[62] India's rejection of Buddhism is disapprovingly mentioned by Robin Alden in *An End of the Hours*:

> India ... made the mistake of millenniums and shackled and ravaged herself for all future times, when she rejected the Buddha and chose the other way.[63]

L.H.Myers again proves an exception in his choice of Buddhism to present a character like Rajah Amar. He represents 'Good' in life as opposed to 'Evil' and his aim in life lies in Becoming and that is the reason he chooses renunciation. Buddha emphasized both the need to overcome evil in life and also the process of Becoming.

Towards Conclusion

Aldous Huxely is another English writer who modelled his enlightened characters upon Buddha, the compassionate one.[64] He was widely read in Buddhism as is evident from the collection of his letters.[65] But it is in his novel *Island* that this interest is most dominantly present. As a matter of fact, Buddha is the presiding deity of the novel and most of the action takes place in full view of a huge stone Buddha by the lotus pool. Huxley has pictured in the novel the society of Pala which has, by following the Buddhist path of compassion, discovered the way to virtually put an end to sorrow and achieve enlightenment. Undoubtedly, the English writers were enthusiastic about Buddhism since it was more familiar and less complex and metaphysical than the other-worldly Hinduism. The fine balance it struck between a life of pleasure and a life of renunciation in its emphasis on the Middle Way, was another plausible reason for this fascination. Unlike Hinduism which was shown in its popular forms, Buddhism is presented in highly idealized forms.[66]

After this detailed examination of the various constituents that go to make the image of India, a brief reference to the two novels that have constantly vied with each other to be regarded as *the* classic on India, is perhaps not out of place. The novels in question are Rudyard Kipling's *Kim* and E.M.Forster's *A Passage to India*. By and large, critics seem to assign the classical status to Forster's work, though Nirad Chaudhuri is the one notable exception who makes out a persuasive case for *Kim*. This is largely because modern critics find in *A Passage to India* a more coherent structure, a greater degree of complexity than in *Kim*. Undoubtedly Forster's novel is a more sophisticated work, but as novels that project an image of India there are some important differences that need to be kept in mind in any comparison of the two.

There is a basic difference in the attitudes of Kipling and Forster towards India. While it is one of total acceptance in *Kim*, it is a sense of scepticism and a tendency to question everything that marks *A Passage to India*. Hence, Kipling can get into his Indian characters with an effortless ease, an ease unparalleled in Anglo-Indian fiction. But Forster despite his liberal stance, finds the land and its people both a mystery and a muddle. For him "the Mediterranean is the human norm"[67] and from this standpoint it is but inevitable that India should seem amorphous and formless. Whereas Kipling responds to India with a loving understanding, Forster can only stand at a distance and pass critical judgements.

Added to this, there was a significant difference in the prevailing political situation of the times. Whereas Kipling wrote at the height of imperial glory, Forster was writing his novel when the empire was no longer thought to be infallible. And as Katherine Moore believes,

> Kipling in the 1880's was convinced that we, the British in India, were loved, and deserved to be loved. Forster in the 1920's is quite sure that we are not loved at all and not sure that we deserve to be. For we no longer love.[68]

And in *Kim*, Kipling for once ignored the political realities completely, perhaps he could afford to do so in that era of confidence. But in *A Passage to India*, the political forms the very basis of Forster's exploration into the Indo-British encounter.

And now to some characters in these novels. Both Hurree Chunder Mookerjee and Aziz are representatives of the Westernized Indian. The former is an intelligent, resourceful spy whose loyalty to the Raj is total. But Aziz is, despite his sensitivity, highly self-conscious, always 'on edge' and struggles to find a proper place in his own society. The crucial difference lies in the treatment they receive at the hands of their creators. In the words of Katherine Moore, "the change into westernized Indian in *Kim* is made a source of amusement ... In *A Passage* the change is a source of tragic conflict."[69] As in this case, there is also a significant difference between the characters of the Lama and Prof. Godbole. Reverence, wonder and humility have gone into Kipling's characterisation of the Lama. The synthesis between the East and the West is shown to be a distinct possibility in the wonderful relationship between him and Kim. However, Forster shows no such reverence for Prof. Godbole who is presented as a caricature that makes him appear totally ridiculous. But even he is shown to have achieved transcendence, thanks to his complete faith in Hindu religion. In this achievement, he comes closer to the Lama.

One could suggest that while Kipling reacted to India like an insider, Forster was only able to respond as an outsider. This is not meant to be taken as a value judgement But by not considering the political implications inherent in the Indian situation, Kipling was able to illuminate different facets of the multifarious reality of India that clearly lay outside Forster's intentions. *A Passage to India* is able to capture at best, a passing phase in the history of British-Indian relations. On the other hand, Kipling attains a completeness in his portrayal of India in *Kim* as he makes us aware of how "within the all-embracing context of India, work and love, public and personal interests, imperial rule and indigenous life can be closely and meaningfully related."[70] In terms of the image of India, *Kim* definitely projects a fuller and comprehensive image of the land and its people while it is only fragmentary in *A Passage to India*.

Raja Rao was included in order to see how an insider responds to his country in striking contrast to the Englishman writing on India. He is one of the three most significant Indians who use the fiction form for their creative expression, the other two being Mulk Raj Anand and R.K.Narayan. While Anand's preoccupations are more to do with the socio-political realities, Narayan treats in his novels both the religious and the philosophical aspects of the Indian reality. On the other hand, Raja Rao reveals a greater sweep and depth in his concerns which are at once, social, religious and metaphysical, though one notices a greater penchant for the philosophic and mataphysical in his later works. It is this comprehensiveness that sets him apart from other Indian writers in English.

While dealing with the Indian village life in his collection of short stories, *The Cow of the Barricades* and the novel, *Kanthapura*, Raja Rao provides us with an insight into the life of the villagers, a life lived close to the soil and nourished and sustained by their myths and religion. Every aspect of this life is taken cognisance of by the writer, for we not only see their exploitation and suffering based on class and caste but also their strengths derived from an unshakeable faith in tradition and religion. As people living close to the soil, they are endowed with a powerful folk imagination and mythoepic conciousness. This is noticed, for instance, in Narsiga and Achakka who grasp the Indian freedom movement in mythical terms. At this point, a slight deviation is made to show how very rarely even an English writer like Edmund Candler is aware of the typical working of the Indian mind. Notice his acute ability to render the freedom struggle in terms of traditional myths:

> The English were the Asuras again, who ravaged the Mother land, which was now in the birth pangs of a new breed of dragon slayers who were to rid her of the evil.[71]

> 'Why he is ruling over us? Why you are afraid of Englishmen? They are not gods but men like yourselves, or rather monsters who have ravaged Sita-like beauty of your country. If there be any Rama among you, let him come

forth to bring back your Sita."[72]

However, it should be kept in mind that Candler is a rare exception. And then an insider like Raja Rao can see how there is a strong sense of acceptance in the Indian village folk which has always been simply dismissed as fatalism by the Anglo-Indian writers. This sense of acceptance make for no escapism but gives them an inner resilience and strength of character. It is clearly seen in the people of Kanthapura at the end of the novel. They might have lost everything, materially speaking; perhaps their spirit is broken but they are not destroyed, for they have experienced something valuable since "something has entered [their] hearts, an abundance like the Himavathy on Gauri's night."(p. 199.) This experience makes for a renewal of hope once again.

In *Kanthapura* as in his other novels, we notice an intimate relationship between the secular and the religious. This constitutes a very important truth about Indian life which has always eluded the grasp of the Anglo-Indian writer. Not only are they wedded to the empirical but they insist on making neat and clear demarcations between the Religious and the Secular, the Spiritual and the Material, the Sacred and the Profane. But the Indian view of life shuns such categorisations and recognizes the value of the Secular, the Material and the Profane, but in the ultimate analysis grants a higher value to the Religious, the Spiritual and the Sacred. However, it acknowledges that the latter cease to have any significance when they are divorced from the former. Unable to understand this, the majority of Anglo-Indian writers have failed to project a satisfactory image of India. Hence, it is but logical that India should remain an insoluble mystery to them. Whereas, in the lives of Moorthy, Ramaswamy and Govindan Nair, to name only a few, this all-embracing view of life is delineated by Raja Rao.

Raja Rao's interest in India is far deeper and profounder than those of his Indian counterparts since a solid philosophical foundation based on the Advaita philosophy of Sankara forms the basis of his novels. In a very important sense, all his stories can be taken as preparations for non- duality. And as he probes into the nature of Ultimate Reality and the various means of achieving Self-Realization — through the paths of Action, Knowledge and Devotion — he achieves a completeness in his treatment of India as a metaphysical idea. But his vision of India attains a totality, since his novels work on two levels

Towards Conclusion

throughout — the realistic and the metaphysical, each illuminating the other. For one like Raja Rao — as in the traditional Indian way — each of them in isolation would be meaningless and they both acquire value and significance only through mutual dependence. And so we see that in all his works, Raja Rao is acutely aware of the Indian social reality but always considers them in the context of a higher reality, so characteristic of even the average Indian mind. It is this wholeness of vision that assures him a singularly unique position in Indian-English literature. Undeniably, his vision prevents him from idealising Hinduism in the manner of a revivalist. As a matter of fact,

> Raja Rao's quest is not that of a revivalist, one has seen in answer (as it did in Gandhi's case) to a pressing political need in *Kanthapura*; it stands intellectual Ramaswamy in good stead in alien soil in *The Serpent and the Rope*, and Govindan Nair in a corrupt ration office in *The Cat and Shakespeare*; and saves a Brahmin in the grip of Marxist ideology in *Comrade Kirillov*. These are supreme examples of the operation of tradition in diverse modern social and political contexts.[73]

And in summing up the achievement of Raja Rao, it could justifiably be said that he is, in his works, trying to understand India by placing Indians in a variety of situations and in pursuit of very different interests. For whoever they are and whatever they do, the metapyhsical India, to use an expression of Jawaharlal Nehru, 'clings' to them. And it is no exaggeration to suggest that of all the Indian-English writers, Raja Rao alone seems to be capable of the Shakespearean kind of approach, the letter to the Renaissance man and the former to the Indian man, by placing him in a variety of contexts and reinforcing a cetain coherent view of an epoch, a nation and an entire way of life.

In Rudyard Kipling, L.H.Myers and Raja Rao we have three writes of genius who reveal different degrees of comprehensiveness in their presentation of the image of India. It would be profitable to consider their success in terms of the insider/outsider paradigm. Kipling, though an Englishman, was born in India and came to love the land and its people dearly. And his own knowledge of Indian life must surely make us consider him an insider to India. But curiously, his image of India turned out to be more precise and accurate when he wrote about the country after getting away from it in 1889. That is to say, the detachment given to him now as an outsider must account for this success. On the other hand, L.H.Myers was indeed an outsider to India, for he never visited the land. Paradoxical though it may seem, even this makes for a certain advantage in the case of Myers as it enabled him to be more disinterested in his presentation of India. But his extraordinary knowledge and understanding of Indian religious and philosophical thought makes him virtually an insider. And in contrast to Kipling and Myers, Raja Rao by virtue of his birth and his inwardness with aspects of Indian life is an insider. But the very fact that he has been staying away from India and that all his works with the exception of a few of his early stories and *The Cat and Shakespeare* were written outside India gives him, in a restricted sense, the status of an outsider. While this distance made for the necessary artistic detachment and the resulting success in *Kanthapura*, it also produced a work like *The Serpent and the Rope* that projects an exalted image of India. More significantly, in the latter work, we have the presence of passages that are sentimental and jingoistic in their references to India. Also, his being an expatriate does contribute to his playing down the social reality in order to emphasise only the timeless India. But happily this tendency disappears completely in his later novels. So it can perhaps be pointed out that while Kipling and Raja Rao belong to the insider-outsider category, Myers is the outsider-insider. And it is only a combination of the two that can produce an authentic response since

> literary art, like any achieved form of perception or cognition, demands a relationship of both objective distance from, and intricate inwardness with, its object.[74]

Raja Rao and L.H.Myers share a common interest in their fascination for Indian religions and philosophy which has led them both to project an image of India as an idea in their fictional works. This fascination finds an echo in the Orientalist's interest in India that produced an immaculate conception of the country. But there is a vital difference between them, in that, while the Orientalists entirely ignored the contemporary social realities, Myers and Raja Rao do not do so because of their acute awareness of the country. As the British and German Orientalists were drawn to Indian Philosophy by the wisdom and profundity inherent in it, Myers also discovered that his moral and ethical problems were clarified by Indian thought. Also, Myers had inevitably to turn to India for "there (was) no assured moral or religious tradition within which the writer can work" in his own country as he found "there (was) no body of vital ideas and beliefs in the society of (his) time on which he can depend."[75] It is one of the supreme ironies of colonialism that the coloniser who always saw himself as the superior and stronger figure had to turn, as in the case of Myers, to the colonised for clarity, if not wisdom, that was not available in his own culture. It is also a reflection of the loss of confidence in European civilization and the disillusionment with material progress that Europe had accomplished. This must indeed explain T.S.Eliot's interest in Hindu philosophy, Ezra Pound's admiration for Chinese thought and D.H.Lawrence's fancy for the Etruscans.[76]

Attention has already been drawn to the various sterotypes in the constituents of the image of India in Anglo-Indian fiction. The tendency to dismiss the sterotypes as patently false and inaccurate and hence not valuable, is to take an entirely lopsided view of the question. That these streotypes occur with an alarming frequency should not disturb us since they point to very important truths in the British response to India. All these stereotyped images of the land and the people of India are not creations of pure fancy. They are all born out of the observation, experience and conviction of the perceiver of the Indian reality. Quite often we notice that these images are not entirely inaccurate in their details, but as generalized pictures they are invariably found to be wanting. This is mainly due to the preconceived notions of the British, notions that are the direct result of the colonial relationship. The writers reveal varying degrees of success at transcending the colonial framework. It is only the more successful among them who are able to go beyond stereotypes and produce authentic images of India.

In concluding this study, the crucial question has to be posed: Why do the vast majority of Anglo-Indian writers fail in their attempts at understanding India? The reasons for this have to be perhaps sought outside literature as well. In *The Cat and Shakespeare* a related question is asked and an answer suggested: "How can you know you are an Indian? You must know India." (p. 95.) In this, lies an obvious but profound truth that merely being born in India does not confer Indianhood on an individual as a matter of birthright. More importantly, he should earn his India. And does the British writer know his India or are there certain limitations built into his situation by virtue of the peculiar nature of his relationship with India? In the words of John Masters,

> To feel India ... You must become Indian, gain one set of qualities and lose another. As a race we don't do it — we

can't.[77]

A very important reason for the failure of the British is suggested in these words. In any endeavour to come to terms with India, one has to learn to imaginatively identify oneself with the Indian point of view. In other words, one has to "gain one set of qualities" that one had not possessed. But it is perhaps not necessary that he should lose his Englishness as Masters would have us believe, for what we expect in an Englishman's picture of India is the *English* view of India and not the Indian view. His Englishness is valuable for this reason, but an essential, civilized Englishness, that is. This apart, what Masters has put forth here is applicable to almost every Anglo-Indian writer. There is also the implicit suggestion of the inability of the British to feel like Indians because of the difference in race. It is true that there is a wide gulf between the East and the West in terms of attitudes, values and philosophical outlooks. Undoubtedly this has prevented the British from looking at India objectively.

Nirad Chaudhuri also offers another possible factor responsible for this failure. He points out intelligently that the European mind was outraged by the Hindus mainly because of their own insistence on three principles, "that of reason, that of order, and that of measure."[78] Such a mind is always predisposed to judge India on the basis of these criteria. That is why even a sensitive writer like E.M.Forster is genuinely baffled by India. And the fate of the lesser writers can surely be imagined. However, one should not overlook the limitations of such a criteria, for the empirical and the rational are indeed not much help in getting to know the complex social, philosophic and metaphysical components of the Indian actuality. Actually they act as a positive hindrance in these writers.

And then, there was the imperialist ideology, which not only resulted in an unbridgeable chasm between the two races but endowed the British with feelings of superiority, supremacy and greatness that made them look down upon Indians and all that is Indian. It also engendered in them an attitude of condescension and superciliousness which could only lead to misunderstanding and distortion. The crux of the problem was that the British writers were reacting as representatives of the ruling race to India, the subject country. When politics enters into human relationship, it hardens both the head and the heart, and in art it results in a blurring of the vision and an incompleteness of perception. This preoccupation with a political ideology also had a definite effect on their treatment of Indian characters whom they tended to see as Indians first and as human beings only next.

Finally to the British insularity. As Hutchins points out, the

> British never became Indianized, as had earlier conquerors. Earlier conquerors had not possessed a foreign home from which they continuously drew their standards and which induced them to look upon India only as a place of permanent exile. The British kept themselves apart with all the exclusiveness of an Indian caste, but unlike a true caste they could never be fitted into the larger Indian society.[79]

Actually by not trying to assimilate anything of the country in which they lived, the British were being true to their proverbial insularity, which like Imperialism results in a partial view of things. It produces a vicious circle of biasses, prejudices and half-truths, all of which ultimately contribute to an absence of genuine understanding.

The foregoing reasons explain, on the one hand, the failure of the British novelists to project an authentic image of India and on the other, point to their anglo-centric concerns. Because of this, they produced images of India which were sadly more *British* than Indian. Hence the emphasis on British *in* India rather than India itself. Most of them did not seem to realise that until one learns to see a country on its own terms, one will not succeed in perceiving it with either clarity or certainty. A writer has to learn to imaginatively identify himself with the people of the country. Only then will he be able to faithfully depict the essential truth about that country and its people. Both artistic detachment and self-effacement become important prerequisites in such an attempt.

It is undeniable that "on account of its vastness and variety India is a treacherous ground for all foreign writers."[80] All the three writers chosen for this study have achieved exceptional success in their presentation of India. Rudyard Kipling is a truly representaive Anglo-Indian writer since he reveals most of the weaknesses of his fellow-writers in some of his stories, and has given us stereotyped images of India and her people. But in his better stories, that is, in terms of art, and in his novel *Kim* we notice that Kipling is able to transcend these limitations and give us new insights unsuspected in a British writer, which in turn makes for memorable vignettes of India. This was possible because Kipling responded to India with not only sympathy but also love since there existed an emotional bond between him and the land of his birth. It is this remarkable achievement of Kipling to see India as an insider that entitles him to the honorific, "Interpreter General from India to the West"[81] among the Anglo-Indian movelists.

L.H.Myers is a less-worked-upon writer even in India which is very unfortunate. It has been established in the course of the chapter on him how Indian thought and religions operate in a central way in his tetralogy *The Near and the Far*, though he professes in his prefaces that he is using India merely as a distancing device. In a very important sense, Myers stands outside the tradition of Anglo-Indian literature since neither did he visit India nor share the predilections of those writers. This gave him a distinct advantage over them since he could regard India in a more dispassionate and disinterested manner. By choosing to set his novel in the sixteenth century India of Akbar's time, he could also escape from the severely restricting influence of a political ideology like Imperialism. It is this pure interest in India that distinguished Myers from the other Western writers on India.

Raja Rao being an Indian writer is altogether in a different category. His inclusive view of India makes for both comprehensive and precise images of the country in his fictional works. He is also successful in extending the frontiers of the fiction form to accommodate the 'new' experience — the quest for Ultimate Reality — that he is trying to convey in his novels and short stories. More significantly, we have in him an exceptional genius who is eminently capable of understanding cultures other than his own, like that of France and England. In this, he offers us a variation on the general disability of the Anglo-Indian writer to get into the heart of India.

Taken together, the fictional works of Rudyard Kipling, L.H.Myers and Raja Rao, give us images of India that help us perceive the multifarious and diverse realities of the country and its culture. Multiple perspectives on India become available to us in these writers enabling us to see the various shades and nuances of the Indian actuality. These images in their entirety offer richly satisfying vignettes of India and assist us in fathoming this "ancient palimpset."[82]

Notes

1. Hutchins, *The Illusion of Permanence*, p. 199.
2. Ibid., p. 118.
3. Shamsul Islam, *Chronicles of the Raj*, pp. 114-15.
4. E.M.Forster, *A Passage to India* (1924; rpt. Harmondsworth: Penguin Books, 1970), p. 135.
5. George Orwell, *Burmese Days* (1934; rpt. London: Secker and Warburg, 1966), p. 43.
6. Ibid., p. 69.
7. Myers, *The Near and the Far*, p. 430.
8. Orwell, *Burmese Days*, p. 45.
9. Greenberger, *The British Image of India*, p. 38.
10. Maud Diver, *The Great Amulet* (London: Blackwood and Sons, 1908), p. 94.
11. Edmund Candler, *Siri Ram Revolutionist: A Transcript from Life 1907-1910* (1912; rpt. London: Constable & Company Ltd., 1913), p. 70.
12. Richard Cook 'Rudyard Kipling and George Orwell,' *Modern Fiction Studies*, Vol. 7, No. 2 (1961), p. 129.
13. Orwell, *Burmese Days*, p. 21.
14. Edward Thompson, *An Indian Day* (1927; rpt. London: Macmillan and Co., 1940), p. 171.
15. Forster, *A Passage to India*, p. 89.
16. Orwell, *Burmese Days*, p. 123.
17. Thompson, *An Indian Day*, p. 97.
18. Ibid., p. 221.
19. Louise Jordan Milne, *The Green Goddess* (London: Hodder and Stoughton, 1924), p. 82.
20. Ibid., p. 93.
21. J.G.Farrell, *The Seige of Krishnapur* (1973; rpt. Harmondsworth: Penguin Books, 1982), p. 82.
22. Hutchins, *The Illusion of Permanence*, p. 187.
23. Edmund Candler, *Abdication* (London: Constable & Company Ltd., 1922), p. 11.
24. Benita Parry, *Delusions and Discoveries*, p. 156.
25. W.Somerset Maugham, "Introduction," *A Choice of Kipling's Prose*, ed. W.Somerset Maugham (London: Macmillan & Co. Ltd., 1952), pp. v-vi.
26. Thompson, *An Indian Day*, p. 95.
27. J.R.Seeley, *The Expansion of England*, p. 213.
28. Kipling, 'In Flood Time,' *Soldiers Three and other Stories*, p. 299.

29. Paul Scott, *The Raj Quartet* (London: Heinemann, 1976), p. 1.
30. Gomathi Narayan, "Paul Scott's Indian Quartet: 'The Story of a Rape' ", *The Literary Criterion*, Vol. XIII, No. 4 (1978), p. 45.
31. Ibid., p. 52.
32. E.M.Forster, 'Reflections in India: I-Too Late? *'The Nation and the Athenaeum*, 30 (21 January 1922), p. 615.
33. Thompson, *An Indian Day*, pp. 123-24.
34. Borges, Jorge Luis, trans., *Labyrinths: Selected Stories & Other Writings*, (New York: A New Directions Book, 1964), p. 181.
35. Raja Rao, *The Serpent and the Rope*, p. 22.
36. Forster, *A Passage to India*, p. 164.
37. Ibid.
38. Greenberger, *The British Image of India*, p. 35.
39. Ibid., p. 38.
40. Hilton Brown, *Potter's Clay: Some Stories of South India* (London: Simpkin, Marshall, Hamilton Kent & Co., Ltd., 1927).
41. Hilton Brown, *One Virginity* (1948; Bombay: Jaico Publishing House, 1960).
42. Maud Diver, *Far to Seek: A Romance of England and India* (Edinburgh and London: W.Blackwood and Sons, 1921), p. 159.
43. Kipling, 'The Bisara of Pooree', *Plain Tales from the Hills*, p. 262.
44. Raja Rao, *The Serpent and the Rope*, p. 30.
45. Maud Diver, *The Great Amulet*, p. 96.
46. Ibid., p. 385.
47. Edward Thompson, *Krishna Kumari: An Historical Drama in Four Acts* (London: Earnest Benn, 1924), p. 61.
48. Flora Annie Steel, 'A Maiden's Prayer,' *The Indian Scene* (London: Arnold, 1933), p. 625.
49. F.E.Penny, *The Swami's Curse* (London: Hodder & Stoughton, 1929), p. 48.
50. Benita Parry, *Delusions and Discoveries*, p. 117.
51. Agehananda Bharati, *The Tantric Tradition* (London: Rider, 1965), p. 18.
52. Ibid., p. 15.
53. E.M.Forster, *The Hill of Devi* (1953; rpt. New Delhi: Arnold-Heinemann, 1977), p. 133. Subsequent quotations referred to in this text are from this edition.
54. Thompson, *An Indian Day*, p. 184.
55. Ibid., p. 185.
56. W.Somerset Maugham, *The Razor's Edge* (1944; rpt. London: Pan Books Ltd., 1983), p. 268. Subsequent Quotations referred to in the text are from this edition.
57. C.D.Narasimhaiah, 'Introduction', *Awakened Conscience,* ed. C.D. Narasimhaiah (New Delhi: Sterling Publishers Pvt. Ltd., 1978), p. xxii.
58. D.W.Harding, 'The Work of L.H.Myers,' *Scrutiny*, 3, No.1 (June 1934), p. 49.
59. Letter to Gai Eaton, 21 May 1943. Quoted in G.H.Bantock, *L.H.Myers: A Critical Study*, p. 134.
60. Somerset Mangham, *A Writer's Notebook* (London: William Heinemann Ltd., 1949.)
61. Maud Diver, *The Great Amulet*, p. 14.
62. Alice Perrin, *Idolatry* (London: Chatto and Windus, 1909), p. 101.
63. Edward Thompson, *An End of the Hours* (London:

Macmillan and Company, 1930), pp. 232-33.
64. S.Krishnamoorthy Aithal, 'In the Image of Buddha, The Compassionate One: Aldous Huxley's Portraits of the Enlightened' (An unpublished paper).
65. Grover Smith, ed. *Letters of Aldous Huxley* (London: Chatto & Windus, 1969).
66. Greenberger, *The British Image of India*, p. 133.
67. Forster, *A Passage to India*, p. 275.
68. Katherine Moore, *Kipling and the White Man's Burden* (London: Faber and Faber, 1968), p. 90.
69. Ibid., p. 93.
70. Shirley Chew, *Vain Empires*, p. 66.
71. Candler, *Siri Ram Revolutionist*, p. 37.
72. Ibid., p. 89.
73. C.D. Narasimhaiah, 'The Indian-English Writer: The Strength of Tradition' in *The Eye of the Beholder: Indian Writing in English*. ed. Maggie Butcher (London: Commonwealth Institute, 1983), p. 31.
74. Terry Eagleton, *Exiles and Emigres*, p. 219.
75. G.H.Bantock, *L.H.Myers: A Critical Study*, p. 88.
76. Jeffrey Meyers, *Fiction and the Colonial Empire*, p. ix.
77. John Masters, *The Nightrunners of Bengal* (London: Michael Joseph, 1951), p. 30.
78. Nirad C. Chaudhuri, *The Continent of Circe*, p. 102.
79. Hutchins, *The Illusion of Permanence*, p. 118.
80. Nirad C.Chaudhuri, 'The Finest Story About India-In English', p. 49.
81. Nelson S.Bushnell, "Kipling's Ken of India," *University of Toronto Quarterly*, p. 62.
82. Jawaharlal Nehru, *The Discovery of India* (1946; rpt. Bombay: Asia Publishing House, 1972), p. 59.

Appendix-A

The Orientalist's Image of India

A consideration of the British Orientalists should rightly begin with Warren Hastings who was the first ruler to evince keen interest in Indian culture and civilization. He got Charles Wilkins to translate *Bhagavadgita* in 1784, and *Hitopadesha* in 1787. No doubt, his encouragement of Oriental Studies had a practical side. He had his own ideas of how India ought to be ruled: which was to rule the conquered in their own, traditional way. This was how the Romans had maintained their empire long ago. The ultimate aim of Hastings was to reconcile British rule with Indian institutions. At this time Sir William Jones (1746-94), interested in Oriental languages and literature and who had mastered Persian, Arabic and Hebrew accepted the appointment of a judge of the Supreme Court at Calcutta so that he could learn Sanskrit and study its literature. When he arrived in India, his reaction to the country was most favourable:

> It gave me an inexpressible pleasure to find myself in the midst of so noble an amphitheatre, almost encircled by the vast regions of *Asia,* which has ever been esteemed the nurse of sciences, the scene of glorious actions, fertile in the productions of human genius, abounding in natural wonders, and infinitely diversified in the forms of religion and government, in the laws, manners, customs and languages, as well as in the features and complexions, of men.[1]

This could well have come from Conservatives like Hastings and Burke with whom Jones Shared an admiration for Indian culture and civilized achievement. Jones's most significant act was to establish Royal Asiatik Society of Bengal in 1784 to encourage both the English and Indians to research and propagate the rich cultural heritage of

India. He himself translated Kalidasa's *Shakuntala* (1789), *Gitagovinda* (1792) and *The Code of Manu* (1794). Another distinguished member of the society, H.T.Colebrooke translated principal sources of Hindu law and also wrote on the Vedas. Jones used Sanskrit drama to argue that the Hindus had a civilization in its own way equal to that of the Greeks. In fact, he ascribed the style of *Shakuntala* to "a highly complex and cultivated civilization."[2] Even when he had read the Indian epics and myths in the Persian versions, he was filled with admiration for their heroes:

> I am in love with Gopia, charmed with Crishen (Krishna), an enthusiastic admirer of Raama and a devout adorer of Brihma (Brahma), Bishen (Vishnu), Mahiser (Maheswara); not to mention that Judishteir, Arjen, Corno and other warriors of the M'hab'harat (Mahabharata) appear greater in my eyes than Agamemnon, Ajax and Achilles appeared when I first read the Iliad.[3]

In his study of Hinduism, Jones was attracted most by the conception of the non-duality of God and the human soul as explained by Sankara in his commentary on the Vedanta and the transmigration of the soul. This fascination of Jones for India came in for severe criticism at the hands of James Mill who said that his descriptions of Hindu life far surpassed the "rhapsodies of Rousseau on the happiness and virtue of savage life."[4] Mill's criticism is far too simplistic since it refuses to take into account Jones's views on India in relation to his estimate of Europe. Actually, Jones was "firmly grounded in the eighteenth century, with its Whig philosophy, classical education and the cult of Reason."[5] And so despite his praise for the greatness of Hindu civilization, its beautiful literature, sublime religion and highly complex metaphysics, Jones did not think, as alleged by Mill, that India was better than Europe. He had always asserted that the superiority of the European lay in ratiocination whereas that of the Indian lay in imagination.

To Jones, the greatest accomplishments of human wisdom were embodied in the British Constitution. In his study of Indian history and culture, he discovered that India and the other nations of Asia had flourished especially in literature and philosophy, but believed that they had failed to produce a satisfactory form of government. What he therefore desired for India was "a British Government true to the Whig principles, the separation of powers, the rule of law, protection of the individual, yet authoritarian and ruling according to the Indian laws."[6] So we see that Jones was one of the very first Englishman who preached liberalism at home but supported authoritarian rule in India.

Jones's interest in Indian religion and philosophy was continued in the nineteenth century by English scholars like Monier Williams, MacDonell and Keith among others. All these Orientalists glorified India's past since they all hoped to achieve a fine fusion of Hindu and European learning in their works if not in their lives. It should be said in fairness to them that there was hardly anything of significant merit in the then contemporary Indian works. The establishing of the Asiatick Society which published *Asiatick Researches* thus called for explorations into the ancient cultural heritage of India. However when the preoccupation with India lay chiefly with her past, as it happened in the case of the Orientalists, there was a tendency to view India in abstract terms without relating it to the immediate present. This produced a rather immaculate conception of India since the sole emphasis was centred on the *idea* of India. There is another important reason for the deliberate ignoring of the present by the late eighteenth and nineteenth century British Orientalists. After all, they saw in their times only the seamier side of Hinduism with such terrible practices like sati, thuggee, female infanticide and child marriage etc. It naturally appeared horrifying to them and they were more than convinced of the all-round decadence of Hindu culture. And so it is no wonder that such an inglorious present should have evoked no curiosity whatsoever.

The Orientalists, especially Sir William Jones, with their theories about the civilization in India and through translations of classical Sanskrit works and the publications in *Asiatick Researches* succeeded in evoking a most sensational reaction all over Europe, especially in Germany. Indian philosophy now available through translations affected German transcendentalism led by Kant, Schiller, Heine and others. Schleigel's work *On the Language and Wisdom of the Indians* (1808) also marked the beginning of German romantic revival. Schopenhauer acknowledged that the growth of his metaphysical system was determined by Indian ideas among other influences:

> I confess... that I do not think that my doctrine could have ever come into existence until the Upanishads, Plato and Kant could together project their rays into the human

mind... [7]

The Indians are for him "the noblest and the ancient people," "with a religion which is the oldest and the most widespread and as such is the foremost religion of mankind with regard to time and space."[8] He believed that the religion of the Indians is "the original religion of our race."[9] He extolled the Vedas as the "fruit of the highest human knowledge and wisdom."[10] Of course, his praise of the *Upanishads* is most memorable:

> That incomparable book stirs the spirit to the very depths of the soul. From every sentence deep, original, and sublime thoughts arise, and the whole is pervaded by a high and holy and earnest spirit. Indian air surrounds us, and original thoughts of kindred spirits... In the whole world there is no study, except that of the originals, so beneficial and so elevating as that of the *Oupnekhat*. It has been the solace of my life, it will be the solace of my death.[11]

Krause in his *Outline of the History of Philosophy* considers Indian philosophy to have significantly enriched his knowledge of the history of human thought:

> Indian philosophy proves to be the first independent and characteristic formulation of knowledge in a complete form which was perfected, keeping in view the basic perception and the organism built therein, of all perception is the most essential on earth, and which can neither be excelled nor elaborated in this respect.[12]

Paul Deusen spoke of Vedanta as "the strongest support of pure morality, the greatest consolation in the sufferings of life and death."[13] Nietzsche was convinced that "Religion and Philosophy have absorbed every practical instinct in India."[14] Among writers, we have Goethe's famous apostrophe to *Shakuntala*. German critics have come to regard the conversation between the poet, the manager and the jester in the prelude to *Faust* to have been modelled upon a similar device in Kalidasa's play.

As the above statements make clear, German response to India was evidently more spontaneous than the British. Their interest in India was certainly purer since they looked to Indian philosophy as a means of enriching their personality and understanding of the human mind. As Nirad C. Chaudhuri perceptively points out, "the German interest was ideological and imaginative, the British practical and objective."[15] In this, perhaps, lay the reason why the English Orientalist never considered the possibility that even the best of Indian thought could enrich his personality. The English Orientalist could never divorce his interest in India from his awareness that he could be of help in the governing of the country. But the irony of it was that the British policy makers sought his help only in the form of information and never as an ideology to influence the administration of the empire. This possibly explains why the English Orientalist's view of India had little impact on the popular view in England, of India as the land of depravity.

Now we should turn to Max Muller, German by birth but English by adoption, for he "avoided both extremes, the callow German enthusiasm and the hardboiled English contempt."[16] As Chaudhuri suggest, he exhibits "the strongest and the most sympathetic features of the interest in [India] of both Englishmen and Germans."[17] However, unlike the English Orientalists, his interest in India led him to Vedic literature as he was convinced that,

> it is with the *Veda*, therefore that Indian philology ought to begin if it is to follow a natural and historical course... it is impossible to find the right point of view for judging of Indian religion, morals, and literature without a knowledge of the literary remains of the Vedic age.[18]

The *Vedas* constituted the *real* India for Max Muller while the other India, "the mere surface India, with its grotesque religion, its pretty poetry, and its fabulous antiquity"[19] held out no interest to him. Just as the English Orientalist overlooked contemporary India, Max Muller completely ignored the post-Vedic Indian society and its literature. Undoubtedly both were prompted by a common desire to locate their ideal idea of India. Max Muller's idea of India is contained in his Cambridge lectures delivered in 1882, later published under the title, *India: What Can It Teach Us?* He reiterated that India from the first century B.C. to the third century A.D. was to be regarded as 'ancient' and 'natural' and the later period as 'modern' and 'artificial.' He felt convinced that it,

> .... was a real misfortune that Sanskrit literature became first known to the learned public in Europe through specimens belonging to the second or what I called the

> Renaissance period ... Although the specimens of this modern Sanskrit literature, when they first became known, served to arouse a general interest, and serve even now to keep alive a certain superficial sympathy for Indian literature, more serious students had soon disposed of these compositions, and while gladly admitting their claim to be called pretty and attractive, could not think of allowing Sanskrit literature a place among the World-literature, a place by the side of Greek and Latin, Italian, French, English or German.[20]

But, on the contrary, he believed that it,

> is different with the ancient literature of India, the literature dominated by the Vedic and the Buddhist religions. That literature opens to us a chapter in what has been called the Education of the Human race, to which we can find no parallel anywhere else.[21]

Max Muller further argued that anybody wishing to know the origins of language, thought, philosophy, religion and other human creations

> must in future pay the same attention to the literature of the Vedic period as to the literature of Greece and Rome and Germany.[22]

His love for the ancient civilization of India and the idea of India thus attains a rhetorical quality, unequalled in the entire response of the Orientalists to India:

> If I were to look over the whole world to find out the country most richly endowed with all the wealth, power, and beauty that nature can bestow — in some parts a very paradise on earth — I should point to India.

> If I were asked under what sky the human mind has most fully developed some of its choicest gifts, has most deeply pondered on the greatest problems of life, and has found solutions of some of them which well deserve the attention even of those who have studied Plato and Kant — I should point to India. And if I were to ask myself from what literature we, here in Europe, we who have been nurtured almost exclusively on the thoughts of Greeks and Romans, and of one Semitic race, the Jewish, may draw that correc-

tive which is most wanted in order to make our inner life more perfect, more comprehensive, more universal, in fact more truly human, a life, not for this life only, but a transfigured and eternal life — again I should point to India.[23]

So we see that Max Muller's love for India stemmed from his love for the Vedas. His view of Indian literature is dominated but also sadly obscured by his obsession with the Aryan man. As is to be expected, he was also repelled by the popular forms of Hinduism prevalent in India during the nineteenth century. But he devoted the better part of his life to Sanskrit studies. It was indeed a labour of love, for he always considered Sanskrit to be his "first love."[24]

The Orientalists on the whole, succeeded in projecting an image of India as a country with a glorious past, full of ripe wisdom embodied in its religion and philosophy. It was "a purely literary creation"[25] made by them. This image has persisted even today but it is interesting to note that it has had a wider influence outside England both in Europe and in America. Only the British imperial rule in India should offer an explanation for this comparative neglect in England.

In conclusion, it has to be conceded that though the Orientalists attempted to understand India, they did nothing to emulate Indian culture. Despite their concern with Hindu civilization, they were not attempting to discover the social history of the times. This was again due to their preoccupation exclusively with philosophical Hinduism and not with its popular forms. On the political plane, however they did contribute to the resurgence of national spirit in the Indians, by giving them self-confidence and pride in themselves when they needed it most.

Notes

1. Quoted in Bearce, p. 21.
2. Quoted in S.N.Mukherjee, *Sir William Jones: A Study in Eighteenth Century British Attitudes to India,* p. 115.
3. Letter to Richard Johnson, 14 August 1784. Quoted in S.N.Mukherjee, p. 117.
4. James Mill, *The History of British India,* II, pp. 139-40.
5. S.N.Mukherjee, p.96.
6. Ibid., p. 136.
7. Quoted in Helmuth Von Glasenapp, trans., *Image of India* (New Delhi: Indian Council for Cultural Relations, 1973), p. 62.
8. Ibid., p. 63.
9. Ibid., p. 64.
10. Ibid., p. 69.
11. Quoted by H.G.Rawlinson, 'India in European Literature and Thought' in *The Legacy of India,* ed. G.T.Garratt (Oxford: Clarendon Press, 1937), p. 3.
12. Quoted in Glasenapp, *Image of India,* p. 57.
13. Quoted by H.G.Rawlinson, *The Legacy of India,* p. 32.
14. Quoted in Glasenap, *Image of India,* p. 93.
15. Nirad C.Chaudhuri, *Scholar Extraordinary: The Life of Fredrich Max Muller* (New Delhi, Orient Paperbacks, 1974), p. 125.
16. Ibid., p. 134.
17. Ibid.
18. Max Muller, *A History of Ancient Sanskrit Literature* (1859; rpt. Varanasi: The Chowkhamba Sanskrit Series Office, 1968), pp. 8-9.
19. Max Muller, *The Life and Letters* (London: Longmans, Green And Co., 1903), II, p. 138.
20. Max Muller, *India: What Can It Teach Us?* (1882; rpt. Delhi: Munshi Ram Manohar Lal, 1961), pp. 81; 83-84.
21. Ibid., p. 80.
22. Ibid.
23. Ibid., p. 6.
24. Max Muller, **The Life And Letters** (London: Longmans, Green, And Co., 1903), I, p. 498.
25. Nirad C.Chaudhuri, *The Continent of Circe,* p. 97.

Appendix-B

The Image of India in British Historians, Indologists and Art Critics

While the eighteenth century British historians were officials interested only in the Company affairs, the nineteenth century historians were preoccupied with the rise of the British power in India, though they were officials as well. James Mill and John Marshman, the baptist missionary, were the two notable exceptions. But they were also, like the officials, "anglo-centric in their attitude"[1] and consequently "the history of modern India in their hands came to be the history of the rise of the British in India."[2] This provides us with the vital clue to the response of the British historian to India. As a result of this bias, the British historian, with very few exceptions, invariably gives an account not so much about India or Indians, nor even about British India but about the British *in* India.

This also explains why Indian history books authored by Englishmen were only political histories. Even the sixth volume in the admirable series, *Cambridge History of India* by H.H.Dodwell does not contain a single chapter on any social historical theme. Only Sir Alfred Lyall's book, *Asiatic Studies* (1882) made some efforts in this direction. On the other hand, the social life of the British in India received more than adequate attention in such books as T.G.P.Spear's *The Nabobs: A Study of the Social Life of the English in Eighteenth Century India* (1932) and Dennis Kincaid's *British Social Life in India: 1608-1937* (1938). In addition, there is also another bias in the British historians towards Muslims seen ever since James Mill's history. The British always felt more at ease with the Muslims, for they found in Islam a religion that was more comprehensible than the mystifying Hinduism. And there was a common bond of sympathy between the two races for they were both, at different times, conquerors of India.

But the twentieth century has seen this rather unfortunate situation set right by books like *The Rise and Fulfilment of the British Rule in India* by Edward Thompson and G.T. Garratt (1934), *History of British India* by P.E. Roberts (1952) and *India, a Modern History* by Percival Spear (1961).

Hence, it has to be reiterated that the 'anglo-centric attitude' of the British historian led him to render India's historical past in such a way as to justify the imperial rule. And we see the English in the foreground, with India and Indians forming a rather hazy and distant background. This strange paradox in works of Indian history need not unduly disturb us when we realise that the British image of India that is projected in Anglo-Indian fiction is again, quite often the image of the British in India rather than the image of Indians in India.

The interest of the Indologist in India was mainly in its classical Sanskrit literature and they all come under the common label of Orientalists. Their response acted as a counter to the Utilitarian's view of India popularised by James Mill. Sanskrit scholars of today believe, with reason, that their early enthusiasm was based on imperfect translations of Sanskrit classics. Nor are they always happy with the judgements of the Orientalists. MacDonell and Keith wrote histories of Sanskrit literature which contain numerous evaluations of the different forms of poetry. Here are two illustrations chosen at random from their works:

> The subject-matter of the later Kavyas, which is derived from the two great epics, becomes more and more mixed up with lyric, erotic and didactic elements. It is increasingly regarded as a means for the display of elaborate conceits, till at last nothing remains but bombast and verbal jugglery.[3]

> The history of the epic, in fact, is one of the decline in taste and growing artificiality in form.[4]

Without going deep into the merits of such criticism, it is not long before one discovers that their critical estimate is based on their own skills in English poetry. In other words, they almost entirely ignore Indian views about poetry and criticism which, in reality should have at least formed some basis for their judgement. But to study a literature and pass pronouncements on it wholly ignoring the tradition of Indian aesthetics is, no doubt, consistent with the criteria adopted by the Englishman in his response to India.

Appendix-B

At this juncture, it is rewarding to once again consider Max Muller's view of India for there is more in it than meets the eye as suggested by the distinguished Sanskrit scholar K. Krishnamoorthy.[5] Despite his birth in Germany, he is now regarded a British indologist and this is confirmed by his English viewpoint as revealed in his *Life and Letters* rather than his well known, scholarly works on India. If he did not display "the callow German enthusiasm and the hardboiled English contempt"[6] in his Indian books, there is a surprising reversal of his position in his *Life and Letters*. A Man who virtually spent all his life in working on *Rig Veda* of which he had so ecstatically spoken in *India: What Can It Teach Us?* speaks in, as it were, another voice in some of his statements found in his *Life and Letters*. Three illustrations should suffice to drive home this contrary view of Max Muller:

> The *Rig-Veda* is the most ancient book of the Aryan world.... These hymns represent the lowest stratum in the growth of the human mind that can be reached anywhere by means of contemporaneous literature.[7]

> .... this edition of mine and the translation of the *Veda* will hereafter tell to a great extent on the fate of India, and on the growth of millions of souls in that country. It is the root of their religion, and to show them what that root is, is I feel sure, the only way of uprooting all that has sprung up from it during the last 3,000 years.[8]

> I do not claim for the ancient Indian literature any more than I should willingly concede to the fables and traditions and songs of savage nations. I simply say that in the Veda we have a nearer approach to a beginning, and an intelligent beginning, than in the wild invocations of the Hottentots and the Bushmen.[9]

Let us now turn to Max Muller's passionate plea for Christianising India. It is true he had said: "the more I see of the so-called heathen religions, the more I feel convinced that they contain germs of highest truth"[10] and also expressed the opinion that,

> A country permeated by such thoughts as were uttered by Ramakrishna cannot be possibly looked upon as a country of ignorant idolaters, to be converted by the same methods which are applicable to the races of Central Africa.[11]

But Max Muller strove ceaselessly to impress his friends in India like Keshub Chunder Sen and B.M.Malabari, that India should embrace Christianity. Note the following two observations:

> .... I have myself the strongest belief in the growth of Christianity in India. There is no country so ripe for Christianity as India....[12]

> .... I have not much faith in the missionaries, medical or otherwise. If we get such men again in India as Rammohun Roy, or Keshub Chunder Sen, and if we get an archbishop at Calcutta who knows what Christianity really is, India will be Christianized in all that is essential in the twinkling of an eye.[13]

He also argued that Christianity was only one step from Brahmo Samaj.

That Max Muller is more English than German becomes transparent when we learn that he is against Indians entering the Civil Service:

> .... To tell you the truth, I do not believe in the efficiency of a *mixed* Civil Service. Oil and Water will not mix – let the oil be at the top, there is plenty of room for the water beneath.[14]

Regarding independence for India, he frankly confesses:

> .... I have all my life been an Indian reformer .... I have all my life been a Liberal and a Gladstonian, but I do not approve of Home Rule.[15]

Max Muller's *Life and Letters* provides a veritable mine of information about the man and his contradictions in his views of India. He is, as the preceding remarks have hopefully shown, an unusual combination of such disparate attitudes as Conservatism, Liberalism and Imperialism. That he could, in the same breath, support British rule in India and also champion India and Indians, is viewed by Nirad Chaudhuri as an evidence of "his balance of mind and capacity to see both sides of any question."[16] This is shying away from facts. In the light of the above evidence, Romila Thapar's view, representative of the traditional assessment of Max Muller, is quite unacceptable:

> .... He [Max Muller] represents a group of European in-

dologists who were extremely sympathetic to Indian culture and acted as a counter to those who were proclaiming despotism and backwardness as symbolic of the Indian past.[17]

By examining in detail the response to India of Max Muller, the greatest of all Indologists, we once again realise the consequences of an opinionated standpoint. He believed, among other things, that Christianity was superior to the religions of India; that popular Hinduism as manifest in nineteenth century India invited nothing but contempt; that the British and the Indians should not mix; that conversion to Christianity will transform India into a more humane society and reinvigorate its stagnant culture; that India did not deserve freedom; that Vedas were the only seventh best sacred book in the world[18] and that the ancient vedic society was not without barbaric elements. This less well known side of Max Muller has been highlighted to demonstrate how the best of minds tend to react to India in a uniform manner, a feature noticed in the historians as well.

We could now attempt a tentative assessment of the British understanding of Indian art. The response of the nineteenth century English scholars who were brought up on the classical tradition was marked by a tendency to view Indian art in terms of the Greek influence on it.[19] The interest was not really in India but on what revelations it would bring to the surface regarding the ancient Greek civilization. Indian art was not considered worthy of independent appreciation. And such an attitude can be explained as an outcome of the status of India as a subject country, a reason exemplified in different ways in both the English historian and the indologist. Curiously even Vincent Smith, a respected historian of India reacts thus to the murals at Ajanta:

> .... This picture, in addition to its interest as a contemporary record of unusual political relations between India and Persia, is one of the highest value as a landmark in the history of art. It not only fixes the date of some of the most important paintings at Ajanta and so establishes a standard by which the date of others can be judged; but also suggests the possibility that the Ajanta school of pictorial art may have been derived from Persia and ultimately from Greece.[20]

It is basically a refusal to grant India the status of an independent civilization.

However, E.B.Havell, the eminent art critic has made a significant contribution to the understanding of Indian culture specially its art, painting and sculpture. In one of his books, he points out how Indian art suffered neglect and prejudice because of the predominantly Utilitarian standpoint in the British. As an instance, he refers to the British Engineers for whom Indian art

> meant no more than a pretty chintz, a rich brocade, or gorgeous carpet, fantastic carving, or curious inlay; and an ancient architecture fascinating to the archaelogist and tourist with its reminiscences of bygone pomp and splendour, but an extinct art useless for the needs and ideals of our prosaic and practical terms.[21]

It is possibly this obsession with the practical needs, that has made the building of the 'dak bungalow Gothic' among the typical contributions of the British to Indian architecture. Another revealing fact is that the British, ever since Lord Curzon, took an interest in Indian art that was solely archaelogical.

Havell was mainly responsible for replacing the traditional British view that Indian art was derivative. He also referred to the tendency among the British art critics to often misinterpret the Indian image like that of the Nataraja and the Kali, which are essentially religious symbols. Havell points out very perceptively what ought to constitute the ideal approach:

> We must, however, always bear in mind that the spiritual significance of a religious symbol must be appraised by what it conveys to the mind of the worshipper and not merely by its aesthetic contents. Ethical and aesthetical values do not always coincide, either in the East or the West, and the Western critic is not the best judge of what an Indian symbol may convey to an instructed mind ....[22]

It is this tendency to make a purely aesthetic response without taking into consideration the cultural factors, that contributed to a failure of the British in reacting favourably to Indian art.

So it could be legitimately said that it is their anglo-centricism that characterises the response of the British historian, indologist and art critic to India. Whereas in the historian, this makes for an exclusive interest in the British rule of India so that India's entire past is viewed in order to justify its rule, the indologist, convinced of the inherent superiority of his culture reveals a bias for his own critical canons in his literary evaluations. Similarly, the art critic makes either a purely aesthetic response to Indian art ignoring the cultural context or judges it on the basis of his ideal, the ancient Greek art. Such a refusal to view India in its own terms, and the predisposition to judge it from the English viewpoint makes them close allies of the Anglo-Indian writers.

Notes

1. Percival Spear, *A History of India,* p. 11.
2. Ibid., pp. 11-12.
3. A.A.MacDonell, *A History of Sanskrit Literature* (1899; rpt. Delhi: Motilal Banarsidass, 1971), p. 277.
4. A.B.Keith, *Classical Sanskrit Literature* (1923; rpt. Calcutta: Y.M.C.A. Publishing House, 1958), p. 39.
5. K.Krishnamoorthy, "Western Response to Sanskrit Literature" in *Commonwealth Literature: Problems of Response,* ed. C.D.Narasimhaiah pp. 55-63.
6. Nirad C.Chaudhuri, *Scholar Extraordinary,* p. 134.
7. Max Muller, *The Life and Letters,* I, p. 285.
8. Letter to his wife, 9 December 1867, *The Life and Letters,* I, p. 346.
9. Quoted in K.Krishnamoorthy, p. 59.
10. Letter to Dean Stanley, 7 December 1878, *The Life and Letters,* II, p. 57.
11. Max Muller, *The Life and Letters,* II, p. 399.
12. Letter to Dr. Milman, 26 February 1867, *The Life and Letters,* I, p. 350.
13. Letter to Sir Henry Acland, 23 November 1898, *The Life and Letters,* II, p. 398.
14. Letter to B.M.Malabari, 5 September 1884, *The Life and Letters,* II, p. 170.
15. Letter to B.M.Malabari, 25 August 1893, *The Life and Letters,* II, p. 318.
16. Nirad Chaudhuri, *Scholar Extraordinary,* p. 343.
17. Romila Thapar, *The Past And Prejudice* (1975; rpt. New Delhi: National Book Trust, 1979), p. 8.
18. Max Muller, *The Life and Letters,* II, p. 339.
19. K.DE B.Codrington, 'Indian Art and Archaelogy' in *The Legacy of India,* p. 73.
20. Vincent A. Smith, *The Early History of India* (1924; rpt. Oxford: Clarendon Press, 1967), p. 442.
21. E.B.Havell, *Indian Sculpture and Painting* (London: Macmillans, 1908), p. 44.
22. E.B.Havell, *The Himalayas In Indian Art* (1928; rpt. Varanasi: Indological Book House, n.d.), p. 69.

Bibliography

RUDYARD KIPLING
WORKS BY RUDYARD KIPLING

Kipling, Rudyard, *Plain Tales from the Hills*. 1888; rpt. London: Macmillan, 1954.

Kipling, Rudyard. *Soldiers Three and Other Stories*. 1888; rpt. London: Macmillan, 1960.

Kipling, Rudyard. *Wee Willie Winkie*. 1888; rpt. London: Macmillan, 1951.

Kipling, Rudyard. *The Light that Failed*. 1890; rpt. Harmondsworth: Penguin Books, 1970.

Kipling, Rudyard. 'The Enlightenments of Pagett, M.P.', *The Contemporary Review*. LVIII (Sept. 1890), pp. 333-55.

Kipling, Rudyard. *Life's Handicap*. 1891; rpt. London: Macmillan, 1952.

Kipling, Rudyard. *The Naulahka*. 1892; rpt. London: Macmillan, 1917.

Kipling, Rudyard. *Many Inventions*. 1893; rpt. London: Macmillan, 1949.

Kipling, Rudyard. *The Jungle Book*. 1894; rpt. London: Macmillan, 1955.

Kipling, Rudyard. *The Second Jungle Book*. 1895; rpt. London: Macmillan, 1956.

Kipling, Rudyard. *The Day's Work*. 1898; rpt. London: Macmillan, 1955.

Kipling, Rudyard. *Stalky & Co.* 1899; rpt. London: Macmillan, 1957.

Kipling, Rudyard. *Kim*. 1901; rpt. London: Macmillan, 1958.

Kipling, Rudyard. *Something of Myself.* 1937; rpt. London: Macmillan, 1951.

Kipling, Rudyard. *Rudyard Kipling's Verse: Definitive Edition.* 1940; rpt. London: Hodder and Stoughton, 1960.

Kipling, Rudyard. *A Choice of Kipling's Verse,* ed. T.S.Eliot. 1941; rpt. London: Faber and Faber, 1954.

Kipling, Rudyard. *A Choice of Kipling's Prose.* ed. Somerset Maugham. London: Macmillan & Co. Ltd., 1952.

WORKS ON RUDYARD KIPLING

(A) Books

Amis, Kingsley. *Rudyard Kipling and his World.* London: Thames and Hudson. 1975.

Birkenhead, Lord. *Rudyard Kipling.* London: Weidenfeld and Nicolson, 1978.

Carrington, Charles. *Rudyard Kipling: His Life and Work.* London: Macmillan, 1955.

Cornell, Louis L. *Kipling in India.* New York: Macmillan, 1966.

Dobree, Bonamy. *Rudyard Kipling: Realist and Fabulist.* London: Oxford University Press, 1967.

Fido, Martin. *Rudyard Kipling.* London: Hamlyn, 1974.

Gilbert, Elliot L. *The Good Kipling: Studies in the Short Story.* London: Manchester University Press, 1972.

Gilbert, Elliot L., ed. *Kipling and the Critics.* London: Peter Owen, 1966.

Green, R.L., ed. *Kipling: The Critical Heritage.* London: Routledge & Kegan Paul, 1971.

Gross, John, ed. *Rudyard Kipling the man, his work and his world.* London: Weidenfeld & Nicolson, 1972.

Harrison, James. *Rudyard Kipling.* Boston: Twayne Publishers, 1982.

Henn, T.R. *Kipling.* Edinburgh and London: Oliver and Boyd, 1967.

Husain, Syed Sajjad. *Kipling and India: An Inquiry into the Nature and Extent of Kipling's Knowledge of the Indian Sub-Continent.* Dacca: University of Dacca, 1964.

Mason, Philip. *Kipling: The Glass, The Shadow and The Fire.* London: Jonathan Cape, 1975.

Moore, Katherine. *Kipling and the White Man's Burden.* London: Faber and Faber, 1968.

Rao, K. Bhaskara. *Rudyard Kipling's India.* Norman: University of Oklahoma Press, 1967.

Rutherford, Andrew, ed. *Kipling's Mind And Art.* Edinburgh and London: Oliver & Boyd, 1964.

Sandison, Alan. *The Wheel of Empire.* London: Macmillan, 1967.

Shahane, Vasant A. *Rudyard Kipling: Activist and Artist.* Carbondale: Southern Illinois University Press, 1973.

Stewart, J.I.M. *Rudyard Kipling.* London: Victor Gollancz Ltd.,1966.

Tompkins, J.M.S. *The Art of Rudyard Kipling.* 1959; rpt. London: Methuen University Paperbacks, 1965.

Wilson, Angus. *The Strange Ride of Rudyard Kipling: His Life and Works.* 1977; rpt. London: Granada Publishing Ltd., 1979.

(B) Articles and Reviews

'An Indian Student.' 'Kipling's Conception of India.' *Lippincott's Monthly Magazine,* 94 (Aug 1914), pp. 177-85.

Belliappa, K.C. "Kipling's 'The Man Who would be King': A Parable of Empire Building," *Commonwealth Quarterly,* 2, No. 8 (Sept. 1978), pp. 27-33.

Belliappa, K.C. 'Love and Racial Encounters in Kipling' in *The Colonial and the Neo-Colonial Encounters in Commonwealth Literature,* ed. H.H.Anniah Gowda, Mysore; University of Mysore,1983.

Bushnell, Nelson N. 'Kipling's Ken of India,' *University of Toronto Quarterly,* 27 (Oct. 1957), pp. 62-78.

Cook, Richard. 'Rudyard Kipling and George Orwell,' *Modern Fiction Studies,* 7, No.2 (1961), pp. 125-35.

Cooperman, Stanley. 'The Imperial Posture and the Shrine of Darkness: Kipling's *The Naulahka* And E.M.Forster's *A Passage to India,*' *English Literature in Transition,* VI, No. 1 (1963), pp. 9-13.

Chaudhuri, Nirad C. 'The Finest Story About India - In English', *Encounter,* VIII, No. 4 (Apr 1957), pp. 47-53.

Dobree, Bonamy. 'Rudyard Kipling,' *The Criterion,* VI, No. 6 (Dec. 1927), pp. 499-515.

Dunman, Jack. 'Rudyard Kipling Re-Estimated,' *Marxism Today* (Aug. 1965-Feb. 1966), pp. 58-60.

Edwardes, Michael. 'Rudyard Kipling and the Imperial Imagination,' *Twentieth Century,* 153 (June 1953), pp. 443- 54.

Ford, Boris. 'A Case for Kipling,' *Scrutiny,* XI, No. 1 (Summer 1942), pp. 23-33.

Fussell, Paul. "Irony, Freemasonry and Humane Ethics in Kipling's 'The Man who would be King,'" *English Literary History,* Vol. 25 (1958), pp. 216-33.

Haward, Edwin. 'Kipling Myths and Traditions in India,' *Nineteenth Century* (Feb. 1939), pp. 194-202.

McLuhan, Herbert Marshall. 'Kipling and Forster,' *Sewanee Review,* 52 (1944), pp. 332-43.

Meyers, Jeffrey. "The Idea of Moral Authority in 'The Man who would be King'", *Studies in English Literature,* VIII, No. 4 (Autumn 1968), pp. 711-23.

Munro, John. 'Kipling's *Kim* and Co-existence,' *English Literature in Transition,* VII, No. 4 (1964), pp. 222-27.

Robinson, Edward Kay. 'Kipling in India: Reminiscences by the Editor of the Newspaper on which Kipling served at Lahore,' *McClure's Magazine,* 7 (Jul., 1896), pp. 99-109.

Roy, Sarath, A.R. 'Rudyard Kipling Seen Through Hindu Eyes,' *North American Review,* 199 (Feb. 1914), pp. 271-81.

Singh, Nihal. 'Indians And Anglo-Indians: As Portrayed To Britons By British Novelists,' *Modern Review.* 36 (Sept. 1924), pp. 251-56.

Tarinayya, M. 'East-West Encounter: Kipling,' *The Literary Criterion,* VII, No. 3 (Winter 1966), pp. 28-41.

Varley, Henry Leland. 'Imperialism and Rudyard Kipling,' *Journal of the History of Ideas,* 14 (Jan.1953), pp. 124-35.

L.H.MYERS

WORKS BY L.H.MYERS

Myers, L.H. *The Root and the Flower.* London: Cape,1935.
Myers, L.H. *Strange Glory.* London: Putnam, 1936.
Myers, L.H. *The Pool of Vishnu.* London: Jonathan Cape, 1940.
Myers, L.H. *The Near and the Far.* 1943; rpt. London: The Reprint Society, 1956.

WORKS ON L.H.MYERS

(A) Books

Bantock, G.H. *L.H.Myers: A Critical Study,* London: Jonathan Cape, 1956.

Eaton, Gai. *The Richest Vein: The Eastern Tradition and Modern Thought.* London: Faber and Faber Ltd., 1949.

Ford, Boris, ed. *The Pelican Guide of English Literature. Volume 7.* 1961; rpt. Harmondsworth: Penguin Books, 1970.

Gillie, Christopher. *Movements in English Literature, 1900-1940.* Cambridge: Cambridge University Press, 1975.

Gupta, B.S. *The Glassy Essence: A Study of E.M.Forster, L.H.Myers and Aldous Huxley in relation to Indian Thought.* Kurukshetra: Kurukshetra University, 1976.

Iyengar, K.R.Srinivasa. *The Adventure of Criticism.* Bombay: Asia Publishing House, 1962.

Neill, Diana. *A Short History of the English Novel.* Ludhiana: Kalyani Publishers, 1971.

Prescott, Orville. *In My Opinion: An Inquiry into the Contemporary Novel.* New York: The Bobbs-Merril Company, Inc., 1952.

Strong, L.A.G. *Personal Remarks.* London: Peter Nevil, 1953.

Van Doren, Mark. *The Private Reader.* New York: Kraus Reprint Co., 1968.

Walter, Inna. *L.H.Myers: Myth and Symbol in his Indian Novels.* New Delhi: Arnold-Heinemann, 1984.

West, Paul. *The Modern Novel.* Vol. 1. 1963; rpt. London: Hutchinson University Library, 1967.

(B) Articles and Reviews

Bottrall, Roland. "L.H.Myers," *A Review of English Literature,* 2,(Apr. 1961), pp. 47-58.

Harding, D.W. "The Work of L.H.Myers," *Scrutiny,* 3, No. 1 (Jun 1934), pp. 44-63.

Harding, D.W. "The Root and the Flower," *Scrutiny,* 4, No. 1 (Jun 1935), pp. 79-81.

Harding, D.W. "A Statement of Positives: *The Pool of Vishnu,*" *Scrutiny,* 9, No. 2 (Sept. 1940), pp. 161-65.

Rudd, Margaret. "L.H.Myers and 'The Near and the Far'", *Mandrake,* 9, (1953), pp. 201-8.

RAJA RAO

WORKS BY RAJA RAO

Raja Rao. *The Cow of the Barricades.* Madras: Geoffrey Cumberlege, Oxford University Press, 1947.

Raja Rao. *Kanthapura.* 1938; rpt. New Delhi: Orient Paperbacks, 1971.

Raja Rao. *The Serpent and the Rope.* 1960; rpt. New Delhi: Orient

Paperbacks, 1968.

Raja Rao. *The Cat and Shakespeare.* 1965; rpt. New Delhi: Orient Paperbacks, 1971.

Raja Rao. *Comrade Kirillov.* New Delhi: Orient Paperbacks, 1976.

Raja Rao. *The Policeman and the Rose.* New Delhi: Oxford University Press, 1978.

WORKS ON RAJA RAO

(A) Books

Amirthanayagam, Guy and Harrex, Syd, ed. *Only Connect: Literary Perspectives East and West.* Adelaide & Honolulu: Centre for Research in New Literatures in English and East- West Center, 1981.

Amur, G.S. *Images and Impressions.* Jaipur: Panchsheel Prakashan, 1979.

Desai, S.K. ed. *Experimentation with Language in Indian Writing in English (Fiction),* Kolhapur: Shivaji University Press, 1974.

Goodwin, K.L. ed. *National Identity.* Melbourne: Heinemann Educational Books Ltd., 1970.

Harrex, S.C. *The Fire and the Offering. Volume Two.* Calcutta: Writers Workshop, 1978.

Iyengar, K.R. Srinivasa. *Indian Writing in English.* 1962; rpt. Bombay: Asia Publishing House, 1973.

Mohan, Ramesh, ed. *Indian Writing in English.* Madras: Orient Longman, 1978.

Mukherjee, Meenakshi. *The Twice Born Fiction: Themes and Techniques of the Indian Novel in English.* 1971; New Delhi: Arnold Heinemann, 1974.

Mukherjee, Meenakshi. ed. *Considerations.* New Delhi: Allied Publishers Pvt. Ltd., 1977.

Naik, M.K. *Raja Rao.* New York: Twayne Publishers, 1972.

Naik, M.K., Desai, S.K., Amur, G.S., ed. *Critical Essays on Indian Writing in English.* 1968; rpt. Madras: Macmillan India Ltd., 1977.

Naik, M.K. ed. *Aspects of Indian Writing in English.* Madras: Macmillan India Ltd., 1979.

Narasimhaiah, C.D. *The Swan and the Eagle.* Simla: Indian Institute of Advanced Study, 1969.

Narasimhaiah, C.D. *Raja Rao.* New Delhi: Arnold-Heinemann. n.d.

Narasimhaiah, C.D., ed. *Fiction and the Reading Public in India.* Mysore: University of Mysore, 1967.

Narasimhaiah, C.D., ed. *Indian Literature of the Past Fifty Years. 1917-1967.* Mysore: University of Mysore, 1970.

Narasimhan, Raji. *Sensibility Under Stress.* New Delhi: Ashajanak Publications, 1976.

Srivastava, Narsingh. *The Mind and Art of Raja Rao.* Bareilly: Prakash Book Depot, 1980.

Williams, Haydn Moore. *Studies in Modern Indian Fiction in English. Volume Two.* Calcutta: Writers Workshop. 1973.

(B) Articles and Reviews

Aithal, S.Krishnamoorthy and Aithal, Rashmi. 'East-West Encounters in Four Indo-English Novels,'*ACLALS Bulletin,* V, No.1 (Nov. 1982), pp. 1-16.

Ali, Ahmed. 'Illusion and Reality: The Art and Philosophy of Raja Rao', *The Journal of Commonwealth Literature,* No. 5 (Jul. 1968), pp. 16-28.

Belliappa, K.C. 'The Question of Form in Raja Rao's *The Serpent and the Rope', World Literature written in English,* 24, No. 2 (1984), pp. 407-16.

Coppola, Carlos. 'Ignazio Silone's *Fontamara* and Raja Rao's *Kanthapura:* A Contrastive Analysis,' *Journal of South Asian Literature,* XVI, No.1 (Winter/Spring 1980), pp. 93-100.

Gemmil, Janet Powres. 'Dualities and Non-Duality in Raja Rao's *The Serpent and the Rope,' World Literature written in English,* 12, No. 2 (Nov. 1973), pp. 247-59.

Gemmil, Janet Powres. 'Raja Rao: Three Tales of Independence,'

World Literature Written in English, 15, No. 1 (Apr. 1976), pp. 121-34.

Guruprasad, Thakur. 'Reflections on Rama: India as depicted in *The Serpent and the Rope,*' *Journal of Indian Writing in English,* 1, No. 1 (Jan 1973), pp. 19-28.

Kaul, R.K. '*The Serpent and the Rope* as a Philosophical Novel', *The Literary Criterion,* XV, No. 1 (1980), pp. 32-43.

Mukherjee, Meenakshi. 'Raja Rao's Shorter Fiction,' *Indian Literature,* X, No. 3 (1967), pp. 66-76.

Mukherjee, Meenakshi. 'Literature of Exile,' *ACLALS Bulletin,* IV, No. 2 (1975), pp. 27-32.

Nagarajan, S. 'A Note on Myth and Ritual in *The Serpent and the Rope,*' *The Journal of Commonwealth Literature,* VII, No. 1 (Jun 1972), pp. 45-48.

Narasimhaiah, C.D. 'Indian Writing in English: An Area of Promise,' *The Journal of Commonwealth Literature,* IX, No. 1 (Aug. 1974), pp. 35-49.

Paniker, K.Ayyappa. 'A Conversation with Raja Rao on *The Cat and Shakespeare,*' *Chandrabhaga.* 2 (1979), pp. 13-17.

Paniker, K. Ayyappa. 'The Frontiers of Fiction: A Study of Raja Rao's *The Cat and Shakespeare, The Literary Criterion,* XV, No.1 (1980), pp. 60-72.

Parthasarathy, R. 'An Interview with Raja Rao,' *Span,* XVIII, No. 9 (Sept. 1977), pp. 28-30.

Rajan, P.K. 'Introducing *Comrade Kirillov*', *Litcrit,* 3, No. 1 (Jun 1977), pp. 51-54.

Shepherd, R. 'Raja Rao: Symbolism in *The Cat and Shakespeare,*' *World Literature written in English,* 14, No. 2 (Nov. 1975), pp. 347-56.

S.V.V. 'Face to Face,' *The Illustrated Weekly of India* (Jan 5,1964), pp. 43-45.

Venugopal, C.V. 'Raja Rao as a Short Story Writer: A Study', *Journal of the Karnatak University,* XIV (1970), pp. 159-70.

Visweswariah, H.S. '*The Serpent and the Rope:* A Stylistic Approach,' *The Literary Endeavour,* 1, No. 1 (Jun 1979), pp. 49-62.

Westbrook, Perry D. 'Theme and Inaction in Raja Rao's *The Serpent* and the Rope,' *World Literature written in English,* 14, No. 2 (Nov 1975), pp. 385-98.

GENERAL

Aithal, S.Krishnamurthy. *'In the Image of the Buddha, The Compassionate One: Aldous Huxley's Portraits of the Enlightened.'* Unpublished Material, TS, pp. 1-14.

Allen, Charles. *Raj: A Scrapbook of British India. 1877- 1947.* 1977; rpt. Harmondsworth: Penguin Books, 1979.

Allen, Charles., ed. *Plain Tales From The Raj.* 1975; rpt. London: Macdonald Futura Publishers, 1981.

Arnold, W.D. *Oakfield:* or, *Fellowship in the East.* 1853; rpt. Leicester: Leicester University Press, 1973.

Bary, Theodre de, ed. *Sources of Indian Tradition.* 1958; rpt. New York: Columbia University Press, 1959.

Basham, A.L. *The Wonder That Was India.* 1954; rpt. Calcutta: Rupa & Co., 1982.

Baugh, Edward. 'Cuckoo and Culture: *In the Castle of My Skin,' Ariel.* 8, No.3 (July 1977), pp. 23-33.

Bearce, George D. *British Attitudes Towards India. 1784-1858.* London: Oxford University Press, 1961.

Bennet, George, ed. *The Concept of Empire: Burke to Atlee, 1774-1947.* London: Black, 1953.

Bharati, Agehananda. *The Tantric Tradition.* London: Rider, 1965.

Bisoondeyal, B. *India in World Literature.* London: Luzac & Co. Ltd., 1976.

Borges, Jorge Luis. *Labyrinths: Selected Stories & Other Writings,* trans. New York: A New Directions Book, 1964.

Brown, Hilton. *Potter's Clay: Some Stories of South India.* London: Simpkin, Marshall, Hamilton Kent & Co., Ltd., 1927.

Brown, Hilton. *One Virginity.* 1948; rpt. Bombay: Jaico Publishing House, 1960.

Bibliography

Butcher, Maggie, ed. *The Eye of the Beholder: Indian Writing in English.* London: Commonwealth Institute, 1983.

Candler, Edmund. *Siri Ram Revolutionist: A Transcript from Life. 1907-1910.* 1912; rpt. London: Constable & Company Ltd., 1913.

Candler, Edmund. *Abdication.* London: Constable & Company Ltd., 1922.

Chakravorty, Dilip. *India in English Fiction.* Calcutta: Prayer Books, 1978.

Chaudhuri, Nirad C. *The Continent of Circe: An Essay on the Peoples of India.* 1965; rpt. Bombay: Jaico Publishing House, 1974.

Chaudhuri, Nirad C. Scholar Extraordinary: *The Life of Friedrich Max Muller.* New Delhi: Orient Paperbacks, 1974.

Chaudhuri, Nirad C. *Clive of India: A Political and Psychological Essay.* London: Barrie & Jenkins, 1975.

Chew, Shirley. *Vain Empires: The Response of Some British Writers to the East.* Diss. Singapore, 1976.

Coomaraswamy, Ananda K. *The Dance of Shiva.* 1918; rpt. New Delhi: Sagar Publications, 1968.

Cowley, Malcolm. *Exile's Return: A Literary Odyssey of the 1920's.* New York: The Viking Press, 1951.

Diver, Maud. *The Great Amulet.* London: Blackwood and Sons, 1908.

Diver, Maud. *Far to Seek: A Romance of England and India.* Edinburgh and London: W.Blackwood and Sons, 1921.

Durant, Will. *The Case for India.* New York: Simon and Schuster, 1930.

Dyson, Ketaki Kushari. *A Various Universe: A Study of the Journals and Memoirs in the Indian Subcontinent 1765-1856.* Delhi: Oxford University Press, 1978.

Eagleton, Terry. *Exiles and Emigrées: Studies in Modern Literature.* London: Chatto & Windus, 1970.

Edwardes, Michael. *British India, 1772-1947: A Survey of the Nature and Effects of Alien Rule.* London: Sidgwick & Jackson, 1967.

Fanon, Frantz. *The Wretched of the Earth,* trans, Constance Farrington. 1961; rpt. Harmondsworth: Penguin Books, 1974.

Farrel, J.G. *The Siege of Krishnapur.* 1973; rpt. Harmondsworth: Penguin Books, 1982.

Forster, E.M. 'Reflections on India: I - Too Late?' *The Nation and the Athenaeum*, 30 (21 January 1922), pp. 612-16.

Forster, E.M. *A Passage to India.* 1924; rpt. Harmondsworth: Penguin Books, 1970.

Forster, E.M. *Two Cheers for Democracy.* London: Edward Arnold, 1951.

Forster, E.M. *The Hill of Devi.* 1953; rpt. New Delhi: Arnold Heinemann, 1977.

Garratt, G.T., ed. *The Legacy of India,* Oxford: Clarendon Press, 1937.

Glasenapp, Helmuth Von. *Image of India,* trans. New Delhi: Indian Council for Cultural Relations, 1973.

Green, Martin. *Dreams of Adventure, Deeds of Empire.* New York: Basic Books, Inc., 1979.

Greenberger, A.J. *The British Image of India. A Study in the Literature of Imperialism.* 1880-1960. London: Oxford University Press, 1960.

Greene, Jay E., ed. *100 Great Thinkers.* 1967; rpt. New York: Pocket Books, 1969.

Havell, E.B. *Indian Sculpture and Painting.* London: Macmillan, 1908.

Havell, E.B. *The Himalayas in Indian Art.* 1928; rpt. Varanasi: Indological Book House, n.d.

Hiriyanna, M. *Outlines of Indian Philosophy.* 1932; rpt. London: George Allen & Unwin Ltd., 1958.

Hutchins, Francis G, *The Illusion of Permanence: British Imperialism in India.* Princeton: Princeton University Press, 1967.

Huxley, Aldous. *Jesting Pilate: The Diary of a Journey.* London: Chatto & Windus, 1957.

Huxley, Aldous. *Island.* 1962; rpt. Harmondsworth: Penguin Books, 1964.

Issaacs, Harold R. *Images of Asia: American Views of China and India.* 1958; rpt. New York: Harper & Row, 1972.

Islam, Shamsul. *Chronicles of the Raj: A Study of Literary Reaction to the Imperial Idea towards the end of the Raj.* London: Macmillan, 1979.

Iyengar, K.R. Srinivasa. 'India in Anglo-American Fiction.' *Tennessee Studies,* (1958), pp. 107-16.

Bibliography

Keith, A.B. *Classical Sanskrit Literature*. 1923; rpt. Calcutta: Y.M.C.A. Publishing House, 1958.

Kiernan, V.G. *The Lords of the Human Kind: European Attitudes Towards the Outside World in the Imperial Age*. 1969; rpt. Harmondsworth: Penguin Books, 1972.

Kincaid, Dennis. *British Social Life in India: 1608-1937*. London: Routledge, 1938.

Kipling, John Lockwood. *Beast and Man in India*. London: Macmillan 1891.

Lannoy, Richard. *The Speaking Tree: A Study of Indian Culture & Society*. 1971; rpt. London: Oxford University Press, 1975.

Leavis, F.R. *The Great Tradition*. 1948; rpt. Harmondsworth: Pelican Books, 1972.

Leavis, F.R. *The Common Pursuit*. 1952; rpt. Harmondsworth: Peregrine Books, 1969.

Lukács, Georg. *The Historical Novel*. 1962; rpt. Harmondsworth: Peregrine Books, 1969.

Macdonell, A.A. *A History of Sanskrit Literature*. 1899; rpt. Delhi: Motilal Banarsidass, 1971.

Macquarrie, John. *Existentialism*. 1973; rpt. Harmondswoth: Penguin Books, 1976.

Mannoni, O. *Prospero and Caliban: The Psychology of Colonization*, trans. 1950; rpt. London: Methuen & Co. Ltd., 1956.

Manuel, M. and Ayyappa Paniker, K. ed. *English and India*. Madras: Macmillan Co. of India Ltd., 1978.

Mascaro, Juan. *The Upanishads,*, trans. 1965, rpt. Harmondsworth: Penguin Books, 1973.

Masters, John. *The Nightrunners of Bengal*. London: Michael Joseph, 1951.

Masters, John. *Bhowani Junction*. 1954; rpt. London: The Reprint Society, 1956.

Maugham, Somerset. *The Razor's Edge*. 1944; rpt. London: Pan Books Ltd., 1983.

Maugham, Somerset. *A Writer's Notebook*. London: William Heinemann. 1949.

Mayo, Katherine. *Mother India*. 1927; rpt. London: Jonathan Cape,

1937.

Memmi, Albert. *The Colonizer and the Colonized*, trans., Howard Greenfeld. New York: The Orion Press, 1965.

Menon, Sri Krishna. *Atmanadopanishat*. Tiruvannamalai: Sri Vidya Samiti, 1946.

Meyers, Jeffery. *Fiction and the Colonial Empire*. Ipswitch: The Boydell Press, 1973.

Mill, James. *The History of British India*. London: Macmillan, 1820.

Milne, Louis Jordan: *The Green Goddess*. London: Hodder and Stoughton, 1924.

Morris, James. *Heaven's Command: An Imperial Progress*. 1973; rpt. Harmondsworth: Penguin Books, 1979.

Morris, James. *Farewell The Trumpets: An Imperial Retreat*. 1978; rpt. Harmondsworth: Penguin Books, 1979.

Morris, James. *Pax Britannica: The Climax of an Empire*. London: Faber and Faber, 1978.

Morris, Jan. *The Spectacle of Empire: Style, Effect and the Pax Britannica*. London: Faber and Faber, 1982.

Mukherjee, S.N. *Sir William Jones: A Study in Eighteenth- Century British Attitudes to India*. Cambridge: Cambridge University Press, 1968.

Muller, Max. *A History of Ancient Sanskrit Literature*. 1859; rpt. Varanasi: The Chowkhamba Sanskrit Series Office, 1968.

Muller, Max. *India: What Can It Teach Us?* 1882; rpt. Delhi: Munshi Ram Manohar Lal. 1961.

Muller, Max. *The Life and Letters. Volume I*. London: Longmans, Green And Co., 1903.

Muller, Max. *The Life and Letters.. Volume II*. London: Longmans, Green And Co., 1903.

Naik, M.K., Desai, S.K., Kallapur, S.T., ed. *The Image of India in Western Creative Writing*. Dharwar and Madras: Karnatak University and Macmillan & Co., Ltd., 1971.

Naipaul, V.S. *An Area of Darkness*. 1964; rpt. Harmondsworth: Penguin Books, 1981.

Naipaul, V.S. *India: A Wounded Civilization*. 1977; rpt. Harmondsworth: Penguin Books, 1979.

Bibliography

Nandy, Ashis. *The Intimate Enemy: Loss and Recovery of Self Under Colonialism.* Delhi: Oxford University Press, 1983.

Narasimhaiah, C.D., ed. *Awakened Conscience.* New Delhi: Sterling Publishers Pvt. Ltd., 1978.

Narasimhaiah, C.D., ed. *Commonwealth Literature: Problems of Response.* Madras: Macmillan India Limited, 1981.

Narayanan, Gomathi. "Paul Scott's Indian Quartet: 'The Story of A Rape' "*The Literary Criterion,* Vol. XIII, No. 4 (1978), pp. 44-53.

Nehru, Jawaharlal. *An Autobiography: With Musings on Recent Events in India.* 1936; rpt. Bombay: Allied Publishers Private Ltd., 1962.

Nehru, Jawaharlal. *The Discovery of India.* 1946; rpt. Bombay: Asia Publishing House, 1972.

Orwell, George. *Burmese Days.* 1934; rpt. London: Secker and Warburg, 1966.

Parry, Benita. *Delusions and Discoveries: Studies on India in the British Imagination. 1880-1930.* rpt. 1972; New Delhi: Orient Longman, 1974.

Prabhavananda, Swami and Manchester, Frederick. *The Upanishads: Breath of the Eternal,* trans. 1948; rpt. New York: Mentor Books. 1957.

Radhakrishan, S. *Eastern Religions and Western Thought.* 1939; rpt. London: Oxford University Press, 1958.

Radhakrishan, S. *Our Heritage.* New Delhi: Orient Paperbacks, 1973.

Radhakrishnan, S. *Religion and Culture.* New Delhi: Orient Paperbacks, 1978.

Raskin, Jonah. *The Mythology of Imperialism.* New York: Random House, 1971.

Reid, John T. *Indian Influences in American Literature.* New Delhi: Indian Council for Cultural Relations, 1965.

Schweitzer, Albert. *Indian Thought And Its Development.* 1935; rpt. Bombay: Wilco Publishing House, 1980.

Scott, Paul. *The Raj Quartet.* London: Heinemann, 1976.

Scott, Paul. *Staying On.* 1977; rpt. New Delhi: Allied Publishers Private Limited, 1978.

Scott, Sir Walter. *The Surgeon's Daughter.* London: Ward. Lock & Co., 1827.

Seeley, J.R. *The Expansion of England*. 1883; rpt. London: Macmillan & Co., Ltd., 1920.

Singh, A.G. Bhupal. *A Survey of Anglo-Indian Fiction*. London: Oxford University Press, 1934.

Smith, Grover, ed. *Letters of Aldous Huxley*. London: Chatto & Windus, 1969.

Smith, Vincent A. *Akbar The Great Moghul, 1542-1605*. 1892; rpt. London: Oxford University Press, 1927.

Smith, Vincent A. *The Early History of India*. 1924; rpt. Clarendon: Oxford University Press, 1967.

Spear, Percival. *A History of India. Volume Two*. 1965; rpt. Harmondsworth: Penguin Books, 1975.

Spear, Percival. *The Nabobs: A Study of the Social Life of the English in Eighteenth Century India*. 1932; rpt. London: Oxford University Press, 1963.

Srinivasachari, P.N. *The Philosophies of Visistadwaita*. Adyar: The Adyar Library, 1943.

Stokes, Eric. *The English Utilitarians And India*. London: Oxford. 1959.

Swinden, Patrick. *Paul Scott: Images of India*. London: Macmillan, 1980.

Thapar, Romila. *A History of India. Volume One*. 1966; rpt. Harmondsworth: Penguin Books, 1977.

Thapar, Romila. *The Past and Prejudice*. 1975; rpt. New Delhi, National Book Trust, 1979.

Thompson, Edward. *Krishna Kumari: An Historical Drama in Four Acts*. London: Earnest Benn, 1924.

Thompson, Edward. *An Indian Day*. 1927; rpt. London: Macmillan and Co., 1940.

Thompson, Edward. *An End of the Hours*. London: Macmillan and Co., 1930.

Thompson, Edward and Garratt, G.T. *The Rise and Fulfilment of British Rule*. London: Macmillan & Co., 1934.

Viswanatham, K. *India in English Fiction*. Waltair: Andhra University Press, 1971.

White, Patrick. 'The Prodigal Son'. *Australian Letters* Vol. 1, No. 1, (April 1958), pp. 37-40.

Index

Abbas, K.A., 213
Alden, Robin, 316, 326
Amherst, 3
Amur, G.S., 261
Anand, Mulk Raj, 207, 213, 223, 329
Anglo Indian fiction, 12-16
    Indian images in, 17-19, see Images of India
Arnold, Edwin, 108
Arnold, William Delafield, 12-17, 45
    Novel by, 12-17
Aurobindo, 191
Austen, Jane, 224
Aziz, 18
Bantock, G.H., 142, 183
Bearce, George D., 3, 11
Bentham, Jeremy, 3
Bharatrihari, 285
Bhaskara Rao, K., 30, 60, 76
Bhatta, Iswara, 242
Bhupal Singh, A.G., 11
Birkenhead, 26
Borges, Jorge, 316
British
    Interest in India, 1-10, 303
    Racial superiority, 9
Brown, Hilton, 319
Buber, Martin, 152, 154
Burke, Edmund, 2, 3, 4
Candler, Edmund, 311, 329, 330
Carrington, Charles, 119
Chamberlain, 8
Chaudhuri, Nirad, C., 78, 89, 108, 327, 334
Clive, 1
Cook, Orwell, 308
Coomarswamy, 158

Cornell, Louis, 31, 32, 118
Cornwallis, 3
Curzon, 8
Dane, Louis, 26
Darwin, 131
    Theory of evolution, 9
D'Cruze, Michele, 36
Diver, Maud, 306, 326
Dobree, Bonamy, 34, 121
Eagleton, Terry, 294
Eaton, Gai, 181
Eliot, T.S., 217, 333
Elizabeth, 133, 309
Emerson, 132
English Literatue
    Anglo-Indian fiction in, 12-16
    Indian images in fiction in, 17-19
    Indian imagination in, 10-17
Ferdinand, Conrad, 168
Fido, Martin, 108
Findlayson, 80, 81, 86
Flaubert, 168, 169
Flory, 306
Foster, E.M., 12, 13, 18, 70, 175, 218, 305, 312-16, 318, 321-23, 327-28, 334
Gandhi, Mahatma, 153, 154, 191, 285, 289, 290
    Non-violence of, 279
Gibbon, 317
Gilbert, Elliot L., 79
Gladstone, 37
Grant, Charles, 6
Greenberger, A.J., 134, 318
Guru, Atmanads, 191
Harding, D.W., 132, 140, 154, 165, 181, 182

Harrex, S.C., 264
Hasting Warren, 1, 2, 3, 4
Heber, Bishop, 6
Hiriyanna, M., 152, 153
Hopkins, 223
Husain, Syed Sajjad, 30
Hutchins, Francis, G., 8, 311, 335
Huxely, Aldous, 327
Huxley, T.H., 131
Images of India in Anglo-English literature, 303-29
    Advaita philosophy in, 330-31
    Britishers limitations in, 306
    Britishers on, 318-20
    Britishers on Hindu religion, 320-26
    Britishers princely life, 304
    Britishers superior, 304, 305
    Buddhism in, 326-27
    By Indians, 307
    Characters in, 313-14, 327-28, 330
    Englishman portrayal in, 303, 306-07, 318
    Eurasians in, 308-09
    Failure in portrayal of, 334-35
    Indian freedom movement, 329
    Indian languages in, 317
    Indian philosophy in, 314-15
    Indians-Englishmen relationship in, 315-17
    Kipling on, 304-05, 307-09, 314-15, 318, 323, 326, 327-29, 331, 335-36
    Kipling, Myers and Raja Rao on, 331-34, 336
        Indian religions and philosophy, 332-33
        Insiders/outsiders, 331-32
    Life in India ignored, 303
    Loyality in, 307
    Muslims over Indians in, 308
    Myers in, 305, 313-17, 321, 323-26, 331-33, 336
    Nationalists in, 311-13
    Natives as helpless in, 307-08
    Political realities in, 328-29
    Prejudices to Indian characters, 312-13
    Privileges to Englishmen, 304
    Raja Rao on, 306, 314, 317, 319, 323, 329-31, 336
    Village life in, 329-30
    Western educated in, 309-11
Johnson, 26
Joyce, James, 201, 223
Kaul, R.K., 249
Kaye, M.M., 303
Kincaid, Dennis, 319
Kipling, Lockwood, 26, 27
Kipling Rudyard, 12, 17-19, 23-129, 216, 218, 304-05, 307-09, 314-15, 318, 323, 326-28, 331, 335-36
    Art work in, 112-13
    Benares images of, 107
    Biography of, 26
    British Indian portrayal by, 43-44, 50, 117
    British rule image in, 57, 59
    Buddhism, 108,
    Caste structure in, 28
    Child portrayed by, 73-74, 78-79
    Civil servants portrayal by, 67-68
    Critics of, 30, 108-09
    Different attitude of life in East and West, 86-90
    Dramatic monologue, 31-32
    Education of, 24
    Englishmen and Indians relations, 69-72, 74-75, 79-81
    Englishmen portrayal by, 44-48
    Englishmen superiority, 36-39, 91-102
    English standard in fiction of, 112-15
    Father's influence on, 25-27
    Hindu Muslim riots, 41-42
    Hindu proverb in, 75, 116
    Horrors of life in India by, 68-69
    Impressions of Bombay by, 23
    Impressions of Hindu Gods, 23, 26, 34-35, 55, 82-88, 105, 114
    Impressions of servants by, 23, 37-39, 60-62, 114
    Indians portrayal by, 39-43, 121
    Indian superstition, 105-06
    Lahore experiments, 63-65, 108, 119-20
    Land of mystery, 67
    Love with women in, 32-33, 48-49, 55-56

Index

Narration technique of, 52-56
Phrases used by, 53
Political beliefs, 59
Religion in, 34-35
Simla image of, 50-51
Soldiers in writings of, 29-30
South India description by, 120
Travels description by, 65, 118
Unpleasant life of British India, 29
Variation in use of English by, 116
Whiteman & native women in, 75-79
Women in, 32-34, 48-50, 104
Writings on India, 25-28, 109
Lawrence, D.H., 333
Leavis, F.R., 132, 181, 182, 184, 185
Lewis, C.S., 47
Lukacs, Georg, 166, 167, 168, 169
Macaulay, 26
Maharishi, Ramana, 191
Maini, D.S., 215, 246, 259, 273
Malinowski, 9
Manners, Daphne, 315
Mannoni, O., 56
Marlowe, Christopher, 10
Maugham, Somerest, 323, 325
Mc Cutchion, David, 251, 252, 253, 259, 260, 264
Melville, 132
Memmi, Albert, 39
Meyers, Jeffrey, 56, 108
Mill, James, 3, 4, 5, 6
Milne, L.J., 309
Minto, 3, 10
Mookerjee, Hurree Chunder, 308
Moore, Katherine, 328
Mukherjee, Meenakshi, 198, 199, 204, 220, 223, 265, 295, 296
Myers, Frederic, W.H., 131
Myers, L.H.; 19, 56, 108, 131-89
    Aestheticism, 131-32, 138, 146, 153, 163-64
    Artistic intensions, 134, 137, 146-49
    Buddhism, 136, 139, 142, 168
    Characters in novels of, 136, 142, 155, 167, 181-83
    Criticism of, 180
    Eastern-Western positions, 157, 160, 162-63
    Education of, 131
    Geographical landscape by, 134, 172-73
    Hindu ideals by, 158-60, 162
    Human relations by, 154
    Indian philosophy by, 148-52, 156-58
    Indian profile by, 132-34, 185-86
    Indian religion by, 134-36, 149, 151-54, 160-61
    Love and sex in, 145
    Moral judgements by, 132, 137-40, 145, 147-48, 181, 186
    Mughal India portrayal by, 186
    Narration methods of, 183-85
    Nature of image of India by, 174-80
        Hindu temple, 175-76
        Society, 178
        Use of language by, 179
        Women description, 177
    Problems of living in civilized society, 135, 139-45, 163, 183
    Representation of historical India by, 165-74
        Awakening through, 166-67
        Characters by, 167-68, 170-72
        Facts in, 173
        Traditions in, 168
Nagarajan, K., 213
Naik, M.K., 152, 153, 175, 179, 204, 208, 222, 254, 261, 264, 272
Narasimhaiah, C.D., 256, 258, 260
Narayan, R.K., 177, 207, 213, 224, 329
Nehru, 282
Norton, C.E., 24
Origo, Marchesa Iris, 184
Orwell, George, 12, 16, 39, 44, 66, 83, 306
Paine, Tom, 3
Pai, Ramakrishna, 266, 267, 268
Parry, Benita, 30, 312, 321
Penny, F.E., 320
Perrin, Alice, 326
Pound, Ezra, 333
Proust, Marcel, 131
Radhakrishnan, S., 86, 136, 153, 157
Raja Rao, 19, 175, 177, 191-301, 306, 314, 317, 319, 323, 329-31, 336

Achivements as a novelist of,
Address and exclamation forms in, 206
Artistic terms in, 268, 294
Ashram life portrayal by, 194-98, 208-10, 222-24, 329
Beauty of women in, 205, 289
Biography of, 191
Buddhism, 233-35, 238-39, 257-58
Caste portrayal by, 192-93, 208-09, 215, 224-28, 240, 248, 266, 274
Characteristic expressions, 205, 215-17, 238-40, 249, 252-53, 267-68, 276, 297
Communism in India, 279-88
Creative use of English, 204-05
Criticism of, 259, 264-67, 279-80
Death in, 202-03, 267
Education of, 191
English language use by, 207-08, 221, 262-63
French translation of, 276
Gandhian impact on South Indian villages, 197-99, 209, 212-14, 272
Historical description by, 254-57, 270
Image of India by, 192, 203, 207-08, 217, 293, 296
Indian culture, 222-23, 243-44
Indian expressions in, 262-64
Indian independence movement by, 200-01, 214, 216, 218-19, 221, 295, 329
Indian intellectual portrayal of, 276-88
Influence on, 191
Landscape reference by, 244-46, 250-51
Local terms used by, 221-22
Man-God relationship in, 269-73
Marriages in, 229-33, 240-43, 256, 258, 266-67, 296
Metaphysical search by, 247-48, 254, 261, 264-65
Money lenders in, 217
Mythical imagination in, 197-98, 249
Novels by, 192
Orthodox in, 220
Philosophical pre-occupation, 255, 266, 268-70, 274-76, 293

Political life in, 197-99
Psychological motivation in, 252-53
Real India image by, 246-48, 264, 273, 294
Religious literature by, 195-96, 209-12, 224, 269
Romanticising by, 290-92
Social and political life in, 292
Spiritual literature by, 191-92, 292-93, 297
Style of, 207-08
Teacher-student relations in, 264, 293
Traditional Indian society by, 194-95, 199, 209, 274, 295
Tragic stories by, 288-90
Upanishads, 255, 261, 274-75
Village life portrayal by, 194-98, 208-10, 222-24, 329
Women in, 206-07, 236-39, 263, 285
Ramanuja, 268, 275
Ripon, 37
Roberts, 29
Robinson, Edward Kay, 25
Russell, Bertrand, 136
Sandison, Alan, 25, 108
Schwitzer, Albert, 162
Scott, Paul, 18, 303, 313, 315, 316
Scott, Walter, 11, 167
Seeley, John, 8
Shahane, Vasant A., 113
Shakespeare, 10, 226
Smith, Vincent, 171, 173
Srinivasachari, P.N., 269
Srivastava, Narsingh, 215
Steel, Flora Annie, 12, 174, 320, 321
Taranath, 191, 197
Thompson, Edward, 12, 18, 306, 309, 312-14
Thomson, James, 63
Thoreau, 132
Tolstoy, 289
Tompkins, J.M.S., 89
Veeraswami, 308
Viswanatham, K., 179, 183
Vivekananda, 153, 154
Vofler, Thomas A., 221
Walcott, Derek, 295

Index

Wellesley, 3
Whiteman, 132
White, Patrick, 295
Wilberforce, 4, 6
Wilkins, Charles, 2
William, H.M., 215, 218

Wilson, Angus, 102, 107
Wilson, Edmund, 100, 101
Wilson, H.H., 5
Woodruff, Philip, 69
Woolf, Virginia, 201
Wordsworth, 118